Personality

SELECTED READINGS IN THEORY

Personality

SELECTED READINGS
IN THEORY

Edited by
Willard B. Frick
Emeritus, Albion College

 F. E. PEACOCK PUBLISHERS, INC. ITASCA, ILLINOIS

In appreciation
for my three friends
Robert Balster (31 years)
Berne Jacobs (18 years)
Johan Stohl (27 years)
whose unique personalities
have greatly enriched my own

Contents

Preface

I have long felt the need for the students in my psychology of personality course to have an opportunity to read from each theorist's own writings, to hear each theorist's own voice. Theories of personality, after all, were created by personalities, and in every theory there is the unmistakable reflection of the richness, style, complexity, and uniqueness of its creator. Textbooks, however, cannot convey these personal styles and idiosyncrasies. This is why it is so important for students of personality to read the original materials and make contact with the human essence that gives life and meaning to each theory. Initially, I addressed these concerns by placing primary materials on reserve in the library. This approach, however, proved to be disappointing and of limited value. Students seemed unwilling or unable to tackle these materials and get involved with them.

The present book, *Personality: Selected Readings in Theory,* provides teachers and students with a core of carefully selected materials from the major writings of ten theorists that is readily and conveniently available to them for use in the classroom. Represented in this group of ten theorists are the psychoanalytic, psychodynamic, psychosocial, learning and behavioristic, and humanistic orientations.

Three major criteria have guided me in the selection of the primary materials:

1. To present the distinctive features of each theoretical position.
2. To select those materials that will be of greatest interest and value to the student.
3. To provide materials that have the potential to serve as a stimulus for classroom discussion.

I believe I have achieved these goals in most of my selections.

Personality: Selected Readings in Theory has a distinctive organization to aid the student in establishing a focus for his or her reading and maximize the value of time spent on the readings.

First, I present a brief autobiographical sketch of each theorist. Second, the selections for each theorist are organized around four major topics. Third, prior to each topic, I present a brief commentary designed to introduce the selections and provide some perspective on their meaning and significance. This organization, I believe, makes for a less fragmented and more coherent presentation. The one exception to this four-topic outline is found in the chapter on Erik Erikson. Since most of Erikson's work revolves around his epigenetic stage theory (the eight stages of man) I focus all of the selections around this one major theory.

In preparing the manuscript, invaluable assistance was provided by Ms. Erika Flores of the psychology department and by Ms. Julie Eagle, our very able student assistant. I wish to thank them both for their generous gift of time and energy on my behalf.

Finally, I wish to express appreciation to Mr. F. Edward Peacock, President of F. E. Peacock Publishers, Inc., for his interest, support, and guidance through the process of publication, and my thanks to Norm Mysliwiec and Dick Welna for guiding me and the manuscript through the editorial and production process.

CHAPTER I

The Psychoanalytic Theory
of Sigmund Freud

BIOGRAPHICAL SKETCH

Sigmund Freud was born in Freiberg, Moravia (Czech Republic) in 1856. The exact month of his birth remains in question. Freud was the firstborn of Jacob and Amalie Nathanson Freud. He had seven siblings and two half-brothers from his father's former marriage. When Sigmund was three, the Freud family moved to Leipzig and, following some financial difficulty, moved to Vienna the following year. Thereafter, Freud lived and worked in Vienna, and for eighty years his life and work would be closely associated with that city.

An early interest in science and human behavior led Freud to pursue a medical career. It was also true, at the time, that most other professions were closed to Jews. Freud graduated from the University of Vienna Medical School in 1881. Following his degree, Freud became more interested in research than in a medical practice, and he did physiological research and taught at the university's physiological institute. He published some early papers related to this research.

In 1885 Freud received a grant to study in Paris with the famous Jean-Martin Charcot. With Charcot he learned the technique of hypnosis as a treatment for hysteria. This experience with Charcot was a highly significant one in Freud's development, for it led to his discovery of the free association technique, a technique crucial to the success of psychoanalysis. From the experience with Charcot and a close friendship with Joseph Breuer, from whom he learned about the importance of catharsis in treating hysterical symptoms, Freud refined his free association method, which became central to his psychoanalytic work. As a result of these early clinical investigations into the treatment of hysteria, Freud and Breuer collaborated on the publication *Studies in Hysteria.*

In 1886 Freud married Bertha Bernays. They had six children, one of whom was Anna Freud, who later became a renowned child analyst. After the death of his father in 1896, Freud felt increasingly estranged and isolated. His intense and important friendship with Wilhelm Fliess had cooled and he had not achieved the fame and recognition he so greatly desired. At mid-life Freud suffered from depression and obsessions of death. His friend and biographer, Ernest Jones, believed that Freud suffered from a severe psychoneurosis during this time. During this emotional crisis, however, Freud continued his work with increasing intensity. Rather than debilitating, it was a creative period for Freud during which time he published what was to be considered his most important work, *The Interpretation of Dreams.* Freud had begun an intense daily self-analysis following the death of his father, and many of his own dreams are the subject of analysis in this now-classic book. *The Interpretation of Dreams* had a very slow beginning both in sales and recognition. In time, however, it brought Freud fame and the widespread recognition that he had always wanted. The rest, we might say, is history.

During the year of his father's death Freud first used the term *psychoanalysis* to describe his methods. It was during this time, also, that Freud made his great "discovery" that childhood seduction by parents was responsible for the development of neuroses in adults. However, Freud abandoned this theory in favor of a childhood fantasy theory in 1897, and the motive for doing so became and continues to be a major controversy in psychoanalytic theory. Why did Freud abandon his seduction theory? There are several hypotheses but no one knows for sure.

In 1902 a small group of Freud's followers, including Alfred Adler and Wilhelm Stekel, formed the Psychological Wednesday Society. This group later evolved into the prestigious International Psychoanalytic Association. In 1910 Carl Jung became its president. For Freud and the devoted followers of psychoanalysis, these heady years were made extremely difficult by the traumatic events of World War I and the defection from the group by Jung and Adler.

In 1923 it was discovered that Freud had mouth cancer. Following this diagnoses Freud went through much suffering, including numerous surgeries for the condition. Throughout his illness, however, Freud continued his writing. His last book, *Outline of Psychoanalysis,* was an unfinished work. Following the occupation of Vienna by the Nazis in 1938, Freud, after much resistance, agreed to move to London, where he died on September 23, 1939.

The Topology and Structure
of the Mind

COMMENTARY

Freud was not the first to entertain the idea of an unconscious component in personality. Many philosophers had long believed in the existence of an unknowable inner world. Freud, however, gave a certain empirical status to this mysterious arena of the mind and, while nineteenth century psychologists were at work charting the contours of consciousness, Freud was busy demonstrating how the unconscious could be understood and made accessible. Indeed, Freud considered the unconscious to be the most important and influential dimension of personality.

Freud's topology encompassed the full range of conscious and unconscious states. His major divisions in this topology were consciousness, the preconscious, and the unconscious. As Freud suggests, the meaning of consciousness is not difficult to apprehend. We know something of its meaning though our own "here and now" experience and awareness. With the preconscious and the unconscious, however, things become more elusive, more ambiguous, and difficult for us to know and grasp.

The preconscious, or what we may call "available memory," functions as a buffer zone between the conscious and unconscious realms. Perhaps we could also think of the preconscious as a sort of relay station between the conscious and the unconscious, since the content of the preconscious is composed of material from both the conscious and unconscious. Thoughts, feelings, and wishes, therefore, may move from the unconscious into the preconscious and, at times, enter conscious experience. Likewise, some previously conscious material may move into the preconscious and then, if sufficiently disturbing, into the darkness of the unconscious.

Rather than representing specific or concrete structures, the id, ego, and superego, having no known correlates in one's biochemistry or neuroanatomy, must be considered (as Freud did) to be *hypothetical constructs,* a way of making some conceptual sense out of complex psychic phenomena.

Unlike many of the theorists you will encounter in this text, Freud's theory is based on a conflict model of personality development. While some other theorists may incorporate elements of conflict in their theories (Erikson and Horney, for example) Freud's theoretical division of personality into the id, ego, and superego, makes internal conflict an essential feature of our experience and a central dynamic in personality formation and growth. Indeed, it is in the resolution of conflicting wishes and impulses at various psychosexual stages of growth that moves personality forward and, hopefully, into some measure of stability and maturity. Throughout our lives, however, we are always fighting a rearguard action against the emergence of latent conflicts and, through the sublimation of our sexual and aggressive nature, making the compromises necessary to achieve some balance between the competing forces of id, ego and superego. Some life events, however, such as marriage, the birth of a child, or the death of a parent or spouse, may unleash unconscious forces that were well sublimated prior to the crisis.

The secondary process of the ego calls upon its "reality testing" ability, making use of a set of cognitive skills, such as thinking, reasoning, planning, and perception. For Freud these rational powers of the ego were in the service of the id. It was these same reality-testing skills, however, that formed the basis for a significant revision of ego theory. In this new theoretical perspective Freud's id psychology has been abandoned and the ego has been given an autonomous status, reflected in Heinz Hartmann's early recognition of a "conflict-free ego sphere" and, more recently, in the ego psychology of Erik Erikson.

1.

SIGMUND FREUD

In the course of this work the distinctions which we describe as psychical qualities force themselves on our notice. There is no need to characterize what we call "conscious": it is the same as the consciousness of philosophers and of everyday opinion. Everything else psychical is in our view "the unconscious." We are soon led to make an important division in this unconscious. Some processes become conscious easily; they may then cease to be conscious, but can become conscious once more without any trouble: as people say, they can be reproduced or remembered. This reminds us that consciousness is in general a highly fugitive state. What is conscious is conscious only for a moment. If our perceptions do not confirm this, the contradiction is only an apparent one; it is explained by the fact that the stimuli which lead to perception may persist for considerable periods, so that meanwhile the perception of them may be repeated. The whole position is made clear in connection with the conscious perception of our thought-

[1] Freud, S. (1949). *An Outline of Psycho-Analysis.* New York: W. W. Norton, pp. 31–32. Reprinted from *An Outline of Psycho-Analysis* by Sigmund Freud, translated by James Strachey, with the permission of W. W. Norton & Company, Inc. Copyright 1949 by W. W. Norton & Company, Inc. Copyright © 1969 by the Institute for Psychoanalysis and Alix Strachey.

processes: these too may persist for some time, but they may just as well pass in a flash. Everything unconscious that behaves in this way, that can thus easily exchange the unconscious state for the conscious one, is therefore preferably described as "capable of becoming conscious"; or as *preconscious.* Experience has taught us that there is hardly a psychical process, however complicated it may be, which cannot on occasion remain preconscious, even though as a rule it will, as we say, push its way forward into consciousness. There are other psychical processes and psychical material which have no such easy access to become conscious but must be inferred, recognized and translated into conscious form in the manner described. For such material we reserve the name of the unconscious proper.

Thus we have attributed three qualities to psychical processes: they are either conscious, preconscious or unconscious. The division between the three classes of material which possess these qualities is neither absolute nor permanent. What is preconscious becomes conscious, as we have seen, without any assistance from us; what is unconscious can, through our efforts, be made conscious, and in the process we may have a feeling that we are often overcoming very strong resistances.

2.

SIGMUND FREUD

. . . we have arrived at the term or concept of the unconscious along another path, by considering certain experiences in which mental *dynamics* play a part. We have found—that is, we have been obliged to assume—that very powerful mental processes or ideas exist (and here a quantitative or *economic* factor comes into question for the first time) which can produce all the effects in mental life that ordinary ideas do (including effects than can in their turn become conscious as ideas), though they themselves do not become conscious. . . .

It is enough to say that at this point psycho-analytic theory steps in and asserts that the reason why such ideas cannot become conscious is that a certain force opposes them, that otherwise they could become conscious, and that it would then be apparent how little they differ from other elements which are admittedly psychical. The fact that in the technique of psycho-analysis a means has been found by which the opposing force can be removed and the ideas in

question made conscious renders this theory irrefutable. The state in which the ideas existed before being made conscious is called by us *repression*, and we assert that the force which instituted the repression and maintains it is perceived as *resistance* during the work of analysis.

Thus we obtain our concept of the unconscious from the theory of repression. The repressed is the prototype of the unconscious for us. We see, however, that we have two kinds of unconscious—the one which is latent but capable of becoming conscious, and the one which is repressed and which is not, in itself and without more ado, capable of becoming conscious. This piece of insight into psychical dynamics cannot fail to affect terminology and description. The latent, which is unconscious only descriptively, not in the dynamic sense, we call *preconscious*; we restrict the term *unconscious* to the dynamically unconscious repressed; so that now we have three terms, conscious (Cs.), preconscious (Pcs.), and unconscious (Ucs.), whose sense is no longer purely descriptive. The Pcs. is presumably a great deal closer to the Cs. than is the Ucs., and since we have called the Ucs. psychical we shall with even less hesitation call the latent Pcs. psychical.

² Freud, S. (1960). *The Ego and the Id.* New York: W. W. Norton , pp. 4–6. Reprinted from *The Ego and the Id* by Sigmund Freud, translated by James Strachey, with the permission of W. W. Norton & Company, Inc. Copyright © 1960 by James Strachey.

3.

SIGMUND FREUD

The core of our being, . . . is formed by the obscure *id*, which has no direct communication with the external world and is accessible even to our own knowledge only through the medium of another agency. Within this id the organic *instincts* operate, which are themselves compounded of fusions of two primal forces (Eros and destructiveness) in varying proportions and are differentiated from one another by their relation to organs or systems of organs. The one and only urge of these instincts is towards satisfaction, which is expected to arise from certain changes in the organs with the help of objects in the external world. But immediate and unheeding satisfaction of the instincts, such as the id demands, would often lead to perilous conflicts with the external world and to extinction. The id knows no solicitude about ensuring survival and no anxiety; or it would perhaps be more correct to say that, though it can generate the sensory elements of anxiety, it cannot make use of them. The processes which are possible in and between the assumed psychical elements in the id (the *primary process*) differ widely from those which are familiar to us through conscious perception in our intellectual and emotional life; nor are they subject to the critical restrictions of logic, which repudiates some of these processes as invalid and seeks to undo them.

The id, cut off from the external world, has a world of perception of its own. It detects with extraordinary acuteness certain changes in its interior, especially oscillations in the tensions of its instinctual needs, and these changes become conscious as feelings in the pleasure-unpleasure series. It is hard to say, to be sure, by what means and with the help of what sensory terminal organs these perceptions come about. But it is an established fact that self-perceptions—coenaesthetic feelings and feelings of pleasure-unpleasure—govern the passage of events in the id with despotic force. The id obeys the inexorable pleasure principle. But not the id alone. It seems that the activity of the other psychical agencies too is able only to modify the pleasure principle but not to nullify it; and it remains a question of the highest theoretical importance, and one that has not yet been answered, when and how it is ever possible for the pleasure principle to be overcome. The consideration that the pleasure principle demands reduction, at bottom the extinction perhaps, of the tensions of instinctual needs (that is, Nirvana) leads to the still unassessed relations between the pleasure principle and the two primal forces, Eros and the death instinct.

[3] Freud, S. (1949). *An Outline of Psycho-Analysis.* New York: W. W. Norton. pp. 84–86, 94–95. Reprinted from *An Outline of Psycho-Analysis* by Sigmund Freud, translated by James Strachey, with the permission of W. W. Norton & Company, Inc. Copyright 1949 by W. W. Norton & Company, Inc. Copyright © 1969 by the Institute for Psychoanalysis and Alix Strachey.

The other agency of the mind, which we believe we know best and in which we recognize ourselves most easily—what is known as the *ego*—has been developed out of the id's cortical layer, which, through being adapted to the reception and exclusion of stimuli, is in direct contact with the external world (*reality*). Starting from conscious perception it has subjected to its influence ever larger regions and deeper strata of the id. . . .

The picture of an ego which mediates between the id and the external world, which takes over the instinctual demands of the former in order to lead them to satisfaction, which derives perceptions from the latter and uses them as memories, which, intent on its self-preservation, puts itself in defense against excessively strong claims from both sides and which, at the same time, is guided in all its decisions by the injunctions of a modified pleasure principle—this picture in fact applies to the ego only up to the end of the first period of childhood, till about the age of five. At about that time an important change has taken place. A portion of the external world has, at least partially, been abandoned as an object and has instead, by identification, been taken into the ego and thus becomes an integral part of the internal world. This new psychical agency continues to carry on the functions which have hitherto been performed by the people (the abandoned objects) in the external world: it observes the ego, gives it orders, judges it and threatens it with punishments, exactly like the parents whose place it has taken. We call this agency the *super-ego* and are aware of it in its judicial functions as our *conscience.*

4.

SIGMUND FREUD

We are warned by a proverb against serving two masters at the same time. The poor ego has things even worse: it serves three severe masters and does what it can to bring their claims and demands into harmony with one another. These claims are always divergent and often seem incompatible. No wonder that the ego so often fails in its task. Its three tyrannical masters are the external world, the super-ego and the id. When we follow the ego's efforts to satisfy them simultaneously —or rather, to obey them simultaneously—we cannot feel any regret at

[4] Freud, S. (1965). *New Introductory Lectures on Psycho-Analysis.* New York: W. W. Norton, pp. 96–98. Reprinted from *New Introductory Lectures on Psycho-Analysis* by Sigmund Freud, translated by James Strachey, with the permission of W. W. Norton & Company, Inc. Copyright 1933 by Sigmund Freud, renewed © 1961 by W. J. H. Sprott. Copyright © 1965, 1964 by James Strachey.

having personified this ego and having set it up as a separate organism. It feels hemmed in on three sides, threatened by three kinds of danger, to which, if it is hard pressed, it reacts by generating anxiety. Owing to its origin from the experiences of the perceptual system, it is earmarked for representing the demands of the external world, but it strives too to be a loyal servant of the id, to remain on good terms with it, to recommend itself to it as an object and to attract its libido to itself. In its attempts to mediate between the id and reality, it is often obliged to cloak the Ucs. commands of the id with its own Pcs. rationalizations, to conceal the id's conflicts with reality, to profess, with diplomatic disingenuousness, to be taking notice of reality even when the id has remained rigid and unyielding. On the other hand it is observed at every step it takes by the strict super-ego, which lays down definite standards for its conduct, without taking any account of its difficulties from the direction of the id and the external world, and which, if those standards are not obeyed, punishes it with intense feelings of inferiority and of guilt. Thus the ego, driven by the id, confined by the super-ego, repulsed by reality, struggles to master its economic task of bringing about harmony among the forces and influences working in and upon it; and we can understand how it is that so often we cannot suppress a cry: 'Life is not easy!' If the ego is obliged to admit its weakness, it breaks out in anxiety—realistic anxiety regarding the external world, moral anxiety regarding the super-ego and neurotic anxiety regarding the strength of the passions in the id.

Libido Theory and Stages of Development

COMMENTARY

Freud has the distinction of being the first, and most nearly comprehensive, personality theorist. With the exception of Bandura, and perhaps Rogers, he helped lay the foundation for all of the other theories presented in this book, theories that either built upon his ideas and concepts or developed as a reaction against them. While dramatic revisions of Freudian theory have taken place in recent years, it continues to have a profound influence on our Western culture. Freud's ideas continue to be an important source of critical analysis in art, music, literature, and biographical study.

Freud, one of the premier minds in the history of Western thought, was certainly aware of his own importance. He compared his shattering influence on our world view to that of Copernicus, who taught us that the world was not the center of the solar system, and to that of Darwin, who rejected the premise of "special creation." Much of Freud's "shattering influence" lay in his theory of the libido and his discovery of childhood sexuality. Thus, Freud's special blow to our self-esteem lay in his clinical evidence that we are irrational creatures, driven by our sexual urges and controlled by unconscious motivations.

We have already pointed out, in our commentary for the Typography and Structure of the Mind, that Freud presented us with a conflict theory of development. In his theory of the libido he introduces us to a "critical periods" hypothesis of personality development. In a biologically determined sequence, the psychosexual stages (oral, anal, phallic, latent, and genital) chart the evolution and vicissitudes of libidinal development. Each stage, therefore, is a critical period in the evolution and maturity of instinctual life. Achieving a resolution of conflict and a balanced gratification within each stage is crucial for the development of a loving and productive personality.

1.

SIGMUND FREUD

There can be no question of restricting one or the other of the basic instincts to one of the provinces of the mind. They must necessarily be met with everywhere. We may picture an initial state as one in which the total available energy of Eros, which henceforward we shall speak of as "libido," is present in the still undifferentiated ego-id and serves to neutralize the destructive tendencies which are simultaneously present. (We are without a term analogous to "libido" for describing the energy of the destructive instinct.) At a later stage it becomes relatively easy for us to follow the vicissitudes of the libido, but this is more difficult with the destructive instinct. . . .

There can be no question but that the libido has somatic sources, that it streams to the ego from various organs and parts of the body. This is most clearly seen in the case of that portion of the libido which, from its instinctual aim, is described as sexual excitation. The most prominent of the parts of the body from which this libido arises are known by the name of "erotogenic zones," though in fact the whole body is an erotogenic zone of this kind. The greater part of what we know about Eros—that is to say, about its exponent, the libido—has been gained from a study of the sexual function, which, indeed, on the prevailing view, even if not according to our theory, coincides with Eros. We have been able to form a picture of the way in which the sexual urge, which is destined to exercise a decisive influence on our life, gradually develops out of successive contributions from a number of component instincts, which represent particular erotogenic zones. . . .

The first organ to emerge as an erotogenic zone and to make libidinal demands on the mind is, from the time of birth onwards, the mouth. To begin with, all psychical activity is concentrated on providing satisfaction for the needs of that zone. Primarily, of course, this satisfaction serves the purpose of self-preservation by means of nourishment; but physiology should

[1] Freud, S. (1949). *An Outline of Psycho-Analysis.* New York: W. W. Norton, pp. 19–26. Reprinted from *An Outline of Psycho-Analysis* by Sigmund Freud, translated by James Strachey, with the permission of W. W. Norton & Company, Inc. Copyright 1949 by W. W. Norton & Company, Inc. Copyright © 1969 by the Institute for Psychoanalysis and Alix Strachey.

not be confused with psychology. The baby's obstinate persistence in sucking gives evidence at an early stage of a need for satisfaction which, though it originates from and is instigated by taking of nourishment, nevertheless strives to obtain pleasure independently of nourishment and for that reason may and should be termed *sexual.*

During this oral phase sadistic impulses already occur sporadically along with the appearance of the teeth. Their extent is far greater in the second phase, which we describe as the sadistic-anal one, because satisfaction is then sought in aggression and in the excretory function. Our justification for including aggressive urges under the libido is based on the view that sadism is an instinctual fusion of purely libidinal and purely destructive urges. . . .

The third phase is that known as the phallic one, which is, as it were, a forerunner of the final form taken by sexual life and already much resembles it. It is to be noted that it is not the genitals of both sexes that play a part at this stage, but only the male ones (the phallus). The female genitals long remain unknown: in children's attempts to understand the sexual processes they pay homage to the venerable cloacal theory—a theory which has a genetic justification.

With the phallic phase and in the course of it the sexuality of early childhood reaches its height and approaches its dissolution. Thereafter boys and girls have different histories. Both have begun to put their intellectual activity at the service of sexual researches; both start off from the premise of the universal presence of the penis. But now the paths of the sexes diverge. The boy enters the Oedipus phase; he begins to manipulate his penis and simultaneously has fantasies of carrying out some sort of activity with it in relation to his mother, till, owing to the combined effect of a threat of castration and the sight of the absence of a penis in females, he experiences the greatest trauma of his life and this introduces the period of latency with all its consequences. The girl, after vainly attempting to do the same as the boy, comes to recognize her lack of a penis or rather the inferiority of her clitoris, with permanent effects on the development of her character; as a result of this first disappointment in rivalry, she often begins by turning away altogether from sexual life.

2.

SIGMUND FREUD

... a still higher degree of interest must attach to the influence of a situation which every child is destined to pass through and which follows inevitably from the factor of the prolonged period during which a child is cared for by other people and lives with his parents. I am thinking of the *Oedipus* complex, so named because its essential substance is to be found in the Greek legend of King Oedipus, which has fortunately been preserved for us in a version by a great dramatist. The Greek hero killed his father and took his mother to wife. That he did so unwittingly, since he did not know them as his parents, is a deviation from the analytic facts which we can easily understand and which, indeed, we shall recognize as inevitable. . . .

The effects of the castration complex in little girls are more uniform and no less profound. A female child has, of course, no need to fear the loss of a penis; she must, however, react to the fact of not having received one. From the very first she envies boys its possession; her whole development may be said to take place under the colours of envy for the penis. She begins by making vain attempts to do the same as boys and later, with greater success, makes efforts to compensate for her defect—efforts which may lead in the end to a normal feminine attitude. If during the phallic phase she tries to get pleasure like a boy by the manual stimulation of her genitals, it often happens that she fails to obtain sufficient satisfaction and extends her judgment of inferiority from her stunted penis to her whole self. As a rule she soon gives up masturbating, since she has no wish to be reminded of the superiority of her brother or playmate, and turns away from sexuality altogether.

² Freud, S. (1949). *An Outline of Psycho-Analysis*. New York: W. W. Norton, pp. 69 and 76. Reprinted from *An Outline of Psycho-Analysis* by Sigmund Freud, translated by James Strachey, with the permission of W. W. Norton & Company, Inc. Copyright 1949 by W. W. Norton & Company, Inc. Copyright © 1969 by the Institute for Psychoanalysis and Alix Strachey.

3.

SIGMUND FREUD

With the transference of the wish for a penis-baby on to her father, the girl has entered the situation of the Oedipus complex. Her hostility to her mother, which did not need to be freshly created, is now greatly intensified, for she becomes the girl's rival, who receives from her father everything that she desires from him. For a long time the girl's Oedipus complex concealed her pre-Oedipus attachment to her mother from our view, though it is nevertheless so important and leaves such lasting fixations behind it. For girls the Oedipus situation is the outcome of a long and difficult development; it is a kind of preliminary solution, a position of rest which is not soon abandoned, especially as the beginning of the latency period is not far distant. And we now are struck by a difference between the two sexes, which is probably momentous, in regard to the relation of the Oedipus complex to the castration complex. In

³ Freud, S. (1965). *New Introductory Lectures on Psycho-Analysis.* New York: W. W. Norton, pp. 160–161. Reprinted from *New Introductory Lectures in Psycho-Analysis* by Sigmund Freud, translated by James Strachey, with the permission of W. W. Norton & Company, Inc. Copyright 1933 by Sigmund Freud, renewed © 1961 by W. J. H. Sprott. Copyright © 1965, 1964 by James Strachey.

a boy the Oedipus complex, in which he desires his mother and would like to get rid of his father as being a rival, develops naturally from the phase of his phallic sexuality. The threat of castration compels him, however, to give up that attitude. Under the impression of the danger of losing his penis, the Oedipus complex is abandoned, repressed and, in the most normal cases, entirely destroyed . . . , and a severe super-ego is set up as its heir. What happens with a girl is almost the opposite. The castration complex prepares for the Oedipus complex instead of destroying it; the girl is driven out of her attachment to her mother through the influence of her envy for the penis and she enters the Oedipus situation as though into a haven of refuge. In the absence of fear of castration the chief motive is lacking, which leads boys to surmount the Oedipus complex. Girls remain in it for an indeterminate length of time; they demolish it late and, even so, incompletely. In these circumstances the formation of the super-ego must suffer; it cannot attain the strength and independence which give it its cultural significance, and feminists are not pleased when we point out to them the effects of this factor upon the average feminine character.

4.

SIGMUND FREUD

... There is no need to feel surprised ... if, in a large number of people, dreams disclose their wish to get rid of their parents and especially of the parent of their own sex. We may assume that this wish is also present in waking life and is even conscious sometimes, if it can be masked by some other motive. ... It is rarely that the hostility alone dominates the relationship; far oftener it is in the background of more affectionate impulses by which it is suppressed, and it must wait until a dream isolates it, as it were. ...

But we have come upon this dream-wish, too, where it has no relevance in real life, and where the adult need never confess to it in his waking life. The reason for this is that the deepest and most invariable motive for estrangement, especially between two people of the same sex, has already made itself felt in early childhood.

What I have in mind is rivalry in love, with a clear emphasis on the subject's sex. While he is still a small child, a son will already begin to develop a special affection for his mother, whom he regards as belonging to him; he begins to feel his father as a rival who disputes his sole possession. And in the same way a little girl looks on her mother as a person who interferes with her affectionate relation to her father and who occupies a position which she herself could very well fill. Observation shows us to what early years these attitudes go back. We refer to them as the "Oedipus complex," because the legend of Oedipus realizes, with only a slight softening, the two extreme wishes that arise from the son's situation—to kill his father and take his mother to wife. I do not wish to assert that the Oedipus complex exhausts the relation of children to their parents: it can easily be far more complicated. The Oedipus complex can, moreover, be developed to a greater or less strength, it can even be reversed; but it is a regular and very important factor in a child's mental life, and there is more danger of our under-estimating rather than over-estimating its influence and that of the developments which proceed from it. Incidentally, children often react in their Oedipus attitude to a stimulus coming from their parents; who are frequently led in their preferences by difference of sex, so that the father will choose his daughter and the mother her son as a favorite, or, in case of a cooling-off in the marriage, as a substitute for a love-object that has lost its value.

[4] Freud, S. (1966). *Introductory Lectures on Psycho-Analysis.* New York: W. W. Norton, pp. 255–257. Reprinted from *Introductory Lectures on Psycho-Analysis* by Sigmund Freud, translated by James Strachey, with the permission of Liveright Publishing Corporation. Copyright 1920, 1935 by Edward L. Bernays. Copyright © 1965, 1964, 1963 by James Strachey. Copyright © 1966 by W. W. Norton & Company, Inc.

Anxiety and Its Three Types: Realistic, Moral, and Neurotic

COMMENTARY

One important caveat should be presented here before you read the selections on anxiety. The experience of anxiety is a normal experience, even a constructive one for most of us, most of the time. It may frequently serve to increase alertness and enhance performance. It is not unusual, however, for us to experience excessive anxiety, at times, that might be explained by the Freudian model. In any case, to suffer from such anxiety occasionally does not suggest a neurosis. This principle holds true for other theories presented in this book that deal with the problem of anxiety and other neurotic developments in the personality.

Anxiety, however, can be one of the most distressing emotional states we experience. It is characterized by feelings of apprehension, premonitions of danger, and disquieting feelings of impending crisis. Because of its painful nature, we are driven, through healthy or unhealthy strategies, to prevent its occurrence or reduce its intensity.

Anxiety is an inevitable aspect of our lives, an aspect of being-in-the-world, and managing this emotion successfully is a key to healthy development. While there are differences of opinion about the object of anxiety or its basic source, most personality theorists would agree that anxiety represents the perception of some fundamental threat to our existence. It is not surprising, therefore, that the concept of anxiety plays a central role in many personality theories.

Anxiety plays a prominent role in Freud's theory of personality development. Although his interpretation of anxiety went through several stages of development, as did many aspects of his theory, in its final stage Freud saw anxiety as an ego function, and he emphasized the important signal function of anxiety in alerting the ego to impending danger.

Freud viewed the ego as responding to threat or potential danger from three primary sources: the environment, id impulses, and the superego. Freud thus identified three primary types of anxiety.

1. *Reality Anxiety* reflects the ego's dependence on the external world, where the environment represents an objective source of danger. This type of anxiety comes the closest to representing an objective, tangible fear state (e.g., anxiety over possible loss of a scholarship) and is least likely to become neurotic in intensity.

2. *Neurotic Anxiety* reflects the ego's dependence on the id and arises when the ego feels pressure from primitive impulses that threaten to become conscious and push the person to behave in an impulsive or destructive manner. Neurotic anxiety is the ego's alarm system, a signal that id impulses are pressing for release and expression. In its original manifestation, neurotic anxiety is identified by its vagueness and ambiguity. Thus, the vague apprehension, dread, and discomfort one feels in neurotic anxiety (without a tangible object, as in reality anxiety) is one of its central features. The unconscious dimension of mental life is obviously at work here. As a means of coping with such anxiety, however, these nebulous feelings may become attached to an object or concrete situation. Neurotic anxiety in this case can often be identified by the intensity of emotion and exaggerated behavior, as in a phobia or a state of panic that may arise when one is in an elevator.

3. *Moral Anxiety* suggests the ego's dependence upon the superego and is aroused when there is a conflict between the ego and superego, for example, when the id initiates some immoral thought or action. The superego, as the moral arm and conscience of the psyche, may also become a threat to the ego's expression of normal developmental needs. Doing or even thinking something contrary to the superego (internalized parental standards) may provoke fears of punishment and arouse intense feelings of anxiety and guilt.

In a final selection, Freud discusses a case where intense anxiety is expressed in (or converted into) phobias and rituals.

1.

SIGMUND FREUD

. . . the dissection of the mental personality into a super-ego, an ego and an id, . . . has obliged us to take our bearings afresh in the problem of anxiety as well. With the thesis that the ego is the sole seat of anxiety—that the ego alone can produce and feel anxiety—we have established a new and stable position from which a number of things take on a new aspect. And indeed it is difficult to see what sense there would be in speaking of an "anxiety of the id" or in attributing a capacity for apprehensiveness to the super-ego. On the other hand, we have welcomed a desirable element of correspondence in the fact that the three

[1] Freud, S. (1965). *New Introductory Lectures on Psycho-Analysis.* New York: W. W. Norton, pp. 106–107 and 488. Reprinted from *New Introductory Lectures on Psycho-Analysis* by Sigmund Freud, translated by James Strachey, with the permission of W. W. Norton & Company, Inc. Copyright 1933 by Sigmund Freud, renewed © 1961 by W. J. H. Sprott. Copyright © 1965, 1964 by James Strachey.

Freud, S. (1966). *Introductory Lectures on Psycho-Analysis.* New York: W. W. Norton, p. 488. Reprinted from *Introductory Lectures on Psycho-Analysis* by Sigmund Freud, translated by James Strachey, with the permission of Liveright Publishing Corporation. Copyright 1920, 1935 by Edward L. Bernays. Copyright © 1965, 1964, 1963 by James Strachey. Copyright © 1966 by W. W. Norton & Company, Inc.

main species of anxiety, realistic, neurotic and moral, can be so easily connected with the ego's three dependent relations—to the external world, to the id and to the super-ego. Along with this new view, moreover, the function of anxiety as a signal announcing a situation of danger (a notion, incidentally, not unfamiliar to us) comes into prominence, the question of what the material is out of which anxiety is made loses interest, and in the relations between realistic and neurotic anxiety have become surprisingly clarified and simplified. It is also to be remarked that we now understand the apparently complicated cases of the generation of anxiety better than those which were considered simple. . . .

I have no need to introduce anxiety itself to you. Every one of us has experienced that sensation, or, to speak more correctly that affective state, at one time or other on our own account. But I think the question has never been seriously enough raised of why neurotics in particular suffer from anxiety so much more and so much more strongly than other people. Perhaps it has been regarded as something self-evident. . . .

2.

SIGMUND FREUD

. . . We believe that in the case of the affect of anxiety we know what the early impression is which it repeats. We believe that it is in the *act of birth* that there comes about the combination of unpleasurable feelings, impulses of discharge and bodily sensations which has become the prototype of the effects of a mortal danger and has ever since been repeated by us as the state of anxiety. . . .

It is, of course, our conviction that the disposition to repeat the first state of anxiety has been so thoroughly incorporated into the organism through a countless series of generations that a single individual cannot escape the affect of anxiety even if, like the legendary Macduff, he "was from his mother's womb untimely ripped" and has therefore not himself experienced the act of birth. We cannot say what has become the prototype of the state of anxiety in the case of creatures other than mammals. And in the same way we do not know either what complex of feelings is in such creatures the equivalent to our anxiety. . . .

If we now pass over to consider neurotic anxiety, what fresh forms and situations are manifested by anxiety in

[2] Freud, S. (1966). *Introductory Lectures on Psycho-Analysis*. New York: W. W. Norton, pp. 492–511. Reprinted from *Introductory Lectures on Psycho-Analysis* by Sigmund Freud, translated by James Strachey, with the permission of Liveright Publishing Corporation. Copyright 1920, 1935 by Edward L. Bernays. Copyright © 1965, 1964, 1963 by James Strachey. Copyright © 1966 by W. W. Norton & Company, Inc.

neurotics? There is much to be described here. In the first place we find a general apprehensiveness, a kind of freely floating anxiety which is ready to attach itself to any idea that is in any way suitable, which influences judgment, selects what is to be expected, and lies in wait for any opportunity that will allow it to justify itself. We call this state "expectant anxiety" or "anxious expectation." People who are tormented by this kind of anxiety always foresee the most frightful of all possibilities, interpret every chance event as a premonition of evil and exploit every uncertainty in a bad sense. A tendency to be an expectation of evil of this sort is to be found as a character trait in many people whom one cannot otherwise regard as sick; one calls them over-anxious or pessimistic. A striking amount of expectant anxiety, however, forms a regular feature of a nervous disorder to which I have given the name of "anxiety neurosis." . . .

A second form of anxiety, in contrast to the one I have just described, is bound physically and attached to particular objects or situations. This is the anxiety of the extremely multifarious and often very strange "phobias." . . .

. . . Listen to all the things that can become the object or content of a phobia: darkness, open air, open spaces, cats, spiders, caterpillars, snakes, mice, thunderstorms, sharp points, blood, enclosed spaces, crowds, solitude, crossing bridges, sea voyages and railways journeys, etc., etc. A first attempt at finding one's way about in this confusion suggests a division into three groups. Some of the dreaded objects and situations have something uncanny about them for normal people as well, some relation to danger; and such phobias, therefore, do not strike us as unintelligible, though their strength is greatly exaggerated. Thus most of us have a sense of repulsion if we meet with a snake. . . . We may refer to a second group of cases in which a relation to a danger is still present, though we are accustomed to minimize the danger and not to anticipate it. The majority of situation phobias belong to this group. We know that there is more chance of an accident when we are on a railway-journey than when we stay at home—the chance of a collision; we know, too, that a ship may go down, in which case there is a probability of being drowned; but we do not think about these dangers, and travel by rail and ship without anxiety. It cannot be disputed that we should fall into the river if the bridge collapsed at the moment we were crossing it; but that happens so exceedingly seldom that it does not arise as a danger. Solitude, too, has its dangers and in certain circumstances we avoid it; but there is no question of our not being able to tolerate it under any condition even for a moment. Much the same is true of crowds, of enclosed spaces, of thunderstorms and so on. What in general appears to us strange in these phobias of neurotics is not so much their content as their intensity. The anxiety of phobias is positively overwhelming. And sometimes we get an impression that what neurotics are afraid of are not at all the same things

and situations which may in certain circumstances cause anxiety in us too and which they describe by the same names.

We are left with a third group of phobias, which is quite beyond our comprehension. When a strong, grown-up man is unable owing to anxiety to walk along a street or cross a square in his own familiar hometown, when a healthy, well-developed woman is thrown into insensate anxiety because a cat has brushed against the edge of her dress or because a mouse has run across the room, how are we to relate these things to the danger which they obviously constitute for the phobic subject? In the case of such animal phobias there can be no question of an exaggeration of universal human antipathies, since, as though to demonstrate the contrary, there are numerous people who cannot pass by a cat without coaxing it and stroking it. The mouse that these women are so much afraid of is also (in German) one of the chief terms of affection; a girl who delighted when her lover calls her one will often scream with terror when she sees the pretty creature which bears that name. In the case of the man with agoraphobia the only explanation that we can reach is that he is behaving like a small child. A child is actually taught as part of his education to avoid such situations as dangerous; and our agoraphobic will in fact be saved from his anxiety if we accompany him across the square.

The two forms of anxiety that I have just described—the freely floating expectant anxiety and the sort which is bound to phobias—are independent of each other. One is not a higher stage, as it were, of the other; and they only appear simultaneously in exceptional cases and, so to speak, accidentally. The most powerful general apprehensiveness need not be expressed in phobias; people whose whole existence is restricted by agoraphobia may be entirely free from pessimistic expectant anxiety. Some phobias—for instance, agoraphobia and railway phobia—are demonstrably acquired at a fairly mature age, while others—such as fear of darkness, thunderstorms, and animals—seem to have been present from the first. Those of the former kind have the significance of severe illnesses; the latter make their appearance rather as eccentricities or whims. If a person exhibits one of these latter, one may suspect as a rule that he will have other similar ones. I must add that we class all these phobias as *anxiety hysteria*; that is to say, we regard them as a disorder closely related to the familiar conversion hysteria.

The third of the forms of neurotic anxiety faces us with the puzzling fact that here the connection between anxiety and a threatening danger is completely lost to view. For instance, anxiety may appear in hysteria as an accompaniment to the hysterical symptoms, or in some chance condition of excitement in which, it is true, we should expect some manifestation of affect but least of all one of anxiety; or it may make its appearance, divorced from any determinants and equally comprehensible to us and to the patient, as an unrelated attack of anxiety. Here there is no sign whatever of any danger or of any cause that could be exaggerated into one. We next learn from these spontaneous attacks that the complex which we describe as

a state of anxiety is capable of fragmentation. The total attack can be represented by a single, intensely developed symptom, by a tremor, a vertigo, by palpitation of the heart, or by dyspnoea; and the general feeling by which we recognize anxiety may be absent or have become indistinct. Yet these conditions, which we describe as 'anxiety-equivalents', have to be equated with anxiety in all clinical and aetiological respects. . . .

Our observations on anxiety neurosis led us to conclude that the deflection of the libido from its normal employment, which causes the development of anxiety, takes place in the region of somatic processes. Analyses of hysteria and obsessional neurosis yield the additional conclusion that a similar deflection with the same outcome may also be the result of a refusal on the part of the *psychical* agencies. This much, therefore, we know about the origin of neurotic anxiety. It still sounds fairly indefinite; but for the moment I see no path that would lead us further. The second problem we set ourselves—of establishing a connection between neurotic anxiety, which is libido put to an abnormal employment, and realistic anxiety, which corresponds to a reaction to danger—seems even harder to solve. One might suppose that these were two quite disparate things; and yet we have no means of distinguishing in our feelings between realistic anxiety and neurotic anxiety.

We finally arrive at the connection we are in search of, if we take as our starting point the opposition we have so often asserted between the ego and the libido. As we know, the generation of anxiety is the ego's reaction to danger and the signal for taking flight. If so, it seems plausible to suppose that in neurotic anxiety the ego is making a similar attempt at flight from the demand by its libido, that it is treating this internal danger as though it were an external one. This would therefore fulfill our expectation that where anxiety is shown there is something one is afraid of. But the analogy could be carried further. Just as the attempt at flight from an external danger is replaced by standing firm and the adoption of expedient measures of defense, so too the generation of neurotic anxiety gives place to the formation of symptoms, which results in the anxiety being bound. . . .

I have said that transformation into anxiety—it would be better to say discharge in the form of anxiety—is the immediate vicissitude of libido which is subjected to repression. I must add that that vicissitude is not the only or the definitive one. In the neuroses processes are in action which endeavor to bind this generating of anxiety and which even succeed in doing so in various ways. In phobias, for instance, two phases of the neurotic process can be clearly distinguished. The first is concerned with repression and the changing of libido into anxiety, which is then bound to an external danger. The second consists in the erection of all the precautions and guarantees by means of which any contact can be avoided with this danger, treated as it is like an external thing. Repression corresponds to an attempt at flight by the ego from libido which is felt as a danger. A phobia may be compared to an entrenchment against an external danger which now represents the dreaded libido. . . .

We thus find ourselves convinced that the problem of anxiety occupies a place in the question of the psychology of the neuroses which may rightly be described as central. We have received a strong impression of the way in which the generation of anxiety is linked to the vicissitudes of the libido and the system of the unconscious. There is only a single point that we have found disconnected—a gap in our views: the single, yet scarcely disputable, fact that realistic anxiety must be regarded as a manifestation of the ego's self-preservative instincts.

3.

SIGMUND FREUD

... the special agency which I am beginning to distinguish in the ego is conscience. But it is more prudent to keep the agency as something independent and to suppose that conscience is one of its functions and that self-observation, which is an essential preliminary to the judging activity of conscience, is another of them. And since when we recognize that something has a separate existence we give it a name of its own, from this time forward I will describe this agency in the ego as the *"super-ego."*

I am now prepared to hear you ask me scornfully whether our ego-psychology comes down to nothing more than taking commonly used abstractions literally and in a crude sense, and transforming them from concepts into things—by which not much would be gained. To this I would reply that in ego-psychology it will be difficult to escape what is universally known; it will rather be a question of new ways of looking at things and new ways of arranging them than of new discoveries. So hold to your contemptuous criticism for the time being and await further explanations. The facts of pathology give our efforts a

background that you would look for in vain in popular psychology. So I will proceed.

Hardly have we familiarized ourselves with the idea of a super-ego like this which enjoys a certain degree of autonomy, follows its own intentions and is independent of the ego for its supply of energy, than a clinical picture forces itself on our notice which throws a striking light on the severity of this agency and indeed its cruelty, and on its changing relations to the ego. I am thinking of the condition of melancholia, or, more precisely, of melancholic attacks, which you too will have heard plenty about, even if you are not psychiatrists. The most striking feature of this illness, of whose causation and mechanism we know much too little, is the way in which the super-ego—"conscience," you may call it, quietly—treats the ego. While a melancholic can, like other people, show a greater or lesser degree of severity to himself in his healthy periods, during a melancholic attack, his super-ego becomes over-severe, abuses the poor ego, humiliates it and ill-treats it, threatens it with the direct punishments, reproaches it for actions in the remotest past which had been taken lightly at the time—as though it had spent the whole interval in collecting accusations and had only been waiting for its present access of strength in order to bring them up and make a condemnatory judgment on their basis. The super-ego applies the strictest moral

³ Freud, S. (1965). *New Introductory Lectures on Psychoanalysis.* New York: W. W. Norton, pp. 75–76. Reprinted from *New Introductory Lectures on Psycho-Analysis* by Sigmund Freud, translated by James Strachey, with the permission of W. W. Norton & Company, Inc. Copyright 1933 by Sigmund Freud, renewed © 1961 by W. J. H. Sprott. Copyright © 1965, 1964 by James Strachey.

standard to the helpless ego which is at its mercy; in general it represents the claims of morality, and we realize all at once that our moral sense of guilt is the expression of the tension between the ego and the super-ego. It is a most remarkable experience to see morality, which is supposed to be given us by God and thus deeply implanted in us, functioning (in these patients) as a periodic phenomenon. For after a certain number of months the whole moral fuss is over, the criticism of the super-ego is silent, the ego is rehabilitated and again enjoys all the rights of man till the next attack. In some forms of the disease, indeed, something of a contrary sort occurs in the intervals; the ego finds itself in a blissful state of intoxication, it celebrates triumph, as though the super-ego had lost all its strength or had melted into the ego; and this liberated, manic ego permits itself a truly uninhibited satisfaction of all its appetites. Here are the happenings rich in unsolved riddles!

4.

SIGMUND FREUD

The Meaning of Symptoms. A well-grown clever girl of 19, the only child of her parents, superior to them in education and intellectual activity, was a wild, high-spirited child, but of late years had become very nervous without any apparent cause. She was very irritable, particularly with her mother, was discontented and depressed, inclined to indecision and doubt, finally confessing that she could no longer walk alone through squares and wide streets. We will not go very closely into her complicated condition, which requires at least two diagnoses: agoraphobia and obsessional neurosis: but will turn our attention to the ritual elaborated by this young girl preparatory to going to bed, as a result of which she caused her parents great distress. In a certain sense, every normal person may be said to carry out a ritual before going to sleep, or at least, he requires certain conditions without which he is hindered in going to sleep; the transition from waking life to sleep has been made into a regular formula which is repeated every night in the same manner. But everything that a healthy person requires as a condition of sleep can be rationally explained, and if the external circumstances make any alteration necessary he adapts himself easily to it without a waste of time. The morbid ritual on the other hand is inexorable, it will be maintained at the greatest sacrifices; it is disguised, too, under rational

---

[4] Freud, S. (1943). *A General Introduction to Psycho-Analysis.* New York: Garden City Publishing Co., Inc., pp. 234–238.

motives and appears superficially to differ from the normal only in a certain exaggerated carefulness of execution. On a closer examination, however, it is clear that the disguise is insufficient, that the ritual includes observances which go far beyond what reason can justify and even some which directly contravene this. As the motive of her nightly precautions, our patient declares that she must have silence at night and must exclude all possibility of noise. She does two things for this purpose; she stops the large clock in her room and removes all other clocks out of the room, including even a tiny wrist-watch on her bed-table. Flower-pots and vases are placed carefully together on the writing-table, so that they cannot fall down in the night and break, and so disturb her sleep. She knows that these precautions have only an illusory justification in the demand for quiet; the ticking of the little watch could not be heard, even if it lay on the table by the bed; and we all know that the regular ticking of a pendulum-clock never disturbs sleep, but is more likely to induce it. She also admits that her fear that the flower-pots and vases, if left in their places at night, might fall down of themselves and break is utterly improbable. For some other practices in her ritual this insistence upon silence as a motive is dropped; indeed, by ordaining that the door between her bedroom and that of her parents shall remain half-open (a condition which she ensures by placing objects in the doorway) she seems, on the contrary, to open the way to sources of noise. The most important observances are concerned with the bed itself, however. The bolster at the head of the bed must not touch the back of the wooden bedstead. The pillow must lie across the bolster exactly in a diagonal position and in no other; she then places her head exactly in the middle of this diamond, lengthways. The eiderdown must be shaken before she puts it over her, so that all the feathers sink to the foot-end; she never fails, however, to press this out and redistribute them all over again.

I will pass over other trivial details of her ritual; they would teach us nothing new and lead us too far from our purpose. Do not suppose, though, that all this is carried out with perfect smoothness. Everything is accompanied by the anxiety that it has not all been done properly; it must be tested and repeated; her doubts fix first upon one, then another, of the precautions; and the result is that one or two hours elapse before the girl herself can sleep, or lets the intimidated parents sleep.

The analysis of these torments did not proceed so simply as that of the former patient's obsessive act. I had to offer hints and suggestions of its interpretation which were invariably received by her with a positive denial or with scornful doubt. After this first reaction of rejection, however, there followed a period in which she herself took up the possibilities suggested to her, noted the associations they aroused, produced memories, and established connections until she herself had accepted all the interpretations in working them out for herself. In proportion as she did this she began to relax the performance of her obsessive precautions and before the end of the treatment she had given up the whole ritual. I must also tell you that analytic work, as we conduct it nowadays, definitely excludes any uninterrupted concentration on a single symptom until its meaning becomes fully clear. It is necessary, on the contrary, to abandon a given theme again and again, in the assurance that one will come upon it anew in another context. The interpretation of the symptom, which I am now going to tell you, is therefore a synthesis of the results which, amid the interruptions of work on other points, took weeks and months to procure.

The patient gradually learnt to understand that she banished clocks and watches from her room at night because they were symbols of the female genitals. Clocks, which we know have other symbolic meanings besides this, acquire this significance of a genital organ by their relation to periodical processes and regular intervals. A woman may be heard to boast that menstruation occurs in her as regularly as clockwork. Now this patient's special fear was that the ticking of the clocks would disturb her during sleep. The ticking of a clock is comparable to the throbbing of the clitoris in sexual excitation. This sensation, which was distressing to her, had actually on several occasions wakened her from sleep; and now her fear of an erection of the clitoris expressed itself by the imposition of a rule to remove all going clocks and watches far away from her during the night. Flower-pots and vases are, like all receptacles, also symbols of the female genitals. Precautions to prevent them from falling and breaking during the night are therefore not lacking in meaning. We know the very widespread custom of breaking a vessel or a plate on the occasion of betrothal; everyone present possesses himself of a fragment in symbolic

acceptance of the fact that he may no longer put forward any claims to the bride, presumably a custom which arose with monogamy. The patient also contributed a recollection and several associations to this part of her ritual. Once as a child she had fallen while carrying a glass or porcelain vessel, and had cut her finger which had bled badly. As she grew up and learnt the facts about sexual intercourse, she developed the apprehension that on her wedding-night she would not bleed and so would prove not to be a virgin. Her precautions against the vases breaking signified a rejection of the whole complex concerned with virginity and with the question of bleeding during the first act of intercourse; a rejection of the anxiety both that she would bleed and that she would not bleed. These precautions were in fact only remotely connected with the prevention of noise.

One day she divined the central idea of her ritual when she suddenly understood her rule not to let the bolster touch the back of the bed. The bolster had always seemed a woman to her, she said, and the upright back of the bedstead a man. She wished therefore, by a magic ceremony, as it were, to keep man and woman apart; that is to say, to separate the parents and prevent intercourse from occurring. Years before the institution of her ritual, she had attempted to achieve this end by a more direct method. She had simulated fear, or had exploited a tendency to fear, so that the door between her bedroom and that of her parents should not be closed. This regulation was still actually included in her present ritual; in this way she managed to make it possible to overhear her parents; a proceeding which at one time had caused her months of sleeplessness. Not content with disturbing her parents in this way, she at a time even succeeded occasionally in sleeping between the father and mother in bed. "Bolster" and "bedstead" were then really prevented from coming together. As she finally grew too big to be comfortable in the same bed with the parents, she achieved the same thing by consciously simulating fear and getting her mother to change places with her and to give up her place by the father. This incident was undoubtedly the starting-point of phantasies, the effect of which was evident in the ritual.

If the bolster was a woman, then the shaking of the eiderdown till all the feathers were at the bottom, making a protuberance there, also had a meaning. It meant impregnating a woman; she did not neglect, though, to obliterate the pregnancy again, for she had for years been terrified that intercourse between her parents might result in another child and present her with a rival. On the other hand, if the large bolster meant the mother then the small pillow could only represent the daughter. Why had this pillow to be placed diamond-wise upon the bolster and her head be laid exactly in its middle lengthways? She was easily reminded that a diamond is repeatedly used in drawings on walls to signify the open female genitals. The part of the man (the father) she thus played herself and replaced the male organ by her own head. . . .

Horrible thoughts, you will say, to run in the mind of a virgin girl. I admit that; but do not forget that I have not invented these ideas, only exposed them. A ritual of this kind before sleep is also peculiar enough, and you cannot deny the correspondence, revealed by the interpretation, between the ceremonies and the phantasies. It is more important to me, however, that you should notice that the ritual was the outcome, not of one single phantasy, but of several together which of course must have had a nodal point somewhere. Note, too, that the details of the ritual reflect the sexual wishes both positively and negatively, and serve in part as expressions of them, in part as defenses against them.

Dream Work

COMMENTARY

Dreams have a very important place in Freudian theory and analysis. Dreams were, for Freud, the "royal road" to the unconscious. Indeed, they were the primary well-spring that led Freud to an empirical validation of the phenomenon of the unconscious. Freud discovered that dreams contained symbols, the distorted substitutes for unconscious thoughts, feelings, and desires. The magnitude of such distortions led Freud to believe that dreams represented temporary psychotic episodes in the life of the dreamer. Because of these distortions, Freud saw the dream in two aspects: *the manifest content*, the remembered and conscious portion of the dream; the dream as we usually tell it to another person, and *the latent content*, the most important dimension of the dream for Freud, which includes all aspects of the dream that are symbolized and distorted. Such distortions reflect or contain deeper meanings that are out of the reach of the dreamer's awareness.

According to Freud's theory of dream work (which refers to the dreamer's dynamic use of the dream), the true purpose of the dream is to fulfill wishes and impulses in a safe and imaginary fashion. Thus, in the dream these wishes and impulses are cloaked in a symbolic disguise in order to protect the dreamer from anxiety and psychic pain. Dreams, therefore, are attempts at symbolic wish fulfillments representing a level of primary process gratification. It was the purpose of psychoanalysis, through the dreamer's many and varied associations to elements of the dream, to arrive at the dream's meaning.

In discussing the evidence of the role of the unconscious id in the formation of dreams, Freud recognizes those dreams that contain archaic remnants of a human prehistory. In this observation, Freud appears to recognize the existence of a "collective unconscious," a concept, as we shall see, that was central to Carl Jung's theory. The construct of the collective unconscious, however, was never given any serious attention by Freud.

SIGMUND FREUD

Revision of the Theory of Dreams

. . . We should turn our attention first to the position of the theory of dreams. It occupies a special place in the history of psycho-analysis and marks a turning point; it was with it that analysis took the step from being a psychotherapeutic procedure to being a depth-psychology. Since then, too, the theory of dreams has remained what is most characteristic and peculiar about the young science, something to which there is no counterpart in the rest of our knowledge, a stretch of new country, which has been reclaimed from popular beliefs and mysticism. The strangeness of the assertions it was obliged to put forward has made it play the part of a shibboleth, the use of which decided who could become a follower of psycho-analysis and to whom

Freud. S. (1965). *New Introductory Lectures on Psycho-Analysis*. New York: W. W. Norton, pp. 8–9, 11–16. Reprinted from *New Introductory Lectures on Psycho-Analysis* by Sigmund Freud, translated by James Strachey, with the permission of W. W. Norton & Company, Inc. Copyright 1933 by Sigmund Freud, renewed © 1961 by W. J. H. Sprott. Copyright © 1965, 1964 by James Strachey.

it remained for ever incomprehensible. I myself found it a sheet-anchor during those difficult times when the unrecognized facts of the neuroses used to confuse my experienced judgment. Whenever I began to have doubts of the correctness of my wavering conclusions, the successful transformation of a senseless and muddled dream into a logical and intelligible mental process in the dreamer would renew my confidence of being on the right track. . . .

. . . What has been called the dream we shall describe as the text of the dream or the *manifest* dream, and what we are looking for, what we suspect, so to say, of lying behind the dream, we shall describe as the *latent* dream-thoughts. Having done this, we can express our two tasks as follows. We have to transform the manifest dream into the latent one, and to explain how, in the dreamer's mind, the latter has become the former. The first portion is a *practical* task, for which dream-interpretation is responsible; it calls for a technique. The second portion is a *theoretical* task, whose business it is to explain the hypothetical dream-work; and it can only be a theory. Both of them, the technique of dream-interpretation and theory of the dream-work, have to be newly created.

With which of the two, then, shall we start? With the technique of dream-interpretation, I think; it will present a more concrete appearance and make a more vivid impression on you.

Well then, the patient has told us a dream, which we are to interpret. We have listened passively, without putting our powers of reflection into action. What do we do next? We decide to concern ourselves as little as possible with what we have heard, with the *manifest* dream. Of course this manifest dream exhibits all sorts of characteristics which are not entirely a matter of indifference to us. It may be coherent, smoothly constructed like a literary composition, or it may be confused to the point of unintelligibility, almost like a delirium; it may contain absurd elements or jokes and apparently witty conclusions; it may seem to the dreamer clear and sharp or obscure and hazy; its pictures may exhibit the complete sensory strength of perceptions or may be shadowy like an indistinct mist; the most diverse characteristics may be present in the same dream, distributed over various portions of it; the dream, finally, may show an indifferent emotional tone or be accompanied by feelings of the strongest joy or distress. You must not suppose that we think nothing of this endless diversity in manifest dreams. We shall come back to it later and we shall find a great deal in it that we can make use of in our interpretations. But for the moment we will disregard it and follow the main road that leads to the interpretation of dreams. That is to say, we ask the dreamer, too, to free

himself from the impression of the manifest dream, to divert his attention from the dream as a whole on to the separate portions of its content and to report to us in succession everything that occurs to him in relation to each of these portions—what associations present themselves to him if he focuses on each of them separately.

That is a curious technique, is it not?—not the usual way of dealing with a communication or utterance. And no doubt you guess that behind this procedure there are assumptions which have not yet been expressly stated. But let us proceed. In what order are we to get the patient to take up the portions of his dream? There are various possibilities open to us. We can simply follow the chronological order in which they appeared in the account of the dream. That is what may be called the strictest, classical method. Or we can direct the dreamer to begin by looking out for the "day's residues" in the dream; for experience has taught us that almost every dream includes the remains of a memory or an allusion to some event (or often to several events) of the day before the dream, and, if we follow these connections, we often arrive with one blow at the transition from the apparently far remote dream-world to the real life of the patient. Or, again, we may tell him to start with those elements of the dream's content which strike him by their special clarity and sensory strength; for we know that he will find it particularly easy to get associations to these. It makes no difference by which of these methods we approach the associations we are in search of.

And next, we obtain these associations. What they bring us is of the most various kinds: memories from the day before, the "dream-day," and from times long past, reflections, discussions, with arguments for and against, confessions and enquiries. Some of them the patient pours out; when he comes to others he is held up for a time. Most of them show a clear connection to some element of the dream; no wonder, since those elements were their starting-point. But it also sometimes happens that the patient introduces them with these words: "This seems to me to have nothing at all to do with the dream, but I tell it to you because it occurs to me."

If one listens to these copious associations, one soon notices that they have more in common with the content of the dream than their starting-points alone. They throw a surprising light on all the different parts of the dream, fill in gaps between them, and make their strange juxtapositions intelligible. In the end one is bound to become clear about the relation between them and the dream's content. The dream is seen to be an abbreviated selection from the associations, a selection made, it is true, according to rules that we have not yet understood: the elements of the dream are like representatives chosen by election from a mass of people. There can be no doubt that by our technique we have got hold of something for which the dream is a substitute and in which lies the dream's psychical value, but which no longer exhibits its puzzling peculiarities, its strangeness and its confusion.

Let there be no misunderstanding, however. The associations to the dream are not yet the latent dream-thoughts. The latter are contained in the associations like an alkali in the mother-liquor, but yet not quite completely contained in them. On the one hand, the associations give us far more than we need for formulating the latent dream-thoughts—namely all the explanations, transitions, and connections which the patient's intellect is bound to produce in the course of his approach to the dream-thoughts. On the other hand, an association often comes to a stop precisely before the genuine dream-thought: it has only come near to it and has only had contact with it through allusions. At that point we intervene on our own; we fill in the hints, draw undeniable conclusions, and give explicit utterance to what the patient has only touched on in his associations. This sounds as though we allowed our ingenuity and caprice to play with the material put at our disposal by the dreamer and as though we misused it in order to interpret *into* his utterances what cannot be interpreted *from* them. Nor is it easy to show the legitimacy of our procedure in an abstract description of it. But you have only to carry out a dream-analysis yourselves or study a good account of one in our literature and you will be convinced of the cogent manner in which interpretative work like this proceeds.

If in general and primarily we are dependent, in interpreting dreams, on the dreamer's associations, yet in relation to certain elements of the dream's content we adopt a quite independent attitude, chiefly because we have to, because as a rule associations fail to materialize in their case. We noticed at an early stage that it is always in connection with the same elements that this happens; they are not very numerous, and repeated experience has taught us that they are to be regarded and interpreted as *symbols* of something else. As contrasted with the other dream-elements, a fixed meaning may be attributed to them, which, however, need not be unambiguous and whose range is determined by special rules with which we are unfamiliar. Since *we* know how to translate these symbols and the dreamer does not, in spite of having used them himself, it may happen that the sense of a dream may at once become clear to us as soon as we have heard the text of the dream, even before we have made any efforts at interpreting it, while it still remains an enigma to the dreamer himself. . . .

CHAPTER II

The Individual Psychology of Alfred Adler

BIOGRAPHICAL SKETCH

Alfred Adler, the second of six children, was born in Vienna in the suburb of Penzig, on February 17, 1870. Although he was born into a lower-middle-class Jewish family (his father was a successful merchant), Adler appeared to be influenced more by the rich Viennese culture than by his ethnic background. He never made an issue of his Jewish heritage, as did Freud, and as an adult he converted to Protestantism.

Adler was weak and sickly throughout his early childhood. He suffered from rickets, almost died of pneumonia at five years of age, and twice was almost killed in street accidents. Thus, in sports and other activities, Adler was unable to compete with his peers and unable to win out in an intense rivalry with his older brother, Sigmund. Adler also had a slow start in school, experiencing a particular struggle with math. He was advised by his teacher at one point to apprentice as a shoemaker. With strong support from his father, however, Adler continued to improve in his studies until be became an outstanding student.

Adler's own experiences with poor health and the death of his younger brother prompted an early interest in medicine and healing, and he followed this interest into the University of Vienna Medical School where he obtained his medical degree in 1895. From an initial interest in opthalmology Adler entered general practice, and as his interest in human behavior expanded, he focused on the study and practice of psychiatry.

In 1897, two years after graduating from medical school, Adler married Raissa Tinofejewa, a wealthy Russian girl who had come to Vienna to study.

After publishing a paper defending Freud's book *The Interpretation of Dreams*, Adler was invited by Freud to join the elite Vienna Psychoanalytic Society, becoming one of Freud's earliest colleagues. In 1911, however, after having served as president only a year, Adler resigned under pressure from the society. Adler's vigorous rejection of Freud's view of infantile sexuality and his concept of the unconscious, led to a permanent separation from Freud and his group.

Soon after his resignation, Adler and his followers formed their own group, known initially as the Society of Free Psychoanalytic Research. Later, the group settled on the term "Individual Psychology" to more clearly identify their commitment to a different set of assumptions about human personality.

After serving in the Austrian army during World War I, Adler began the development of child guidance clinics for the public schools of Vienna, applying his ideas in a practical way to child development, education, and family life. In this work he was an early pioneer in the area of community psychiatry. These theoretical and practical contributions brought Adler wide attention and recognition, and he was in demand as a lecturer all over the world.

Freud's view of Adler's contributions was different, however. He claimed that Adler offered nothing new and only changed the terminology. In 1926 Adler made his first visit to the United States, where in 1927 he became a lecturer at Columbia University and a professor of medical psychology at the Long Island College of Medicine. In 1934 Adler and his wife took up residence in New York City, and in 1935 they made the United States their permanent home.

Adler was a highly popular and indefatigable speaker all over the world. It was while he was on one of his many speaking tours, in Aberdeen, Scotland, that he died of a heart attack on May 28, 1937.

Following his death, Adler's impact waned. In the past two decades, however, due in no small part to the interpretive work of Heinz and Rowena Ansbacher, Adler's theories have once again become well known and extremely influential.

There is a journal devoted to the theory and practice of Adlerian psychology, and there are active centers for Adlerian study around the world. Several of these, including the Adlerian Institute in Chicago, offer advanced degrees in the practice and theory of Individual Psychology. Over the years, Adler has also been extremely influential on other psychologists and the development of their ideas. These include, among many others, Abraham Maslow, Carl Rogers, Gordon Allport, Rollo May, Karen Horney, and Erich Fromm.

Adler's theories continue to be ones of substance and relevance.

Inferiority Feelings and Strivings for Superiority

COMMENTARY

In his early thinking Adler stressed organic conditions and the essential weakness and dependency in infancy as the primary source of all later inferiority feelings in the child. In subsequent writings, as in these selections, he emphasized a variety of situations in the child's life that had the potential to provoke feelings of inferiority. Many of these situations refer to the school environment and the insensitivity of teachers.

It is important to remember that, while the feeling of inferiority is "the driving force" behind all strivings for superiority, Adler increasingly recognized that the striving for superiority was not *merely* a compensation for inferiority feelings but was, itself, a dynamic motivation. Thus, feelings of inferiority and the striving for superiority constituted a dynamic interaction, a dialectic force for the upward movement of the personality.

The creative agency in the personality is also given attention here. Adler emphasizes that it is the child's perception and interpretation of his/her situation that is the most important consideration in understanding the child's position and assessing the form that the superiority strivings take. Neurotic symptom formation, for Adler, represented an extreme sense of inferiority and a maladaptive way of dealing with these feelings. To identify this condition of the personality he gave us the term "inferiority complex." The expressions of superiority in neurotic individuals were thus misdirected into false goals, inappropriate behavior, and a maladaptive lifestyle. Individual Psychology, therefore, emphasized the dynamic nature of symptom formation but differed sharply from the psychoanalytical view that the meaning of symptoms lay in repressed sexual conflict and destructive urges.

1.

ALFRED ADLER

One must remember that every child occupies an inferior position in life; were it not for a certain quantum of social feeling on the part of his family he would be incapable of independent existence. One realizes that the beginning of every life is fraught with a more or less deep feeling of inferiority when one sees the weakness and helplessness of every child. Sooner or later every child becomes conscious of his inability to cope single-handed with the challenges of existence. This feeling of inferiority is the driving force, the starting point from which every childish striving originates. It determines how this individual child acquires peace and security in life, it determines the very goal of his existence, and prepares the path along which this goal may be reached.

The basis of a child's educability lies in this peculiar situation which is so closely bound up with his organic potentialities. Educability may be

[1] Adler, A. (1927). *Understanding Human Nature.* New York: Garden City Publishing Co., pp. 69–71. Reprinted by permission of the Estate of Alfred Adler. From *Understanding Human Nature,* by Alfred Adler. Copyright © 1927. Renewed 1955 by Kurt Adler.

shattered by two factors. One of these factors is an exaggerated, intensified, unresolved feeling of inferiority, and the other is a goal which demands not only security and peace and social equilibrium, but a striving to express power over the environment, a goal of dominance over one's fellows. Children who have such goals are always easily recognized. They become "problem" children because they interpret every experience as a defeat, and because they consider themselves always neglected and discriminated against both by nature and by man. One need but consider all these factors to see with what compulsive necessity a crooked, inadequate error-ridden development may occur in the life of a child. Every child runs the danger of mistaken development. Every child finds itself in a situation which is precarious, at some time or another.

Since every child must grow up in an environment of adults he is predisposed to consider himself weak, small, incapable of living alone; he does not trust himself to do those simple tasks that one thinks him capable of doing, without mistakes, errors, or clumsiness. Most of our errors in education begin at this point. In demanding more than the child can do, the idea of his own helplessness is thrown into his face. Some children are even consciously made to feel their smallness and helplessness. Other children are regarded as toys, as animated dolls; others, again, are treated as valuable property that must be carefully watched, while others still are made to feel they are so much useless human freight. A combination of these attitudes on the part of the parents and adults often leads a child to believe that there are but two things in his power, the pleasure or displeasure of his elders. The type of inferiority feeling produced by the parents may be further intensified by certain peculiar characteristics of our civilization. The habit of not taking children seriously belongs in this category. A child gets the impression that he is a nobody, without rights; that he is to be seen, not heard, that he must be courteous, quiet, and the like. Numerous children grow up in the constant dread of being laughed at. Ridicule of children is well-nigh criminal. It retains its effect upon the soul of the child, and is transferred into the habits and actions of his adulthood. An adult who was continually laughed at as a child may be easily recognized; he cannot rid himself of the fear of being made ridiculous again. Another aspect of this matter of not taking children seriously is *the* custom of telling children palpable lies, with the result that the child begins to doubt not only his immediate environment but also to question the seriousness and reality of life.

2.

ALFRED ADLER

The Normal Inferiority Feeling

The degree of the feeling of insecurity and inferiority depends primarily

[2] Excerpt from p. 116 from *The Individual Psychology of Alfred Adler* by Heinz L. Ansbacher and Rowena R. Ansbacher. Copyright © 1956 by Basic Books, Inc. Copyright renewed 1984 by Heinz L. and Rowena R. Ansbacher. Reprinted by permission of BasicBooks, a division of HarperCollins Publishers, Inc.

on the interpretation of the child. Certainly the degree of objective inferiority is significant and will make itself felt. But we must not expect that the child will make correct appraisals in this connection, any more than will the adult. One child will grow up in such complicated circumstances that an error regarding the degree of his inferiority and insecurity is almost certain, while another child will be able to appraise his situation more correctly. By and large, however, it is always the feeling of the child which must be considered. At first this fluctuates daily until eventually it becomes somehow consolidated and expresses itself as a self-appraisal.

3.

ALFRED ADLER

Feelings of Inferiority and Superiority

The "inferiority complex," one of the most important discoveries of Individual Psychology, seems to have become world-famous. Psychologists of many schools have adopted the term and use it in their own practice. I am not at all sure, however, that they understand it or use it with the right meaning. It never helps us, for example, to tell a patient that he is suffering from an inferiority complex; to do so would only stress his feelings of inferiority without showing him how to overcome them. We must recognize the specific discouragement which he shows in his style of life; we must encourage him at the precise point where he falls short in courage. Every neurotic has an inferiority complex. No neurotic is distinguished from other neurotics by the fact that he has an inferiority complex and the others have none. He is distinguished from the others by the kind of situation in which he feels unable to continue on the useful side of life; by the limits he has put to his strivings and activities. It would no more help him to be more courageous if we said to him, "You are suffering from an inferiority complex," than it would help someone with a headache if we said, "I can tell you what is wrong with you. You have a headache!"

Many neurotics, if they were asked whether they felt inferior, would answer, "No." Some would even answer, "Just the opposite. I know quite well that I am superior to the people around me." We do not need to ask: we need only watch the individual's behavior. It is there that we shall notice what tricks he uses to reassure himself of his importance. If we see someone who is arrogant, for example, we can guess that he feels, "Other people are apt to overlook me. I must show that I am somebody." If we see someone who gesticulates strongly when he speaks, we can guess that he feels, "My words would not carry any weight if I did not emphasize them." Behind every one who behaves as if he were superior to others, we can suspect

[3] Adler, A. (1980). *What Life Should Mean to You.* London: George Allen and Unwin, pp. 49–52. From *What Life Should Mean to You* by Alfred Adler. Copyright © 1931. Renewed 1959 by Kurt Adler. Reprinted by permission of the Estate of Alfred Adler.

a feeling of inferiority which calls for very special efforts of concealment. It is as if a man feared that he was too small and walked on tiptoe to make himself seem larger. Sometimes we can see this very behavior if two children are comparing their height. The one who is afraid that he is smaller will stretch up and hold himself very tensely; he will try to seem bigger than he is. If we asked such a child, "Do you think you are too small?" we should hardly expect him to acknowledge the fact.

It does not follow, therefore, that an individual with strong feelings of inferiority will appear to be a submissive, quiet, restrained, inoffensive sort of person. Inferiority feelings can express themselves in a thousand ways. Perhaps I can illustrate this by an anecdote of three children who were taken to the zoo for the first time. As they stood before the lion's cage, one of them shrank behind his mother's skirts and said, "I want to go home." The second child stood where he was, very pale and trembling, and said, "I'm not a bit frightened." The third glared at the lion fiercely and asked his mother, "Shall I spit at it?" All three children felt inferior, but each expressed his feelings in his own way, consonant with his style of life.

Inferiority feelings are in some degree common to all of us, since we all find ourselves in positions which we wish to improve. If we have kept our courage, we shall set about ridding ourselves of these feelings by the only direct, realistic and satisfactory means—by improving the situation. No human being can bear a feeling of inferiority for long; he will be thrown into a tension which necessitates some

kind of action. But suppose an individual is discouraged; suppose he cannot conceive that if he makes realistic efforts he will improve the situation. He will still be unable to bear his feelings of inferiority; he will still struggle to get rid of them; but he will try methods which bring him no farther ahead. His goal is still "to be superior to difficulties," but instead of overcoming obstacles he will try to hypnotize himself, or auto-intoxicate himself, into *feeling* superior. Meanwhile his feelings of inferiority will accumulate, because the situation which produces them remains unaltered. The provocation is still there. Every step he takes will lead him father into self-deception, and all his problems will press in upon him with greater and greater urgency. If we looked at his movements without understanding we should think them aimless. They would not impress us as designed to improve the situation. As soon as we see, however, that he is occupied like everyone else, in struggling for a feeling of adequacy but has given up hope of altering the objective situation, all his movements begin to fall into coherence. If he feels weak, he moves into circumstances where he can feel strong. He does not train to be stronger, to be more adequate; he trains to appear stronger in his own eyes. His efforts to fool himself will meet with only a partial success. If he feels unequal to the problems of occupation, he may attempt to reassure himself of his importance by being a domestic tyrant. In this way he may drug himself; but the real feelings of inferiority will remain. They will be the same old feelings of inferiority provoked by the same old situation. They will be the lasting undercurrent of his psychic life. In such a case we may truly speak of an inferiority complex.

It is time now to give a definition of the inferiority complex. The inferiority complex appears before a problem for which an individual is not properly adapted or equipped, and expresses his conviction that he is unable to solve it. From this definition we can see that anger can be as much an expression of an inferiority complex as tears or apologies. As inferiority feelings always produce tension, there will always be a compensatory movement towards a feeling of superiority; but it will no longer be directed towards solving the problem. The movement towards superiority will thus be towards the useless side of life. The real problem will be shelved or excluded. The individual will try to restrict his field of action and will be more occupied in avoiding defeat than in pressing forward to success. He will give the picture of hesitating, of being at a standstill, or even of retreating, before his difficulties.

4.

ALFRED ADLER

To some degree or other, every neurotic restricts his field of action, his contacts with the whole situation. He tries to keep at a distance the three real confronting problems of life and confines himself to circumstances in which he feels able to dominate. In this way he builds for himself a narrow stable, closes the door and spends his life away from the wind, the sunlight and the fresh air. Whether he dominates by bullying or by whining will depend on his training: he will choose the device in which he has tested best and found most effective for his purposes. Sometimes if he is dissatisfied with one method, he will try the other. In either case the goal is the same—to gain a feeling of superiority without working to improve the situation. The discouraged child which finds that it can tyrannize best by tears will be a cry-baby; and a direct line of development leads from the cry-baby to the adult melancholiac. Tears and complaints—the means which I called "water power"—can be an extremely capable weapon for disturbing cooperation and reducing others to a condition of slavery. With such people, as with those who suffer from shyness, embarrassment and feelings of guilt, we should find the inferiority complex on the surface; they would readily admit their weakness and their inability to look after themselves. What they

[4] Adler, A. (1980). *What Life Should Mean to You*. London: George Allen and Unwin, pp. 53–58. From *What Life Should Mean To You* by Alfred Adler. Copyright © 1931. Renewed 1959 by Kurt Adler. Reprinted by permission of the Estate of Alfred Adler.

would hide from view would be their heightened goal of supremacy, their desire to be the first at all costs. A child given to boasting, on the other hand, displays its superiority complex at first view; if we examined its behavior rather than its words, we should soon discover the unadmitted feelings of inferiority. . . .

We have said that inferiority feelings are not in themselves abnormal. They are the cause of all improvements in the position of mankind. Science itself, for example, can arise only when people feel their ignorance and their need to foresee the future: it is the result of the strivings of human beings to improve their whole situation, to know more of the universe and to be able to control it better. Indeed, it seems to me that all our human culture is based upon feelings of inferiority. . . .

Nobody will worry, I think, over the fact we cannot finally reach the highest goal of our lives. If we could imagine a single individual, or mankind on the whole, as having reached a position where there were no further difficulties, we should think that life in those circumstances must be very dull. Everything then could be foreseen, everything calculated in advance. Tomorrow would bring no unexpected opportunities; there would be nothing to look forward to in the future. Our interest in life comes mainly from our lack of certainty. If we were all sure, if we knew everything, there would no longer be discussions or discoveries. Science would have come to an end; the universe around us would be nothing but a twice-told tale. Art and religion, which cheer us with the imagination of our unattained goals, would no longer have

any meaning. It is our good fortune that life is not so easily exhausted. The strivings of men are continuous and we can always find or invent new problems, and make new opportunities for cooperation and contribution. The neurotic is blocked at the beginning; his solutions remain at a low level and his difficulties are correspondingly great. The more normal individual puts behind himself an increasingly full solution for his problems; he can advance to new difficulties and arrive at new solutions. In this way he is enabled to contribute to others: he does not lag behind and become a liability for his fellow men; he does not need or demand special consideration; but he proceeds with courage and independence to solve his problems in accordance with social feeling.

The goal of superiority, with each individual, is personal and unique. It depends upon the meaning he gives to life; and this meaning is not a matter of words. It is built up in his style of life and runs through it like a strange melody of his own creation. In his style of life he does not express his goal so that we can formulate it once for all. He expresses it vaguely, so that we must guess at it from the indications he gives. Understanding a style of life is similar to understanding the work of a poet. A poet must use words; but his meaning is more than the mere words he uses. The greatest part of his meaning must be guessed at; we must read between the lines. So too, with that profoundest and most intricate creation, an individual style of life. The psychologists must learn to read between the lines; he must learn the art of appreciating life-meanings.

Birth Order and Personality Development

COMMENTARY

For Adler, one of the most important subjective determiners of personality development is the order of one's birth within the family constellation. While birth order itself is an objective factor, it is a subjective influence in that it is the perception of one's situation in the family that is crucial.

Adler's idea on the importance of birth order in personality development has led to over 400 research studies and has stimulated more research than any other Adlerian concept. Given the complex nature of the variables in the family constellation, this has proved to be a difficult area of research. In addition to the objective rank order of each child, the sex of each child, the span of years between them, and the subjective perception of one's ordinal situation all have an influence on birth order and personality development.

While most research studies in this area have been equivocal, some supporting Adler's observations and others disclaiming them, most would agree with Adler that birth order *is* an important influence on personality development. The specifics, however, are difficult to determine, and due to the complex variables mentioned above, it seems likely that considerable variability is possible in response to each ordinal position.

1.

ALFRED ADLER

Birth Order Position

It is a common fallacy to imagine that children of the same family are formed in the same environment. Of course there is much which is the same for all children in the same home, but the psychological situation of each child is individual and differs from that of others, because of the order of their succession.

There has been some misunderstanding of my custom of classification

according to position in the family. It is not, of course, the child's number in the order of successive births which influences his character, but the situation into which he is born and the way in which he interprets it. Thus, if the eldest child is feeble-minded or suppressed, the second child may acquire a style of life similar to that of an eldest child; and in a large family, if two are born much later than the rest, and grow up together separated from the older children, the elder of these may develop like a first child. Such differences also happen sometimes in the case of twins.

[1] Adler, A. (1964). *Problems of Neurosis.* New York: Harper and Row, p. 96. Reprinted by the Estate of Alfred Adler. From *Problems of Neurosis* by Alfred Adler. Copyright © 1929, London, Copyright © 1964 Harper & Row Publishers.

2.

ALFRED ADLER

The Oldest Child

The first-born child is generally given a good deal of attention and spoiling. Too often it is quite suddenly

and sharply that he finds himself ousted from his position. Another child is born and he is no longer unique. Now he must share the attention of his mother and father with a rival. We can often find in problem children, neurotics, criminals, drunkards, and perverts that their difficulties began in such circumstances.

The first-born is in a unique situation; for a while he is an only child and sometime later he is "dethroned."

[2] Selected excerpts from pages 377–382 from *The Individual Psychology of Alfred Adler* by Heinz L. Ansbacher and Rowena R. Ansbacher. Copyright © 1956 by Basic Books, Inc. Copyright renewed 1984 by Heinz L. and Rowena R. Ansbacher. Reprinted by permission of BasicBooks, a division of HarperCollins Publishers, Inc.

This expression chosen by me depicts the change in the situation so exactly that later writers, as Freud, for example, when they do justice to such a case, cannot do without this figurative expression. The time elapsed before this "dethronement" is important for the impression it makes on the child and for the way this impression is utilized. If the time is three years or more, this even meets with an already established style of life and is responded to accordingly. When the time interval is less, the whole process takes place without words and concepts; hence it is not susceptible to a correction by later experiences but only by Individual Psychological understanding of the context. These wordless impressions, of which there are many in early childhood, would be interpreted differently by Freud and Jung. They would regard them not as experiences, but as unconscious instincts or as the atavistic collective unconscious, respectively. Impulses of hate, however, or occasional death wishes are the artificial products of an incorrect training in social interest. They are well-known to us, but we find them only in pampered children, and they are often directed by the first-born against the second child. Similar moods and ill-feelings are found also in later children, especially again if they were pampered. This is sufficient evidence of relegating to the region of fable the idea that a more severe birth trauma is the reason for failures among the first-born.

When other children lose their position in the same way, they will probably not feel it so strongly, since they have already had the experience of cooperating with another child. They have never been the sole object of consideration and care. Of course, if the parents have allowed the first-born to feel sure of their affection, if he knows that his position is secure, and, above all, if he is prepared for the arrival of a younger child and has been trained to cooperate in its care, the crisis will pass without ill effects.

Among such oldest children we find individuals who develop a striving to protect others and help them. They train to imitate their fathers or mothers; often they play the part of a father or a mother with the younger children, look after them, teach them, and feel themselves responsible for their welfare. Sometimes they develop a great talent for organization. These are the favorable cases, though even a striving to protect others may be exaggerated into a desire to keep those others dependent and to rule over them.

Among many peoples and classes an advantageous status of the oldest child has become traditional. Even where this tradition has not actually become crystallized, the oldest child is usually the one whom one accredits with enough strength and intelligence to be a coworker and supervisor. Imagine what it must mean to a child to be constantly entrusted with the full confidence of his environment.

Generally the first-born is not prepared for the new baby which in fact does deprive him of attention, love, and appreciation. He begins trying to pull his mother back to him and thinking how he can regain attention. He fights for his mother's love. In every case of such a fight, we must inquire into the individual circumstances. If the mother fights back at him, the child will become high-tempered, wild, critical, and disobedient. When he turns against his mother, it often happens that his father gives him a chance to renew the old favorable position. Oldest children frequently prefer their fathers and lean towards their side. Such a fight lasts a long time, sometimes through a whole life.

Oldest children generally show, in one way or another, an interest in the past. All their movements and expressions are directed towards the bygone time when they were the center of attention. They admire the past and are pessimistic about the future. Sometimes a child who has lost his power, the small kingdom he ruled, understands better than others the importance of power and authority. When he grows up, he likes to take part in the exercise of authority and exaggerates the importance of rules and laws. Everything should be done by rule, and no rule should ever be changed; power should always be preserved in the hands of those entitled to it. Influences like these in childhood give a strong tendency towards conservatism. In my experience the greatest proportion of problem children are oldest children; and close behind them come the youngest children.

The Second Child

The second child is in a quite different position. From the time he is born, he shares attention with another child, and is therefore a little nearer to cooperation than an oldest child. If the oldest is not fighting against him and pushing him back, he is very well situated. Throughout his childhood he has a pacemaker; there is always a child ahead of him, and he is stimulated to

exert himself and catch up. A typical second child is very easy to recognize. He behaves as if he were in a race, is under full steam all the time, and trains continually to surpass his older brother and conquer him. The Bible gives us many marvelous psychological hints, and the typical second child is beautifully portrayed in the story of Jacob. He wished to be the first, to take away Esau's position, to best Esau and excel him. The second child is often more talented and successful than the first. If he goes ahead faster, it is because he trained more. Even when he is grown up and outside the family circle, he often still makes use of a pacemaker by comparing himself with someone whom he thinks more advantageously placed, and tries to go beyond him.

These characteristics leave their mark on all expressions and are easily found in dreams. Oldest children often dream of falling; they are on top, but are not sure that they can keep superiority. Second children often picture themselves running after trains and riding in bicycle races. Sometimes this hurry in his dreams is sufficient by itself to allow us to guess that the individual is a second child.

Here we see the restlessness, a striving which is less aimed at facts than at semblances, but which is unconquerable until either the goal has been reached, i.e., the man ahead has been outdistanced, or in case of defeat, the retreat begins which often results in neurosis. The mood of the second-born is comparable to the envy of the dispossessed with the prevailing feeling of having been slighted. His goal may be placed so high that he will suffer from it for the rest of his life, and his inner harmony be destroyed in consequence.

This was well expressed by a little boy of four, who cried out, weeping, "I am so unhappy because I can never be as old as my brother."

In his later life, the second child is rarely able to endure the strict leadership of others or to accept the idea of eternal laws. He will be much more inclined to believe, rightly or wrongly, that there is no power in the world which cannot be overthrown. Beware of his revolutionary subtleties! Though it is possible to endanger a ruling power with slander, there are more insidious ways. For example, by means of excessive praise he may idealize and glorify a man or a method until the reality cannot stand up to the idea. Both ways are employed in Antony's oration in *Julius Caesar*. I have shown elsewhere how Dostoievsky made masterly use of the latter means, perhaps unconsciously, to undermine the pillars of old Russia. Those who remember his representation of Father Zosima in *The Brothers Karamazov*, and who also recall the fact that he was a second son, will easily agree with my suggestion regarding the influence played by position in the family.

I need hardly say that the style of life of a second child, like that of the first, may also appear in another child, one in a different chronological position in the family, if the situation is of a similar pattern.

The Youngest Child

All other children can be dethroned, but never the youngest. He has no followers but many pacemakers. He is always the baby of the family, probably the most pampered, and faces the difficulties of a pampered child. But, because he is so much stimulated and has many chances for competition, he often develops in an extraordinary way, runs faster than the other children, and overcomes them all. The position of the youngest has not changed in human history; the oldest stories of mankind tell how the youngest child excelled his brothers and sisters.

In every fairy tale the youngest child surpasses all his brothers and sisters; in German, Russian, Scandinavian, or Chinese fairy tales the youngest is always the conqueror. In the Bible we can find excellent descriptions of youngest children which coincide exactly with our experience, e.g., the stories of Joseph, David, and Saul. Although Joseph had a younger brother Benjamin, he was born when Joseph was seventeen years old, so that as a child Joseph was the youngest.

Joseph's style of life is typical of a youngest child. Even in his dreams he asserts his superiority. The others must bow down before him; he outshines them all. His brothers understood his dreams very well, which was not hard for them, since they had Joseph with them, and his attitude was clear enough. The feelings which Joseph aroused in his dreams they also had felt. They feared him and wanted to get rid of him. From being the last, however, Joseph became the first. In later days he was the pillar and support of the whole family, as the youngest child so often is.

And yet, the second largest proportion of problem children comes from among the youngest, because all the family spoils them. A spoiled child can never be independent. Sometimes a youngest child will not admit to any single ambition, but this is because he wishes to excel in everything, be unlimited and unique. Sometimes a youngest child may suffer from extreme inferiority feelings; everyone in the environment is older, stronger, and more experienced.

The Only Child

The only child has a problem of his own. His rival is not a brother or a sister; his feelings of competition are directed against his father. An only child is pampered by his mother. She is afraid of losing him and wants to keep him under her attention. He develops what is called a "mother complex"; he is tied to his mother's apron strings and wishes to push his father out of the family picture. Often an only child is scared to death lest he should have brothers and sisters following him. When friends of the family say, "You ought to have a little brother or sister," he dislikes the prospect immensely. He wants to be the center of attention all the time. He really feels that it is a right of his, and if his position is challenged, he thinks it a great injustice. In later life, when he is no longer the center of attention, he has many difficulties.

Another point of danger for his development is that he is born into a timid environment. We often find only children in a family where we could expect more children. But the parents are timid and pessimistic; they feel they will not be able to solve the economic problem of having more than one child. The whole atmosphere is full of anxiety and the child suffers badly.

If the children are spaced many years apart, each child will have some of the features of an only child.

Other Sibling Situations

An only boy brought up in a family of girls has a hard time before him. He is in a wholly feminine environment, since the father is absent most of the day. Feeling that he is different, he may grow up isolated. On the other hand, he may fight strongly against this atmosphere and lay great stress on his masculinity. He will feel that he must assert his difference and superiority; but there will always be tension. His development will proceed by extremes, he will train to be either very strong or very weak.

In a rather similar way, an only girl among boys is apt to develop very feminine or very masculine qualities. Frequently she is pursued through life by feelings of insecurity and helplessness.

The preeminence of one of the siblings in early childhood, whether pronounced or unpronounced, often becomes the disadvantage of the other. With amazing frequency the failures of one child are found beside the excellencies of the other. The greater activity of the one may bring about the passivity of the other; the height, the good looks, or the strength of the one may cast a shadow on the other.

Fictional Final Goal

COMMENTARY

Two major principles of Adlerian psychology are addressed in these selections: Adler's concept of the fictional final goal identifies the phenomenological orientation of Individual Psychology. One's goals and life plan are formulated out of one's "personal schema of apperception" as Adler put it, rather than determined by environmental forces in some cause-effect manner. In this respect, the creative agency within the child is clearly at work in the choice of goals and the direction of the life plan.

The holistic nature of Adler's Individual Psychology is also strongly emphasized here. In his holistic view of personality formation, the totality of psychic life, with its many part-functions, is integrated around one's goals and the means of pursuing these goals. This suggests that personality and behavior can only be understood in relation to one's goals and unified life plan. Indeed, we may go so far as to say that life's meaning is embodied in the individual's fictional goals.

When we speak of goals, of course, we are referring to the fictional ideas that give direction to the striving for superiority.

1.

ALFRED ADLER

The science of Individual Psychology developed out of the effort to understand that mysterious creative power of life—that power which expresses itself in the desire to develop, to strive and to achieve—and even to compensate for defeats in one direction by striving for success in another. This power is *teleological*—it expresses itself in the striving after a goal, and in this striving every bodily and psychic movement is made to co-operate. It is thus absurd to study bodily movements and mental conditions abstractly without relation to an individual whole. It is absurd, for instance, that in criminal psychology we should pay so much more attention to the crime than to the criminal. It is the criminal, not the crime that counts, and no matter how much we contemplate the criminal act we shall never understand its criminality unless we see it as an episode in the life of a particular individual. The same outward act may be criminal in one case and not criminal in another. The important thing is to understand the individual context—the goal of an individual's life which marks the line of direction for all his acts and movements. This goal enables us to understand the hidden meaning behind the various separate acts—we see them as parts of a whole. Vice versa, when we study the

parts—provided we study them as parts of a whole—we get a better sense of the whole.

In the author's own case the interest in psychology developed out of the practice of medicine. The practice of medicine provided the teleological or purposive viewpoint which is necessary for the understanding of psychological facts. In medicine we see all organs striving to develop toward definite goals. They have definite forms which they achieve upon maturity. Moreover, in cases where there are organic defects we always find nature making special efforts to overcome the deficiency, or else to compensate for it by developing another organ to take over the functions of the defective one. Life always seeks to continue, and the life force never yields to external obstacles without a struggle.

Now the movement of the psyche is analogous to the movement of organic life. In each mind there is the conception of a goal or ideal to get beyond the present deficiencies and difficulties by postulating a concrete aim for the future. By means of this concrete aim or goal the individual can think and feel himself superior to the difficulties of the present because he has in mind his success of the future. Without the sense of a goal individual activity would cease to have any meaning.

All evidence points to the fact that the fixing of this goal—giving it concrete form—must take place early in life, during the formative period of childhood. A kind of prototype or

---

[1] Adler, A. (1969). *The Science of Living*. New York: Doubleday and Company, Inc., pp. 1–5. Reprinted by the Estate of Alfred Adler, Copyright © 1929. Renewed by Kurt A. Adler in 1957.

model of a matured personality begins to develop at this time. We can imagine how the process takes place. A child, being weak, feels inferior and finds itself in a situation which it cannot bear. Hence it strives to develop, and it strives to develop along a line of direction fixed by the goal which it chooses for itself. The material used for development at this stage is less important than the goal which decided the line of direction. How this goal is fixed it is difficult to say, but it is obvious that such a goal exists and that it dominates the child's every movement. Little is indeed understood about power, impulses, reasons, abilities or disabilities at this early period. As yet there is really no key, for the direction is definitely established only after the child has fixed its goals. Only when we see the direction in which a life is tending can we guess what steps will be taken in the future.

Schema of Apperception

When the prototype—that early personality which embodies the goal—is formed, the line of direction is established and the individual becomes definitely oriented. It is the fact which enables us to predict what will happen later in life. The individual's apperceptions are from then on bound to fall into a groove established by the line of direction. The child will not perceive given situations as they actually exist, but according to a personal schema of apperception—that is to say, he will perceive situations under the prejudice of his own interests. . . .

The child is steeped in a schema of relativity, and in this he is indeed like the rest of us—none of us is blessed with the knowledge of the absolute truth. Even our science is not blessed with absolute truth. It is based on common sense, which is to say that it is ever changing and it is content gradually to replace big mistakes by smaller ones. We all make mistakes, but the important thing is that we can correct them. Such correction is easier at the time of the formation of the prototype. And when we do not correct them at that time, we may correct the mistakes later on by recalling the whole situation of that period. Thus if we are confronted with the task of treating a neurotic patient, our problem is to discover, not the ordinary mistakes he makes in later life, but the very fundamental mistakes made early in his life in the course of the constitution of his prototype. If we discover these mistakes, it is possible to correct them by appropriate treatment.

2.

ALFRED ADLER

If we look at the matter more closely, we shall find the following law holding in the development of all psychic happenings: *we cannot think, feel, will, or act without the perception of some goal.* For all the causalities in the world would not suffice to conquer the chaos of the future nor obviate the planlessness to which we would be bound to fall a victim. All activity would persist in the state of uncontrolled gropings; the economy visible in our psychic life unattained; we should be unintegrated and in every aspect of our physiognomy, in every personal touch, similar to organisms of the rank of the amoeba.

No one will deny that by assuming an objective for our psychic life we accommodate ourselves better to reality. This can be easily demonstrated. For its truth in individual examples, where phenomena are torn from their proper connections, no doubt exists. Only watch, from this point of view, the attempts at walking made by a small child or a woman recovering from a confinement. Naturally he who approaches this whole matter without any theory is likely to find its deeper significance escape him. Yet it is a fact that before the first step has been taken the objective of the person's movement has already been determined.

In the same way it can be demonstrated that all psychic activities are given a direction by means of a previously determined goal. All the temporary and partially visible objectives, after the short period of psychic development of childhood, are under the domination of an imagined terminal goal, a final point felt and conceived of as definitely fixed. In other words, the psychic life of man is made to fit into the fifth act like a character drawn by a good dramatist.

The conclusion thus to be drawn from the unbiased study of any personality viewed from the standpoint of Individual Psychology leads us to the following important proposition: *Every psychic phenomenon, if it is to give us any understanding of a person, can only be grasped and understood if regarded as a preparation for some goal. . . .*

Our science demands markedly individualizing procedure and is consequently not much given to generalizations. For general guidance I would like to propound the following rule: *As soon as the goal of a psychic movement or its life-plan has been recognized, then we are to assume that all the movements of its constituent parts will coincide with both the goal and the life-plan.*

This formulation, with some minor provisos, is to be maintained in the widest sense. It retains its value even if inverted: *The properly understood part-movements must when combined, give the picture of an integrated life-plan and final goal.* Consequently we

[2] Adler, A. (1951). *Individual Psychology: Practice and Theory.* New York: The Humanities Press, pp. 3–8. Reprinted by permission of Routledge & Kegan Paul.

insist that, without worrying about the *tendencies, milieu and experiences,* all psychical powers are under the control of a directive idea and all expressions of emotion, feeling, thinking, willing, acting, dreaming as well as psycho-pathological phenomena, are permeated by one unified life-plan. Let me, by a slight suggestion, prove and yet soften down these heroical propositions: More important than tendencies, objective experience and milieu is *the subjective evaluation,* an evaluation which stands furthermore in a certain often strange, relation to realities. Out of this evaluation however, which generally results in the development of a permanent mood *of the nature of a feeling of inferiority* there arises, depending upon the unconscious technique of our thought-apparatus, an imagined goal, an attempt at a planned final compensation and a life-plan. . . .

This then being my assumption, I shall in the following present to you the most important results of our study of psychic life. Let me emphasize the fact that the dynamics of psychic life that I am about to describe hold equally for healthy and diseased. What distinguishes the nervous from the healthy individual is the stronger safeguarding tendency with which the former's life-plan is filled. With regard to the "positing of a goal" and the life-plan adjusted to it there are no fundamental differences.

I shall consequently speak of a general goal of man. A thorough-going study has taught us that we can best understand the manifold and diverse movements of the psyche as soon as our *most general pre-supposition,* that the psyche has as its objective the *goal of superiority,* is recognized. Great thinkers have given expression to much of this; in part everyone knows it, but in the main it is hidden in mysterious darkness and comes definitely to the front only in insanity or in ecstatic conditions. Whether a person desires to be an artist, the first in his profession, or a tyrant in his home, to hold converse with God or humiliate other people; whether he regards his suffering as the most important thing in the world to which everyone must show obeisance, whether he is chasing after unattainable ideals or old deities, overstepping all limits and norms, at every part of his way he is guided and spurred on by his longing for superiority, the thought of his godlikeness, the belief in his special magical power. In his love he desires to experience his power over his partner. In his purely optional choice of profession the goal floating before his mind manifests itself in all sorts of exaggerated anticipations and fears, and thirsting for revenge, he experiences in suicide a triumph over all obstacles. In order to gain control over an object or over a person, be capable of proceeding along a straight line, bravely, proudly, overbearing, obstinate, cruel; or he may on the other hand prefer, forced by experience, to resort to by-paths and circuitous routes, to gain his victory by obedience, submission, mildness and modesty. Nor have traits of character an independent existence, for they are also adjusted to the individual life-plan, really representing the most important preparations for conflict possessed by the latter.

This goal of complete superiority, with its strange appearance at times, does not come from the world of reality. Inherently we must place it under "fictions" and "imaginations." Of these Vaihinger (*The philosophy of "as if"*) rightly says that their importance lies in the fact that whereas in themselves without meaning, they nevertheless possess in practice the greatest importance. For our case this coincides to such an extent that we may say *that this fiction of a goal of superiority, so ridiculous from the view-point of reality, has become the principal conditioning factor of our life as hitherto known.* It is this that teaches us to differentiate, gives us poise and security, moulds and guides our deeds and activities and forces our spirit to look ahead and to perfect itself. There is of course also an obverse side, for *this goal introduces into our life a hostile and fighting tendency,* robs us of the simplicity of our feelings and is always the cause for an estrangement from reality since it puts near to our hearts the idea of attempting to overpower reality. Whoever takes this goal of godlikeness seriously or literally, will soon be compelled to flee from real life and compromise, by seeking a life within life; if fortunate in art, but more generally in pietism, neurosis or crime.

I cannot give you particulars here. A clear indication of this super-mundane goal is to be found in every individual. Sometimes this is to be gathered from a man's carriage, sometimes it is disclosed only in his demands and expectations. Occasionally one comes upon its tack in obscure memories, phantasies and dreams. If purposely sought it is rarely obtained. However, every bodily or mental attitude indicates clearly its origin in a striving for power and carries within itself the ideal of a kind of perfection and infallibility. In those cases that lie on the confines of neurosis there is always to be discovered a reinforced pitting of oneself against the environment, against the dead or heroes of the past.

Style of Life

COMMENTARY

The terms *inferiority complex* and *lifestyle* have become the two most popularized concepts adopted from Adler's work. The common usage of the term *lifestyle,* however, bears only a superficial resemblance to Adler's meaning and the significance he attributed to it. Style of life is, perhaps, the most encompassing and holistic concept in Adler's theory of personality. It represents the integration of all those attributes and forces of personality that contribute to the individual's striving for superiority. The person's style of life, his life plan, is organized around this movement toward the goal.

Adler discriminates between the "normal" lifestyle, free from neurotic tensions and basic mistakes, and its more pathological forms. Adler's major criterion for a healthy lifestyle is the degree to which the life plan incorporates social interest into its overall design.

In the following selections, Adler also discusses the three major ways of understanding lifestyle and predicting the course of its development. First, the lifestyle of a person is revealed under the impact of a crisis or an unfavorable situation. A dependent personality, for example, might function relatively well when surrounded by the support of other people. If forced to live alone, however, she/he is apt to reveal the underlying nature of lifestyle by becoming depressed, resorting to drugs, etc.

The use of early recollections and a knowledge of birth order and its impact on the individual are also important to Adler in revealing the true nature of one's style of life. These are discussed in greater detail in the sections on birth order and early recollections.

ALFRED ADLER

The Style of Life

If we look at a pine tree growing in the valley we will notice that it grows differently from one on top of a mountain. It is the same kind of a tree, but there are two distinct styles of life. Its style on top of the mountain is different from its style when growing in the valley. The style of life of a tree is the individuality of a tree expressing itself and moulding itself in an environment. We recognize a style when we see it against a background of an environment different from what we expect, for then we realize that every tree has a life pattern and is not merely a mechanical reaction to the environment.

It is much the same way with human beings. We see the style of life under certain conditions of environment and it is our task to analyze its exact relation to the existing circumstances, inasmuch as mind changes with alteration of the environment. As long as a person is in a favorable situation we cannot see his style of life clearly. In new situations, however, where he is confronted with difficulties, the style of life appears clearly and distinctly. A trained psychologist could perhaps understand a style of life of a human being even in a favorable situation, but it becomes apparent to everybody when

Adler, A. (1969) *The Science of Living.* New York: Doubleday and Company, Inc., pp. 38–46. Reprinted by the Estate of Alfred Adler, Copyright © 1929. Renewed by Kurt A. Adler in 1957.

the human subject is put into unfavorable or difficult situations.

Now life, being something more than a game, does not lack difficulties. There are always situations in which human beings find themselves confronted with difficulties. It is while the subject is confronted with these difficulties that we must study him and find out his different movements and characteristic distinguishing marks. As we have previously said, the style of life is a unity because it has grown out of the difficulties of early life and out of the striving for a goal.

But we are interested not so much in the past as in the future. And in order to understand a person's future we must understand his style of life. Even if we understand instincts, stimuli, drive, etc., we cannot predict what must happen. Some psychologists indeed try to reach conclusions by noting certain instincts, impressions or traumas, but on closer examination it will be found that all these elements presuppose a consistent style of life. Thus whatever stimulates, stimulates only to *save* and *fix* a style of life.

. . . We have seen how human beings, . . . because they face difficulties and feel insecure, suffer from a feeling or complex of inferiority. But as human beings cannot endure this for long, the inferiority feeling stimulates them, as we have seen, to movement and action. This results in a person having a goal. Now Individual Psychology has long called the consistent movement toward this goal a plan of life. But because this name has sometimes led to mistakes among students, it is now called a style of life.

Because an individual has a style of life, it is possible to predict his future sometimes just on the basis of talking to him and having him answer questions. It is like looking at the fifth act of a drama, where all the mysteries are solved. We can make predictions in this way because we know the phases, the difficulties and the questions of life. Thus from experience and knowledge of a few facts we can tell what will happen to children who always separate themselves from others, who are looking for support, who are pampered and who hesitate in approaching situations. What happens in the case of a person whose goal it is to be supported by others? Hesitating, he stops or escapes the solution of the questions of life. We know now he can hesitate, stop, or escape, because we have seen the same thing happen a thousand times. We know that he does not want to proceed alone but wants to be pampered. He wants to stay far away from the great problems of life, and he occupies himself with useless things rather than struggle with the useful ones. He lacks social interest, and as a result he may develop into a problem child, a neurotic, a criminal or a suicide—that final escape. All these things are now better understood than formerly.

We realize, for instance, that in looking for the style of life of a human being we may use the normal style of life as a basis for measurement. We use the socially adjusted human being as a standard, the norm, and measure the individual variations from the norm. . . .

Understanding a Style of Life

. . . The normal man is an individual who lives in society and whose mode of life is so adapted that whether he wants it or not society derives a certain advantage from his work. Also from a psychological point of view he has enough energy and courage to meet the problems and difficulties as they come along. Both of these qualities are missing in the case of psychopathic persons: they are neither socially adjusted nor are they psychologically adjusted to the daily tasks of life.

As an illustration we may take the case of a certain individual, a man of thirty who was always at the last moment escaping the solution of his problems. He had a friend but was very suspicious of him, and as a result this friendship never prospered. Friendship cannot grow under such conditions because the other partner feels the tension in the relation. We can readily see how this man really had no friends despite the fact that he was on speaking terms with a large number of persons. He was not sufficiently interested nor adjusted socially to make friends. In fact he did not like to go out, and was always silent in company. He explained this on the ground that in company he never had any ideas and therefore he had nothing to say.

Moreover, the man was bashful. He had pink skin which flushed from time to time when he talked. When he could overcome this bashfulness he would speak quite well. What he really needed was to be helped in this direction without criticism. Of course when he was in this state he did not present a nice picture and was not very much liked by his neighbors. He felt this, and as a result his dislike for speech increased. One might say that his style of life was such that when he approached other persons in company he called attention to himself.

Next to social life and the art of getting along with friends, is the question of occupation. Now our patient always had the fear that he might fail in his occupation, and so he studied day and night. He overworked and overstrained himself. And because he overstrained himself he put himself out of commission for solving the question of occupation.

If we compare our patient's approach to the first and second questions in his life, we see that he was always in too great a tension. This is a sign that he had a great feeling of inferiority. He undervalued himself and looked on others and on new situations as things that were unfriendly to him. He acted as though he were in an enemy country.

We now have enough data to picture the style of life of this man. We can see that he wants to go on but at the same time he is blocked because he fears defeat. It is as if he stood before an abyss, straining and always at a tension. He manages to go forward but only conditionally, and he would prefer to stay at home and not mingle with others.

The third question with which this man was confronted—and it is a question for which most persons are not very well prepared—is the question of love. He hesitated to approach the other sex. He found that he wanted to love and to get married, but on account of his great feeling of inferiority he was too frightened to face the prospect. He could not accomplish what he

wanted, and so we see his whole behavior and attitude summed up in the words, "Yes . . . but!" We see him in love with one girl and then in love with another. This is of a frequent occurrence with neurotic persons because in a sense two girls are less than one. This truth sometimes accounts for a tendency towards polygamy.

And now let us take up the reasons for this style of life. Individual Psychology undertakes to analyze the causes for a style of life. This man established his style of life during the first four or five years. At that time some tragedy happened which moulded and formed him, and so we have to look for the tragedy. We can see that something made him lose his normal interest in others and gave him the impression that life is simply one great difficulty and that it is better not to go on at all than to be always confronting difficult situations. Therefore he became cautious, hesitant, and a seeker of ways of escape.

We must mention the fact that he was a first child. We have already spoken about the great significance of this position. We have shown how the chief problem in the case of a first child arises from the fact that he is for years the center of attention, only to be displaced from his glory and to have another preferred. In a great many cases where a person is bashful and afraid to go on, we find the reason to be that another person has been preferred. Hence in this case it is not difficult to find out where the trouble lies.

In many cases we need only ask a patient: Are you the first, second or third child? then we have all we need. We can also use an entirely different method: We can ask for early recollections. . . . This method is worthwhile because these recollections or first pictures are a part of the building up of the early style of life which we have called the prototype. One comes upon an actual part of the prototype when a person tells of his early recollections. Looking back, everybody remembers certain important things, and indeed what is fixed in memory is always important.

There are schools of psychology which act on the opposite assumption. They believe that what a person has forgotten is the most important point, but there is really no great difference between the two ideas. Perhaps a person can tell us his conscious recollections, but he does not know what they mean. He does not see their connection with his actions. Hence the result is the same, whether we emphasize the hidden or forgotten significance of conscious memories or the importance of forgotten memories.

Little descriptions of early recollections are highly illuminating. Thus a man might tell you that when he was small, his mother took him and his younger brother to market. That is enough. We can then discover his style of life. He pictures himself and a younger brother. Therefore we see it must have been important to him to have had a younger brother. Lead him further and you may find a situation similar to a certain one in which a man recalled that it began to rain that day. His mother took him in her arms, but when she saw the younger brother she put him down to carry the little one. Thus we can picture his style of life. He always has the expectation that another person will be preferred. And so we can understand why he cannot speak in company, for he is always looking around to see if another will not be preferred. The same is true with friendship. He is always thinking that another is more preferred by his friend, and as a result he can never have a true friend. He is constantly suspicious, looking out for little things that disturb friendship.

We can also see how the tragedy he has experienced has hindered the development of his social interest. He recalls that his mother took the younger brother in her arms and we see that he feels that this baby took more of his mother's attention than he did. He feels that the younger brother is preferred and is looking constantly for confirmation of this idea. He is wholly convinced he is right, and so he is always under strain—always under the great difficulty of trying to accomplish things when someone else is preferred. . . .

It is our task to give such a person the social interest demanded of a well-adjusted human being. How is this to be done? the great difficulty with persons trained in this way is that they are overstrained and are always looking for a confirmation of their fixed ideas. It thus becomes impossible to change their ideas unless somehow we penetrate into their personality in a manner that will disarm their preconceptions. To accomplish this it is necessary to use a certain art and a certain tact. And it is best if the adviser is not closely related or interested in the patient. For if one is directly interested in the case, one will find that one is acting for one's own interest and not for the interest of the patient. The patient will not fail to notice this and will become suspicious.

The important thing is to decrease the patient's feeling of inferiority. It cannot be extirpated altogether, and in fact we do not want to extirpate it because a feeling of inferiority can serve as a useful foundation on which to build. What we have to do is change the goal. We have seen that his goal has been one of escape just because someone else is preferred, and it is around this complex of ideas that we must work. We must decrease his feeling of inferiority by showing him that he really undervalues himself. We can show him the trouble with his movements and explain to him his tendency to be over-tense, as if standing before a great abyss or as if living in an enemy country and always in danger. We can indicate to him how his fear that others may be preferred is standing in the way of his doing his best work and making the best spontaneous impression. . . .

Let us now look at another specific case—a case of depression. This is a very common disorder, but it can be cured. Such persons are distinguishable very early in life. In fact, we notice many children who in their approach to a new situation show signs of depression. This depressed man of whom we are speaking had about ten attacks, and these always occurred when he took a new position. As long as he was in his old position he was nearly normal. But he did not want to go out in company and he wanted to rule others. Consequently he had no friends and at fifty he had not married.

Let us look at his childhood in order to study his style of life. He had been very sensitive and quarrelsome, always ruling his older brothers and sisters by emphasizing his pains and weaknesses. When playing on a couch one day, he pushed them all off. When his aunt reproached him for this, he said, "Now my whole life is ruined because you have blamed me!" And at that time he was only four or five years old.

Such was his style of life—always trying to rule others, always complaining of his weakness and of how he suffered. This trait led in his later life to depression, which in itself is simply an expression of weakness. Every patient with depression uses almost the same words: "My whole life is ruined. I have lost everything." Frequently such a person has been pampered and is so no longer and this influences his style of life.

CHAPTER III

The Analytical Psychology of Carl Jung

BIOGRAPHICAL SKETCH

Carl Gustav Jung was born in the small Swiss town of Kesswil in 1875. He was nine years older than his sister and grew up as an only child. His father, Paul Jung, was pastor of a Swiss Reformed church. Eight of his uncles were also clergymen. Religion, therefore, was a dominant theme in his family and in his own life. Even as a child, however, Jung became irritated with his father's inability to connect his religious faith to human passions and aspirations. He viewed his father's religion as dogmatic, disconnected, and centered primarily on church doctrine. Jung came to believe, quite strongly, that religion should be viewed within the context of deeply felt human experience and psychic development.

Due in part to his parents' arguments, his mother's unpredictable nature, and his position as an only child, Jung became increasingly lonely and isolated and more and more preoccupied with his own dreams, fantasies, and visions. These internal experiences and explorations also followed a family tradition of interest in mysticism and occult phenomena, for which Jung seemed to have a natural proclivity. His description of many such experiences are exquisitely recorded in his autobiography *Memories, Dreams, Reflections* (1961). This early preoccupation with dreams, fantasies, and the mysteries of life served as an important foundation for Jung's later investigations into the nature of the human psyche.

In 1900 Jung received his medical degree from the University of Basel, with a specialty in psychiatry that combined his strong interest in both the sciences and the humanities.

Working with Eugen Bleuler in a Zürich mental hospital, Jung became fascinated with the symptoms and complexities of schizophrenia. He also became interested in Freud's work, and after reading Freud's book *The Interpretation of Dreams* Jung initiated a correspondence with Freud, meeting him for the first time in 1907. An intense relationship quickly developed between the two men, and Freud became so impressed with Jung that he soon viewed him as his successor and as the future spokesperson for the rapidly emerging field of psychoanalysis. In 1909 Freud and Jung traveled to the United States together to deliver a series of lectures at Clark University. Jung's contribution to this lecture series was to present his research on the word association test he used to investigate the various complexes of the personal unconscious. The Clark lectures were an important and historic occasion, but early in the trip the seeds were sewn for later personal and theoretical disharmony between the two men. Jung offended Freud's sense of ethics by suggesting that, for American audiences, he should tone down his emphasis on sex.

In 1910, at Freud's urging, Jung was elected first president of the International Psychoanalytic Association. Subsequently, however, Jung began to have more serious reservations about Freud's exclusively sexual interpretation of libidinal energy, and Freud, in turn, became increasingly uncomfortable over Jung's interest in spiritual and occult phenomena. By 1913, the conflict between the two men became as intense as their earlier attraction had been, and in 1914 Jung resigned his presidency of the Psychoanalytic Association. The two men were never in contact again.

This clash and breakup with Freud had a profound impact on Jung. He became disoriented and was obsessed with feelings of doubt and uncertainty. For four years he was preoccupied with his own dreams and fantasies and pursued an intense inner search for truth. He was, during this time, on the edge of madness. Many have viewed this period in Jung's life as a psychotic episode. Remarkably, Jung maintained both his family and his psychiatric practice during these chaotic years.

As is the case for many who undergo such an intense personal crisis, Jung emerged from this "creative illness" as a stronger and more creative man than before. The inner turmoil and suffering led to a profound spiritual awakening that transformed Jung's thoughts and priorities. His personal search was transformed into a search for universal psychic elements and forces that both afflict and ennoble the human personality.

Jung continued to explore the depths and boundaries of the human psyche until his death in June 1961 at the age of 86. Carl Jung stands as a monumental figure in the history of psychology. Although his influence has not been as pervasive as Freud's, his unique contributions to our understanding of personality have been considerable.

Jung was perhaps the most scholarly of all the personality theorists, and although his theories were derived primarily from inner searches and experiences with patients in psychotherapy, he also drew upon important secondary sources in support of his ideas. In addition to his own medical and psychiatric training, Jung had a scholarly command of comparative religion, mythology, cultural anthropology, philosophy, and history. In important ways, Jung brought this vast storehouse of knowledge from many disciplines to support his multidimensional theory of personality, a theory that recognized the wholeness, uniqueness, and the deep creative resources of the human personality.

The Structure of the Psyche: Ego Consciousness and the Personal and Collective Unconscious

COMMENTARY

Jung proposed that the psyche, or personality, is composed of three autonomous but interacting structures: the ego, the personal unconscious, and the collective unconscious. Personality, as a *total* phenomenon, which Jung called *the self*, encompasses all three structures. As the sun is the center of the solar system, the self is the central archetype of the collective unconscious. The *self*, therefore, represents the primary organizing principle of the psyche, with the potential to create unity and integration between the three primary structures.

Jung's concepts of the ego and the personal unconscious are relatively easy to understand. Both correspond quite closely to Freud's ego and his view of the unconscious. The contents of Freud's unconscious, however, are more exclusively sexual in nature, whereas Jung introduces the *complexes* as important components of the personal unconscious. The complexes are clusters of feelings, ideas, and experiences centered around significant themes in one's life: themes such as mother, father, power, or sex. Each complex, therefore, is an emotionally charged core of related psychic material that has the power to assimilate other closely related feelings, ideas, and experiences.

Jung referred to these complexes as "splinter psyches," thus stressing their inner coherence and autonomous nature. The theory of complexes, these "splinter psyches," is similar to the idea of "subpersonalities" that some psychologists give attention and credence to today.

Jung believed that the complexes, which can be both personal and collective phenomena, were the unconscious source of dreams and symptoms. In the outbreak of a neurosis, however, aspects of the complex enter

63

consciousness. Having both personal and collective components, and with access into consciousness, the complex provides us with a good example of the interaction of the three structures of the psyche.

Jung's theory of the collective unconscious, perhaps his most significant contribution to our understanding of the human psyche, is more difficult to comprehend than the ego or the personal unconscious. Unlike the personal unconscious, the collective psyche represents not a personal history but a neural and racial history. In the collective unconscious, as Jung emphasized, we are reliving and retelling the story of mankind while bringing our own individual and unique contributions to the story.

One must bring a certain "suspension of disbelief" to the theory of the collective unconscious in order to fully appreciate its validity and significance. I remember my own struggle, rebellion, and disbelief when, many years ago, I first encountered the idea of the collective unconscious in a graduate course in personality theory. Much later, I realized I had misinterpreted the meaning of Jung's theory, seeing it, at that time, as a complicated version of Lamarck's theory of the inheritance of acquired characteristics. If I had only read Jung's caveat on this issue, my skepticism might have been assuaged. As if he were speaking to me, Jung said, "It should on no account be imagined that there are such things as *inherited ideas*. Of that there can be no question. There are, however, innate possibilities of ideas, a priori conditions for fantasy production; though these innate conditions do not produce any contents themselves, they give definite form to contents that have already been acquired. Being a part of the inherited structure of the brain, they are the reason for the identity of symbols and myth motifs in all parts of the world."

Jung was both a scientist and a mystic. With his painstaking research into the historical, mythological, and anthropological dimensions of the collective unconscious, he brought both of these worlds together in a compatible relationship.

1.

CARL JUNG

The Ego

Investigation of the psychology of the unconscious confronted me with facts which required the formulation

[1] Jung, Carl G. *Aion: Researches into the Phenomenology of the Self*, pp. 3–7. Copyright © 1968 by Princeton University Press. Reprinted by permission of Princeton University Press.

of new concepts. One of these concepts is the *self*. The entity so denoted is not meant to take the place of the one that has always been known as the *ego*, but includes it in a supraordinate concept. We understand the ego as the complex factor to which all conscious contents are related. It forms, as it were, the centre of the field of consciousness;

and, in so far as this comprises the empirical personality, the ego is the subject of all personal acts of consciousness. The relation of a psychic content to the ego forms the criterion of its consciousness, for no content can be conscious unless it is represented to a subject.

With this definition we have described and delimited the *scope* of the subject. Theoretically, no limits can be set to the field of consciousness, since it is capable of indefinite extension. Empirically, however, it always finds its limit when it comes up against the *unknown*. This consists of everything we do not know, which, therefore, is not related to the ego as the center of the field of consciousness. The unknown falls into two groups of objects: those which are outside and can be experienced by the senses, and those which are inside and are experienced immediately. The first group comprises the unknown in the outer world; the second the unknown in the inner world. We call this latter territory the *unconscious.*

The ego, as a specific content of consciousness, is not a simple or elementary factor but a complex one which, as such, cannot be described exhaustively. Experience shows that it rests on two seemingly different bases: the *somatic* and the *psychic*. The somatic basis is inferred from the totality of endosomatic perceptions, which for their part are already of a psychic nature and are associated with the ego, and are therefore conscious. They are produced by endosomatic stimuli, only some of which cross the threshold of consciousness. A considerable proportion of these stimuli occur unconsciously, that is, subliminally. The fact that they are

subliminal does not necessarily mean that their status is merely physiological, any more than this would be true of a psychic content. Sometimes they are capable of crossing the threshold, that is, of becoming perceptions. But there is no doubt that a large proportion of these endosomatic stimuli are simply incapable of consciousness and are so elementary that there is no reason to assign them a psychic nature—unless of course one favors the philosophical view that all life-processes are psychic anyway. The chief objection to this hardly demonstrable hypothesis is that it enlarges the concept of the psyche beyond all bounds and interprets the life-process in a way not absolutely warranted by the facts. Concepts that are too broad usually prove to be unsuitable instruments because they are too vague and nebulous. I have therefore suggested that the term "psychic" be used only where there is evidence of a will capable of modifying reflex or instinctual processes. . . .

The somatic basis of the ego consists, then, of conscious and unconscious factors. The same is true of the psychic basis: on the one hand the ego rests on the *total field of consciousness,* and on the other, on the *sum total of unconscious contents.* These fall into three groups: first, temporarily subliminal contents that can be reproduced voluntarily (memory); second, unconscious contents that cannot be reproduced voluntarily; third, contents that are not capable of becoming conscious at all. Group two can be inferred from the spontaneous irruption of subliminal contents into consciousness. Group three is hypothetical; it is a logical inference from the facts underlying group two. It contains contents which have not yet irrupted into consciousness, or which never will.

When I said that the ego "rests" on the total field of consciousness I do not mean that it *consists* of this. Were that so, it would be indistinguishable from the field of consciousness as a whole. The ego is only the latter's point of reference, grounded on and limited by the somatic factor described above.

Although its bases are in themselves relatively unknown and unconscious, the ego is a conscious factor par excellence. It is even acquired, empirically speaking, during the individual's lifetime. It seems to arise in the first place from the collision between the somatic factor and the environment, and, once established as a subject, it goes on developing from further collisions with the outer world and the inner.

Despite the unlimited extent of its bases, the ego is never more and never less than consciousness as a whole. As a conscious factor the ego could, theoretically at least, be described completely. But this would never amount to more than a picture of the *conscious personality*; all those features which are unknown or unconscious to the subject would be missing. A total picture would have to include these. But a total description of the personality is, even in theory, absolutely impossible, because the unconscious portion of it cannot be grasped cognitively. This unconscious portion, as experience has abundantly shown, is by no means unimportant. On the contrary, the most decisive qualities in a person are often unconscious and can be perceived only by others, or have to be laboriously discovered with outside help.

Clearly, then, the *personality as a total phenomenon* does not coincide with the ego, that is, with the conscious personality, but forms an entity that has to be distinguished from the ego. Naturally the need to do this is incumbent only on a psychology that reckons with the fact of the unconscious, but for such a psychology the distinction is of paramount importance. Even for jurisprudence it should be of some importance whether certain psychic facts are conscious or not—for instance, in adjudging the question of responsibility.

I have suggested calling the total personality which, though present, cannot be fully known, the *self*. The ego is, by definition, subordinate to the self and is related to it like a part to the whole. Inside the field of consciousness it has, as we say, free will. By this I do not mean anything philosophical, only the well-known psychological fact of "free choice," or rather the subjective feeling of freedom. But, just as our free will clashes with necessity in the outside world, so also it finds its limits outside the field of consciousness in the subjective inner world, where it comes into conflict with the facts of the self. And just as circumstances or outside events "happen" to us and limit our freedom, so the self acts upon the ego like an *objective occurrence* which free will can do very little to alter. It is, indeed, well known that the ego not only can do nothing against the self, but is sometimes actually assimilated by unconscious components of the personality that are in the process of development and is greatly altered by them.

It is, in the nature of the case, impossible to give any general description of the ego except a formal one. Any other mode of observation would have to take account of the *individuality* which attaches to the ego as one of its main characteristics. Although the numerous elements composing this complex factor are, in themselves, everywhere the same, they are infinitely varied as regards clarity, emotional coloring, and scope. The result of their combination—the ego—is therefore, so far as one can judge, individual and unique, and retains its identity up to a certain point. Its stability is relative, because far-reaching changes of personality can sometimes occur. Alterations of this kind need not always be pathological; they can also be developmental and hence fall within the scope of the normal.

Since it is the point of reference for the field of consciousness, the ego is the subject of all successful attempts at adaptation so far as these are achieved by the will. The ego therefore has a significant part to play in the psychic economy. Its position there is so important that there are good grounds for the prejudice that the ego is the center of the personality, and that the field of consciousness is the psyche *per se*. If we discount certain suggestive ideas in Leibnitz, Kant, Schelling, and Schopenhauer, and the philosophical excursions of Carus and von Hartmann, it is only since the end of the nineteenth century that modern psychology, with its inductive methods, has discovered the foundations of consciousness and proved empirically the existence of a psyche outside consciousness. With this discovery the position of the ego, till then absolute, became relativized; that is to say, though it retains its quality as the center of the field of consciousness, it is questionable whether it is the center of the personality. It is part of the personality but not the whole of it. As I have said, it is simply impossible to estimate how large or how small its share is; how free or how dependent it is on the qualities of this "extra-conscious" psyche. We can only say that its freedom is limited and its dependence proved in ways that are often decisive. In my experience one would do well not to underestimate its dependence on the unconscious. Naturally there is no need to say this to persons who already overestimate the latter's importance. . . .

2.

CARL JUNG

The Personal Unconscious

. . . if we reject the exclusively sexual theory of the unconscious and put in its place an energic view of the psyche, we must say that the unconscious contains everything psychic that has not reached the threshold of consciousness, or whose energy-charge is not sufficient to maintain it in consciousness, or that will reach consciousness only in the future. We can then picture to ourselves how the unconscious must be constituted. We have already taken cognizance of repressions as contents of the unconscious, and to these we must add *everything that we have forgotten.* When a thing is forgotten, it does not mean that it is extinguished; it simply means that the memory has become subliminal. Its energy-charge has sunk so low that it can no longer appear in consciousness; but, though lost to consciousness, it is not lost to the unconscious. . . . I would like to make what I mean clear by a hypothetical example. Suppose there are two people, one of whom has never read a book and the other has read a thousand. From the minds of both of them we expunge all memory of the ten years in which the first was merely living and the second was reading his thousand books. Each now knows as little as the other, and yet anyone will be able to find out

which of them has read the books and, be it noted, understood them. The experience of reading, though long forgotten, leaves traces behind it, and from these traces the previous experience can be recognized. This long-lasting, indirect influence is due to a fixing of impressions, which are still preserved even when they are no longer capable of reaching consciousness.

Besides things that have been forgotten, subliminal perceptions form part of the contents of the unconscious. These may be sense perceptions occurring below the stimulus-threshold of conscious hearing, or in the peripheral field of vision; or they may be apperceptions, by which are meant perceptions of endopsychic or external processes.

All this material constitutes the *personal unconscious.* We call it personal because it consists entirely of acquisitions deriving from personal life. Therefore, when anything falls into the unconscious it is taken up in the network of associations formed by this unconscious material. Associative connections of high intensity may then be produced, which cross over or rise up into consciousness in the form of inspirations, intuitions, "lucky ideas," and so on.

The concept of a personal unconscious does not, however, enable us fully to grasp the nature of the unconscious. If the unconscious were only personal, it would in theory be possible to trace all the fantasies of

---

[2] Jung, Carl G. *Civilization in Transition,* pp. 8–11. Copyright © 1964 by Princeton University Press. Reprinted by permission of Princeton University Press.

an insane person back to individual experiences and impressions. No doubt a large proportion of the fantasy-material could be reduced to his personal history, but there are certain fantasies whose roots in the individual's previous history one would seek for in vain. What sort of fantasies are these? They are, in a word, *mythological fantasies*. They are elements which do not correspond to any events or experiences of personal life, but only to myths. . . .

The Collective Unconscious

Where do these mythological fantasies come from, if they do not spring from the personal unconscious and hence from the experiences of personal life? Indubitably, they come from the brain—indeed, precisely from the brain and not from personal memory-traces, but from the inherited brain-structure itself. Such fantasies always have a highly original and "creative" character. They are like new creations; obviously they derive from the creative activity of the brain and not simply from its mnemonic activity. We receive along with our body a highly differentiated brain which brings with it its entire history, and when it becomes creative it creates out of this history—out of the history of mankind. By "history" we usually mean the history which we "make," and we call this "objective history." The truly creative fantasy activity of the brain has nothing to do with this kind of history, but solely with that age-old natural history which has been transmitted in living form since the remotest times, namely, the history of the brain-structure. And this structure

tells its own story of mankind: the unending myth of death and rebirth, and the multitudinous figures who weave in and out of this mystery.

This unconscious buried in the structure of the brain and disclosing its living presence only through the medium of creative fantasy, is the *suprapersonal unconscious*. It comes alive in the creative man, it reveals itself in the vision of the artist, in the inspiration of the thinker, in the inner experience of the mystic. The suprapersonal unconscious, being distributed throughout the brain-structure, is like an all-pervading, omnipresent, omniscient spirit. It knows man as he always was, and not as he is at this moment; it knows him as myth. For this reason, also, the connection with the suprapersonal or *collective* unconscious means an extension of man beyond himself; it means death for his personal being and a rebirth in a new dimension, as was literally enacted in certain of the ancient mysteries. It is certainly true that without the sacrifice of man as he is, man as he was—and always will be—cannot be attained. And it is the artist who can tell us most about this sacrifice of the personal man, if we are not satisfied with the message of the Gospels.

It should on no account be imagined that there are such things as *inherited ideas*. Of that there can be no question. There are, however, innate possibilities of ideas, *a priori* conditions for fantasy-production, which are somewhat similar to the Kantian categories. Though these innate conditions do not produce any contents of themselves, they give definite form to contents that have already been acquired. Being a part of the inherited structure of the brain, they are the reason for the identity of symbols and myth-motifs in all parts of the earth. The collective unconscious forms the dark background against which the adaptive function of consciousness stands out in sharp relief. One is almost tempted to say that everything of value in the psyche is taken up into the adaptive function, and that everything useless goes to form that inchoate background from which, to the terror of primitive man, menacing shadows and nocturnal specters detach themselves, demanding sacrifices and ceremonies which to our biologically oriented minds seem futile and meaningless. We laugh at primitive superstitions, thinking ourselves superior, but we completely forget that we are influenced in just as uncanny a fashion as the primitive by this background, which we are wont to scoff at as a museum of stupidities. Primitive man simply has a different theory—the theory of witchcraft and spirits. I find this theory very interesting and very sensible—actually more sensible than the academic views of modern science. Whereas the highly educated modern man tries to figure out what diet best suits his nervous intestinal catarrh and to what dietetic mistakes the new attack may be due, the primitive, quite correctly, looks for psychological reasons and seeks a psychologically effective method of cure. The processes in the unconscious influence us just as much as they do primitives; we are possessed by the demons of sickness no less than they, our psyche is just as much in danger of being struck by some hostile influence, we are just as much the prey of malevolent spirits of the dead, or the victims of a magic spell cast by a strange personality. Only, we call these things by different names, and that is the only advantage we have over primitive man. It is, as we know, a little thing, yet it makes all the difference. For mankind it was always like a deliverance from a nightmare when the new name was found.

3.

CARL JUNG

The necessary and needful reaction from the collective unconscious expresses itself in archetypally formed ideas. The meeting with oneself is, at first, the meeting with one's own shadow. The shadow is a tight passage, a narrow door, whose painful constriction no one is spared who goes down to the deep well. But one must learn to know oneself in order to know who one is. For what comes after the door is, surprisingly enough, a boundless expanse full of unprecedented uncertainty, with apparently no inside and no outside, no above

---

[3] Jung, Carl G. *The Archetypes and the Collective Unconscious*, pp. 21–22. Copyright © 1968 by Princeton University Press. Reprinted by permission of Princeton University Press.

and no below, no here and no there, no mine and no thine, no good and no bad. It is the world of water, where all life floats in suspension; where the realm of sympathetic system, the soul of everything living, begins; where I am indivisibly this *and* that; where I experience the other in myself and the other-than-myself experiences me.

No, the collective unconscious is anything but an encapsulated personal system; it is sheer objectivity, as wide as the world and open to all the world. There I am the object of every subject, in complete reversal of my ordinary consciousness, where I am always the subject that has an object. There I am utterly one with the world, so much a part of it that I forget all too easily who I really am. "Lost in oneself" is a good way of describing this state. But this self is the world, if only a consciousness could see it. That is why we must know who we are.

The unconscious no sooner touches us than we *are* it—we become unconscious of ourselves. That is the age-old danger, instinctively known and feared by primitive man, who himself stands so very close to this pleroma. His consciousness is still uncertain, wobbling on its feet. It is still childish, having just emerged from the primal waters. A wave of the unconscious may easily roll over it, and then he forgets who he was and does things that are strange to him. Hence primitives are afraid of uncontrolled emotions, because consciousness breaks down under them and gives way to possession. All man's strivings have therefore been directed towards the consolidation of consciousness. This was the purpose of rite and dogma; they were dams and walls to keep back the dangers of the unconscious, the "perils of the soul." Primitive rites consists accordingly in the exorcising of spirits, the lifting of spells, the averting of the evil omen, propitiation, purification and the production by sympathetic magic of helpful occurrences. . . .

4.

CARL JUNG

The transference is in itself no more than a projection of unconscious contents. At first the so-called superficial contents of the unconscious are projected, as can be seen from symptoms,

⁴ Jung, Carl G. *Two Essays on Analytical Psychology,* pp. 64–66. Copyright © 1966 by Princeton University Press. Reprinted by permission of Princeton University Press.

dreams, and fantasies. In this state the doctor is interesting as a possible lover. . . . Then he appears more in the role of the father: either the good, kind father or the "thunderer," depending on the qualities which the real father had for the patient. Sometimes the doctor has a maternal significance, a fact that seems somewhat peculiar, but is still within the bounds of possibility. All these fantasy projections are founded on personal memories.

Finally there appear forms of fantasy that possess an extravagant character. The doctor is then endowed with uncanny powers: he is a magician or a wicked demon, or else the corresponding personification of goodness, a savior. Again, he may appear as a mixture of both. Of course it is to be understood that he need not necessarily appear like this to the patient's conscious mind; it is only the fantasies coming to the surface which picture him in this guise. Such patients often cannot get it into their heads that their fantasies really come from themselves and have little or nothing to do with the character of the doctor. This delusion rests on the fact that there are no personal grounds in the memory for this kind of projection. It can sometimes be shown that similar fantasies had, at a certain period in childhood, attached themselves to the father or mother, although neither father nor mother provided any real occasion for them. . . .

There are present in every individual, besides his personal memories, the great "primordial" images, as Jacob Burckhardt once aptly called them, the inherited possibilities of human imagination as it was from time immemorial. The fact of this inheritance explains the truly amazing phenomenon that certain motifs from myths and legends repeat themselves the world over in identical forms. It also explains why it is that our mental patients can reproduce exactly the same images and associations that are known to us from the old texts. . . .

In this further stage of treatment, then, when fantasies are produced which no longer rest on personal memories, we have to do with the manifestations of a deeper layer of the unconscious where the primordial images common to humanity lie sleeping. I have called these images or motifs "archetypes," also "dominants" of the unconscious. . . .

This discovery means another step forward in our understanding: the recognition, that is, of two layers in the unconscious. We have to distinguish between a personal unconscious and an *impersonal* or *transpersonal unconscious*. We speak of the latter also as the *collective unconscious*, because it is detached from anything personal and is common to all men, since its contents can be found everywhere, which is naturally not the case with the personal contents. The personal unconscious contains lost memories, painful ideas that are repressed (i.e., forgotten on purpose), subliminal perceptions, by which are meant sense-perceptions that were not strong enough to reach consciousness, and finally, contents that are not yet ripe for consciousness. . . .

Archetypes of the Collective Unconscious

COMMENTARY

It must be emphasized that the archetypes do not come into being with specific content. They are, rather, forms without content to be activated by experiences that relate to a particular archetypical image. Hall and Nordby* are helpful here in their suggestion that an archetype is not a photograph but should be conceived more as a negative to be developed by experience. Following this analogy, the archetypical form *mother* would be the negative. The experiences with one's own mother, and with mothers in general, would provide the specific images, fantasies, desires, fears, loves, and hates that relate to this archetypical form, with its potential for an infinite variety of responses.

Jung observed that there are as many archetypes as there are universal human situations and experiences in life. It is possible, therefore, to identify numerous archetypal encounters in our own lives that reflect the earliest experiential history and evolution of our ancestral past. Throughout our lives we are destined to be touched by many of these primordial images and forces. Among them birth, death, rebirth, pageantry and ritual, the stranger, the intruder, the healer, the child, the hero, mother, father, and all the cycles, rhythms, and creations of the great earth mother. When we are transfixed by the rising of a full moon on a warm summer night, when we are awed, perhaps moved to tears, by the miracle of childbirth, when we feel the uplifting presence of a spiritual force in our lives, when

---

* C. S. Hall and V. J. Nordby. *A Primer of Jungian Psychology.* New York: New American Library, 1973.

we are captivated by the slight-of-hand skills of the magician, when we are frightened on Halloween by the shadowy presence of ghosts, ghouls, and goblins, we have touched, and have been touched by, the archetypes.

Our urge to explore and discover, to venture into new worlds, is rooted in the timeless archetype of discovery, or the hero's quest. The highly popular television and movie series *Star Trek* undoubtedly represents a call from this archetype.

As the following selections suggest, however, there are less benign, more complicated and insistent archetypical forms with which we are confronted. These archetypes contain hidden dangers for personality development, for they are more powerful and more difficult to integrate into ego consciousness. This is particularly true of the shadow and the anima and animus. If the archetypes remain unconscious we may be caught in the grip of irrationality, the victims of seemingly alien forces.

The shadow is the most primitive and sinister portion of the collective psyche. It is the source of our basest, most animal-like instincts, with tendencies toward aggression, immorality, and cruelty. In short, the shadow is the source of our propensity for evil. To assimilate these darker tendencies into consciousness is our greatest challenge and, according to Jung, the primary measure of one's courage. Remaining unconscious, the shadow can only find expression in dreams and fantasies and in irrational projections. The most shameful moments in history have resulted from the unconscious projections of the shadow onto innocent victims. Indeed, history is replete with evidence of the cruelty that these acted-out projections, "psychic epidemics" as Jung called them, have inflicted upon others. If we allow shadow aspects of our personality into consciousness, however, thus accepting our full humanness, we can utilize its energy for constructive and creative developments. It is this creative and productive potential of the shadow that distinguishes it from Freud's id. The great actors and actresses of stage and screen are undoubtedly drawing on these archetypal forms to identify with their roles and give their performances the imaginative power to stimulate the emotional involvement of their audiences.

Healthy psychic development depends, in large measure, on allowing these unconscious forms into consciousness, to become differentiated and utilized to enhance our unique qualities and individual selves. Thus, the process of individuation, that movement toward integration and wholeness, requires a growing balance between conscious and unconscious components.

The reader might well ask, "How can I become conscious of these archetypical forces that are so deeply embedded in my unconscious?" My answer to this very reasonable question is this: You have already started on the process of integration as you read, study, and contemplate the theories and concepts of Jung. It is my belief that the awareness of the collective psyche and its archetypes will enable you to give these constructs an important reality within the context of your development and experiences and will activate many of them as constructive forces in your own life. This principle, the conceptual foundation for self-actualization, is certainly not limited to Jung's contributions but will hold true for many of the other concepts and theories you will encounter during your study of personality and its development.

1.

CARL JUNG

Provided that we do not again exaggerate and so fall a victim to unrestrained "psychologizing," it seems to me that the critical standpoint here defined is inescapable. It constitutes the essence, origin, and method of modern psychology. There *is* an *a priori* factor in all human activities, namely the inborn, preconscious and unconscious individual structure of the psyche. The preconscious psyche—for example, that of a new-born infant—is not an empty vessel into which, under favorable conditions, practically anything can be poured. On the contrary, it is a tremendously complicated, sharply defined individual entity which appears indeterminate to us only because we cannot see it directly. But the moment the first visible manifestations of psychic life begin to appear, one would have to be blind not to recognize their individual character, that is, the unique personality behind them. It is hardly possible to suppose that all

these details come into being only at the moment in which they appear. When it is a case of morbid predispositions already present in the parents, we infer hereditary transmission through the germ-plasm; it would not occur to us to regard epilepsy in the child of an epileptic mother as an unaccountable mutation. Again, we explain by heredity the gifts and talents which can be traced back through whole generations. We explain in the same way the reappearance of complicated instinctive actions in animals that have never set eyes on their parents and therefore could not possibly have been "taught" by them.

Nowadays we have to start with the hypothesis that, so far as predisposition is concerned, there is no essential difference between man and all other creatures. Like every animal, he possesses a preformed psyche which breeds true to his species and which, on closer examination, reveals distinct features traceable to family antecedents. We have not the slightest reason to suppose that there are certain human activities or functions that could be exempted from this rule. We are

[1] Jung, Carl G. *The Archetypes and the Collective Unconscious,* pp. 77–80. Copyright © 1968 by Princeton University Press. Reprinted by permission of Princeton University Press.

unable to form any idea of what those dispositions or aptitudes are which make instinctive actions in animals possible. And it is just as impossible for us to know the nature of the preconscious psychic disposition that enables a child to react in a human manner. We can only suppose that his behavior results from patterns of functioning, which I have described as *images*. The term "image" is intended to express not only the form of the activity taking place, but the typical situation in which the activity is released. These images are "primordial" images in so far as they are peculiar to whole species, and if they ever "originated" their origin must have coincided at least with the beginning of the species. They are the "human quality" of the human being, the specifically human form his activities take. This specific form is hereditary and is already present in the germ-plasm. The idea that it is not inherited but comes into being in every child anew would be just as preposterous as the primitive belief that the sun which rises in the morning is a different sun from that which set the evening before.

Since everything is preformed, this must also be true of the individual functions, especially those which derive directly from the unconscious predisposition. The most important of these is creative fantasy. In the products of fantasy the primordial images are made visible, and it is here that the concept of the archetype finds its specific application. I do not claim to have been the first to point out this fact. The honor belongs to Plato. The first investigator in the field of ethnology to draw attention to the widespread occurrence of certain "elementary ideas"

was Adolf Bastian. Two later investigators . . . speak of "categories" of the imagination. And it was no less an authority than Hermann Usener who first recognized unconscious preformation under the guise of "unconscious thinking." If I have any share in these discoveries, it consists in my having shown that archetypes are not disseminated only by tradition, language, and migration, but that they can rearise spontaneously, at any time, at any place, and without any outside influence.

The far-reaching implications of this statement must not be overlooked. For it means that there are present in every psyche forms which are unconscious but nonetheless active—living dispositions, ideas in the Platonic sense, that preform and continually influence our thoughts and feelings and actions.

Again and again I encounter the mistaken notion that an archetype is determined in regard to its content, in other words that it is a kind of unconscious idea (if such an expression be admissible). It is necessary to point out once more that archetypes are not determined as regards their content, but only as regards their form and then only to a very limited degree. A primordial image is determined as to its content only when it has become conscious and is therefore filled out with the material of conscious experience. Its form, however, as I have explained elsewhere, might perhaps be compared to the axial system of a crystal, which, as it were, preforms the crystalline structure in the mother liquid, although it has no material existence of its own. This first appears according to the specific way in which the ions and molecules aggregate. The archetype in itself is empty and purely formal, nothing but a *facultas praeformandi*, a possibility of representation which is given *a priori*. The representations themselves are not inherited, only the forms, and in that respect they correspond in every way to the instincts, which are also determined in form only. The existence of the instincts can no more be proved than the existence of the archetypes, so long as they do not manifest themselves concretely. With regard to the definiteness of the form, our comparison with the crystal is illuminating inasmuch as the axial system determined only the stereometric structure but not the concrete form of the individual crystal. This may be either large or small, and it may vary endlessly by reason of the different size of its planes or by the growing together of two crystals. The only thing that remains constant is the axial system, or rather, the invariable geometric proportions underlying it. The same is true of the archetype. In principle, it can be named and has an invariable nucleus of meaning—but always only in principle, never as regards its concrete manifestation. In the same way, the specific appearance of the mother-image at any given time cannot be deduced from the mother archetype alone, but depends on innumerable other factors.

2.

CARL JUNG

There are as many archetypes as there are typical situations in life. Endless repetition has engraved these experiences into our psychic constitution, not in the form of images filled with content, but at first only as *forms without content*, representing merely the possibility of a certain type of perception and action. When a situation occurs which corresponds to a given archetype, that archetype becomes activated and a compulsiveness appears, which, like an instinctual drive, gains its way against all reason and will, or else produces a conflict of pathological dimensions, that is to say, a neurosis.

Method of Proof. We must now turn to the question of how the existence of archetypes can be proved. Since archetypes are supposed to produce certain psychic forms, we must discuss how and where one can get hold of the material demonstrating these forms. The main source, then, is *dreams*, which have the advantage of being involuntary, spontaneous products of the unconscious psyche and are therefore pure products of nature not falsified by

---

[2] Jung, Carl G. *The Archetypes and the Collective Unconscious,* pp. 48–53. Copyright © 1968 by Princeton University Press. Reprinted by permission of Princeton University Press.

any conscious purpose. By questioning the individual one can ascertain which of the motifs appearing in the dream are known to him. From those which are unknown to him we must naturally exclude all motifs which might be known to him. . . . Consequently, we must look for motifs which could not possibly be known to the dreamer and yet behave functionally in his dream in such a manner as to coincide with the functioning of the archetype known from historical sources.

Another source for the material we need is to be found in "active imagination." By this I mean a sequence of fantasies produced by deliberate concentration. I have found that the existence of unrealized, unconscious fantasies increases the frequency and intensity of dreams, and that when these fantasies are made conscious the dreams change their character and become weaker and less frequent. From this I have drawn the conclusion that dreams often contain fantasies which "want" to become conscious. The sources of dreams are often repressed instincts which have a natural tendency to influence the conscious mind. In cases of this sort, the patient is simply given the task of contemplating any one fragment of fantasy that seems significant to him—a chance idea, perhaps, or something he has become conscious of in a dream—until its context becomes visible, that is to say, the relevant associative material in which it is embedded. It is not a question of the "free association" recommended by Freud for the purpose of dream-analysis, but of elaborating the fantasy by observing the further fantasy material that adds itself to the fragment in a natural manner.

This is not the place to enter upon a technical discussion of the method. Suffice it to say that the resultant sequence of fantasies relieves the unconscious and produces material rich in archetypal images and associations. Obviously, this is a method that can only be used in certain carefully selected cases. The method is not entirely without danger, because it may carry the patient too far away from reality. A warning against thoughtless application is therefore in place.

Finally, very interesting sources of archetypal material are to be found in the delusions of paranoiacs, the fantasies observed in trance-states, and the dreams of early childhood, from the third to the fifth year. Such material is available in profusion, but it is valueless unless one can adduce convincing mythological parallels. It does not, of course, suffice simply to connect a dream about a snake with the mythological occurrence of snakes, for who is to guarantee that the functional meaning of the snake in the dream is the same as in the mythological setting? In order to draw a valid parallel, it is necessary to know the functional meaning of the individual symbol, and then to find out whether the apparently parallel mythological symbol has a similar context and therefore the same functional meaning. Establishing such facts not only requires lengthy and wearisome researches, but is also an ungrateful subject for demonstration. As the symbols must not be torn out of their context, one has to launch forth into exhaustive descriptions, personal as well as symbological, and this is practically impossible in the framework of a lecture. I have repeatedly tried it at the risk of sending one half of my audience to sleep.

An example. I am choosing as an example a case which, though already published, I use again because its brevity makes it peculiarly suitable for illustration.

About 1906 I came across a very curious delusion in a paranoid schizophrenic who had been interned for many years. The patient had suffered since his youth and was incurable. He had been educated at a State school and been employed as a clerk in an office. He had no special gifts, and I myself knew nothing of mythology or archaeology in those days, so the situation was not in any way suspect. One day I found the patient standing at the window, wagging his head and blinking into the sun. He told me to do the same, for then I would see something very interesting. When I asked him what he saw, he was astonished that I could see nothing, and said: "Surely you see the sun's penis—when I move my head to and fro, it moves too, and that is where the wind comes from." Naturally I did not understand this strange idea in the least, but I made a note of it. Then about four years later, during my mythological studies, I came upon a book by the late Albrecht Dieterich, the well-known philologist, which threw light on this fantasy. The work, published in 1910, deals with Greek papyrus in the Bibliothéque Nationale, Paris. Dieterich believed he had discovered a Mithraic ritual in one part of the text. The text is undoubtedly a religious prescription for carrying out certain incantations in which Mithras is named. It comes from the Alexandrian school of mysticism and shows affinities with certain passages in the Leiden papyri and *Corpus Hermeticum.* In Dieterich's text we read the following directions:

Draw breath from the rays, draw in three times as strongly as you can and you will feel yourself raised up and walking towards the height, and you will seem to be in the middle of the aerial region. . . . The path of the visible gods will appear through the disc of the sun, who is God my father. Likewise the so-called tube, the origin of the ministering wind. For you will see hanging down from the disc of the sun something that looks like a tube. And towards the regions westward it is as though there were an infinite east wind. . . .

It is obviously the author's intention to enable the reader to experience the vision which he had, or which at least he believes in. The reader is to be initiated into the inner religious experience either of the author, or—what seems more likely—one of those mystic communities of which Philo Judaeus gives contemporary accounts. The fire- or sun-god here invoked is a figure which has close historical parallels, for instance with the Christ-figure of the Apocalypse. It is therefore a "représentation collective," as are also the ritual actions described, such as the imitating of animal noises, etc. The vision is embedded in a religious context of a distinctly ecstatic nature and describes a kind of initiation into mystic experience of the Deity.

Our patient was about ten years older than I. In his megalomania, he thought he was God and Christ in one person. His attitude towards me was patronizing; he liked me probably because I was the only person with any sympathy for his abstruse ideas. His delusions were mainly religious, and when he invited me to blink into the sun like he did and waggle my head he obviously wanted to let me share his vision. He played the role of the mystic sage and I was the neophyte. He felt he was the sun-god himself, creating the wind by wagging his head to and fro. The ritual transformation into the deity is attested by Apuleius in the Isis mysteries, and moreover in the form of a Helios apotheosis. The meaning of the "ministering wind" is probably the same as the procreative pneuma, which streams from the sun-god into the soul and fructifies it. The association of sun and wind frequently occurs in ancient symbolism.

It must now be shown that this is not a purely chance coincidence of two isolated cases. We must therefore show that the idea of a wind-tube connected with God or the sun exists independently of these two testimonies and that it occurs at other times and in other places. Now there are, as a matter of fact, medieval paintings that depict the fructification of Mary with a tube or hose-pipe coming down from the throne of God and passing into her body, and we can see the dove of the Christ-child flying down it. The dove represents the fructifying agent, the wind of the Holy Ghost.

Now it is quite out of the question that the patient could have had any knowledge whatever of a Greek papyrus published four years later, and it is in the highest degree unlikely that his vision had anything to do with the rare medieval representations of the Conception, even if through some incredibly improbable chance he had ever seen a copy of such a painting. The patient was certified in his early twenties. He had never traveled. And there is no such picture in the public art gallery in Zürich, his native town.

I mention this case not in order to prove that the vision is an archetype but only to show you my method of procedure in the simplest possible form. If we had only such cases, the task of investigation would be relatively easy, but in reality the proof is much more complicated. First of all, certain symbols have to be isolated clearly enough to be recognizable as typical phenomena, not just matters of chance. This is done by examining a series of dreams, say a few hundred, for typical figures, and by observing their development in the series. The same method can be applied to the products of active imagination. In this way it is possible to establish certain continuities or modulations of one and the same figure. You can select any figure which gives the impression of being an archetype by its behavior in the series of dreams or visions. If the material at one's disposal has been well observed and is sufficiently ample, one can discover interesting facts about the variations undergone by a single type. Not only the type itself but its variants too can be substantiated by evidence from comparative mythology and ethnology. . . .

3.

CARL JUNG

The Shadow

Whereas the contents of the personal unconscious are acquired during the individual's lifetime, the contents of the collective unconscious are invariably archetypes that were present from the beginning. . . . The archetypes most clearly characterized from the empirical point of view are those which have the most frequent and the most disturbing influence on the ego. These are the *shadow*, the *anima*, the *animus*. The most accessible of these, and the easiest to experience, is the shadow, for its nature can in large measure be inferred from the contents of the personal unconscious. The only exceptions to this rule are those rather rare cases where the positive qualities of the personality are repressed, and the ego in consequence plays an essentially negative or unfavorable role.

The shadow is a moral problem that challenges the whole ego-personality, for no one can become conscious of the shadow without considerable moral effort. To become conscious of it involves recognizing the dark aspects of the personality as present and real. This act is the essential condition for any kind of self-knowledge, and it therefore, as a rule, meets with considerable resistance. Indeed, self-knowledge as a psycho-therapeutic measure frequently requires much painstaking work extending over a long period.

Closer examination of the dark characteristics—that is, the inferiorities constituting the shadow—reveals that they have an *emotional* nature, a kind of autonomy, and accordingly an obsessive or, better, possessive quality. Emotion, incidentally, is not an activity of the individual but something that happens to him. Affects occur usually where adaptation is weakest, and at the same time they reveal the reason for its weakness, namely a certain degree of inferiority and the existence of a lower level of personality. On this lower level with its uncontrolled or scarcely controlled emotions one behaves more or less like a primitive, who is not only the passive victim of his affects but also singularly incapable of moral judgment.

Although, with insight and good will, the shadow can to some extent be assimilated into the conscious personality, experience shows that there are certain features which offer the most obstinate resistance to moral control and prove almost impossible to influence. These resistances are usually bound up with *projections*, which are not recognized as such, and their recognition is a moral achievement beyond the ordinary. While some traits peculiar to the shadow can be recognized without too much difficulty as one's own personal qualities, in this case both insight and

[3] Jung, Carl G. *Aion: Researches into the Phenomenology of the Self,* pp. 8–9. Copyright © 1968 by Princeton University Press. Reprinted by permission of Princeton University Press.

good will are unavailing because the cause of the emotion appears to lie, beyond all possibility of doubt, in the other person. No matter how obvious it may be to the neutral observer that it is a matter of projections, there is little hope that the subject will perceive this himself. He must be convinced that he throws a very long shadow before he is willing to withdraw his emotionally-toned projections from their object.

4.

CARL JUNG

The Anima and the Animus

In the course of my exposition so far, I have kept exclusively to *masculine* psychology. The anima, being of feminine gender, is exclusively a figure that compensates the masculine consciousness. In woman the compensating figure is of a masculine character, and can therefore appropriately be termed the *animus*. If it was no easy task to describe what is meant by the anima, the difficulties become almost insuperable when we set out to describe the psychology of the animus.

The fact that a man naively ascribes his anima reactions to himself, without seeing that he really cannot identify himself with an autonomous complex, is repeated in feminine psychology, though if possible in even more marked form. This identification with an autonomous complex is the essential reason why it is so difficult to understand and describe the problem,

⁴ Jung, Carl G. *Two Essays on Analytical Psychology.*, pp. 205–211. Copyright © 1966 by Princeton University Press. Reprinted by permission of Princeton University Press.

quite apart from its inherent obscurity and strangeness. We always start with the naive assumption that we are masters in our own house. Hence we must first accustom ourselves to the thought that, in our most intimate psychic life as well, we live in a kind of house which has doors and windows to the world, but that, although the objects or contents of this world act upon us, they do not belong to us. For many people this hypothesis is by no means easy to conceive, just as they do not find it at all easy to understand and to accept the fact that their neighbor's psychology is not necessarily identical with their own. My reader may think that the last remark is something of an exaggeration, since in general one is aware of individual differences. But it must be remembered that our individual conscious psychology develops out of an original state of unconsciousness and therefore of non-differentiation. . . . Consequently, consciousness of differentiation is a relatively late achievement of mankind, and presumably but a relatively small sector of the indefinitely large field of original identity. Differentiation is the essence, the *sine qua non* of consciousness. Everything unconscious is undifferentiated, and everything that happens unconsciously proceeds on the basis of non-differentiation—that is to say, there is no determining whether it belongs or does not belong to oneself. It cannot be established "a priori" whether it concerns me, or another, or both. Nor does feeling give us any sure clues in this respect.

An inferior consciousness cannot *eo ipso* be ascribed to women; it is merely different from masculine consciousness. But, just as a woman is often clearly conscious of things which a man is still groping for in the dark, so there are naturally fields of experience in a man which, for woman, are still wrapped in the shadows of non-differentiation, chiefly things in which she has little interest. Personal relations are as a rule more important and interesting to her than objective facts and their interconnections. The wide fields of commerce, politics, technology, and science, the whole realm of the applied masculine mind, she relegates to the penumbra of consciousness; while, on the other hand, she develops a minute consciousness of personal relationships, the infinite nuances of which usually escape the man entirely.

We must therefore expect the unconscious of woman to show aspects essentially different from those found in man. If I were to attempt to put in a nutshell the difference between man and woman in this respect, i.e., what it is that characterizes the animus as opposed to the anima, I could only say this: as the anima produces *moods*, so the animus produces *opinions*; and as the moods of a man issue from a shadowy background, so the opinions of a woman rest on equally unconscious prior assumptions. Animus opinions very often have the character of solid convictions that are not lightly shaken, or of principles whose validity is seemingly unassailable. If we analyze these opinions, we immediately come upon unconscious assumptions whose existence must first be inferred; that is to say, the opinions are apparently conceived *as though* such assumptions existed. But in reality the opinions are not thought out at all: they exist ready made, and they are held so positively and with so much conviction that the woman never has the shadow of doubt about them.

One would be inclined to suppose that the animus, like the anima, personifies itself in a single figure. But this, as experience shows, is true only up to a point, because another factor unexpectedly makes its appearance, which brings about an essentially different situation from that existing in a man. The animus does not appear as one person, but as a plurality of persons. In H. G. Wells' novel *Christina Alberta's Father*, the heroine, in all that she does or does not do, is constantly under the surveillance of a supreme moral authority, which tells her with remorseless precision and dry matter-of-factness what she is doing and for what motives. Wells calls this authority a "Court of Conscience." This collection of condemnatory judges, a sort of College of Preceptors, corresponds to a personification of the animus. The animus is rather like an assembly of fathers or dignitaries of some kind who lay down incontestable, "rational," *ex cathedra* judgments.

On closer examination these exacting judgments turn out to be largely sayings and opinions scraped together more or less unconsciously from childhood on, and compressed into a canon of average truth, justice, and reasonableness, a compendium of preconceptions which, whenever a conscious and competent judgment is lacking (as not infrequently happens), instantly obliges with an opinion. Sometimes these opinions take the form of so-called sound common sense, sometimes they appear as principles which are like a travesty of education: "People have always done it like this," or "Everybody says it is like that."

It goes without saying that the animus is just as often projected as the anima. The men who are particularly suited to these projections are either walking replicas of God himself, who know all about everything, or else they are misunderstood word-addicts with a vast and windy vocabulary at their command, who translate common or garden reality into the terminology of the sublime. It would be insufficient to characterize the animus merely as a conservative, collective conscience; he is also a neologist who, in flagrant contradiction to his correct opinions, has an extraordinary weakness for difficult and unfamiliar words which act as a pleasant substitute for the odious task of reflection.

Like the anima, the animus is a jealous lover. He is an adept at putting, in place of the real man, an opinion about him, the exceedingly disputable grounds for which are never submitted to criticism. Animus opinions are invariably collective, and they override individuals and individual judgments in exactly the same way as the anima thrusts her emotional anticipations and projections between man and wife. If the woman happens to be pretty, these animus opinions have for the man something rather touching and childlike about them, which makes him adopt a benevolent, fatherly, professorial manner. But if the woman does not stir his sentimental side, and competence is expected of her rather than appealing helplessness and stupidity, then her animus opinions irritate the man to death, chiefly because they are based on nothing but opinion for opinion's sake, and "everybody has a right to his own opinions." Men can be pretty venomous here, for it is an inescapable fact that the animus always plays up the anima—and *vice versa*, of course—so that all further discussion becomes pointless.

In intellectual women the animus encourages a critical disputatiousness and would-be highbrowism, which, however, consists essentially in harping on some irrelevant weak point and nonsensically making it the main one. Or a perfectly lucid discussion gets tangled up in the most maddening way through the introduction of a quite different and if possible perverse point of view. Without knowing it, such women are solely intent upon exasperating the man and are, in consequence, the more completely at the mercy of the animus. "Unfortunately I am always right," one of these creatures once confessed to me.

However, all these traits, as familiar as they are unsavory, are simply and solely due to the extraversion of the animus. The animus does not belong to the function of conscious relationship; his function is rather to facilitate relations with the unconscious. Instead of the woman merely associating opinions with external situations—situations which she ought to think about consciously—the animus, as an associative function, should be directed inwards, where it could associate the contents of the unconscious. The technique of coming to terms with the animus is the same in principle as in the case of the anima; only here the woman must learn to criticize and hold her opinions at a distance; not in order to repress them, but, by investigating their origins, to penetrate more deeply into the background, where she will then discover the primordial images, just as the man does in his dealings with the anima. The animus is the deposit, as it were, of all women's ancestral experiences of man—and not only that, he is also a creative and procreative being, not in the sense of masculine creativity, but in the sense that he brings forth . . . the spermatic word. Just as man brings forth his work as a complete creation out of his inner feminine nature, so the inner masculine side of a woman brings forth creative seeds which have the power to fertilize the feminine side of the man. This would be the *femme inspiratrice* who, if falsely cultivated, can turn into the worst kind of dogmatist and high-handed pedagogue—a regular "animus hound," as one of my women patients aptly expressed it.

A woman possessed by the animus is always in danger of losing her femininity, her adapted feminine person (persona), just as a man in like circumstances runs the risk of effeminacy. These psychic changes of sex are due entirely to the fact that a function which belongs inside has been turned outside. The reason for this perversion is clearly the failure to give adequate recognition to an inner world which stands autonomously opposed to the outer world, and makes just as serious demands on our capacity for adaptation.

With regard to the plurality of the animus as distinguished from what we might call the "uni-personality" of the anima, this remarkable fact seems to me to be a correlate of the conscious attitude. The conscious attitude of woman is in general far more exclusively personal than that of man. Her world is made up of fathers and mothers, brothers and sisters, husbands and children. The rest of the world consists likewise of families, who nod to each other but are, in the main, interested essentially in themselves. The man's world is the nation, the state, business concerns, etc. His family is simply a means to an end, one of the foundations of the state, and his wife is not necessarily *the* woman for him (at any rate not as the woman means it when she says "my man"). The general means more to him than the personal; his world consists of a multitude of co-ordinated factors, whereas her world, outside her husband, terminates in a sort of cosmic mist. A passionate exclusiveness therefore attaches to the man's anima, and an indefinite variety to the woman's animus. Whereas the man has, floating before him, in clear outlines the alluring form of a Circe or a Calypso, the animus is better expressed as a bevy of Flying Dutchmen or unknown wanderers from over the sea, never quite clearly grasped, protean, given to persistent and violent motion. These personifications appear especially in dreams, though in concrete reality they can be famous tenors, boxing champions, or great men in faraway, unknown cities.

These two crepuscular figures from the dark hinterland of the psyche—truly the semi-grotesque "guardians of the threshold," to use the pompous jargon of theosophy—can assume an almost inexhaustible number of shapes, enough to fill whole volumes. Their complicated transformations are as rich and strange as the world itself, as manifold as the limitless variety of their conscious correlate, the persona. They inhabit the twilight sphere, and we can just make out that the autonomous complex of anima and animus is essentially a psychological function that has usurped, or rather retained, a "personality" only because this function is itself autonomous and undeveloped. But already we can see how it is possible to break up the personifications, since by making them conscious we convert them into bridges to the unconscious. It is because we are not using them purposefully as functions that they remain personified complexes. So long as they are in this state they must be accepted as relatively independent personalities. They cannot be integrated into consciousness while their contents remain unknown. The purpose of the dialectical process is to bring these contents into the light; and only when this task has been completed, and the conscious mind has become sufficiently familiar with the unconscious processes reflected in the anima, will the anima be felt simply as a function.

I do not expect every reader to grasp right away what is meant by animus and anima. But I hope he will at least have gained the impression that it is not a question of anything "metaphysical," but far rather of empirical facts which could equally well be expressed in rational and abstract language. I have purposely avoided too abstract a terminology because, in matters of this kind, which hitherto have been so inaccessible to our experience, it is useless to present the reader with an intellectual formulation. It is far more to the point to give him some conception of what the actual possibilities of experience are. Nobody can really understand these things unless he has experienced them himself. I am therefore much more interested in pointing out the possible ways to such experience than in devising intellectual formulae which, for lack of experience must necessarily remain an empty web of words. Unfortunately there are all too many who learn the words by heart and add the experiences in their heads, thereafter abandoning themselves, according to temperament, either to credulity or to criticism. We are concerned here with a new questioning, a new—and yet age-old—field of psychological experience. We shall be able to establish relatively valid theories about it only when the corresponding psychological facts are known to a sufficient number of people. The first things to be discovered are always facts, not theories. Theory-building is the outcome of discussion among many.

5.

CARL JUNG

The autonomy of the collective unconscious expresses itself in the figures of anima and animus. They personify those of its contents which, when withdrawn from projection, can be integrated into consciousness. To this extent, both figures represent *functions* which filter the contents of the collective unconscious through to the conscious mind. They appear or behave as such, however, only so long as the tendencies of the conscious and unconscious do not diverge too greatly. Should any tension arise, these functions, harmless till then, confront the conscious mind in personified form and behave rather like systems split off from the personality, or like part souls. This comparison is inadequate in so far as nothing previously belonging to the ego-personality has split off from it; on the contrary, the two figures represent a disturbing accretion. The reason for their behaving in this way is that though the *contents* of anima and animus can be integrated they themselves cannot, since they are archetypes. As such they are the foundation stones of the psychic structure, which in its totality exceeds the limits of consciousness and therefore can never become the object of direct cognition. Though the effects of anima and animus can be made conscious, they themselves are factors transcending consciousness and beyond the reach of perception and volition. Hence they remain autonomous despite the integration of their contents, and for this reason they should be borne constantly in mind. This is extremely important from the therapeutic standpoint, because constant observation pays the unconscious a tribute that more or less guarantees its co-operation. The unconscious as we know can never be "done with" once and for all. It is, in fact, one of the most important tasks of psychic hygiene to pay continual attention to the symptomatology of unconscious contents and processes, for the good reason that the conscious mind is always in danger of becoming one-sided, of keeping to well-worn paths and getting stuck in blind alleys. The complementary and compensating function of the unconscious ensures that these dangers, which are especially great in neurosis, can in some measure be avoided. It is only under ideal conditions, when life is still simple and unconscious enough to follow the serpentine path of instinct without hesitation or misgiving, that the compensation works with entire success. The more civilized, the more unconscious and complicated a man is the less he is able to follow his instincts. . . .

⁵ Jung, Carl G. *Aion: Researches into the Phenomenology of the Self,* pp. 20–21. Copyright © 1968 by Princeton University Press. Reprinted by permission of Princeton University Press.

6.

CARL JUNG

The Persona

The persona is a complicated system of relations between the individual consciousness and society, fittingly enough a kind of mask, designed on the one hand to make a definite impression upon others, and, on the other, to conceal the true nature of the individual. That the latter function is superfluous could be maintained only by one who is so identified with his persona that he no longer knows himself; and that the former is unnecessary could only occur to one who is quite unconscious of the true nature of his fellows. Society expects, and indeed must expect, every individual to play the part assigned to him as perfectly as possible, so that a man who is a parson must not only carry out his official functions objectively, but must at all times and in all circumstances play the role of parson in a flawless manner. Society demands this as a kind of surety; each must stand at his post, here a cobbler, there a poet. No man is expected to be both. Nor is it advisable to be both, for that would be "odd." Such a man would be "different" from other people, not quite reliable. In the academic world he would be a dilettante, in politics an "unpredictable" quantity, in religion a free-thinker—in short, he would always be suspected of unreliability and

incompetence, because society is persuaded that only the cobbler who is not a poet can supply workmanlike shoes. To present an unequivocal face to the world is a matter of practical importance: the average man—the only kind society knows anything about—must keep his nose to one thing in order to achieve anything worth while, two would be too much. Our society is undoubtedly set on such an ideal. It is therefore not surprising that everyone who wants to get on must take these expectations into account. Obviously no one could completely submerge his individuality in these expectations; hence the construction of an artificial personality becomes an unavoidable necessity. The demands of propriety and good manners are an added inducement to assume a becoming mask. What goes on behind the mask is then called "private life." This painfully familiar division of consciousness into two figures, often preposterously different, is an incisive psychological operation that is bound to have repercussions on the unconscious.

The construction of a collectively suitable persona means a formidable concession to the external world, a genuine self-sacrifice which drives the ego straight into identification with the persona, so that people really do exist who believe they are what they pretend to be. The "soullessness" of such an attitude is, however, only apparent, for under no circumstances will the unconscious tolerate this shifting of the center of gravity. When we examine such cases critically, we find that the excellence of the mask is compensated by the "private life" going on behind it. The pious Drummond once lamented that "bad temper is the vice of the virtuous." Whoever builds up too good a persona for himself naturally has to pay for it with irritability. Bismarck had hysterical weeping fits, Wagner indulged in correspondence about the belts of silk dressing-gowns. Nietzsche wrote letters to his "dear lama," Goethe held conversations with Eckermann, etc. But there are subtler things than the banal lapses of heroes. I once made the acquaintance of a venerable personage—in fact, one might easily call him a saint. I stalked round him for three whole days, but never a mortal failing did I find in him. My feeling of inferiority grew ominous, and I was beginning to think seriously of how I might better myself. Then, on the fourth day, his wife came to consult me. . . . Well, nothing of the sort has ever happened to me since. But this I did learn: that any man who becomes one with his persona can cheerfully let all disturbances manifest themselves through his wife without her noticing it, though she pays for her self-sacrifice with a bad neurosis.

These identifications with a social role are a very fruitful source of neuroses. A man cannot get rid of himself in favor of an artificial personality without punishment. Even the attempt to do so brings on, in all ordinary cases, unconscious reactions in the form of bad moods, affects, phobias, obsessive ideas, backslidings, vices, etc. The social "strong man" is in his private life often a mere child where his own states

of feeling are concerned; his discipline in public (which he demands quite particularly of others) goes miserably to pieces in private. His "happiness in his work" assumes a woeful countenance at home; his "spotless" public morality looks strange indeed behind the mask—we will not mention deeds, but only fantasies, and the wives of such men would have a pretty tale to tell. As to his selfless altruism, his children have decided views about that.

To the degree that the world invites the individual to identify with the mask, he is delivered over to influences from within. "High rests on low," says Lao-tzu. An opposite forces its way up from inside; it is exactly as though the unconscious suppressed the ego with the very same power which drew the ego into the persona. The absence of resistance outwardly against the lure of the persona means a similar weakness inwardly against the influence of the unconscious. Outwardly an effective and powerful role is played, while inwardly an effeminate weakness develops in face of every influence coming from the unconscious. Moods, vagaries, timidity, even a limp sexuality (culminating in impotence) gradually gain the upper hand.

The persona, the ideal picture of a man as he should be, is inwardly compensated by feminine weakness, and as the individual outwardly plays the strong man, so he becomes inwardly a woman, i.e., the anima, for it is the anima that reacts to the persona. But because the inner world is dark and invisible to the extraverted consciousness, and because a man is all the less capable of conceiving his weaknesses the more he is identified with the persona, the persona's counterpart, the anima, remains completely in the dark and is at once projected, so that our hero comes under the heel of his wife's slipper. If this results in a considerable increase of her power, she will acquit herself none too well. She becomes inferior, thus providing her husband with the welcome proof that it is not he, the hero, who is inferior in private, but his wife. In return the wife can cherish the illusion, so attractive to many, that at least she has married a hero, unperturbed by her own uselessness. This little game of illusion is often taken to be the whole meaning of life.

Just as, for the purpose of individuation, or self-realization, it is essential for a man to distinguish between what he is and how he appears to himself and to others, so it is also necessary for the same purpose that he should become conscious of his invisible system of relations to the unconscious, and especially of the anima, so as to be able to distinguish himself from her. One cannot of course distinguish oneself from something unconscious. In the matter of the persona it is easy enough to make it clear to a man that he and his office are two different things. But it is very difficult for a man to distinguish himself from his anima, the more so because she is invisible. Indeed, he has first to contend with the prejudice that everything coming from inside him springs from the truest depths of his being. The "strong man" will perhaps concede that in private life he is singularly undisciplined, but that, he says, is just his "weakness" with which, as it were, he proclaims his solidarity. Now there is in this tendency a cultural legacy that is not to be despised; for when a man recognizes that his ideal persona is responsible for his anything but ideal anima, his ideals are shattered, the world becomes ambiguous, he becomes ambiguous even to himself. He is seized by doubts about goodness, and what is worse, he doubts his own good intentions. When one considers how much our private idea of good intentions is bound up with vast historical assumptions, it will readily be understood that it is pleasanter and more in keeping with our present view of the world to deplore a personal weakness than to shatter ideals.

The Basic Attitudes and Functions: Introversion and Extraversion; Thinking, Feeling, Sensation, and Intuition

COMMENTARY

Psychological Types, published in 1921 after twenty years of research, shows that Jung had achieved a breakthrough in understanding how and why people differ so markedly in personality and temperament. He discovered that such differences were not random and capricious but were based on the presence of very specific psychic structures and processes involved in psychological development. Jung not only identified these fundamental structures and processes but, in so doing, pioneered in establishing a psychology of individual differences.

The two basic attitudes or orientations, extraversion and introversion, are identified primarily by the focus and attachment of psychic energy. In the introvert this energy is directed toward the self, focused on one's inner world of ideas, imagination, feelings, and perceptions. In the extravert, however, psychic energy is directed outward and forms attachments to people, activities, and external objects.

While both of these attitudes are present in each of us, one is usually more dominant (more conscious and differentiated) than the other. The inferior, or poorly developed, attitude remains relatively unconscious, and we are less in control of its expressions and potential.

The attitudes of extraversion and introversion provide us with an excellent example of a fundamental principle in Jungian psychology, the principle of *compensation*. This principle recognizes an unconscious and innate striving to maintain or restore psychic balance throughout the psyche, and, while never fully achieved, there will be numerous compensations for one-sidedness in the personality. Thus, the two basic attitudes of extraversion and introversion stand in a compensatory relationship to each other. Corrections for an imbalance of power between the two attitudes will often come from the unconscious in the form of dreams. In the dream the unconscious sends the dreamer a message on the state of his/her psyche. I will illustrate this principle with one of my own dreams.

Several years ago, while in therapy with a Jungian analyst, I was preparing to direct a weekend workshop where twelve to fifteen people would be participating. Being a confirmed introvert, I became frightened and anxious at the prospect of interacting with and entertaining a group of people. After several weeks of working through my dilemma I had a dream. I dreamed I was Liberace, the flamboyant and extraverted pianist and entertainer of the 1960s and 70s who walked onto the stage in elaborate costumes and sequined gowns and had candelabra on his piano. Liberace was a talented performer who could always entertain and captivate his audience. This dream, a compensatory message from my unconscious, was urging me to create a more equitable balance between my highly dominant introversion and my relatively unconscious and undifferentiated extraversion and to recognize my potential for doing so. This dream, with the help of my therapist, strengthened my inferior attitude, freed me from a dominating introversion, and gave me more energy and confidence to interact with the people at my workshop.

When the two attitudes, *extraversion* and *introversion*, are combined with the four functions, *thinking, feeling, sensing*, and *intuiting*, eight type variants are produced. They are as follows:

Extraverted thinking type   Extraverted sensation type
Introverted thinking type   Introverted sensation type
Extraverted feeling type   Extraverted intuitive type
Introverted feeling type   Introverted intuitive type

It must be remembered, as Jung suggests in the following selection, that there are no pure types. There is a polarity involved for each of the attitudes and functions.

The focus of most of the research on Jung's theories has been devoted to studies of his type theory. Much of this research followed the development of the Myers-Briggs Type Indicator (MBTY), a self-report questionnaire designed to measure individual differences centered on Jung's typology. The MBTY, in addition to measuring the two basic attitudes and the four functions, incorporates the additional dimension of judgment vs. perception. Most studies show the MBTY to be a fairly reliable (stable and consistent) and valid measure of Jung's typology. Its use has been invaluable in marriage and family therapy and in occupational-vocational counseling.

1.

CARL JUNG

In my practical medical work with nervous patients I have long been struck by the fact that besides the many individual differences in human psychology there are also typical differences. Two types especially become clear to me; I have termed them the introverted and the extraverted types.

When we consider the course of human life, we see how the fate of one individual is determined more by the objects of his interest, while in another it is determined more by his own inner self, by the subject. Since we all swerve rather more towards one side or the other, we naturally tend to understand everything in terms of our own type.

I mention this circumstance at once in order to avoid possible misunderstandings. It will be apparent that it is one which considerably aggravates the difficulty of a general description of types. I must presume unduly upon the good will of the reader if I may hope to be rightly understood. It would be relatively simple if every reader knew to which category he belonged. But it is often very difficult to find out whether a person belongs to one type or the other, especially in regard to oneself. In respect of one's own personality one's judgment is as a rule extraordinarily clouded. This subjective clouding of judgment is particularly common because in every

pronounced type there is a special tendency to compensate the one-sidedness of that type, a tendency which is biologically purposive since it strives constantly to maintain the psychic equilibrium. The compensation gives rise to secondary characteristics, or secondary types, which present a picture that is extremely difficult to interpret, so difficult that one is inclined to deny the existence of types altogether and to believe only in individual differences.

I must emphasize this difficulty in order to justify certain peculiarities in my presentation. It might seem as if the simplest way would be to describe two concrete cases and to dissect them side by side. But everyone possesses both mechanisms, extraversion as well as introversion, and only the relative predominance of one or the other determines the type. Hence, in order to throw the picture into the necessary relief, one would have to retouch it rather vigorously, and this would amount to a more or less pious fraud. Moreover, the psychological reactions of a human being are so complicated that my powers of description would hardly suffice to draw an absolutely correct picture. From sheer necessity, therefore, I must confine myself to a presentation of principles which I have abstracted from a wealth of facts observed in many different individuals. In this there is no question of a *deductio a priori*, as it might appear; it is rather a deductive presentation of empirically gained insights. These insights will, I

[1] Jung, Carl G. *Psychological Types,* pp. 3–6. Copyright © 1971 by Princeton University Press. Reprinted by permission of Princeton University Press.

hope, help to clarify a dilemma which, not only in analytical psychology but in other branches of science as well, and especially in the personal relations of human beings with one another, has led and still continues to lead to misunderstanding and discord. For they explain how the existence of two distinct types is actually a fact that has long been known: a fact that in one form or another has struck the observer of human nature or dawned upon the brooding reflection of the thinker, presenting itself to Goethe's intuition, for instance, as the all-embracing principle of systole and diastole. The names and concepts by which the mechanisms of extraversion and introversion have been grasped are extremely varied, and each of them is adapted to the standpoint of the observer in question. But despite the diversity of the formulations the fundamental idea common to them all constantly shines through: in one case an outward movement of interest towards the object, and in the other a movement of interest away from the object to the subject and his own psychological processes. In the first case the object works like a magnet upon the tendencies of the subject; it determines the subject to a large extent and even alienates him from himself. His qualities may become so transformed by assimilation to the object that one might think it possessed some higher and decisive significance for him. It might almost seem as if it were an absolute determinant, a special purpose of life or fate that he should abandon himself wholly to the object. But in the second case the subject is and remains the centre of every interest. It looks, one might say, as though all the life-energy were ultimately seeking the

subject, and thus continually preventing the object from exercising any overpowering influence. It is as though the energy were flowing away from the object, and the subject were a magnet drawing the object to itself.

It is not easy to give a clear and intelligible description of this two-way relationship to the object without running the risk of paradoxical formulations which would create more confusion than clarity. But in general one could say that the introverted standpoint is one which sets the ego and the subjective psychological process above the object and the objective process, or at any rate seeks to hold its ground against the object. This attitude, therefore, gives the subject a higher value than the object, and the object accordingly has a lower value. It is of secondary importance; indeed, sometimes the object represents no more than an outward token of a subjective content, the embodiment of an idea, the idea being the essential thing. If it is the embodiment of a feeling, then again the feeling is the main thing and not the object in its own right. The extraverted standpoint, on the contrary, subordinates the subject to the object, so that the object has the higher value. In this case the subject is of secondary importance, the subjective process appearing at times as no more than a disturbing or superfluous appendage of objective events. It is clear that the psychology resulting from these contrary standpoints must be classed as two totally different orientations. The one sees everything in terms of his own situation, the other in terms of the objective event.

These contrary attitudes are in themselves no more than correlative mechanisms: a diastolic going out and seizing of the object, and a systolic concentration and detachment of energy from the object seized. Every human being possesses both mechanisms as an expression of his natural life-rhythm, a rhythm which Goethe, surely not by chance, described physiologically in terms of the heart's activity. A rhythmical alternation of both forms of psychic activity would perhaps correspond to the normal course of life. But the complicated outer conditions under which we live and the even more complicated conditions of our individual psychic make-up seldom permit a completely undisturbed flow of psychic energy. Outer circumstances and inner disposition frequently favor one mechanism and restrict or hinder the other. One mechanism will naturally predominate, and if this condition becomes in any way chronic a *type* will be produced; that is, an habitual attitude in which one mechanism predominates permanently, although the other can never be completely suppressed since it is an integral part of the psychic economy. Hence there can never be a pure type in the sense that it possesses only one mechanism with the complete atrophy of the other. A typical attitude always means merely the relative predominance of one mechanism.

The hypothesis of introversion and extraversion allows us, first of all, to distinguish two large groups of psychological individuals. Yet this grouping is of such a superficial and general nature that it permits no more than this very general distinction. Closer investigation of the individual psychologies that fall into one group or the other will at once show great differences between individuals who nevertheless belong to the same group. If, therefore, we wish to determine wherein lie the differences between individuals belonging to a definite group, we must take a further step. Experience has taught me that in general individuals can be distinguished not only according to the broad distinction between introversion and extraversion, but also according to their basic psychological functions.

2.

CARL JUNG

. . . It has come to light on closer investigation that either type has a predilection to marry its opposite, each being unconsciously complementary to the other. The reflective nature of the introvert causes him always to think and consider before acting. This naturally makes him slow to act. His shyness and distrust of things induce hesitation, and so he always has difficulty in adapting to the external world. Conversely the extravert has a positive relation to things. He is, so to speak, attracted to them. New, unknown situations fascinate him. In order to make

[2] Jung, Carl G. *Two Essays on Analytical Psychology*, pp. 55–59. Copyright © 1966 by Princeton University Press. Reprinted by permission of Princeton University Press.

closer acquaintance with the unknown he will jump into it with both feet. As a rule he acts first and thinks afterwards. Thus his action is swift, subject to no misgivings and hesitations. The two types therefore seem created for a symbiosis. The one takes care of reflection and the other sees to the initiative and practical action. When the two types marry they may effect an ideal union. So long as they are fully occupied with their adaptation to the manifold external needs of life they fit together admirably. But when the man has made enough money, or if a fine legacy should drop from the skies and external necessity no longer presses, they have time to occupy themselves with one another. Hitherto they stood back to back and defended themselves against necessity. But now they turn face to face and look for understanding—only to discover that they have never understood one another. Each speaks a different language. Then the conflict between the two types begins. This struggle is envenomed, brutal, full of mutual depreciation, even when conducted quietly and in the greatest intimacy. For the value of the one is the negation of value for the other. It might reasonably be supposed that each, conscious of his own value, could peaceably recognize the other's value, and that in this way any conflict would be superfluous. I have seen a good number of cases where this line of argument was adopted, without, however, arriving at a satisfactory goal. Where it is a question of normal people, such critical periods of transition will be overcome fairly smoothly. By "normal" I mean a person who can somehow exist under all circumstances which afford him the minimum needs of life. But many people cannot do this; therefore not so many people are normal. What we commonly mean by a "normal person" is actually an ideal person whose happy blend of character is a rare occurrence. By far the greater number of more or less differentiated persons demand conditions of life which offer considerably more than the certainty of food and sleep. For these the ending of a symbiotic relationship comes as a severe shock.

It is not easy to understand why this should be so. Yet if we consider that no man is simply introverted or simply extraverted, but has both attitudes potentially in him—although he had developed only one of them as a function of adaptation—we shall immediately conjecture that with the introvert extraversion lies dormant and undeveloped somewhere in the background, and that introversion leads a similar shadowy existence in the extravert. And this is indeed the case. The introvert does possess an extraverted attitude, but it is unconscious, because his conscious gaze is always turned to the subject. He sees the object, of course, but has false or inhibiting ideas about it, so that he keeps his distance as much as possible, as though the object were something formidable and dangerous. I will make my meaning clear by a simple illustration:

Let us suppose two youths rambling in the country. They come to a fine castle; both want to see inside it. The introvert says, "I'd like to know what it's like inside." The extravert answers, "Right, let's go in," and makes for the gateway. The introvert draws back— "perhaps we aren't allowed in," says he, with visions of policemen, fines, and fierce dogs in the background. Whereupon the extravert answers, "Well, we can ask. they'll let us in all right"—with visions of kindly old watchmen, hospitable seigneurs, and the possibility of romantic adventures. On the strength of extraverted optimism they at length find themselves in the castle. But now comes the dénouement. The castle has been rebuilt inside, and contains nothing but a couple of rooms with a collection of old manuscripts. As it happens, old manuscripts are the chief joy of the introverted youth. Hardly has he caught sight of them than he becomes as one transformed. He loses himself in contemplation of the treasures, uttering cries of enthusiasm. He engages the caretaker in conversation so as to extract from him as much information as possible, and when the result is disappointing, he asks to see the curator in order to propound his questions to him. His shyness has vanished, objects have taken on a seductive glamour, and the world wears a new face. But meanwhile the spirits of the extraverted youth are ebbing lower and lower. His face grows longer and he begins to yawn. No kindly watchmen are forthcoming here, no knightly hospitality, not a trace of romantic adventure—only a castle made over into a museum. There are manuscripts enough to be seen at home. While the enthusiasm of the one rises, the spirits of the other fall, the castle bores him, the manuscripts remind [him] of a library, library is associated with university, university with studies and menacing examinations. Gradually a veil of gloom descends over the once so interesting and enticing castle. The object becomes negative. "Isn't it marvelous," cries the introvert, "to have stumbled on this wonderful collection?" "The place bores me to extinction," replies the other with undisguised ill humor. This annoys the introvert, who secretly vows never again to go rambling with an extravert. The latter is annoyed with the other's annoyance, and he thinks to himself that he always knew the fellow was an inconsiderate egotist who would, in his own selfish interest, waste all the lovely spring day that could be enjoyed so much better out of doors.

What has happened? Both were wandering together in happy symbiosis until they discovered the fatal castle, . . . At this point the types invert themselves: the introvert, who at first resisted the idea of going in, cannot now be induced to go out, and the extravert curses the moment when he set foot inside the castle. The former is now fascinated by the object, the latter by his negative thoughts. When the introvert spotted the manuscripts, it was all up with him. His shyness vanished, the object took possession of him, and he yielded himself willingly. The extravert, however, felt a growing resistance to the object and was eventually made the prisoner of his own ill-humored subjectivity. The introvert became extraverted, the extravert introverted. But the extraversion of the introvert is different from the extraversion of the extravert, and vice versa. So long as both were wandering along in joyous harmony, neither fell foul of the other, because each was in his natural character. Each was positive to the other, because their attitudes were complementary. They were complementary, however, only because the attitude of the one included the other. We can see this from the short conversation at the gateway. Both wanted to enter the castle. The doubt of the introvert as to whether an entry were possible also held good for the other. The initiative of the extravert likewise held good for the other. Thus the attitude of the one includes the other, and this is always in some degree true if a person happens to be in the attitude natural for him, for this attitude has some degree of collective adaptation. The same is true of the introvert's attitude, although this always starts from the subject. It simply goes from subject to object, while the extravert's attitude goes from object to subject.

But the moment when, in the case of the introvert, the object overpowers and attracts the subject, his attitude loses its social character. He forgets the presence of his friend, he no longer includes him, he becomes absorbed into the object and does not see how very bored his friend is. In the same way the extravert loses all consideration for the other as soon as his expectations are disappointed and he withdraws into subjectivity and moodiness.

We can therefore formulate the occurrence as follows: in the introvert the influence of the object produces an inferior extraversion, while in the extravert an inferior introversion take the place of his social attitude. And so we come back to the proposition from which we started: "The value of the one is the negation of value for the other." . . .

And yet it is necessary for the development of character that we should allow the other side, the inferior function, to find expression. We cannot in the long run allow one part of our personality to be cared for symbiotically by another; for the moment when we might have need of the other function may come at any time and find us unprepared, as the above example shows. And the consequences may be bad: the extravert loses his indispensable relation to the object, and the introvert loses his to the subject. Conversely, it is equally indispensable for the introvert to arrive at some form of action not constantly bedeviled by doubts and hesitations, and for the extravert to reflect upon himself, yet without endangering his relationships.

In extraversion and introversion it is clearly a matter of two antithetical, natural attitudes or trends, which Goethe once referred to as diastole and systole. They ought, in their harmonious alternation, to give life a rhythm, but it seems to require a high degree of art to achieve such a rhythm. Either one must do it quite unconsciously, so that the natural law is not disturbed by any conscious act, or one must be conscious in a much higher sense, to be capable of willing and carrying out the antithetical movements. Since we cannot develop backwards into animal unconsciousness, there remains only the more strenuous way forwards into higher consciousness. Certainly that consciousness, which would enable us to live the great Yea and Nay of our own free will and purpose, is an altogether superhuman idea. Still, it is a goal. Perhaps our present mentality only allows us consciously to will the Yea and to hear with the Nay. When that is the case, much is already achieved.

3.

CARL JUNG

The Four Functions: Thinking, Feeling, Sensation, and Intuition. The contrast between introversion and extraversion is simple enough, but simple formulations are unfortunately the most open to doubt. . . .

What struck me now was the undeniable fact while people may be classed as introverts or extraverts, this does not account for the tremendous differences between individuals in either class. So great, indeed, are these differences that I was forced to doubt whether I had observed correctly in the first place. It took nearly ten years of observation and comparison to clear up this doubt.

The question as to where the tremendous differences among individuals of the same type came from entangled me in unforeseen difficulties which for a long time I was unable to master. To observe and recognize the differences gave me comparatively little trouble, the root of my difficulties being now, as before, the problem of criteria. How was I to find suitable terms for the characteristic differences? Here I realized for the first time how young psychology really is. It is still little more than a chaos of arbitrary opinions and dogmas, produced for the most part in the study or consulting room by spontaneous generation from the isolated and Jove-like

brains of learned professors, with complete lack of agreement. Without wishing to be irreverent, I cannot refrain from confronting the professor of psychology with, say, the psychology of women, of the Chinese, or of the Australian aborigines. Our psychology must get down to brass tacks, otherwise we simply remain stuck in the Middle Ages.

I realized that no sound criteria were to be found in the chaos of contemporary psychology, that they had first to be created, not out of thin air, but on the basis of the invaluable preparatory work done by many men whose names no history of psychology will pass over in silence. . . .

I cannot possibly mention all the separate observations that led me to pick out certain *psychic* functions as criteria for the differences under discussion. I will only state very broadly what the essential differences are, so far as I have been able to ascertain them. An introvert, for example, does not simply draw back and hesitate before the object, but he does so in a quite definite way. Moreover he does not behave just like every other introvert, but again in a way peculiar to himself. Just as the lion strikes down his enemy or his prey with his forepaw, in which his specific strength resides, and not with his tail like the crocodile, so our habitual mode of reaction is normally characterized by the use of our most reliable and efficient function, which is an expression of our particular strength. However, this does

[3] Jung, Carl G. *Psychological Types*, pp. 535–541. Copyright © 1971 by Princeton University Press. Reprinted by permission of Princeton University Press.

not prevent us from reacting occasionally in a way that reveals our specific weakness. According to which function predominates, we shall seek out certain situations while avoiding others, and shall thus have experiences specific to ourselves and different from those of other people. An intelligent man will adapt to the world through his intelligence, and not like a sixth-rate pugilist, even though now and then, in a fit of rage, he may make use of his fists. In the struggle for existence and adaptation everyone instinctively uses his most developed function, which thus becomes the criterion of his habitual mode of reaction.

How are we to sum up these functions under general concepts, so that they can be distinguished from the welter of merely individual events? A rough typization of this kind has long since existed in social life, in the figures of the peasant, the worker, the artist, the scholar, the fighter, and so forth, or in the various professions. But this sort of typization has little or nothing to do with psychology, for, as a well-known savant once maliciously remarked, there are certain scholars who are no more than "intellectual porters."

A type theory must be more subtle. It is not enough, for example, to speak of intelligence, for this is too general and too vague a concept. Almost any kind of behavior can be called intelligent if it works smoothly, quickly, effectively and to a purpose. Intelligence, like stupidity, is not a function but a modality; the word tells us no more than *how* a function is working, not *what* is functioning. The same holds true of moral and aesthetic criteria. We must be able to designate what it is that functions outstandingly in the individual's habitual way of reacting. We are thus forced to revert to something that at first glance looks alarmingly like the old faculty psychology of the eighteenth century. In reality, however, we are only returning to ideas current in daily speech, perfectly accessible and comprehensible to everyone. When, for instance, I speak of "thinking," it is only the philosopher who does not know what it means; no layman will find it incomprehensible. He uses the word every day, and always in the same general sense, though it is true he would be at a loss if suddenly called upon to give an unequivocal definition of thinking. The same is true of "memory" or "feeling." However difficult it is to define these purely psychological concepts scientifically, they are easily intelligible in current speech. Language is a storehouse of concrete images; hence concepts which are too abstract and nebulous do not easily take root in it, or quickly die out again for lack of contact with reality. But thinking and feeling are such insistent realities that every language above the primitive level has absolutely unmistakable expressions for them. We can therefore be sure that these expressions coincide with quite definite psychic facts, no matter what the scientific definition of these complex facts may be. Everyone knows, for example, what consciousness means, and nobody can doubt that it coincides with a definite psychic condition, however far science may be from defining it satisfactorily.

And so it came about that I simply took the concepts expressed in current speech as designations for the corresponding psychic functions, and used them as my criteria in judging the differences between persons of the same attitude-type. For instance, I took thinking, as it is generally understood, because I was struck by the fact that many people habitually do more thinking than others, and accordingly give more weight to thought when making important decisions. They also use their thinking in order to understand the world and adapt to it, and whatever happens to them is subjected to consideration and reflection or at least subordinated to some principle sanctioned by thought. Other people conspicuously neglect thinking in favor of emotional factors, that is, of feeling. They invariably follow a policy dictated by feeling, and it takes an extraordinary situation to make them reflect. They form an unmistakable contrast to the other type, and the difference is most striking when the two are business partners or are married to each other. It should be noted that a person may give preference to thinking whether he be extraverted or introverted, but he will use it only in the way that is characteristic of his attitude-type, and the same is true of feeling.

The predominance of one or the other of these functions does not explain all the differences that occur. What I call the thinking and feeling types comprise two groups of persons who again have something in common which I cannot designate except by the word *rationality*. No one will dispute that thinking is essentially rational, but when we come to feeling, weighty objections may be raised which I would not like to brush aside. On the contrary, I freely admit that this problem of feeling has been one that has

caused me much brain-racking. . . . The chief difficulty is that the word "feeling" can be used in all sorts of different ways. This is especially true in German, but is noticeable to some extent in English and French as well. First of all, then, we must make a careful distinction between feeling and *sensation*, which is a sensory function. And in the second place we must recognize that a feeling of regret is something quite different from a "feeling" that the weather will change or that the price of our aluminum shares will go up. I have therefore proposed using *feeling* as a proper term in the first example, and dropping it—so far as its psychological usage is concerned—in the second. Here we should speak of *sensation* when sense impressions are involved, and of *intuition* if we are dealing with a kind of perception which cannot be traced back directly to conscious sensory experience. Hence I define sensation as perception via conscious sensory functions, and intuition as perception via the unconscious.

Obviously we could argue until Doomsday about the fitness of these definitions, but ultimately it is only a question of terminology. It is as if we were debating whether to call a certain animal a leopard or a panther, when all we need to know is what name we are giving to what. Psychology is virgin territory, and its terminology has still to be fixed. As we know, temperature can be measured according to Réaumur, Celsius, or Fahrenheit, but we must indicate which system we are using.

It is evident, then, that I take feeling as a function *per se* and distinguish it from sensation and intuition. Whoever confuses these last two functions with feeling in the strict sense is obviously not in a position to acknowledge the rationality of feeling. But once they are distinguished from feeling, it becomes quite clear that feeling values and feeling judgments—indeed, feelings in general—are not only rational but can also be as logical, consistent and discriminating as thinking. This may seem strange to the thinking type, but it is easily explained when we realize that in a person with a differentiated thinking function the feeling function is always less developed, more primitive, and therefore contaminated with other functions, these being precisely the functions which are not rational, not logical, and not discriminating or evaluating, namely, sensation and intuition. These two are by their very nature opposed to the rational functions. When we think, it is in order to judge or to reach a conclusion, and when we feel, it is in order to attach a proper value to something. Sensation and intuition, on the other hand, are perceptive functions—they make us aware of what is happening, but do not interpret or evaluate it. They do not proceed selectively, according to principles, but are simply receptive to what happens. But "what happens" is essentially irrational. There is no inferential method by which it could ever be proved that there must be so and so many planets, or so and so many species of warm-blooded animals. Irrationality is a vice where thinking and feeling are called for, rationality is a vice where sensation and intuition should be trusted.

Now there are many people whose habitual reactions are irrational because they are based either on sensation or on intuition. They cannot be based on both at once, because sensation is just as antagonistic to intuition as thinking is to feeling. When I try to assure myself with my eyes and ears of what is actually happening, I cannot at the same time give way to dreams and fantasies about what lies around the corner. As this is just what the intuitive type must do in order to give the necessary free play to his unconscious or to the object, it is easy to see that the sensation type is at the opposite pole to the intuitive. Unfortunately, time does not allow me to go into the interesting variations which the extraverted or introverted attitude produces in the irrational types.

Instead, I would like to add a word about the effects regularly produced on the other functions when preference is given to one function. We know that a man can never be everything at once, never quite complete. He always develops certain qualities at the expense of others, and wholeness is never attained. But what happens to those functions which are not consciously brought into daily use and are not developed by exercise? They remain in a more or less primitive and infantile state, often only half conscious, or even quite unconscious. These relatively undeveloped functions constitute a specific inferiority which is characteristic of each type and is an integral part of his total character. The one-sided emphasis on thinking is always accompanied by an inferiority of feeling, and differentiated sensation is injurious to intuition and vice versa.

Whether a function is differentiated or not can easily be recognized from its strength, stability, consistency, reliability, and adaptedness. But inferiority in a function is often not so easy to recognize or to describe. An essential criterion is its lack of self-sufficiency and consequent dependence on people and circumstances, its disposing us to moods and crotchetiness, its unreliable use, its suggestible and labile character. The inferior function always puts us at a disadvantage because we cannot direct it, but are rather its victims.

Since I must restrict myself here to a mere sketch of the ideas underlying a psychological theory of types, I must forgo a detailed description of each type. The total result of my work in this field up to the present is the establishing of two general attitude-types, extraversion and introversion, and four function-types, thinking feeling, sensation, and intuition. Each of these function-types varies according to the general attitude and thus eight variants are produced.

I have often been asked, almost accusingly, why I speak of four functions and not of more or fewer. That there are exactly four was a result I arrived at on purely empirical grounds. But as the following consideration will show, these four together produce a kind of totality. Sensation establishes what is actually present, thinking enables us to recognize its meaning, feeling tells us its value, and intuition points to possibilities as to whence it came and whither it is going in a given situation. In this way we can orient ourselves with respect to the immediate world as completely as when we locate a place geographically by latitude and longitude. The four functions are somewhat like the four points of the compass; they are just as arbitrary and just as indispensable. Nothing prevents our shifting the cardinal points as many degrees as we like in one direction or the other, or giving them different names. It is merely a question of convention and intelligibility.

But one thing I must confess: I would not for anything dispense with this compass on my psychological voyages of discovery. This is not merely for the obvious, all-too-human reason that everyone is in love with his own ideas. I value the type theory for the objective reason that it provides a system of comparison and orientation which makes possible something that has long been lacking, a critical psychology.

Individuation and Self-Actualization

COMMENTARY

Life begins in a state of unconscious and undifferentiated wholeness. From this primitive stage we embark on a dramatic psychic journey to achieve increasing individuation and completeness of personality. The ultimate goal of this journey, therefore, is to achieve self-realization, which, like a seed, exists as potential within every child. This striving, according to Jung, represents the unfolding of an inborn, autonomous, and archetypal process.

We can say, therefore, that Jung's psychology of personality development is teleological. The development of the self is oriented toward the future as we are drawn toward our destination of self-realization and wholeness. This teleological principle is also important in Abraham Maslow's theory of self-actualization and in Alfred Adler's concept of upward movement toward realization of a fictional final goal. In Maslow, Adler, and Jung, therefore, the personality is seen as striving for the realization of some intrinsic purpose or goal.

For Jung, the ultimate expression and embodiment of this teleological principle is found in his concept of *vocation*. As the process of individuation and differentiation unfolds, as we move away from the collective psyche and its norms, we are asked to heed an inner calling that will unite us with our true vocation—what we are destined to be or become. The law of vocation, this inner calling, is present within each of us, but it may be weakened by the strength of the collective psyche or group norms.

While Jung focused much of his attention on individual psychic development, he also stressed the social character of individuation and emphasized the importance of preserving collective standards while allowing for the emergence of individuality and uniqueness. Ideally, in this didactic relationship, the individual does not become alienated from society but participates in a mutually reinforcing relationship. This suggests an ideal state of synergy, a term used by the anthropologist Ruth Benedict to refer to the holistic unity or harmony between the needs of the individual and the needs (directions) of the society or culture.

In addition to Jung's many attributes as a personality theorist, he was also a developmental psychologist. Jung recognized that the process of individuation unfolds within the context of certain developmental stages with their own laws of growth and differentiation. For Jung these stages were childhood, youth and young adulthood, middle age, and old age. Each of these stages has its own special requirements and potentials for psychic growth, its own characteristic relationship with conscious and unconscious dynamics.

1.

CARL JUNG

Definition of Individuation. The concept of individuation plays a large role in our psychology. In general, it is the process by which individual beings are formed and differentiated; in particular, it is the development of the psychological *individual* as being distinct from the general, collective psychology. Individuation, therefore, is a process of *differentiation*, having for its goal the development of the individual personality.

Individuation is a natural necessity inasmuch as its prevention by a leveling down to collective standards is injurious to the vital activity of the individual. Since *individuality* is a prior psychological and physiological datum, it also expresses itself in psychological ways. Any serious check to individuality, therefore, is an artificial stunting. It is obvious that a social group consisting of stunted individuals cannot be a healthy and viable institution; only a society that can preserve its internal cohesion and collective values, while at the same time granting the individual the greatest possible freedom, has any prospect of enduring vitality. As the individual is not just a single, separate being, but by his very existence presupposes a collective relationship, it follows that the process of individuation must lead to more intense and

[1] Jung, Carl G. *Psychological Types*, pp. 448–450. Copyright © 1971 by Princeton University Press. Reprinted by permission of Princeton University Press.

broader collective relationships and not to isolation.

Individuality is closely connected with the *transcendent function* . . . since this function creates individual lines of development which could never be reached by keeping to the path prescribed by collective norms.

Under no circumstances can individuation be the sole aim of psychological education. Before it can be taken as a goal, the educational aim of adaptation to the necessary minimum of collective norms must first be attained. If a plant is to unfold its specific nature to the full, it must first be able to grow in the soil in which it is planted.

Individuation is always to some extent opposed to collective norms, since it means separation and differentiation from the general and a building up of the particular—not a particularity that is *sought out*, but one that is already ingrained in the psychic constitution. The opposition to the collective norm, however, is only apparent, since closer examination shows that the individual standpoint is not *antagonistic* to it, but only *differently oriented*. The individual way can never be directly opposed to the collective norm, because the opposite of the collective norm could only be another, but contrary, norm. But the individual way can, by definition, never be a norm. A norm is the product of the totality of individual ways, and its justification and beneficial effect are contingent upon the existence of individual ways that need from time to time to orient to a norm. A norm serves no purpose when it possesses absolute validity. A real conflict with the collective norm arises only when an individual way is raised to a norm, which is the actual aim of extreme individualism. Naturally this aim is pathological and inimical to life. It has, accordingly, nothing to do with individuation, which, though it may strike out on an individual bypath, precisely on that account needs the norm for its *orientation* to society and for the vitally necessary relationship of the individual to society. Individuation, therefore, leads to a natural esteem for the collective norm, but if the orientation is exclusively collective the norm becomes increasingly superfluous and morality goes to pieces. The more a man's life is shaped by the collective norm, the greater is his individual immorality.

Individuation is practically the same as the development of consciousness out of the original state of *identity*. It is thus an extension of the sphere of consciousness, an enriching of conscious psychological life.

2.

CARL JUNG

. . . Individuation means becoming an "individual," and, in so far as "individuality" embraces our innermost, last, and incomparable uniqueness, it also implies becoming one's own self. We could therefore translate individuation as "coming to selfhood" or "self-realization."

. . . Individualism means deliberately stressing and giving prominence to some supposed peculiarity rather than to collective considerations and obligations. But individuation means precisely the better and more complete fulfillment of the collective qualities of the human being, since adequate consideration of the peculiarity of the individual is more conducive to a better social performance than when the peculiarity is neglected or suppressed. The idiosyncrasy of an individual is not to be understood as any strangeness in his substance or in his components, but rather as a unique combination, or gradual differentiation, of functions and faculties which in themselves are universal. Every human face has a nose, two eyes, etc., but these universal factors are variable, and it is this variability which makes individual peculiarities possible. Individuation, therefore, can only mean a process of psychological development that fulfills the individual qualities given; in other words, it is a process by which a man becomes the

definite, unique being he in fact is. In so doing he does not become "selfish" in the ordinary sense of the word, but is merely fulfilling the peculiarity of his nature, and this, as we have said, is vastly different from egotism or individualism.

Now in so far as the human individual, as a living unit, is composed of purely universal factors, he is wholly collective and therefore in no sense opposed to collectivity. Hence the individualistic emphasis on one's own peculiarity is a contradiction of this basic fact of the living being. Individuation, on the other hand, aims at a living co-operation of all factors. But since the universal factors always appear only in individual form, a full consideration of them will also produce an individual effect, and one which cannot be surpassed by anything else, least of all by individualism.

The aim of individuation is nothing less than to divest the self of the false wrappings of the persona on the one hand, and of the suggestive power of primordial images on the other. . . . But when we turn to the other side, namely to the influence of the collective unconscious, we find we are moving in a dark interior world that is vastly more difficult to understand than the psychology of the persona, which is accessible to everyone. Everyone knows what is meant by "putting on official airs" or "playing a social role." Through the persona a man tries to appear as this or that, or he hides behind a mask, or he may even build up a definite persona as a barricade. So the

² Jung, Carl G. *Two Essays on Analytical Psychology*, pp. 173–182. Copyright © 1966 by Princeton University Press. Reprinted by permission of Princeton University Press.

problem of the persona should present no great intellectual difficulties.

It is, however, another thing to describe, in a way that can be generally understood, those subtle inner processes which invade the conscious mind with such suggestive force. . . .

So far as our present experience goes, we can lay it down that the unconscious processes stand in a compensatory relation to the conscious mind. I expressly use the word "compensatory" and not the word "contrary" because conscious and unconscious are not necessarily in opposition to one another, but complement one another to form a totality, which is the *self*. According to this definition the self is a quantity that is supraordinate to the conscious ego. It embraces not only the conscious but also the unconscious psyche, and is therefore, so to speak, a personality which we *also* are. It is easy enough to think of ourselves as possessing part-souls. Thus we can, for instance, see ourselves as a persona without too much difficulty. But it transcends our powers of imagination to form a clear picture of what we are as a self, for in this operation the part would have to comprehend the whole. There is little hope of our ever being able to reach even approximate consciousness of the self, since however much we may make conscious there will always exist an indeterminate and indeterminable amount of unconscious material which belongs to the totality of the self. Hence the self will always remain a supraordinate quantity.

The unconscious processes that compensate the conscious ego contain all those elements that are necessary for the self-regulation of the psyche as a whole. On the personal level, these are not the consciously recognized personal motives which appear in dreams, or the meanings of daily situations which we have overlooked, or conclusions we have failed to draw, or affects we have not permitted, or criticisms we have spared ourselves. But the more we become conscious of ourselves through self-knowledge, and act accordingly, the more the layer of the personal unconscious that is superimposed on the collective unconscious will be diminished. In this way there arises a consciousness which is no longer imprisoned in the petty, over-sensitive, personal world of the ego, but participates freely in the wider world of objective interests. This widened consciousness is no longer that touchy, egotistical bundle of personal wishes, fears, hopes, and ambitions which always has to be compensated or corrected by unconscious counter-tendencies; instead, it is a function of relationship to the world of objects, bringing the individual into absolute, binding, and indissoluble communion with the world at large. The complications arising at this stage are no longer egotistic wish-conflicts, but difficulties that concern others as much as oneself. At this stage it is fundamentally a question of collective problems, which have activated the collective unconscious because they require collective rather than personal compensation. We can now see that the unconscious produces contents which are valid not only for the person concerned, but for others as well, in fact for a great many people and possibly for all. . . .

We should certainly not conclude from these compensations that, as the conscious mind becomes more deeply engrossed in universal problems, the unconscious will bring forth correspondingly far-reaching compensations. There is what one might call a legitimate and an illegitimate interest in impersonal problems. Excursions of this kind are legitimate only when they arise from the deepest and truest needs of the individual; illegitimate when they are either mere intellectual curiosity or a flight from unpleasant reality. In the latter case the unconscious produces all too human and purely personal compensations, whose manifest aim is to bring the conscious mind back to ordinary reality. People who go illegitimately mooning after the infinite often have absurdly banal dreams which endeavor to damp down their ebullience. Thus, from the nature of the compensation, we can at once draw conclusions as to the seriousness and rightness of the conscious strivings.

3.

CARL JUNG

What, in the last analysis, induces a man to choose his own way and so to climb out of unconscious identity with the mass as out of a fog bank? It cannot be necessity, for necessity comes to many and they all save themselves in convention. It cannot be moral choice, for as a rule a man decides for convention. What is it, then, that inexorably tilts the beam in favor of the *extraordinary*?

It is what is called vocation: an irrational factor that fatefully forces a man to emancipate himself from the herd and its trodden paths. True personality always has vocation and believes in it, has fidelity to it as to God, in spite of the fact that, as the ordinary man would say, it is only a feeling of individual vocation. But this vocation acts like a law of God from which there is no escape. That many go to ruin upon their own ways means nothing to him who has vocation. He must obey his own law, as if it were a demon that whisperingly indicated to him new and strange ways. Who has vocation hears the voice of the inner man; he is *called.* . . .

To have vocation means in the original sense *to be addressed by a voice.* We find the clearest examples of this in the confessions of the Old Testament prophets. Nor is this merely an ancient manner of speech, as is shown by the confessions of historic personalities such as Goethe and Napoleon, to mention two familiar examples, who made no secret of their feeling of vocation.

Now, vocation, or the feeling of vocation, is not perchance the prerogative of great personalities, but also belongs to the small ones all the way

³ Jung, C. G. (1939). *The Integration of the Personality.* Copyright © 1939 by Farrar and Rinehard, Inc., pp. 291–297. Reprinted by permission of Routledge & Kegan Paul.

down to the duodecimo format; only, with the decrease of proportions, it becomes more veiled and unconscious. It is as if the voice of the inner demon moved further and further off and spoke more rarely and indistinctly. The smaller the personality is, so much the more unclear and unconscious it becomes, till it finally merges into one with society, surrendering its own wholeness and dissolving instead into the wholeness of the group. In the place of the inner voice appears the voice of the social group and its conventions, and in the place of vocation the collective necessities.

But it happens to not a few, even in this unconscious social state, to be summoned by the individual voice, whereupon they are at once differentiated from the others and feel themselves confronted by a problem that the others do not know about. It is generally impossible for a man to explain to his fellow beings what has happened, for understanding is cut off by a wall of the strongest prejudices. "I am just like everyone else"; there is "no such thing," or if there is, then, of course, it is "morbid" and moreover quite inexpedient; it is "monstrous presumption to suppose that anything of that sort could have any significance"; indeed, it is "nothing but psychology."

This last objection is highly popular today. It arises from a singular undervaluation of psychic life, which people apparently regard as something personal, arbitrary, and therefore completely futile. And this, paradoxically enough, along with the present-day enthusiasm for psychology. After all, the unconscious is "nothing but fantasy"! He "merely thought" so and so,

etc. People take themselves for magicians who conjure the psychic hither and yon and mold it to suit their moods. They deny what is uncomfortable, sublimate the unwished for, explain away anything that causes anxiety, correct faults, and suppose in the end that they have finally arranged everything beautifully. In the meanwhile they have forgotten the main point, which is that psychic life is only to the smallest extent identical with consciousness and its sleight-of-hand tricks, while for much the greater part it is unconscious fact that lies there hard and heavy as granite, immovable and inaccessible, yet ready, whenever unknown laws shall dictate, to plunge down upon us. The gigantic catastrophes that threaten *us* are not elemental happenings of a physical or biological kind, but are psychic events. We are threatened in a fearful way by wars and revolutions that are nothing else than psychic epidemics. At any moment a few million people may be seized by a madness, and then we have another world war or a devastating revolution. Instead of being exposed to wild beasts, tumbling rocks, and inundating waters, man is exposed today to the elemental forces of his own psyche. Psychic life is a world-power that exceeds by many times all the powers of the earth. The enlightenment, which stripped nature and human institutions of gods, overlooked the one god of fear who dwells in the psyche. Fear of God is in place, if anywhere, before the dominating power of psychic life.

But these are all mere abstractions. Everyone knows that the intellect—that handy man—can put it this way and in quite a different way too. It is wholly a different matter when this objective, psychic fact, hard as granite and heavy as lead, confronts the individual as an inner experience and says to him in an audible voice, "This is what will and must happen." Then he feels himself called, just as do the social groups when a war is on, or a revolution, or any other madness. Not for nothing is it just our own epoch that calls for the liberating personality, for the one who distinguishes himself from the inescapable power of collectivity, thus freeing himself at least in a psychic way, and who lights a hopeful watchfire announcing to others that at least *one* man has succeeded in escaping from the fateful identity with the group soul. The fact is that the group, because of its unconsciousness, has no freedom of choice, so that, within it, psychic life works itself out like an uncontrolled law of nature. There is set going a causally connected process that comes to rest only in catastrophe. The people always long for a hero, a slayer of dragons, when it feels the danger of psychic forces; thence, the cry for personality.

But what has the single personality to do with the need of the many? First of all, he is a part of the people as a whole and as exposed to the force that moves the whole as are all the others. The only thing that distinguishes this person from all the others is his vocation. He has been called away from the all-powerful, all-oppressing psychic life that is his own and his people's affliction. If he listens to the voice, then he is different and isolated, for he has decided to follow the law that confronts him from within. His "own" law, everyone will cry. He alone knows better—has to know better: it is *the* law, *the* vocation, as little his "own" as the lion that fells him, although it is undoubtedly this particular lion that kills him, and not any other lion. Only in this sense can he speak of "his" vocation, "his" law.

With the very decision to put his own way above all other ways he has already in large part fulfilled his liberating vocation. He has canceled the validity of all other ways for himself. He has placed *his* law above all conventions, and so has shoved aside, as far as he is concerned, all those things that not only failed to prevent the great danger, but actually brought it on. For conventions are in themselves soulless mechanisms that can never do more than grasp the routine of life. Creative life is always on the yonder side of convention. This is how it comes about that, when the mere routine of life in the form of traditional conventions predominates, a destructive outbreak of the creative forces *must* follow. But such an outbreak is only catastrophic as a *mass phenomenon*, and never in the individual who consciously subordinates himself to these higher powers and places his abilities at their service. The mechanism of convention keeps people *unconscious*, and then, like wild game, they can follow their customary runways without the necessity of conscious choice. This unintentional effect of even the best conventions is unavoidable, and it is also a terrible danger. For when new conditions not provided for by the old conventions arise, then panic seizes the human being who has been held unconscious by routine, much as it seizes an animal, and with equally unpredictable results.

But personality does not allow itself to be seized by the panic of those who are just awakening, for it already has terror behind it. It is equal to the changing conditions brought by time, and is unknowingly and unwillingly a *leader*.

Certainly, all human beings resemble one another, for otherwise they could not succumb to the same delusion; and the foundation of the psyche, upon which individual consciousness rests, is universally the same, beyond a doubt, for otherwise people could never reach a common understanding. In this sense, personality with its peculiar psychic make-up is itself not something absolutely unique and happening but once. The uniqueness holds only for the *individuality* of the personality, as it does for each and every individuality. To become a personality is not the absolute prerogative of the man of genius. He may even have genius without either having personality or being a personality. In so far as every individual has his own inborn law of life, it is theoretically possible for every man to follow this law before all others and so to become a personality—that is, to achieve completeness. But since life can only exist in the form of living units, which is to say, of individuals, the law of life in the last analysis always

tends towards a life that *is individually lived*. Although, at bottom, one cannot conceive the objective-psychic in any other way than as an actuality that is universal and uniform, and although this means that all men share the same primary, psychic condition, still the objective-psychic must individuate itself as soon as it manifests itself, for there is no way in which it can express itself except through the single individual. The only exception to this is when it seizes upon the group; but in that case it leads by rules of nature to a catastrophe, and for the simple reason that it acts only through unconscious channels and is not assimilated by any consciousness so as to be assigned its place among all the other conditions of life.

Only the man who is able *consciously* to affirm the power of the vocation confronting him from within becomes a personality; he who succumbs to it falls a prey to the blind flux of happening and is destroyed. The greatness and the liberating effect of all genuine personality consists in this, that it subjects itself of free choice to its vocation and consciously translates into its own individual reality what would lead only to ruin if it were lived unconsciously by the group.

4.

CARL JUNG

The Child Archetype and Individuation. One of the essential features of the child motif is its futurity. The child is potential future. Hence the occurrence of the child motif in the psychology of the individual signifies as a rule an anticipation of future developments, even though at first sight it may seem like a retrospective configuration. Life is a flux, a flowing into the future, and not a stoppage or a backwash. It is therefore not surprising that so many of the mythological saviours are child gods. This agrees exactly with our experience of the psychology of the individual, which shows that the "child" paves the way for a future change of personality. In the individuation process, it anticipates the figure that comes from the synthesis of conscious and unconscious elements in the personality. It is therefore a symbol which unites the opposites; a mediator,

bringer of healing, that is, one who makes whole. Because it has this meaning, the child motif is capable of the numerous transformations mentioned above: it can be expressed by roundness, the circle or sphere. . . . The goal of the individuation process is the synthesis of the self. From another point of view the term "entelechy" might be preferable to "synthesis." There is an empirical reason why "entelechy" is, in certain conditions, more fitting: the symbols of wholeness frequently occur at the beginning of the individuation process, indeed they can often be observed in the first dreams of early infancy. This observation says much for the a priori existence of potential wholeness, and on this account the idea of entelechy instantly recommends itself. But in so far as the individuation process occurs, empirically speaking, as a synthesis, it looks, paradoxically enough, as if something already existent were being put together. From this point of view, the term "synthesis" is also applicable.

---

[4] Jung, Carl G. *The Archetypes and the Collective Unconscious,* pp. 164–165. Copyright © 1968 by Princeton University Press. Reprinted by permission of Princeton University Press.

CHAPTER IV

The Psychoanalytic Social Theory of Karen Horney

BIOGRAPHICAL SKETCH

Karen Horney, born Karen Danielson in 1885, was the daughter of a Norwegian sea captain and a socially prominent Dutch mother. Karen's father, Henrick Danielson, was a stern religious fundamentalist, given to fits of anger and inclined to view women with contempt. Her mother, Clotilde Marie von Ronzelen, on the other hand, was intelligent, liberal and free thinking. Not surprisingly, their temperamental differences often led to serious conflicts.

Throughout her early years Karen was both intimidated by and attracted to her dominant and powerful father, who took her on several of his voyages and introduced her to exotic artifacts and trinkets from around the world.

Karen did not have a happy childhood. She felt unloved and unwanted and was plagued by self-doubts and feelings of unattractiveness. Emotional problems continued throughout much of her life, and there were periods of time when she was suicidal.

In 1906, at the age of twenty-one, Karen became one of the first women in Germany permitted to enter medical school. She had decided, early on, to compensate for her perceived unattractiveness by developing her intellect. It was while she was studying medicine at the University of Freiburg that she met her husband, Oskar Horney, who was studying economics and political science at another university. They were married in 1909. This marital union produced three daughters.

Following her marriage, Horney continued her studies, receiving her medical degree from the University of Berlin in 1915. Shortly after receiving her degree she published her first paper, which was written well within the bounds of psychoanalytic tradition. This article showed little of the radical departure from classical theory that Horney was to take in the later years.

Following her medical degree, Karen spent five years of training in psychoanalysis at the Berlin Psychoanalytic Institute. After these intense years of training, during which she suffered from numerous episodes of depression, Karen's life was further burdened with serious personal problems. Her marriage to Oskar Horney rapidly disintegrated, her brother died prematurely, and both her mother and father died within a year. In 1927 she and her husband separated, but they were not divorced until 1939.

The most positive and promising period of Karen's life began soon after her separation from Oskar Horney. She continued her teaching at the Berlin Psychoanalytic Institute and became increasingly involved in her private practice, her professional writing, and traveling.

In 1932, Karen Horney was invited by the psychoanalyst Franz Alexander to come to the United States. After serving as Associate Director of the Chicago Institute of Psychoanalysis for two years, she moved to New York where she taught at the New York Psychoanalytic Institute and established a private practice.

As Horney moved further and further away in her thinking from classical analytic theory there was an inevitable clash between her unorthodox ideas and the traditional Freudian doctrine that prevailed at the Institute. It was during this time that her book *New Ways in Psychoanalysis* (1939) was published. This book focused on some of her differences with Freudian theory and stressed the social influences on personality. Horney openly rebelled at the established traditions of the Institute and was finally forced to limit her work and influence there. Under pressure, Horney resigned from her position at the New York Psychoanalytic Institute in 1941 and founded her own group, the American Institute for Psychoanalysis. One of Horney's most creative and independent expressions of her own theories and concepts came with the publication of *Neurosis and Human Growth* in 1950. Karen Horney remained with the American Institute until her death from cancer in 1952.

Throughout her life Karen Horney was plagued with conflict and emotional turmoil. These negative features of her life, however, did not detract from her courage to take on the Freudian "establishment" and from the considerable contributions she made to the revision and evolution of psychoanalytic theory.

The Three Neurotic Trends: Moving Toward Others, Moving Against Others, Moving Away from Others

COMMENTARY

When it comes to understanding the complexities of the neurotic personality and the process by which such distortions occur, Karen Horney has no peer. She spent her long and distinguished career studying and treating neurotic individuals. Fortunately, Horney was also a writer, and the richness of her clinical experience and the depth of her understanding of neurotic conflicts and the neurotic process are available to us through three primary works: *The Neurotic Personality of Our Time* (1937); *Our Inner Conflicts* (1945); and *Neurosis and Human Growth* (1950). In these works Horney details her theory of the neurotic condition. It is a theory that departs from the Freudian view by emphasizing the importance of interpersonal and cultural factors in personality development. Although Horney focused on the development of the neurotic personality, she also deepened our understanding of the needs, conflicts, and coping strategies common to us all. Throughout her works, Horney emphasized again and again that the crucial conflicts around which a neurosis develops are usually the same conflicts we all share within our culture.

The following selections present Horney's central thesis regarding neurotic developments in personality. In these selections we are introduced to her important concepts of *basic anxiety, the three neurotic trends,* the generic or *basic conflict,* and the *search for glory*.

In order to cope with *basic anxiety*, feelings of being isolated and helpless in a hostile world, the child is driven by an inner necessity toward one of the three neurotic trends: moving toward people, moving against people, and moving away from people. In the neurotic personality these three

116

neurotic directions are unconscious, exaggerated, and maladaptive. In the normal person, however, they function in an adaptive and flexible manner and are complementary, making for a "harmonious whole."

The important distinction is that in the neurotic orientation to life these trends become compulsive, rigid, and indiscriminate. In neurotic persons, for example, their very existence, happiness, and security depend upon the need for love, for power, or for freedom and isolation. Although one of these trends will eventually dominate the personality, the *central neurotic conflict* lies in the fact that the neurotic, like all of us, has a need for a balanced satisfaction in all three areas, and this cannot be achieved.

For Horney, the *search for glory,* represents the final consolidation and integration of the neurotic personality. Horney shows how the neurotic creates a virtue out of neurotic necessity. The neurotic abandons all connections with the *real self* and thus creates an idealized self-image of heroic proportions wherein all neurotic traits and conflicts are glorified. The search for glory becomes the ultimate resolution of the basic neurotic conflict. In these selections Horney discusses the tragic implications of this final development.

1.

KAREN HORNEY

To approach the problem genetically we must go back to what I have called basic anxiety, meaning by this the feeling a child has of being isolated and helpless in a potentially hostile world. A wide range of adverse factors in the environment can produce this insecurity in a child: direct or indirect domination, indifference, erratic behavior, lack of respect for the child's individual needs, lack of real guidance, disparaging attitudes, too much admiration or the absence of it, lack of reliable warmth, having to take sides in parental disagreements, too much or too little responsibility, over-protection, isolation from other children, injustice, discrimination, unkept promises, hostile atmosphere, and so on and so on. . . .

Harassed by these disturbing conditions, the child gropes for ways to keep going, ways to cope with this menacing world. Despite his own weakness and fears he unconsciously shapes his tactics to meet the particular forces operating in his environment.

[1] Horney, K. (1945). Reprinted from *Our Inner Conflicts*, pp. 41–42, by Karen Horney, by permission of W. W. Norton & Company, Inc. Copyright © 1945 by W. W. Norton & Company, Inc., renewed © 1972 by Renate Mintz, Marianne von Eckardt, and Brigitte Horney Swarzenski.

In doing so, he developed not only *ad hoc* strategies but lasting character trends which become part of his personality. I have called these "neurotic trends". . . .

At first a rather chaotic picture may present itself, but out of it in time three main lines crystallize: a child can move *toward* people, *against* them, or *away from* them. . . .

2.

KAREN HORNEY

Moving Toward People

In sum, this type needs to be liked, wanted, desired, loved; to feel accepted, welcomed, approved of, appreciated; to be needed, to be of importance to others, especially to one particular person; to be helped, protected, taken care of, guided. . . .

Where the patient errs is in claiming that all his frantic beating about for affection and approval is genuine, while in reality the genuine portion is heavily over-shadowed by his insatiable urge to feel safe.

The need to satisfy this urge is so compelling that everything he does is oriented toward its fulfillment. In the process he develops certain qualities and attitudes that mold his character. Some of these could be called endearing: he becomes sensitive to the needs of others—within the frame of what

he is able to understand emotionally. For example, though he is likely to be quite oblivious to a detached person's wish to be aloof, he will be alert to another's need for sympathy, help, approval, and so on. He tries automatically to live up to the expectations of others, or to what he believes to be their expectations, often to the extent of losing sight of his own feelings. He becomes "unselfish," self-sacrificing, undemanding—except for his unbound desire for affection. He becomes compliant, over-considerate—within the limits possible for him—overappreciative, overgrateful, generous. He blinds himself to the fact that in his heart of hearts he does not care much for others and tends to regard them as hypocritical and self-seeking. But—if I may use conscious terms for what goes on unconsciously—he persuades himself that he likes everyone, that they are all "nice" and trustworthy, a fallacy which not only makes for heartbreaking disappointments but adds to his general insecurity.

These qualities are not as valuable as they appear to the person himself,

---

[2] Horney, K. (1945). Reprinted from *Our Inner Conflicts,* pp. 51–95, by Karen Horney, by permission of W. W. Norton & Company, Inc. Copyright © 1945 by W. W. Norton & Company, Inc., renewed © 1972 by Renate Mintz, Marianne von Eckardt, and Brigitte Horney Swarzenski.

particularly since he does not consult his own feelings or judgment but gives blindly to others all that he is driven to want from them—and because he is profoundly disturbed if the returns fail to materialize.

Along with these attributes and overlapping them goes another lot, aimed at avoiding black looks, quarrels, competition. He tends to subordinate himself, takes second place, leaving the limelight to others; he will be appeasing, conciliatory, and— at least consciously—bears no grudge. . . .

. . . We will not fully understand how rigidly all the attitudes and beliefs are adhered to unless we are aware of the extent to which the repression of opposing trends reinforces the dominant ones. So we shall take a brief glance at the reverse side of the picture. When analyzing the compliant type we find a variety of aggressive tendencies strongly repressed. In decided contrast to the apparent oversolicitude, we come upon a callous lack of interest in others, attitudes of defiance, unconscious parasitic or exploiting tendencies, propensities to control and manipulate others, relentless needs to excel or to enjoy vindictive triumphs.

Moving Against People

Just as the compliant type clings to the belief that people are "nice," and is continually baffled by evidence to the contrary, so the aggressive type takes it for granted that everyone is hostile, and refuses to admit that they are not. To him life is a struggle of all against all, and the devil take the hindmost. Such exceptions as he allows are made reluctantly and with reservation. His attitude is sometimes quite apparent, but more often it is covered over with a veneer of suave politeness, fairmindedness and good fellowship. . . .

A strong need to exploit others, to outsmart them, to make them of use to himself, is part of the picture. Any situation or relationship is looked at from the standpoint of "What can I get out of it?"—whether it has to do with money, prestige, contacts, or ideas. The person himself is consciously or semiconsciously convinced that everyone acts this way, and so what counts is to do it more efficiently than the rest. The qualities he develops are almost diametrically opposed to those of the compliant type. He becomes hard and tough, or gives that appearance. He regards all feelings, his own as well as others', as "sloppy sentimentality." Love, for him, plays a negligible role. Not that he is never "in love" or never has an affair or marries, but what is of prime concern is to have a mate who is eminently desirable, one through whose attractiveness, social prestige, or wealth he can enhance his own position. He sees no reason to be considerate of others. . . .

Why, though, does he reject the softer human sentiments with such violence? Why is he likely to feel nauseated at the sight of affectionate behavior in others? Why is he so contemptuous when someone shows sympathy at what he considers the wrong moment? He acts like the man who chased beggars from his door because they were breaking his heart. He may indeed literally be abusive to beggars; he may refuse the simplest request with a vehemence quite out of proportion. Reactions like these are typical of him and can readily be observed as the aggressive trends become less rigid during analysis. Actually, his feelings on the score of "softness" in others are mixed. He despises it in them, it is true, but he welcomes it as well, because it leaves him all the freer to pursue his own goals. Why else should he so often feel drawn toward the compliant type—just as the latter is so often drawn toward him? The reason his reaction is so extreme is that it is prompted by his need to fight all softer feelings within himself. . . .

The inner logic of his struggle is in principle identical with that presented in the case of the compliant type and therefore need only be briefly indicated here. For the aggressive type any feeling of sympathy, or obligation to be "good," or attitude of compliance would be incompatible with the whole structure of living he has built up and would shake its foundations. Moreover, the emergence of these opposing tendencies would confront him with his basic conflict and so destroy the organization he has carefully nurtured—the organization for unity. The consequence will be that repression of the softer tendencies will reinforce the aggressive one, making them all the more compulsive.

Moving Away from People

What all detached persons have in common is . . . their capacity to look at themselves with a kind of objective interest, as one would look at a work of art. Perhaps the best way to describe it would be to say that they have the same "on-looker" attitude toward themselves that they have toward life in general. They may often, therefore,

be excellent observers of the processes going on within them. . . .

What is crucial is their inner need to put emotional distance between themselves and others. More accurately, it is their conscious and unconscious determination not to get emotionally involved with others in any way, whether in love, faith, co-operation, or competition. They draw around themselves a kind of magic circle which no one may penetrate. And this is why, superficially, they may "get along" with people. The compulsive character of the need shows up in their reaction of anxiety when the world intrudes upon them.

All the needs and qualities they acquire are directed toward this major need of not getting involved. Among the most striking is a need for *self-sufficiency*. Its most positive expression is resourcefulness. The aggressive type also tends to be resourceful—but the spirit is different; for him it is a prerequisite for fighting one's way in a hostile world and for wanting to defeat others in the fray. In the detached type the spirit is like Robinson Crusoe's: he has to be resourceful in order to live. It is the only way he can compensate for his isolation. . . .

He can take pleasure in an occasional evening with a few friends but dislikes general gregariousness and social functions. Similarly, he avoids competition, prestige, and success. . . . He may bitterly resent illness, considering it a humiliation because it forces him to depend upon others. . . .

Another pronounced need is his need for privacy. He is like a person in a hotel room who rarely removes the "Do-Not-Disturb" sign from his door. Even books may be regarded as intruders, as something from outside. Any question put to him about his personal life may shock him; he tends to shroud himself in a veil of secrecy. . . .

As a rule he prefers to work, sleep, eat, alone. In distinct contrast to the compliant type he dislikes sharing any experience—the other person might disturb him. . . .

The all-important function of neurotic detachment then, is to keep major conflicts out of operation. It is the most radical and most effective of the defenses erected against them. One of the many neurotic ways of creating an artificial harmony, it is an attempt at solution through evasion. But it is no true solution because the compulsive cravings for closeness as well as for aggressive domination, exploitation, and excelling remain, and they keep harassing if not paralyzing their carrier. Finally no real inner peace or freedom can ever be attained as long as the contradictory sets of values continue to exist.

3.

KAREN HORNEY

In each of these three attitudes, one of the elements involved in basic anxiety is overemphasized: helplessness in the first, hostility in the second, and isolation in the third. But the fact is that the child cannot make any one of these moves wholeheartedly, because under the conditions in which the attitudes develop, all are bound to be present. What we have seen from our panoramic view is only the predominant move. . . .

The predominant attitude, however, is the one that most strongly determines actual conduct. It represents those ways and means of coping with others in which the particular person feels most at home. Thus a detached person will as a matter of course, use all the unconscious techniques for keeping others at a safe distance because he feels at a loss in any situation that requires close association with them. Moreover, the ascendant attitude is often but not always the one most acceptable to the person's conscious mind. . . .

From the point of view of the normal person there is no reason why the three attitudes should be mutually exclusive. One should be capable of giving in to others, of fighting, and of keeping to oneself. The three can complement each other and make for a harmonious whole. If one predominates, it merely indicates an overdevelopment along one line.

But in neurosis there are several reasons why these attitudes are irreconcilable. The neurotic is not flexible; he is driven to comply, to fight, to be aloof, regardless of whether the move is appropriate in the particular circumstance, and he is thrown into a panic if he behaves otherwise. Hence when all three attitudes are present in any strong degree, he is bound to be caught in a severe conflict. . . .

My contention is that the conflict born of incompatible attitudes constitutes the core of neurosis and therefore deserves to be called *basic*. And let me add that I use the term *core* not merely in the figurative sense of its being significant but to emphasize the fact that it is the dynamic center from which neuroses emanate.

4.

KAREN HORNEY

The Search for Glory

Self-idealization always entails a general self-glorification, and thereby gives the individual the much-needed feeling of significance and of superiority over others. But it is by no means a blind self-aggrandizement. Each person builds up his personal idealized image from the materials of his own special experiences, his earlier fantasies, his particular needs, and also his given faculties. If it were not for the personal character of the image, he would not attain a feeling of identity and unity. He idealizes, to begin with, his particular "solution" of his basic

conflict: compliance becomes goodness; love, saintliness; aggressiveness becomes strength, leadership, heroism, omnipotence; aloofness becomes wisdom, self-sufficiency, independence. What—according to his particular solution—appear as shortcomings or flaws are always dimmed out or retouched.

He may deal with his contradictory trends in one of three different ways. They may be glorified, too, but remain in the background. It may, for instance, appear only in the course of analysis that an aggressive person, to whom love seems unpermissible softness, is in his idealized image not only a knight in shining armor but also a great lover.

Secondly, contradictory trends, besides being glorified, may be so isolated in the person's mind that they no longer constitute disturbing conflicts. One patient was, in his image, a

⁴ Horney, K. (1970). Reprinted from *Neurosis and Human Growth,* pp. 22–24, by Karen Horney, by permission of W. W. Norton & Company, Inc. Copyright © 1950 by W. W. Norton & Company, Inc., renewed © 1978 by Renate Mintz, Marianne von Eckardt, and Brigitte Horney Swarzenski.

benefactor of mankind, a wise man who had achieved a self-contained serenity, and a person who could without qualms kill his enemies. These aspects—all of them conscious—were to him not only uncontradictory but also even unconflicting. In literature this way of removing conflicts by isolating them has been presented by Stevenson in *Doctor Jekyll and Mr. Hyde.*

Lastly, the contradictory trends may be exalted as positive faculties or accomplishments so that they become compatible aspects of a rich personality . . . a gifted person turned his compliant trends into Christlike virtues, his aggressive trends into a unique faculty for political leadership, and his detachment into the wisdom of a philosopher. Thus the three aspects of his basic conflict were at once glorified and reconciled each with the others. He became, in his own mind, a sort of modern equivalent to *l'uomo universale* of the Renaissance.

Eventually the individual may come to identify himself with his idealized, integrated image. Then it does not remain a visionary image which he secretly cherishes; imperceptibly he becomes this image: the idealized image becomes an *idealized self.* And this idealized self becomes more real to him than his real self, not primarily because it is more appealing but because it answers all his stringent needs. This transfer of his center of gravity is an entirely inward process; there is no observable or conspicuous outward change in him. The change is in the core of his being, in his feeling about himself. It is a curious and exclusively human process. It would

hardly occur to a cocker spaniel that he "really" is an Irish setter. And the transition can occur in a person only because his real self has previously become indistinct. While the healthy course of this phase of development—and at *any* phase—would be a move toward his real self, he now starts to abandon it definitely for the idealized self. The latter begins to represent to him what he "really" is, or potentially is—what he could be, and should be. It becomes the perspective from which he looks at himself, the measuring rod with which he measures himself.

Self-idealization, in its various aspects, is what I suggest calling a *comprehensive neurotic solution*—i.e., a solution not only for a particular conflict but one that implicitly promises to satisfy all the inner needs that have arisen in an individual at a given time. Moreover, it promises not only a riddance from his painful and unbearable feelings (feeling lost, anxious, inferior, and divided), but in addition an ultimately mysterious fulfillment of himself and his life. No wonder, then, that when he believes he has found such a solution he clings to it for dear life. No wonder that, to use a good psychiatric term, it becomes *compulsive.* The regular occurrence of self-idealization in neurosis is the result of the regular occurrence of the compulsive needs bred in a neurosis-prone environment.

We can look at self-idealization from two major vantage points: it is the logical outcome of an early development and it is also the beginning of a new one. It is bound to have a far reaching influence upon the further development because there simply is no more consequential step to be taken than the abandoning of the real self. But the main reason for its revolutionary effect lies in another implication of this step. *The energies driving toward self-realization are shifted to the aim of actualizing the idealized self.* This shift means no more and no less than a change in the course of the individual's whole life and development.

The Tyranny of the Should

COMMENTARY

You will recall that in the search for glory, driven by the need for personal perfection, the individual creates an idealized self-image. This illusion of perfection is supported by a system of inner dictates and rigid expectations which Horney designates as "the tyranny of the should." These unreasonable and unrealistic expectations become an essential part of the idealized self-image ("I should always be kind and generous" becomes "I am always kind and generous") and thus builds a psychic fortress against vulnerability.

The primary difficulty is that these shoulds do not represent genuine desires and feelings. They are, rather, make-believe feelings that are out of touch with the reality of the self. Appropriate feelings, therefore, do not accompany the self-imposed shoulds. For example, a person may think, "I should always be charitable to others," but will seldom have any genuine feelings of charity toward others. Thus, the individual becomes unable to discriminate between "real" feelings and the pseudo or manufactured ones.

The personal difficulties created by the shoulds become much greater where these shoulds are in conflict. "I should be a perfect mother and wife. I should also be an outstanding community leader." It is clear that such serious discrepancies between the conflicting shoulds will lead to serious difficulties in decision making.

Since they can never be gratified (perfection can never be attained) living a life based on shoulds rather than upon genuine feelings and desires and a realistic appraisal of the self, can only lead to bitter frustration, disappointment, and discouragement and to an even lower self-regard. Horney tells us, however, that the ultimate damage of the shoulds, especially in the neurotic, is that they lead to self-hate.

The negative impact of the shoulds upon our relationships with others is enormous. In the relentless striving for a state of perfection, the person not only imposes these unrealistic shoulds upon himself or herself, but is likely to impose such standards upon others, demanding that they be perfect as well. The damage to interpersonal relationships is likely to be severe.

I believe that Horney's concept of the shoulds also gives us insight into the commonly experienced failure of New Year's resolutions that usually end, for most of us, in a sense of disappointment and personal failure. Many, if not most, of these resolutions are based on our creation of shoulds. They do not aim at any real change in our personality or behavior but at achieving an immediate and absolute perfection.

It is important to see that Horney's concept of the shoulds applies not only to the neurotic personality but to everyone to a greater or lesser degree. We are all tempted to escape the challenge of self-discovery, genuine change, and authentic living in favor of a persona of pseudo-feelings and false standards.

KAREN HORNEY

We shall now discuss that aspect of self-actualization . . . in which the focus is within himself. Unlike Pygmalion, who tried to make another person into a creature fulfilling his concept of beauty, the neurotic sets to work to mold himself into a supreme being of his own making. He holds

Horney, K. (1950). Reprinted from *Neurosis and Human Growth,* pp. 64–68, 72–73, 81–82, by Karen Horney, by permission of W. W. Norton & Company, Inc. Copyright © 1950 by W. W. Norton & Company, Inc., renewed © 1978 by Renate Mintz, Marianne von Eckardt, and Brigitte Horney Swarzenski.

before him his image of perfection and unconsciously tells himself: "Forget about the disgraceful creature you actually *are*; this is how you *should* be; and to be this idealized self is all that matters. . . .

The inner dictates comprise all that the neurotic should be able to do, to be, to feel, to know—and taboos on how and what he should not be. . . .

He should be the utmost of honesty, generosity, considerateness, justice, dignity, courage, unselfishness. He should be the perfect lover, husband, teacher. He should be able to endure everything, should like everybody, should love his parents, his wife, his country; or, he should not be attached to anything or anybody, nothing should matter to him, he should never feel hurt, and he should always be serene and unruffled. He should always enjoy life; or, he should be above pleasure and enjoyment. He should be spontaneous; he should always control his feelings. He should know, understand, and foresee everything. He should be able to solve every problem of his own, or of others, in no time. He should be able to overcome every difficulty of his as soon as he sees it. He should never be tired or fall ill. He should always be able to find a job. He should be able to do things in one hour which can only be done in two or three hours. . . .

What strikes us first is the same *disregard for feasibility* which pervades the entire drive for actualization. Many of these demands are of a kind which no human being could fulfill. They are plainly fantastic, although the person himself is not aware of it. He cannot help recognizing it, however, as soon as his expectations are exposed to the clear light of critical thinking. Such an intellectual realization, however, usually does not change much, if anything. Let us say that a physician may have clearly realized that he cannot do intensive scientific work in addition to a nine-hour practice and an extensive social life; yet, after abortive attempts to cut down one or another activity, he keeps going at the same pace. His demands that limitations in time and energies should not exist for him are stronger than reason. Or take a more subtle illustration. At an analytic session a

patient was dejected. She had talked with a friend about the latter's marital problems, which were complicated. My patient knew the husband only from social situations. Yet, although she had been in analysis for several years and had enough understanding of the psychological intricacies involved in any relationship between two people to know better, she felt that she should have been able to tell her friend whether or not the marriage was tenable.

I told her that she expected something of herself which was impossible for anybody, and pointed out the multitude of questions to be clarified before one could even begin to have a more than dim impression of the factors operating in the situation. It turned out then that she had been aware of most of the difficulties I had pointed out. But she had still felt that she should have a kind of sixth sense penetrating all of them. . . .

The inner dictates, exactly like political tyranny in a police state, operate with a supreme *disregard for the person's own psychic condition*—for what he can feel or do as he is at present. One of the frequent shoulds, for instance, is that one should never feel hurt. As an absolute (which is implied in the "never") anyone would find this extremely hard to achieve. How many people have been, or are, so secure in themselves, so serene, as never to feel hurt? This could at best be an ideal toward which we might strive. To take such a project seriously must mean intense and patient work at our unconscious claims for defense, at our false pride—or, in short, at every factor in our personality that makes us vulnerable. But the person who feels that he should never feel hurt does not have too concrete a program in mind. He simply issues an absolute order to himself, denying or overriding the fact of his existing vulnerability. . . .

In trying to account for the amazing blindness of the shoulds, we again have to leave many loose ends. This much, however, is understandable from their origin in the search for glory and their function to make oneself over into one's idealized self: *the premise on which they operate is that nothing should be, or is, impossible for oneself.* If that is so, then, logically, existing conditions need not be examined. . . .

The more we get a feeling for the nature of the shoulds, the more clearly do we see that the difference between them and real moral standards or ideals is not a quantitative but a qualitative one. It was one of Freud's gravest errors to regard the inner dictates (some of the features of which he had seen and described as superego), as constituting morality in general. To begin with, their connection with moral questions is not too close. True enough, the commands for moral perfection do assume a prominent place among the shoulds, for the simple reason that moral questions are important in all our lives. But we cannot separate these particular shoulds from others, just as insisted, which are plainly determined by unconscious arrogance, such as "I should be able to get out of a Sunday afternoon traffic jam" or "I should be able to paint without laborious training and working." We must also remember that many demands conspicuously lack even a moral pretense, among them "I should be able to get away with

anything," "I should always get the better of others," and "I should always be able to get back at others." Only by focusing on the totality of the picture are we able to get the proper perspective on the demands for moral perfection. Like the other shoulds, they are permeated by the spirit of arrogance and aim at enhancing the neurotic's glory and at making him godlike. They are, in this sense, the neurotic counterfeit of normal moral strivings. When one adds to all this the unconscious dishonesty necessarily involved in making blemishes disappear, one recognizes them as an immoral rather than a moral phenomenon. It is necessary to be clear about these differences for the sake of the patient's eventual reorientation from a make-believe world into the development of genuine ideals. . . .

The *effects* the shoulds have on a person's personality and life vary to some extent with his way of responding to them or experiencing them. But certain effects show inevitably and regularly, though to a greater or lesser degree. The shoulds always produce a feeling of *strain*, which is all the greater the more a person tries to actualize his shoulds in his behavior. He may feel that he stands on tiptoe all the time, and may suffer from a chronic exhaustion. Or he may feel vaguely cramped, tense, or hemmed in. Or, if his shoulds coincide with attitudes culturally expected of him, he may feel merely an almost imperceptible strain. It may be strong enough, however, to contribute to a desire in an otherwise active person to retire from activities or obligations.

Furthermore, because of externalizations, the shoulds always contribute to *disturbances in human relations* in one way or another, the most general disturbance on this score is hypersensitivity to criticism. Being merciless toward himself, he cannot help experiencing any criticism on the part of others—whether actual or merely anticipated, whether friendly or unfriendly—as being just as condemnatory as his own. We shall understand the intensity of this sensitivity better when we realize how much he hates himself for any lagging behind his self-imposed standards. Otherwise the kinds of disturbance in human relations depend upon the kind of prevailing externalization. They may render him too critical and harsh of others or too apprehensive, too defiant, or too compliant.

Most important of all, the shoulds further *impair the spontaneity* of feelings, wishes, thoughts, and beliefs—i.e., the ability to feel his own feelings, etc. . . . . The person, then, can at best be "spontaneously compulsive" (to quote a patient) and express "freely" what she *should* feel, wish, think, or believe. We are accustomed to think that we cannot control feelings but only behavior. In dealing with others we can enforce labor but we cannot force anybody to love his work. Just so, we are accustomed to think that we can force ourselves to act as if we were not suspicious but we cannot enforce a feeling of confidence. This remains essentially true. And, if we needed a new proof, analysis could supply it. But if the shoulds issue an order as to feelings, imagination waves its magic wand and the border line between what we *should* feel and what we *do* feel evaporates. We consciously believe or feel then as we should believe or feel.

This appears in analysis when the spurious certainty of pseudo-feelings is shaken, and the patient then goes through a period of bewildering uncertainty which is painful but constructive. A person for instance who believed she liked everybody because she should do so may then ask: Do I really like my husband, my pupils, my patients? Or anybody at that? And at that point the questions are unanswerable because only now can all the fears, suspicions, and resentments that have always prevented a free flow of positive feelings, and yet were covered up by the shoulds, be tackled. I call this period constructive because it represents a beginning search for the genuine.

Masculine and Feminine Psychology

COMMENTARY

One of Karen Horney's strongest and most courageous expressions of rebellion against the psychoanalytic tradition was her rejection of Freud's sacrosanct theory that "anatomy is destiny." Women, according to Freud, suffer from penis envy and are forever destined, in one form or another, to be or to feel, inferior. The psychology of the woman, throughout her life, was determined by this anatomical difference. Thus, the male's possession of the penis and the woman's jealousy of this possession was the major premise upon which Freud based his belief in the superiority of the male. Horney considered this view to be a degrading one. While rejecting this strict biological basis for woman's inferior status, it should not be overlooked that Horney interpreted the woman's desire to be a male as a means of resolving the Oedipal attachment to the father. Thus, Horney did not totally abandon Freudian theory in this case. Horney stressed, however, that cultural factors were of far greater significance than biological ones in determining the psychology of both men and women. She sought to establish that a woman's inferiority was not biologically determined but was culturally induced by a masculine-dominated civilization, a civilization where every major institution—economic, legal, political, educational, and religious—were developed and controlled by men. Women feel inferior to men, therefore, because their lives are controlled by economic, political, and psychological dependence on men. As Hergenhahn has observed, it isn't the penis that women envy but the power to participate in their culture freely.

It is true, however, as Horney pointed out, that the reaction of many women to this state of affairs has been one of unhealthy compensation, either to aspire to become more "masculine" or to become even more dependent on men through the overvaluation of love, leading to a renunciation of their potential powers and aspirations.

While Horney focuses much of her attention on the psychology of women and their problems, she also raises issues related to male psychology and the male-female relationship. In this sense, Horney was a humanist who sought to develop a psychology of the person, with a deeper understanding of both males and females.

It is obvious that Karen Horney's views were well ahead of her time. They represented a radical departure from Freud's theory and were extremely controversial at the time. Today, however, she sounds quite "modern" in her position. The basic issues she raised, quite apart from her rejection of the theory of penis envy, are important and ongoing ones and certainly have not been resolved. It is unfortunate that Horney did not live to see the feminist revolution well in place.

1.

KAREN HORNEY

Like all sciences and all valuations, the psychology of women has hitherto been considered only from the point of view of men. It is inevitable that the man's position of advantage should cause objective validity to be attributed to his subjective, affective relations to the woman, and . . . the psychology of women hitherto actually represents a deposit of the desires and disappointments of men.

An additional and very important factor in the situation is that women have adapted themselves to the wishes of men and felt as if their adaptation were their true nature. That is, they see or saw themselves in the way that their men's wishes demanded of them; unconsciously they yielded to the suggestion of masculine thought.

If we are clear about the extent to which all our being, thinking, and doing conform to these masculine standards, we can see how difficult it is for the individual man and also for the individual woman really to shake off this mode of thought.

The question then is how far analytical psychology also, when its researches have women for their object, is under the spell of this way of thinking, insofar as it has not yet wholly left behind the stage in which frankly and as a matter of course masculine

[1] Horney, K. (1967). Reprinted from *Feminine Psychology,* pp. 56–57, 63–64, 66–67, 69–70, by Karen Horney, by permission of W. W. Norton & Company, Inc. Copyright © 1967 by W. W. Norton & Company, Inc.

development only was considered. In other words, how far has the evolution of women, as depicted to us today by analysis, been measured by masculine standards and how far therefore does this picture fail to present quite accurately the real nature of women. . . .

In order to approach this problem we must first of all realize that our empirical material with regard to the masculinity complex in women is derived from two sources of very different importance. The first is the direct observation of children, in which the subjective factor plays a relatively insignificant part. Every little girl who has not been intimidated displays penis envy frankly and without embarrassment. We see that the presence of this envy is typical and understand quite well why this is so; we understand how the narcissistic mortification of possessing less than the boy is reinforced by a series of disadvantages arising out of the different pregenital cathexes: the manifest privileges of the boy in connection with urethral eroticism, the scoptophilic instinct, and onanism.

I should like to suggest that we should apply the term *primary* to the little girl's penis envy, which is obviously based simply on the anatomical difference.

The second source upon which our experience draws is to be found in the analytical material produced by adult women. Naturally it is more difficult to form a judgment on this, and there is therefore more scope for the subjective element. We see here in the first instance that penis envy operates as a factor of enormous dynamic power. We see patients rejecting their feminine functions, their unconscious

motive in so doing being the desire to be male. We meet with fantasies of which the content is: "I once had a penis; I am a man who has been castrated and mutilated," from which proceed feelings of inferiority that have for after-effect all manner of obstinate hypochondriacal ideas. We see a marked attitude of hostility toward men, sometimes taking the form of depreciation and sometimes of a desire to castrate or maim them, and we see how the whole destinies of certain women are determined by this factor.

It was natural to conclude—and especially natural because of the male orientation of our thinking—that we could link these impressions on to the primary penis envy and to reason *a posteriori* that this envy must possess an enormous intensity, an enormous dynamic power, seeing that it evidently gave rise to such effects. Here we overlooked the fact, more in our general estimation of the situation than in details, that this desire to be a man, so familiar to us from the analyses of adult women, had only very little to do with that early, infantile, primary penis envy, but that it is a secondary formation embodying all that has miscarried in the development toward womanhood.

From beginning to end, my experience has proved to me with unchanging clearness that the Oedipus complex in women leads (not only in extreme cases where the subject has come to grief, but *regularly*) to a regression to penis envy, naturally in every possible degree and shade. The difference between the outcome of the male and the female Oedipus complexes seems to me in average cases to be as follows. In boys the mother as a sexual object is renounced owing to the fear of castration, but the male role itself is not only affirmed in further development but is actually overemphasized in the reaction to the fear of castration. We see this clearly in the latency and prepubertal period in boys and generally in later life as well. Girls, on the other hand, not only renounce the father as a sexual object but simultaneously recoil from the feminine role altogether. . . .

Under the pressure of this anxiety the girl now takes refuge in a fictitious male role.

What is the economic gain of this flight? Here I would refer to an experience that all analysts have probably had: They find that the desire to be a man is generally admitted comparatively willingly and that when once it is accepted, it is clung to tenaciously, the reason being the desire to avoid the realization of libidinal wishes and fantasies in connection with the father. Thus the wish to be a man subserves the repression of these feminine wishes or the resistance against their being brought to light. This constantly recurring, typical experience compels us, if we are true to analytical principles, to conclude that the fantasies of being a man were at an earlier period devised for the very purpose of securing the subject against libidinal wishes in connection with the father. The fiction of maleness enabled the girl to escape from the female role now burdened with guild and anxiety. It is true that this attempt to deviate from her own line to that of the male inevitably brings about a sense of inferiority, for the girl begins to measure herself by pretensions and values that are foreign to her specific biological nature and

confronted with which she cannot but feel herself inadequate. . . .

Now these typical motives for flight into the male role—motives whose origin is the Oedipus complex—are reinforced and supported by the actual disadvantage under which women labor in social life. Of course we must recognize that the desire to be a man, when it springs from this last source, is a peculiarly suitable form of rationalization of those unconscious motives. But we must not forget that this disadvantage is actually a piece of reality and that it is immensely greater than most women are aware of. . . .

Here we probably have the explanation also of the underestimation of this factor in analytical literature. In actual fact a girl is exposed from birth onward to the suggestion-inevitable, whether conveyed brutally or delicately—of her inferiority, an experience that constantly stimulates her masculinity complex.

There is one further consideration. Owing to the hitherto purely masculine character of our civilization, it has been much harder for women to achieve any sublimation that would really satisfy their nature, for all the ordinary professions have been filled by men. This again must have exercised an influence upon women's feelings of inferiority, for naturally they could not accomplish the same as men in these masculine professions and so it appeared that there was a basis in fact for their inferiority. It seems to me impossible to judge to how great a degree the unconscious motives for the flight from womanhood are reinforced by the actual social subordination of women. One might conceive of the connection as an interaction of psychic and social factors. But I can only indicate these problems here, for they are so grave and so important that they require a separate investigation.

The same factors must have quite a different effect on the man's development. On the one hand they lead to a much stronger repression of his feminine wishes, in that these bear the stigma of inferiority; on the other hand it is far easier for him successfully to sublimate them.

2.

KAREN HORNEY

The Overvaluation of Love

Woman's efforts to achieve independence and an enlargement of her field of interests and activities are continually met with skepticism which insists that such efforts should be made only in the face of economic necessity, and they run counter to her inherent character and her natural tendencies. Accordingly, all efforts of this sort are said to be without any vital significance for woman, whose every thought, in point of fact, should center exclusively upon the male or upon motherhood, in much the manner expressed in Marlene Dietrich's famous song, "I know only love, and nothing else."

Various sociological considerations immediately suggest themselves in this connection; they are, however, of too familiar and obvious a character to require discussion. This attitude toward woman, whatever its basis and however it may be assessed, represents the patriarchal ideal of womanhood, of woman as one whose only longing is to love a man and be loved by him, to admire him and serve him, and even to pattern herself after him. Those who maintain this point of view mistakenly infer from external behavior of the existence of an innate instinctual disposition thereto; whereas, in reality, the latter cannot be recognized as such, for the reason that biological factors never manifest themselves in pure and undisguised form, but always as modified by tradition and environment. . . .

It is comprehensible, therefore—speaking solely from the sociological standpoint—that women who nowadays obey the impulse to their independent development of their abilities are able to do so only at the cost of a struggle against both external opposition and such resistances within themselves as created by an intensification of the traditional ideal of the exclusively sexual function of woman.

It would not be going too far to assert that at the present time this conflict confronts every woman who ventures upon a career of her own and

[2] Horney, K. (1973). Reprinted from *Feminine Psychology,* pp. 182–184, by Karen Horney, by permission of W. W. Norton & Company, Inc. Copyright © 1967 by W. W. Norton & Company, Inc.

who is at the same time unwilling to pay for her daring with the renunciation of her femininity. The conflict in question is therefore one that is conditioned by the altered position of woman and confined to those women who enter upon or follow a vocation, who pursue special interests, or who aspire in general to an independent development of their personality.

Sociological insight makes one fully cognizant of the existence of conflicts of this kind, of their inevitability, and in broad outline, of many of the forms in which they are manifested and of their more remote effects. It enables one—to give but a single instance—to understand how there result attitudes that vary from the extreme of complete repudiation of femininity on the one hand to the opposite extreme of total rejection of intellectual or vocational activities on the other.

Cultural Influences on Personality

COMMENTARY

The major revisionists of Freudian theory, while pursuing their own individual lines of departure, held one emphasis in common: the important role of ego processes and the critical play of cultural forces in personality formation and development. Erik Erikson, Erich Fromm, and Karen Horney were perhaps the key revisionists in this new theoretical development. Erikson, as we shall see in greater detail in the next chapter, viewed the evolution of ego development and maturity as inexorably linked to the historical and cultural forces that impinged upon the eight critical stages of ego development that emerged, sequentially, throughout the life span.

Erich Fromm extended the boundaries of psychoanalytic thought by emphasizing the crucial role of the social, economic, and political factors in shaping not only individual character and personality, but in determining the health or sickness of national character as well.

Fromm identified five existential, or human, needs, and he analyzed the social and cultural conditions necessary to meet these needs in order to nurture healthy and productive personalities. In a pervasive analysis, Fromm demonstrated how the social and economic climate molds the character structure of the individual. Personality, according to Fromm, could never be understood without considering these forces as they impact upon the individual at a particular moment in history.

Karen Horney was one of the most courageous of the revisionists in abandoning Freud's biological-instinctual line of thought in favor of interpersonal and social dynamics. Throughout her writings she speaks to Freud's disregard of the importance of cultural factors on personality development, and she accused Freud of being blinded to these important realities.

Horney emphasized that personality development was not merely an intrapsychic phenomenon nor based exclusively on isolated individual experiences but was, rather, closely related to the specific cultural conditions under which we live—a soil which either nourishes or contaminates psychic life and health. Individual experiences, therefore, rather than being self-contained phenomena, take their form and expression from prevailing social values, traditions, and ideologies. The interpretation and style of parenting, for example, creating formative childhood perceptions and experiences, arise out of tendencies and conditions within the culture. Feelings and attitudes toward one's self and others are influenced by such conditions. According to Horney, therefore, the individual and the culture are "inseparably interwoven."

Throughout her writings, Horney emphasizes that both neurotic and normal personalities have a common social environment and cultural heritage that helps create many of the common problems we all face. Fear, anxiety, depression, and feelings of isolation are shared experiences arising out of prevailing cultural patterns, expectations, and values.

In the following selection, Horney identifies some of the more dominant cultural influences on personality.

KAREN HORNEY

When we have recognized that neurotic persons in our culture are impelled by the same underlying conflicts, and that in a diminished degree the normal person is also subject to them, we are confronted again with the question that was raised at the beginning: what are the conditions in our culture which are responsible for the fact that neuroses center around these particular conflicts I have described, and not others? . . .

There are certain typical difficulties inherent in our culture, which mirror themselves as conflicts in every individual's life and which, accumulated, may lead to the formation of neuroses. Since I am not a sociologist I shall merely point out briefly the main trends which have a bearing on the problem of neurosis and culture.

Horney, K. (1937). Reprinted from *The Neurotic Personality of Our Time*, pp. 282, 284–289, by Karen Horney, by permission of W. W. Norton & Company, Inc. Copyright © 1937 by W. W. Norton & Company, Inc., renewed © 1964 by Renate Mintz, Marianne von Eckardt and Brigitte Horney Swarzenski.

Modern culture is economically based on the principle of individual competition. The isolated individual has to fight with other individuals of the same group, has to surpass them and, frequently, thrust them aside. The advantage of the one is frequently the disadvantage of the other. The psychic result of this situation is a diffuse hostile tension between individuals. Everyone is the real or potential competitor of everyone else. This situation is clearly apparent among members of the same occupational group, regardless of strivings to be fair or of attempts to camouflage by polite considerateness. It must be emphasized, however, that competitiveness, and the potential hostility that accompanies it, pervades all human relationships. Competitiveness is one of the predominant factors in social relationships. It pervades the relationships between men and men, between women and women, and whether the point of competition is by popularity, competence, attractiveness or any other social virtue, it greatly impairs the possibilities of reliable friendship. It also, as already indicated, disturbs the relations between men and women, not only in the choice of the partner but in the entire struggle with him for superiority. It pervades school life. And perhaps most important of all, it pervades the family situation, so that as a rule the child is inoculated with this germ from the very beginning. The rivalry between father and son, mother and daughter, one child and another, is not a general human phenomenon but is the response to culturally conditioned stimuli. It remains one of Freud's great achievements to have seen the role of rivalry in the family, as expressed in his concept of the Oedipus complex and in other hypotheses. It must be added, however, that this rivalry itself is not biologically conditioned but is a result of given cultural conditions and, furthermore, that the family situation is not the only one to stir up rivalry, but that the competitive stimuli are active from the cradle to the grave. . . .

All these factors together—competitiveness and its potential hostilities between fellow-beings, fears, diminished self-esteem—result psychologically in the individual feeling that he is isolated. Even when he has many contacts with others, even when he is happily married, he is emotionally isolated. Emotional isolation is hard for anyone to endure; it becomes a calamity, however, if it coincides with apprehensions and uncertainties about one's self.

It is this situation which provokes, in the normal individual of our time, an intensified need for affection as a remedy. Obtaining affection makes him feel less isolated, less threatened by hostility and less uncertain of himself. Because it corresponds to a vital need, love is overvalued in our culture. It becomes a phantom—like success—carrying with it the illusion that it is a solution for all problems. Love itself is not an illusion—although in our culture it is most often a screen for satisfying wishes that have nothing to do with it—but it is made an illusion by our expecting much more of it than it can possibly fulfill. . . .

When we remember that in every neurosis there are contradictory tendencies which the neurotic is unable to reconcile, the question arises as to whether there are not likewise certain definite contradictions in our culture, which underlie the typical neurotic conflicts. It would be the task of the sociologist to study and describe these cultural contradictions. It must suffice for me to indicate briefly and schematically some of the main contradictory tendencies.

The first contradiction to be mentioned is that between competition and success on the one hand, and brotherly love and humility on the other. On the one hand everything is done to spur us toward success, which means that we must be not only assertive but aggressive, able to push others out of the way. On the other hand we are deeply imbued with Christian ideals which declare that it is selfish to want anything for ourselves, that we should be humble, turn the other cheek, be yielding. For this contradiction there are only two solutions within the normal range: to take one of these striving seriously and discard the other; or to take both seriously with the result that the individual is seriously inhibited in both directions.

The second contradiction is that between the stimulation of our needs and our factual frustrations in satisfying them. For economic reasons needs are constantly being stimulated in our culture by such means as advertisements, "conspicuous consumption," the ideal of "keeping up with the Joneses." For the great majority, however, the actual fulfillment of these needs is closely restricted. The psychic consequence for the individual is a constant discrepancy between his desires and their fulfillment.

Another contradiction exists between the alleged freedom of the individual and all his factual limitations. The individual is told by society that he is free, independent, can decide his life according to his own free will; "the great game of life" is open to him, and he can get what he wants if he is efficient and energetic. In actual fact, for the majority of people all these possibilities are limited. What has been said facetiously of the impossibility of choosing one's parents can well be extended to life in general—choosing and succeeding in an occupation, choosing ways of recreation, choosing a mate. The result for the individual is a wavering between a feeling of boundless power in determining his own fate and a feeling of entire helplessness.

These contradictions embedded in our culture are precisely the conflicts which the neurotic struggles to reconcile: his tendencies toward aggressiveness and his tendencies toward yielding; his excessive demands and his fear of never getting anything; his striving toward self-aggrandizement and his feeling of personal helplessness. The difference from the normal is merely quantitative. While the normal person is able to cope with the difficulties without damage to his personality, in the neurotic all the conflicts are intensified to a degree that makes any satisfactory solution impossible.

CHAPTER V

The Psychosocial Theory of Erik Erikson

BIOGRAPHICAL SKETCH

Erik Erikson was born in 1902 near Frankfurt, Germany. His parents separated soon after his birth, and the identity of his Danish father remains a mystery. Three years later his mother, Karla Abrahamsen, married Dr. Theodor Homberger, a pediatrician. Erikson took the name Homberger and, for several years, believed Dr. Homberger to be his real father. When he became a naturalized American citizen in 1939 he preferred to adopt his original name.

After graduating from high school, rejecting his stepfather's wish that he study medicine, Erikson became a wanderer, traveling throughout central Europe. Although Erikson was rebellious, restless, and somewhat confused about the direction of his life, his travels were not entirely without focus. He spent much of his time studying art and visiting art galleries. Looking back on this seemingly aimless period of Erikson's life, one can see it as a prophetic metaphor for his later work on identity formation, with special attention to the "identity crisis" in young people.

In 1927 Erikson terminated his travels to accept an unexpected invitation from analyst Peter Blos to teach in a private school in Vienna. Through his work in this school, founded by Anna Freud for the children of parents studying psychoanalysis, Erikson became acquainted with Freud and his family and began the study of psychoanalysis. During this time he also began his own analysis with Anna Freud. While in Vienna, Erikson met and married Joan Serson who later became an important collaborator in some of his work. They had three children.

In 1933, after graduating from the Vienna Psychoanalytic Society, the

Eriksons came to the United States where he became Boston's first child analyst and one of the first in the United States. Without benefit of a college education, Erikson quickly gained a national reputation for his work. In the ensuing years he held teaching positions at Harvard University and Yale University.

To further his special interest in the cultural forces on personality development, Erikson left Yale in 1938 to spend a year observing and studying the Sioux Indian children on a reservation in South Dakota. Following this year he took a post with the Institute of Child Welfare of the University of California, where he studied children of Yurok Indians. Out of these experiences he wrote one of his most influential books, *Childhood and Society,* first published in 1950. This, his first book, quickly brought him international recognition.

Prior to his retirement in 1970, Erikson returned to Harvard as Professor of Human Development. He advanced the study of psychohistory and psychobiography with his publications of *Young Man Luther* (1958) and *Ghandi's Truth* (1969). For this latter work he was awarded the Pulitzer Prize and the National Book Award for Philosophy and Religion.

In retirement with his wife, Erikson continued his writing and research until his death in 1994.

Growth and Crisis of the Healthy Personality: The Eight Stages of Ego Development

COMMENTARY

Erik Erikson stands as a central figure within the lineage of post-Freudians who liberated the ego from servitude and acknowledged the importance of historical forces and cultural conditions in the formation of ego and its subsequent evolution. As other important voices contributing to this radical departure from classical psychoanalytic theory the names of Heinz Hartmann, Karen Horney and Erich Fromm come to mind.

Hartmann proposed, in 1939, a "conflict-free ego sphere" stressing autonomous ego development and its integrated functions. Horney rejected Freud's doctrine that "anatomy is destiny," and she emphasized environmental factors and cultural forces in shaping stereotypical sex roles and in the creation of neurosis. Eric Fromm stressed the crucial economic and social arrangements within a society that created alienation and neurosis. He believed that these arrangements shaped the social character of the individual as well as the character of an entire society.

It was Erikson, however, who presented the most unified post-Freudian theory of the autonomous ego and its development. In this theory, Erikson viewed personality development as a dialectic engagement between the genetic maturation and requirements of the ego and the historical and cultural forces within which the emergence of the ego takes place.

Erikson proposed eight critical stages in ego development throughout the life span. At each stage the demands of culture and the genetic requirements of ego present the individual with a developmental task to be mastered. As the conflict within each stage is resolved, the individual incorporates a new component of ego strength into the personality. Failure to resolve the crisis, on the other hand, diminishes the personality and produces a "weak link" in the developmental sequence. In the selection on identity vs. identity diffusion, for example, Erikson states that "A lasting ego identity cannot begin to exist without the trust of the first oral stage."

Thus, while presenting a crisis theory of human development Erikson, unlike Freud, was decidedly optimistic in his view of human growth. In resolving the psychosocial crisis at each stage of ego development, the individual strengthens his/her capacity to grow and mature. As each crisis unfolds and is resolved, the ego acquires greater coherence, strength, and integrity.

In his theory, Erikson shifts from a traditional id psychology to an ego psychology, stressing the autonomous character of the ego and the cultural context within which it develops. In his theory of the eight stages of ego development, from birth to old age, Erikson also introduces us to the concept of life-span development. Whereas Freud saw the rudiments of personality development completed at the end of the Oedipal period, around the age of six, Erikson viewed personality as evolving and undergoing critical changes throughout the life span. The first of his eight stages of ego development, establishing "basic trust," begins at birth, while the final stage of accomplishment, "ego integrity," is reserved for old age.

Although Erikson never considered his work as a radical departure from psychoanalytic theory, his psychosocial theory represents a totally new perspective on the psychoanalytic tradition. While it is true that his first four stages parallel Freud's oral, anal, phallic, and latency periods, Erikson's four additional stages of ego development clearly recognize that ego formation is never a "finished" product or a static entity but always moves toward a "functioning whole." This is clearly brought forth in the following selections.

1.

ERIK ERIKSON

On Health and Growth

Whenever we try to understand growth, it is well to remember the *epigenetic principle* which is derived from the growth of organisms in *utero.* Somewhat generalized, this principle states that anything that grows has a *ground plan,* and that out of this ground plan the *parts* arise, each part having its *time* of special ascendancy, until all parts have arisen to form a *functioning whole.* At birth the baby leaves the chemical exchange of the womb for the social exchange system of

[1] Erikson, E. (1959). "Identity and the Life Cycle," *Psychological Issues* 1:1. pp. 52–77. Reprinted from *Identity and the Life Cycle* by Erik H. Erikson, with the permission of W. W. Norton & Company, Inc. Copyright © 1959 by International Universities Press, Inc. Copyright © 1980 by W. W. Norton & Company, Inc.

his society, where his gradually increasing capacities meet the opportunities and limitations of his culture. How the maturing organism continues to unfold, not by developing new organs, but by a prescribed sequence of locomotor, sensory, and social capacities, is described in the child-development literature. Psychoanalysis has given us an understanding of the more idiosyncratic experiences and especially the inner conflicts, which constitute the manner in which an individual becomes a distinct personality. But here, too, it is important to realize that in the sequence of his most personal experiences the healthy child, given a reasonable amount of guidance, can be trusted to obey inner laws of development, laws which create a *succession of potentialities for significant interaction* with those who tend him. While such interaction varies from culture to culture, it must remain within the *proper rate* and the *proper sequence* which govern the *growth of a personality* as well as that of an organism. Personality can be said to develop according to steps predetermined in the human organism's readiness to be driven toward, to be aware of, and to interact with, a widening social radius, beginning with the dim image of a mother and ending with mankind, or at any rate that segment of mankind which "counts" in the particular individual's life. . . .

Each comes to its ascendance, meets its crisis, and finds its lasting solution (in ways to be described here) *toward the end of the stages* mentioned. All of them exist in the beginning in some form, although we do not make a point of this fact, and we shall not confuse things by calling these components different names at earlier or later stages.

A baby may show something like "autonomy" from the beginning, for example, in the particular way in which he angrily tries to wriggle his hand free when tightly held. However, under normal conditions, it is not until the second year that he begins to experience the whole *critical alternative between being an autonomous creature and being a dependent one;* and it is not until then that he is ready for a *decisive encounter* with his environment, an environment which, in turn, feels called upon to convey to him its *particular ideas and concepts of autonomy and coercion* in ways decisively contributing to the character, the efficiency, and the health of his personality in his culture.

It is this *encounter,* together with the resulting crisis, which is to be described for each stage. Each stage becomes a crisis because incipient growth and awareness in a significant part function goes together with a shift in instinctual energy and yet causes specific vulnerability in that part. One of the most difficult questions to decide, therefore, is whether or not a child at a given stage is weak or strong. Perhaps it would be best to say that he is always vulnerable in some respects and completely oblivious and insensitive in others, but that at the same time he is unbelievably persistent in the same respects in which he is vulnerable. It must be added that the smallest baby's weakness gives him power; out of his very dependence and weakness he makes signs to which his environment (if it is guided well by a responsiveness based both on instinctive and traditional patterns) is peculiarly sensitive. A baby's presence exerts a consistent and persistent domination over the outer and inner lives of every member of a household. Because these members must reorient themselves to accommodate his presence, they must also grow as individuals and as a group. It is as true to say that babies control and bring up their families as it is to say the converse. A family can bring up a baby only by being brought up by him. His growth consists of a series of challenges to them to serve his newly developing potentialities for social interaction.

Each successive step, then, is a potential crisis because of a radical *change in perspective.* There is, at the beginning of life, the most radical change of all: from intrauterine to extrauterine life. But in postnatal existence, too, such radical adjustments of perspective as lying relaxed, sitting firmly, and running fast must all be accomplished in their own good time. With them, the interpersonal perspective, too, changes rapidly and often radically, as is testified by the proximity in time of such opposites as "not letting mother out of sight" and "wanting to be independent." Thus, *different capacities use different opportunities* to become full-grown components of the ever-new configuration that is the growing personality.

Basic Trust Versus Basic Mistrust

For the first component of a healthy personality I nominate a sense of *basic trust,* which I think is an attitude toward oneself and the world derived from the experiences of the first year of life. By "trust" I mean what is commonly implied in reasonable trustfulness as far as others are concerned and a simple sense of trustworthiness as far

as oneself is concerned. (When I say "basic," I mean that neither this component nor any of those that follow are, either in childhood or in adulthood, especially conscious. In fact, all of these criteria, when developed in childhood and when integrated in adulthood, blend into the total personality. Their crises in childhood, however, and their impairment in adulthood are clearly circumscribed.)

In describing this growth and its crises as a development of a series of alternative basic attitudes, we take recourse to the term *"a sense of."* Like a "sense of health" or a "sense of not being well," such "senses" pervade surface and depth, consciousness and the unconscious. They are ways of conscious *experience,* accessible to introspection (where it develops); ways of *behaving,* observable by others; and unconscious *inner states* determinable by test and analysis. It is important to keep these three dimensions in mind, as we proceed.

In *adults* the impairment of basic trust is expressed in a *basic mistrust.* It characterizes individuals who withdraw into themselves in particular ways when at odds with themselves and with others. These ways, which often are not obvious, are more strikingly represented by individuals who regress into psychotic states in which they sometimes close up, refusing food and comfort and becoming oblivious to companionship. In so far as we hope to assist them with psychotherapy, we must try to reach them again in specific ways in order to convince them that they can trust the world and that they can trust themselves. . . .

What we here call "trust" coincides with what Therese Benedek has called "confidence." If I prefer the word "trust," it is because there is more naiveté and more mutuality in it: an infant can be said to be trusting, but it would be assuming too much to say that he "has confidence." The general state of trust, furthermore, implies not only that one has learned to rely on the sameness and continuity of the outer providers but also that one may trust oneself and the capacity of one's own organs to cope with urges; that one is able to consider oneself trustworthy enough so that the providers will not need to be on guard or to leave. . . .

At any rate, the psychiatrists, obstetricians, pediatricians, and anthropologists, to whom I feel closest, today would agree that the *firm establishment of enduring patterns for the balance of basic trust over basic mistrust* is the first task of the budding personality and therefore first of all a task for maternal care. But it must be said that the *amount of trust* derived from earliest infantile experience does not seem to depend on absolute *quantities of food or demonstrations of love* but rather on the *quality* of the maternal relationship. Mothers create a sense of trust in their children by that kind of administration which in its quality combines sensitive care of the baby's individual needs and a firm sense of personal trustworthiness within the trusted framework of their community's life style.

Autonomy Versus Shame and Doubt

The over-all significance of this stage lies in the maturation of the muscle system, the consequent ability (and doubly felt inability) to coordinate a number of highly conflicting action patterns such as "holding on" and "letting go," and

the enormous value with which the still highly dependent child begins to endow his autonomous will.

Psychoanalysis has enriched our vocabulary with the word "anality" to designate the particular pleasurableness and willfulness which often attach to the eliminative organs at this stage. The whole procedure of evacuating the bowels and the bladder as completely as possible is, of course, enhanced from the beginning by a premium of "feeling good" which says in effect, "well done." This premium, at the beginning of life, must make up for quite frequent discomfort and tension suffered as the bowels learn to do their daily work. Two developments gradually give these anal experiences the necessary volume: the arrival of better formed stool and the general coordination of the muscle system which permits the development of voluntary release, of dropping and throwing away. This new dimension of approach to things, however, is not restricted to the sphincters. A general ability, indeed, a violent need, develops to drop and to throw away and to alternate withholding and expelling at will.

As far as anality proper is concerned, at this point everything depends on whether the cultural environment wants to make something of it. There are cultures where the parents ignore anal behavior and leave it to older children to lead the toddler out to the bushes so that his compliance in this matter may coincide with his wish to imitate the bigger ones. Our Western civilization, and especially certain classes within it, have chosen to take the matter more seriously. It is here that the machine age has added the ideal of a mechanically trained, faultlessly functioning, and always clean, punctual, and deodorized body. In addition it has been more or less consciously assumed that early and rigorous training is absolutely necessary for the kind of personality which will function efficiently in a mechanized world which says "time is money" and which calls for orderliness, punctuality, and thrift. Indications are that in this, we have gone too far; that we have assumed that a child is an animal which must be broken or a machine which must be set and tuned—while, in fact, human virtues can grow only by steps. At any rate our clinical work suggests that the neurotics of our time include the "overcompulsive" type, who is stingy, retentive, and meticulous in matters of affection, time, and money, as well as in matters concerning his bowels. Also, bowel and bladder training has become the most obviously disturbing item of child training in wide circles of our society.

What, then, makes the anal problem potentially important and difficult?

The anal zone lends itself more than any other to the expression of stubborn insistence on conflicting impulses because, for one thing, it is the model zone for two contradictory modes which must become alternating; namely, *retention* and *elimination*. Furthermore, the sphincters are only part of the muscle system with its general ambiguity of rigidity and relaxation, of flexion and extension. This whole stage, then, becomes a battle for *autonomy*. For as he gets ready to stand on his feet more firmly, the infant delineates his world as "I" and "you," "me" and "mine." Every mother knows how astonishingly

pliable a child may be at this stage, if and when he has made the decision that he *wants* to do what he is supposed to do. It is impossible, however, to find a reliable formula for making him want to do just that. Every mother knows how lovingly a child at this stage will snuggle and how ruthlessly he will suddenly try to push the adult away. At the same time the child is apt both to hoard things and to discard them, to cling to possessions and throw them out of the windows of houses and vehicles. All of the seemingly contradictory tendencies, then, we include under the formula of the retentive-eliminative modes.

The matter of mutual regulation between adult and child now faces its severest test. If outer control by too rigid or too early training insists on robbing the child of his attempt *gradually* to control his bowels and other functions willingly and by his free choice, he will again be faced with a double rebellion and a double defeat. Powerless in his own body (sometimes afraid of his bowels) and powerless outside, he will again be forced to seek satisfaction and control either by regression or by fake progression. In other words, he will return to an earlier, oral control, that is, by sucking his thumb and becoming whiny and demanding; or he will become hostile and willful, often using his feces (and, later, dirty words) as ammunition; or he will pretend an autonomy and an ability to do without anybody to lean on which he has by no means really gained.

This stage, therefore, becomes decisive for the ratio between love and hate, for that between cooperation and willfulness, and for that between the freedom of self-expression and its suppression. From a sense of *self-control without loss of self-esteem* comes a lasting sense of autonomy and pride; from a sense of muscular and anal impotence, of loss of self-control, and of parental overcontrol comes a lasting sense of doubt and shame. . . .

Initiative Versus Guilt

Having found a firm solution of his problem of autonomy, the child of four and five is faced with the next step—and with the next crisis. Being firmly convinced that he *is* a person, the child must now find out *what kind* of a person he is going to be. And here he hitches his wagon to nothing less than a star: he wants to be like his parents, who to him appear very powerful and very beautiful, although quite reasonably dangerous. He "identities with them," he plays with the idea of how it would be to be them. *Three strong developments* help at this stage, yet also serve to bring the child closer to his crisis: (1) he learns to *move around* more freely and more violently and therefore establishes a wider and, so it seems to him, an unlimited radius of goals; (2) his sense of *language* becomes perfected to the point where he understands and can ask about many things just enough to misunderstand them thoroughly; and (3) both language and locomotion permit him to expand his *imagination* over so many things that he cannot avoid frightening himself with what he himself has dreamed and thought up. Nevertheless, out of all this he must emerge with a sense of *unbroken initiative* as a basis for a high and yet realistic sense of ambition and independence.

One may ask here—one may, indeed—what are the criteria for such an unbroken sense of initiative? The criteria for all the senses discussed here are the same: a crisis, beset with fears, or at least a general anxiousness or tension, seems to be resolved, in that the child suddenly seems to "grow together" both psychologically and physically. He seems to be "more himself," more loving and relaxed and brighter in his judgment (such as it is at this stage). Most of all, he seems to be, as it were, self-activated; he is in the free possession of a certain surplus of energy which permits him to forget failures quickly and to approach what seems desirable (even if it also seems dangerous) with undiminished and better aimed effort. In this way the child and his parents face the next crisis much better prepared. . . .

This is also the stage of infantile sexual curiosity, genital excitability, and occasional preoccupation and overconcern with sexual matters. This "genitality" is, of course, rudimentary, a mere promise of things to come; often it is not particularly noticeable as such. If not specifically provoked into precocious manifestation by especially strict and pointed prohibitions ("if you touch it, the doctor will cut it off") or special customs (such as sex play in groups), it is apt to lead to no more than a series of fascinating experiences which soon become frightening and pointless enough to be repressed. This leads to the ascendancy of that human specialty which Freud called the "latency" period, that is, the long delay separating infantile sexuality (which in animals is followed by maturity) and physical sexual maturation.

2.

ERIK ERIKSON

Industry vs. Inferiority

With the oncoming latency period, the normally advanced child forgets, or rather sublimates, the necessity to "make" people by direct attack or to become papa and mama in a hurry: he now learns to win recognition by producing things. He has mastered the ambulatory field and the organ modes. He has experienced a sense of finality regarding the fact that there is no workable future within the womb of his family, and thus becomes ready to apply himself to given skills and tasks, which go far beyond the mere playful expression of his organ modes or the pleasure in the function of his limbs. He develops a sense of industry—i.e., he adjusts himself to the inorganic laws of the tool world. He can become an eager and absorbed unit of a productive situation. To bring a productive situation to completion is an aim which gradually supersedes the whims and wishes of play. His ego boundaries include his tools and skills: the work principle (Ives Hendrick) teaches him the pleasure of work completion by steady attention and persevering diligence. In all cultures, at this stage, children receive some *systematic instruction*, although, as we saw in the chapter on American Indians, it is by no means always in the kind of school which literate people must organize around special teachers who have learned how to teach literacy. In preliterate people and in non-literate pursuits much is learned from adults who become teachers by dint of gift and inclination rather than by appointment, and perhaps the greatest amount is learned from older children. Thus the *fundamentals of technology* are developed, as the child becomes ready to handle the utensils, the tools, and the weapons used by the big people. Literate people, with more specialized careers, must prepare the child by teaching him things which first of all make him literate, the widest possible basic education for the greatest number of possible careers. . . .

The child's danger, at this stage, lies in a sense of inadequacy and inferiority. If he despairs of his tools and skills or of his status among his tool partners, he may be discouraged from identification with them and with a section of the tool world. To lose the hope of such "industrial" association may pull him back to the more isolated, less tool-conscious familial rivalry of the oedipal time. The child despairs of his equipment in the tool world and in anatomy, and considers himself doomed to mediocrity or inadequacy. It is at this point that wider society becomes significant in its ways of admitting the child to an understanding of meaningful roles in its technology and economy. Many a

² Erikson, E. (1963). *Childhood and Society*, pages 258–269. Reprinted from *Childhood and Society*, Second Edition, by Erik H. Erikson, by permission of W. W. Norton & Company, Inc. Copyright © 1963 by W. W. Norton & Company, Inc., renewed © 1978, 1991 by Erik H. Erikson.

child's development is disrupted when family life has failed to prepare him for school life, or when school life fails to sustain the promises of earlier stages. . . .

Identity vs. Role Confusion

The integration now taking place in the form of ego identity is, as pointed out, more than the sum of the childhood identifications. It is the accrued experience of the ego's ability to integrate all identifications with the vicissitudes of the libido, with the aptitudes developed out of endowment, and with the opportunities offered in social roles. The sense of ego identity, then, is the accrued confidence that the inner sameness and continuity prepared in the past are matched by the sameness and continuity of one's meaning for others, as evidence in the tangible promise of a "career." . . .

The danger of this stage is role confusion. Where this is based on a strong previous doubt as to one's sexual identity, delinquent and outright psychotic episodes are not uncommon. If diagnosed and treated correctly, these incidents do not have the same fatal significance which they have at other ages. In most instances, however, it is the inability to settle on an occupational identity which disturbs individual young people. To keep themselves together they temporarily overidentify, to the point of apparent complete loss of identity, with the heroes of cliques and crowds. This initiates the stage of "falling in love," which is by no means entirely, or even primarily, a sexual matter—except where the mores demand it. To a considerable extent adolescent love is an attempt to

arrive at a definition of one's identity by projecting one's diffused ego image on another and by seeing it thus reflected and gradually clarified. This is why so much of young love is conversation. . . .

Intimacy vs. Isolation

. . . Thus, the young adult, emerging from the search for and the insistence on identity, is eager and willing to fuse his identity with that of others. He is ready for intimacy, that is, the capacity to commit himself to concrete affiliations and partnerships and to develop the ethical strength to abide by such commitments, even though they may call for significant sacrifices and compromises. Body and ego must now be masters of the organ modes and of the nuclear conflicts, in order to be able to face the fear of ego loss in situations which call for self-abandon: in the solidarity of close affiliations, in orgasms and sexual unions, in close friendships and in physical combat, in experiences of inspiration by teachers and of intuition from the recesses of the self. The avoidance of such experiences because of a fear of ego loss may lead to a deep sense of isolation and consequent self-absorption. . . .

Strictly speaking, it is only now that *true genitality* can fully develop; for much of the sex life preceding these commitments is of the identity-searching kind, or is dominated by phallic or vaginal strivings which make of sex life a kind of genital combat. On the other hand, genitality is all too often described as a permanent state of reciprocal sexual bliss. This then, may be the place to complete our discussion of genitality.

The danger of this stage is isolation, that is, the avoidance of contacts which commit to intimacy. In psychopathology, this disturbance can lead to severe "character-problems." On the other hand, there are partnerships which amount to an isolation à deux, protecting both partners from the necessity to face the next critical development—that of generativity.

Generativity vs. Stagnation

. . . The fashionable insistence on dramatizing the dependence of children on adults often blinds us to the dependence of the older generation on the younger one. Mature man needs to be needed, and maturity needs guidance as well as encouragement from what has been produced and must be taken care of.

Generativity, then, is primarily the concern in establishing and guiding the next generation, although there are individuals who, through misfortune or because of special and genuine gifts in other directions, do not apply this drive to their own offspring. And indeed, the concept generativity is meant to include such more popular synonyms as *productivity* and *creativity*, which, however, cannot replace it.

It has taken psychoanalysis some time to realize that the ability to lose oneself in the meeting of bodies and minds leads to a gradual expansion of ego-interests and to a libidinal investment in that which is being generated. Generativity thus is an essential stage on the psychosexual as well as on the psychosocial schedule. Where such enrichment fails altogether, regression to an obsessive

need for pseudo-intimacy takes place, often with a pervading sense of stagnation and personal impoverishment. Individuals, then, often begin to indulge themselves as if they were their own—or one another's—one and only child; and where conditions favor it, early invalidism, physical or psychological, becomes the vehicle of self-concern. The mere fact of having or even wanting children, however, does not "achieve" generativity. In fact, some young parents suffer, it seems, from the retardation of the ability to develop this stage. The reasons are often to be found in early childhood impressions; in excessive self-love based on a too strenuously self-made personality; and finally (and here we return to the beginnings) in the lack of some faith, some "belief in the species," which would make a child appear to be a welcome trust of the community. . . .

Ego Integrity vs. Despair

Only in him who in some way has taken care of things and people and has adapted himself to the triumphs and disappointments adherent to being, the originator of others or the generator of products and ideas—only in him may gradually ripen the fruit of these seven stages. I know no better word for it than ego integrity. Lacking a clear definition, I shall point to a few constituents of this state of mind. It is the ego's accrued assurance of its proclivity for order and meaning. It is a post-narcissistic love of the human ego—not of the self—as an experience which conveys some world order and spiritual sense, no matter how dearly paid for. It is the acceptance of one's one and only life cycle as something that had to be and that, by necessity, permitted of no substitutions: it thus means a new, a different love of one's parents. It is a comradeship with the ordering ways of distant times and different pursuits, as expressed in the simple products and sayings of such times and pursuits. Although aware of the relativity of all the various life styles which have given meaning to human striving, the possessor of integrity is ready to defend the dignity of his own life style against all physical and economic threats. For he knows that an individual life is the accidental coincidence of but one life cycle with but one segment of history; and that for him all human integrity stands or falls with the one style of integrity of which he partakes. . . .

The lack or loss of this accrued ego integration is signified by fear of death: the one and only life cycle is not accepted as the ultimate of life. Despair expresses the feeling that the time is now short, too short for the attempt to start another life and to try out alternate roads to integrity.

CHAPTER VI

The Behavioral Theory of B. F. Skinner

BIOGRAPHICAL SKETCH

Burrhus Frederic Skinner was born in the town of Susquehanna, Pennsylvania, on March 20, 1904. Skinner, the oldest of two sons (his brother Ed died at age 16), enjoyed the privilege of growing up in a comfortable, upper-middle-class home where the emphasis was upon the eternal verities of honesty, hard work, and family values.

Skinner demonstrated an early aptitude for design and construction. As a child, he made roller-skate scooters, sleds, wagons, model planes and kites. Later, this talent was to be used to great advantage in the design and construction of the sophisticated apparatus needed for his operant conditioning experiments. By the time Skinner entered high school, however, he had developed a growing interest in the arts. He learned to play the piano and saxophone and experimented in the writing of poems, plays, songs, and novels. Following graduation from high school, Skinner entered Hamilton College in Clinton, New York, where he continued these artistic interests, playing in a jazz band and an orchestra.

Skinner graduated from Hamilton College with an English major, a Phi Beta Kappa key, and a passion to become a creative writer. This was not to be. After two years of work, Skinner abandoned his dream, deciding that he really had nothing to say. Disillusioned, he spent the following summer traveling in Europe. Many years later Skinner was to realize something of his creative ambitions with the publication of his utopian novel *Walden II* in 1948.

Prior to his entering the Harvard University graduate program in psychology in 1928, Skinner's early identity crisis, his failure as a writer, was resolved with his reading of the works of Ivan Pavlov and John B. Watson, the behaviorist. His father, a lawyer, wanted his son to study law, but Skinner became, instead, a passionate and devoted student of behaviorism. His daily routine as a graduate student at Harvard reflected this commitment. His life was confined primarily to studies, laboratories, and libraries. He seldom deviated from this pattern and read nothing but physiology and psychology.

Skinner received his Ph.D. from Harvard in three years but stayed on five more years to pursue his research with a post-doctoral fellowship, partly supported by the National Research Council. Having been at Harvard for eight years with much of his time spent in the laboratory, Skinner felt ill-prepared for his first teaching position at the University of Minnesota in 1936. He claimed that throughout his graduate studies he had never completely read a standard psychology text. While at Minnesota in 1938, however, Skinner established a national reputation with the publication of his now classic book, *The Behavior of Organisms,* an introduction to his pioneering research on operant conditioning. In 1948, after three years at Indiana University, Skinner returned to Harvard where he remained until his retirement in 1974. He continued to write and lecture until his death on August 18, 1990, at the age of 86, as a result of complications from leukemia.

B. F. Skinner was a brilliant, highly productive, and creative scientist with many important books, countless articles, and numerous awards and recognitions, including the American Psychological Association Distinguished Contribution Award (1958) and the National Medal of Science Award for distinguished scientific achievement (1968).

The Myth of Autonomous Man: Internal Variables vs. Environmental Contingencies

COMMENTARY

Most theories of personality attribute some important role to inner determinants. Freud's unconscious dynamics, Jung's archetypes, Adler's strivings for perfection, Allport's traits, Bandura's reciprocal determinism, and Rogers' actualizing tendency all emphasize the importance of certain internal forces and structures in the development of personality. Even the post-Freudian theories of Horney and Erikson, with their emphasis on cultural and social forces, do not abandon internal forces as important causal agents in personality formation and behavior. B. F. Skinner's radical behaviorism, however, presents us with an entirely different picture. For Skinner all behaviors and developments of personality are due to the lawful interactions of emitted behaviors and the environmental response to these behaviors. These operant behaviors "operate" on the environment to produce consequences. In the repertoire of behaviors that become established in the human organism, the environmental consequences have been reinforcing. Thus, in Skinner's view, the shape of personality is due to the individual's unique reinforcement history.

With his extreme environmentalism Skinner has been accused of representing an "empty organism" theory. This is an incorrect view of his position. Skinner has always acknowledged the presence of internal states. However, he strongly rejects such internal states as the causes or autonomous agents of behavior. For example, one might say of one's roommate "She didn't go to class today because she felt depressed" (internal causation). Skinner would shout "Absolutely not!" The depression has no validity as a causal agent in determining her behavior, which can only be

155

understood by examining the non-reinforcing properties of the classroom environment.

For Skinner such mental states have absolutely no explanatory power and, thus, play no significant role in personality or behavior. In fact, these internal states are established in much the same way as any other behavior. The basic nature of events, therefore, is the same whether these events take place internally or in the environment. Given Skinner's total rejection of inner determinants in personality formation and behavior, we may want to ask, "Should Skinner be regarded as a personality theorist?"

1.

B. F. SKINNER

Inner "Causes"

Every science has at some time or other looked for causes of action inside the things it has studied. Sometimes the practice has proved useful, sometimes it has not. There is nothing wrong with an inner explanation as such, but events which are located inside a system are likely to be difficult to observe. For this reason we are encouraged to assign properties to them without justification. Worse still, we can invent causes of this sort without fear of contradiction. The motion of a rolling stone was once attributed to its *vis viva*. The chemical properties of bodies were thought to be derived from the *principles or essences* of

which they were composed. Combustion was explained by the *phlogiston* inside the combustible object. Wounds healed and bodies grew well because of a *vis medicatric*. It has been especially tempting to attribute the behavior of a living organism to the behavior of an inner agent, as the following examples may suggest.

Neural Causes. The layman uses the nervous system as a ready explanation of behavior. The English language contains hundreds of expressions which imply such a causal relationship. At the end of a long trial we read that the jury shows signs of *brain fag,* that the *nerves* of the accused are *on edge,* that the wife of the accused is on the verge of a *nervous breakdown,* and that his lawyer is generally thought to have lacked the *brains* needed to stand up to the prosecution. Obviously, no direct observations have been made of the nervous systems of any of these

¹ Skinner. B. F. (1953). Reprinted with the permission of The Free Press, a division of Macmillan, Inc. from *Science and Human Behavior,* pp. 27–31, by B. F. Skinner. Copyright © 1953 by Macmillan Publishing Company, renewed 1981 by B. F. Skinner.

people. Their "brains" and "nerves" have been invented on the spur of the moment to lend substance to what might otherwise seem a superficial account of their behavior.

The sciences of neurology and physiology have not divested themselves entirely of a similar practice. Since techniques for observing the electrical and chemical processes in nervous tissue had not yet been developed, early information about the nervous system was limited to its gross anatomy. Neural processes could only be inferred from the behavior which was said to result from them. Such inferences were legitimate enough as scientific theories, but they could not justifiably be used to explain the very behavior upon which they were based. The hypotheses of the early physiologist may have been sounder than those of the layman, but until independent evidence could be obtained, they were no more satisfactory as explanations of behavior. Direct information about many of the chemical and electrical processes in the nervous system is now available. Statements about the nervous system are no longer necessarily inferential or fictional. But there is still a measure of circularity in much physiological explanation, even in the writing of specialists. In World War I a familiar disorder was called "shell shock." Disturbances in behavior were explained by arguing that violent explosions had damaged the structure of the nervous system, though no direct evidence of such damage was available. In World War II the same disorder was classified as "neuropsychiatric." The prefix seems to show a continuing unwillingness to abandon explanations in terms of hypothetical neural damage.

Eventually, a science of the nervous system based upon direct observation rather than inference will describe the neural states and events which immediately precede instances of behavior. We shall know the precise neurological conditions which immediately preceded, say, the response, "No, thank you." These events in turn will be found to be preceded by other neurological events, and these in turn by others. This series will lead us back to events outside the nervous system and, eventually, outside the organism. . . .

Psychic Inner Causes. An even more common practice is to explain behavior in terms of an inner agent which lacks physical dimensions and is called "mental" or "psychic." The purest form of the psychic explanation is seen in the animism of primitive peoples. From the immobility of the body after death it is inferred that a spirit responsible for movement has departed. The *enthusiastic* person is, as the etymology of the word implies, energized by a "god within." It is only a modest refinement to attribute every feature of the behavior of the physical organism to a corresponding feature of the "mind" or of some inner "personality." The inner man is regarded as driving the body very much as the man at the steering wheel drives a car. The inner man wills an action, the outer executes it. The inner loses his appetite, the outer stops eating. The inner man wants and the outer gets. The inner has the impulse which the outer obeys.

It is not the layman alone who resorts to these practices, for many reputable psychologists use a similar dualistic system of explanation. The inner man is sometimes personified clearly, as when delinquent behavior is attributed to a "disordered personality," or he may be dealt with in fragments, as when behavior is attributed to mental processes, faculties, and traits. Since the inner man does not occupy space, he may be multiplied at will. It has been argued that a single physical organism is controlled by several psychic agents and that its behavior is the resultant of their several wills. The Freudian concepts of the ego, superego, and id are often used in this way. They are frequently regarded as nonsubstantial creatures, often in violent conflict, whose defeats or victories lead to the adjusted or maladjusted behavior of the physical organism in which they reside.

Direct observation of the mind comparable with the observation of the nervous system has not proved feasible. It is true that many people believe that they observe their "mental states" just as the physiologist observes neural events. . . . Introspective psychology no longer pretends to supply direct information about events which are the causal antecedents, rather than the mere accompaniments, of behavior. It defines its "subjective" events in ways which strip them of any usefulness in a causal analysis. The events appealed to in early mentalistic explanations of behavior have remained beyond the reach of observation. Freud insisted upon this by emphasizing the role of the unconscious—a frank recognition that important mental processes are not directly observable. The Freudian literature supplies many examples of behavior from which unconscious wishes, impulses, instincts, and emotions are inferred. Unconscious

thought-processes have also been used to explain intellectual achievements. Though the mathematician may feel that he knows "how he thinks," he is often unable to give a coherent account of the mental processes leading to the solution of a specific problem. But any mental event which is unconscious is necessarily inferential, and the explanation is therefore not based upon independent observations of a valid cause.

The fictional nature of this form of inner cause is shown by the ease with which the mental process is discovered to have just the properties needed to account for the behavior. When a professor turns up in the wrong classroom or gives the wrong lecture, it is because his *mind* is, at least for the moment, *absent.* If he forgets to give a reading assignment, it is because it has slipped his *mind* (a hint from the class may *remind him* of it). He begins to tell an old joke but pauses for a moment, and it is evident to everyone that he is trying to make up his *mind* whether or not he has already used the joke that term. His lectures grow more tedious over the years, and questions from the class confuse him more and more, because his *mind* is failing. What he says is often disorganized because his ideas are confused. He is occasionally unnecessarily emphatic because of the force of his *ideas.* When he repeats himself, it is because he has an *idée fixe;* and when he repeats what others have said, it is because he borrows his *ideas.* Upon occasion there is nothing in what he says because he lacks *ideas.* In all this it is obvious that the mind and the ideas, together with their special characteristics, are being invented on the spot to provide spurious explanations. A science of behavior can hope to gain very little from so cavalier a practice. Since mental or psychic events are asserted to lack the dimensions of physical science, we have an additional reason for rejecting them.

Conceptual Inner Causes. The commonest inner causes have no specific dimensions at all, either neurological or psychic. When we say that a man eats *because* he is hungry, smokes a great deal *because* he has the tobacco habit, fights *because* of the instinct of pugnacity, behaves brilliantly *because* of his intelligence, or plays the piano well *because* of his musical ability, we seem to be referring to causes. But on analysis these phrases prove to be merely redundant descriptions. A single set of facts is described by the two statements: "He eats" and "He is hungry." a single set of facts is described by the two statements: "He smokes a great deal" and "He has the smoking habit." A single set of facts is described by the two statements: "He plays well" and "He has musical ability." The practice of explaining one statement in terms of the other is dangerous because it suggests that we have found the cause and therefore need

search no further. Moreover, such terms as "hunger," "habit," and "intelligence" convert what are essentially the properties of a process or relation into what appear to be things. Thus we are unprepared for the properties eventually to be discovered in the behavior itself and continue to look for something which may not exist.

The Variables of Which Behavior Is a Function. The practice of looking inside the organism for an explanation of behavior has tended to obscure the variables which are immediately available for scientific analysis. These variables lie outside the organism, in its immediate environment and in its environmental history. They have a physical status to which the usual techniques of science are adapted, and they make it possible to explain behavior as other subjects are explained in science. These independent variables are of many sorts and their relations to behavior are often subtle and complex, but we cannot hope to give an adequate account of behavior without analyzing them.

2.

B. F. SKINNER

A Functional Analysis. The external variables of which behavior is a

[2] Skinner. B. F. (1953). Reprinted with the permission of Macmillan Publishing Company from *Science and Human Behavior,* pp. 35–36, by B. F. Skinner. Copyright © 1953 by Macmillan Publishing Company, renewed 1981 by B. F. Skinner.

function provide for what may be called a causal or functional analysis. We undertake to predict and control the behavior of the individual organism. This is our "dependent variable"—the effect for which we are to find the cause. Our "independent variables" the causes of behavior—are the external conditions of which behavior is a function. Relations between the two—the "cause-and-effect relationships" in behavior—are the laws of a science. A synthesis of these laws expressed in quantitative terms yields a comprehensive picture of the organism as a behaving system.

This must be done within the bounds of a natural science. We cannot assume that behavior has any peculiar properties which require unique methods or special kinds of knowledge. It is often argued that an act is not so important as the "intent" which lies behind it, or that it can be described only in terms of what it "means" to the behaving individual or to others whom it may affect. If statements of this sort are useful for scientific purposes, they must be based upon observable events, and we may confine ourselves to such events exclusively in a functional analysis. We shall see later that although such terms as "meaning" and "intent" appear to refer to properties of behavior, they usually conceal references to independent variables. This is also true of "aggressive," "friendly," "disorganized," "intelligent," and other terms which appear to describe properties of behavior but in reality refer to its controlling relations.

The independent variables must also be described in physical terms. An effort is often made to avoid the labor of analyzing a physical situation by guessing what it "means" to an organism or by distinguishing between the physical world and a psychological world of "experience." This practice also reflects a confusion between dependent and independent variables. The events affecting an organism must be capable of description in the language of physical science. It is sometimes argued that certain "social forces" or the "influences" of culture or tradition are exceptions. But we cannot appeal to entities of this sort without explaining how they can affect both the scientist and the individual under observation. The physical events which must then be appealed to in such an explanation will supply us with alternative material suitable for physical analysis.

By confining ourselves to these observable events, we gain a considerable advantage, not only in theory, but in practice. A "social force" is no more useful in manipulating behavior than an inner state of hunger, anxiety, or skepticism. Just as we must trace these inner events to the manipulable variables of which they are said to be functions before we may put them to practical use, we must identify the physical events through which a "social force" is said to affect the organism before we can manipulate it for purposes of control. In dealing with the directly observable data we need not refer to either the inner state or the outer force.

3.

B. F. SKINNER

An important role of autonomous man has been to give human behavior direction, and it is often said that in dispossessing an inner agent we leave man himself without a purpose. As one writer has put it, "Since a scientific psychology must regard human behavior objectively, as determined by necessary laws, it must represent human behavior as unintentional." But "necessary laws" would have this effect only if they referred exclusively to antecedent conditions. Intention and purpose refer to selective consequences, the effects of which can be formulated in "necessary laws." Has

life, in all the forms in which it exists on the surface of the earth, a purpose, and is this evidence of intentional design? The primate hand evolved *in order that* things might be more successfully manipulated, but its purpose is to be found not in a prior design but rather in the process of selection. Similarly, in operant conditioning the purpose of a skilled movement of the hand is to be found in the consequences which follow it. A pianist neither acquires nor executes the behavior of playing a scale smoothly because of a prior intention of doing so. Smoothly played scales are reinforcing for many reasons, and they select skilled movements. In neither the evolution of the human hand nor in the acquired use of the hands is any prior intention or purpose at issue.

[3] Skinner, B. F. (1971). From *Beyond Freedom and Dignity,* pp. 194–195, by B. F. Skinner. Copyright © 1971 by B. F. Skinner. Reprinted by permission of Alfred A. Knopf, Inc. New York. Alfred A. Knopf, Inc.

4.

B. F. SKINNER

An experimental analysis shifts the determination of behavior from autonomous man to the environment—an

environment responsible both for the evolution of the species and for the repertoire acquired by each member. Early versions of environmentalism were inadequate because they could not explain how the environment worked, and much seemed to be left for autonomous man to do. But environmental contingencies now take over functions

[4] Skinner, B. F. (1971). From *Beyond Freedom and Dignity,* pp. 205–206, by B. F. Skinner. Copyright © 1971 by B. F. Skinner. Reprinted by permission of Alfred A. Knopf, Inc. New York. Alfred A. Knopf, Inc.

once attributed to autonomous man, and certain questions arise. Is man then "abolished"? Certainly not as a species or an individual achiever. It is the autonomous inner man who is abolished, and that is a step forward. But does man not then become merely a victim or passive observer of what is happening to him? He is indeed controlled by his environment, but we must remember that it is an environment largely of his own making. The evolution of a culture is a gigantic exercise in self-control. It is often said that a scientific view of man leads to wounded vanity, a sense of hopelessness, and nostalgia. But no theory changes what it is a theory about; man remains what he has always been. And a new theory may change what can be done with its subject matter. A scientific view of man offers exciting possibilities. We have not yet seen what man can make of man.

5.

B. F. SKINNER

Obstacles to a Science of Behavior

Obstacle 1: Humanistic Psychology. Many people find the implications of a behavioral analysis disturbing. The traditional direction of action of organism and environment seems to be reversed. Instead of saying that the organism sees, attends to, perceives, "processes," or otherwise acts upon stimuli, an operant analysis holds that stimuli acquire control of behavior through the part they play in contingencies of reinforcement. Instead of saying that an organism stores copies of the contingencies to which it is exposed and later retrieves and responds to them again, it says that the organism is changed by the contingencies and later responds as a changed organism, the contingencies having passed into history. The environment takes over the control formerly assigned to an internal, originating agent.

Some long-admired features of human behavior are then threatened. Following the lead of evolutionary theory, an operant analysis replaces creation with variation and selection. there is no longer any need for a creative mind or plan, or for purpose or goal direction. Just as we say that species-specific behavior did not evolve in *order that* a species could adapt to the environment but rather evolved *when* it adapted, so we say that operant behavior is not strengthened by reinforcement *in order that* the individual can adjust to the environment but is strengthened *when* the

[5] Skinner, B. F. (1987). "Whatever Happened to Psychology As the Science of Behavior?" *The American Psychologist,* 42:8 (August 1987), pp. 782–784. Copyright © 1987 by the American Psychological Association. Reprinted by permission.

individual adjusts (where "adapt" and "adjust" mean "behave effectively with respect to").

The disenthronement of a creator seems to threaten personal freedom (Can we be free if the environment is in control?) and personal worth (Can we take credit for our achievements if they are nothing more than the effects of circumstance?). It also seems to threaten ethical, religious, and governmental systems that hold people responsible for their conduct. Who or what is responsible if unethical, immoral, or illegal behavior is due to heredity or personal history? Humanistic psychologists have attacked behavioral science along these lines. Like creationists in their attack on secular humanists (with the humanists on the other side), they often challenge the content or selection of textbooks, the appointment of teachers and administrators, the design of curricula, and the allocation of funds.

Obstacle 2: Psychotherapy. Certain exigencies of the helping professions are another obstacle in the path of a scientific analysis of behavior. Psychotherapists must talk with their clients and, with rare exceptions, do so in everyday English, which is heavy laden with references to internal causes—"I ate because I was *hungry,*" "I could do it because I *knew* how to do it," and so on. All fields of science tend to have two languages, of course. Scientists speak one with casual acquaintances and the other with colleagues. In a relatively young science, such as psychology, the use of the vernacular may be challenged. How often have behaviorists heard, "You just said 'It crossed my mind!' I thought there wasn't supposed to be any mind." It has been a long time since anyone challenged a physicist who said, "that desk is made of solid oak," by protesting, "But I thought you said that matter was mostly empty space."

The two languages of psychology raise a special problem. What we feel when we are hungry or when we know how to do something are states of our bodies. We do not have very good ways of observing them, and those who teach us to observe them usually have no way at all. We were taught to say "I'm hungry," for example, by persons who knew perhaps only that we had not eaten for some time ("You missed your lunch; you must be hungry") or had observed something about our behavior ("You are eating ravenously. You must be *hungry*"). Similarly, we were taught to say "I know" by persons who had perhaps only seen us doing something ("Oh, you *know* how to do that!") or had told us how to do something and then said "Now you *know.*" The trouble is that private states are almost always poorly correlated with the public evidence.

References to private events are, nevertheless, often accurate enough to be useful. If we are preparing a meal for a friend, we are not likely to ask, "How long has it been since you last ate?" or "Will you probably eat a great deal?" We simply ask, "How *hungry* are you?" If a friend is driving us to an appointment, we are not likely to ask, "Have you driven there before?" or "Has anyone told you where it is?" Instead we ask, "Do you *know* where it is?" Being hungry and knowing where something is are states of the body resulting from personal histories, and what is said about them may be the only available evidence of those histories. Nevertheless, how much a person eats does depend upon a history of deprivation, not upon how a deprived body feels, and whether a person reaches a given destination does depend upon whether he or she has driven there before or has been told how to get there, not upon introspective evidence of the effects.

Psychotherapists must ask people what has happened to them and how they feel because the confidential relationship of therapist and client prevents direct inquiry. (It is sometimes argued that what a person remembers may be more important than what actually happened, but that is true only if something else has happened, of which it would also be better to have independent evidence.) But although the use of reports of feelings and states of mind can be justified on practical grounds, there is no justification for their use in theory making. The temptation, however, is great. Psychoanalysts, for example, specialize in feelings. Instead of investigating the early lives of their patients or watching them with their families, friends, or business associates, they ask them what has happened and how they feel about it. It is not surprising that they should then construct theories in terms of memories, feelings, and states of mind or that they should say that an analysis of behavior in terms of environmental events lacks "depth."

Obstacle 3: Cognitive Psychology. A curve showing the appearance of the word *cognitive* in the psychological literature would be interesting. A first rise could probably be seen around 1960; the subsequent acceleration would be exponential. Is there any field of psychology today in which something does not seem to be gained by adding that charming adjective to the occasional noun? The popularity may not be hard to explain. When we became psychologists, we learned new ways of talking about human behavior. If they were "behavioristic," they were not very much like the old ways. The old terms were taboo, and eyebrows were raised when we used them. But when certain developments seemed to show that the old ways might be right after all, everyone could relax. Mind was back.

Information theory was one of those developments, computer technology another. Troublesome problems seemed to vanish like magic. A detailed study of sensation and perception was no longer needed; one could simply speak of processing information. It was no longer necessary to construct settings in which to observe behavior; one could simply describe them. Rather than observe what people actually did, one could simply ask them what they would probably do.

That mentalistic psychologists are uneasy about these uses of introspection is clear from the desperation with which they are turning to brain science, asking it to tell them what perceptions, feelings, ideas, and intentions "really are." And brain scientists are happy to accept the assignment. To complete the account of an episode of behavior (for example, to explain what happens when a reinforcement brings an organism under the control of a given stimulus) is not only beyond the present range of brain science, it would lack the glamour of a revelation about the nature of mind. But psychology may find it dangerous to turn to neurology for help. Once you tell the world that another science will explain what your key terms really mean, you must forgive the world if it decides that the other science is doing the important work.

Cognitive psychologists like to say that "the mind is what the brain does," but surely the rest of the body plays a part. The mind is what the *body* does. It is what the *person* does. In other words, it is behavior, and that is what behaviorists have been saying for more than half a century. To focus on an organ is to rejoin the Homeric Greeks.

SECTION B

Operant Conditioning and Behavior

COMMENTARY

In important respects, the history of behaviorism and learning theory has been the history of American psychology, and B. F. Skinner stands at the apex in this evolution. It will enlarge our perspective on Skinner, therefore, if we take a brief look at two of the important precursors to his work; the Russian physiologist, Ivan Pavlov, and the American psychologist and father of behaviorism, John B. Watson.

Around the turn of the century Ivan Pavlov was involved in the investigation of the process of digestion in dogs. During his research he made a dramatic discovery. His dogs had started salivating to the sound of the attendant's footsteps before seeing or receiving the food. Following a period of intense inner struggle and conflict with colleagues, Pavlov decided to abandon his established research on digestion to pursue this newly discovered phenomenon, which in 1901 he called the "conditioned reflex."

In continuing their investigations, Pavlov and his co-workers established that when the presentation of food was paired frequently with any neutral stimulus, the sound of footsteps, the sound of a bell tone, etc., the dog would begin to salivate to the neutral stimulus without the presentation of the food. In the process of his research, Pavlov also discovered several other important principles in relation to this stimulus-response type of learning. For example, if food were permanently withdrawn the conditioned response to the neutral stimulus would disappear and *extinction* would occur. *Stimulus generalization* would take place if a number of tones of different frequencies were paired with food, so that the dog "learned" to salivate to a whole range of tones.

Pavlov's important research gave an early impetus to the development of behaviorism and laid the foundation for the development of over a half century of learning theory.

John B. Watson, the American behaviorist, was greatly influenced by Pavlov's work. Watson saw in this research the basis for a scientific psychology that would parallel the natural sciences in its precision, control, and ability to work with quantifiable data. Thus, in his famous 1913 manifesto, Watson asserted that the time had come when psychology must discard all references to consciousness in the interest of creating a purely objective, experimental science. In this new vision for psychology, introspection as a method of psychological inquiry would no longer be acceptable, and no mental states would be recognized as sources for psychological data. Watson later used the Pavlovian classical conditioning model to study the learning process in infants and children and their acquisition of fears.

Pavlov's research and Watson's passionate crusade for a scientific psychology became a clarion call for Skinner as he realized his ambitions to become a creative writer were not to be. He read both Pavlov and Watson assiduously. Skinner, however, became interested in pursuing another form of conditioning. Rather than following Pavlov's classical stimulus-response model, where a specific response is elicited by a known stimulus (salivation to the sound of the bell), Skinner focused on the behaviors that are emitted by the organism without any known stimulus. As we have seen, these emitted behaviors, in turn, "operate" on the environment to produce consequences, the most important of which is reinforcement. Skinner demonstrated that reinforcement of an emitted behavior increases the frequency and strength of that behavior. It is this fundamental relationship between the operant behavior and the environmental response that, for Skinner, forms the foundation for human development, learning, and, as we shall see in Section D, social engineering. Controlling this relationship between emitted behavior and environmental response, therefore, becomes of paramount importance. Thus, "personality" for Skinner meant nothing more or less than the patterns of behavior that issue forth from the individual's personal reinforcement history.

1.

B. F. SKINNER

Selection by Consequences. The history of human behavior, if we may

[1] Skinner, B. F. (1987). "Selection by Consequences," *Science* 213 (31 July, 1981), pp. 501–503. Copyright © 1981 by the AAAS. Used by permission.

take it to begin with the origin of life on earth, is possibly exceeded in scope only by the history of the universe. Like the astronomer and cosmologist, the historian proceeds only by reconstructing what may have happened rather than by reviewing recorded facts. The story presumably began not with a big bang, but with that extraordinary moment when a molecule that had the power to reproduce itself came into existence. It was then that selection by consequences made its appearance as a causal mode. Reproduction was itself a first consequence, and it led, through natural selection, to the evolution of cells, organs, and organisms that reproduced themselves under increasingly diverse conditions.

What we call behavior evolved as a set of functions furthering the interchange between organism and environment. In a fairly stable world it could be as much a part of the genetic endowment of a species as digestion, respiration, or any other biological function. The involvement with the environment, however, posed limitations. The behavior functioned well only under conditions fairly similar to those under which it was selected. Reproduction under a much wider range of conditions became possible with the evolution of two processes through which individual organisms acquired behavior appropriate to novel environments. Through respondent (Pavlovian) conditioning, responses prepared in advance by natural selection could come under the control of new stimuli. Through operant conditioning, new responses could be strengthened *(reinforced)* by events that immediately followed them.

A Second Kind of Selection. Operant conditioning is a second kind of selection by consequences. It must have evolved in parallel with two other products of the same contingencies of natural selection—a susceptibility to

reinforcement by certain kinds of consequences and a supply of behavior less specifically committed to eliciting or releasing stimuli. (Most operants are selected from behavior that has little or no relation to such stimuli.)

When the selecting consequences are the same, operant conditioning and natural selection work together redundantly. For example, the behavior of a duckling in following its mother is apparently the product not only of natural selection (ducklings tend to move in the direction of large moving objects) but also of an evolved susceptibility to reinforcement by proximity to such an object. . . . The common consequence is that the duckling stays near its mother. (Imprinting is a different process, close to respondent conditioning.)

Because a species that quickly acquires behavior appropriate to a given environment has less need for an innate repertoire, operant conditioning could not only supplement the natural selection of behavior but also replace it. There were advantages favoring such a change. When members of a species eat a certain food simply because eating it has had survival value, the food does not need to be, and presumably is not, a reinforcer. Similarly, when sexual behavior is simply a product of natural selection, sexual contact does not need to be, and presumably is not, a reinforcer. But when, through the evolution of special susceptibilities, food and sexual contact become reinforcing, new forms of behavior can be set up. New ways of gathering, processing, and ultimately cultivating foods and new ways of behaving sexually or of behaving in ways that lead only eventually to sexual reinforcement can be shaped and maintained. The behavior so conditioned is not necessarily adaptive: Foods are eaten that are not healthful, and sexual behavior strengthened that is not related to procreation.

Much of the behavior studied by ethnologists—courtship, mating, care of the young, intraspecific aggression, defense of territory, and so on—is social. It is within easy range of natural selection because other members of a species are one of the most stable features of the environment of a species. Innate social repertoires are supplemented by imitation. By running when others run, for example, an animal responds to "releasing stimuli" to which it has not itself been exposed. A different kind of imitation, with a much wider range, results from the fact that contingencies of reinforcement that induce one organism to behave in a given way will often affect another organism when it behaves in the same way. An imitative repertoire that brings the imitator under the control of new contingencies is therefore acquired.

The human species presumably became much more social when its vocal musculature came under operant control. Cries of alarm, mating calls, aggressive threats, and other kinds of vocal behavior can be modified through operant conditioning. . . .

The ability of the human species to acquire new forms through selection by consequences presumably resulted from the evolution of a special innervation of the vocal musculature, together with a supply of vocal behavior not strongly under the control of eliciting or "releasing" stimuli, such as the babbling of children, from which verbal operants are selected. No new

susceptibility to reinforcement was needed because the consequences of verbal behavior are distinguished only by the fact that they are mediated by other people.

The development of environmental control of the vocal musculature greatly extended the help one person receives from others. By behaving verbally people cooperate more successfully in common ventures. By taking advice, heeding warnings, following instructions, and observing rules, they profit from what others have already learned. Ethical practices are strengthened by being codified in laws, and special techniques of ethical and intellectual self-management are devised and taught. Self-observation or awareness emerges when one person asks another a question such as "What are you going to do?" or "Why did you do that?" The invention of the alphabet spread these advantages over great distances and periods of time. They have long been said to give the human species its unique position, although it is possible that what is unique is simply the extension of operant control to the vocal musculature.

A Third Kind of Selection. Verbal behavior greatly increased the importance of a third kind of selection by consequences, the evolution of social environments—cultures. The process presumably begins at the level of the individual. A better way of making a tool, growing food, or teaching a child is reinforced by its consequence—the tool, the food, or a useful helper, respectively. A culture evolves when practices originating in this way contribute to the success of the practicing group in solving its problems. It is the effect on the group, not the reinforcing consequences for individual members, that is responsible for the evolution of the culture.

In summary, then, human behavior is the joint product of (1) the contingencies of survival responsible for the natural selection of the species and (2) the contingencies of reinforcement responsible for the repertoires acquired by its members, including (3) the special contingencies maintained by an evolved social environment. (Ultimately, of course, it is all a matter of natural selection, since operant conditioning is an evolved process, of which cultural practices are special applications.)

Similarities and Differences. Each of the three levels of variation and selection has its own discipline—the first, biology; the second, psychology; and the third, anthropology. Only the second, operant conditioning, occurs at a speed at which it can be observed from moment to moment. Biologists and anthropologists study the processes through which variations arise and are selected, but they merely reconstruct the evolution of a species or culture. Operant conditioning is selection in progress. It resembles a hundred million years of natural selection or a thousand years of the evolution of a culture compressed into a very short period of time.

2.

B. F. SKINNER

Operant Behavior. . . . When a bit of behavior has the kind of consequence called reinforcing, it is more likely to occur again. A positive reinforcer strengthens any behavior that produces it: a glass of water is positively reinforcing when we are thirsty, and if we then draw and drink a glass of water, we are more likely to do so again on similar occasions. A negative reinforcer strengthens any behavior that reduces or terminates it: when we

take off a shoe that pinches, the reduction in pressure is negatively reinforcing, and we are more likely to do so again when a shoe pinches.

The process supplements natural selection. Important consequences of behavior which could not play a role in evolution because they were not sufficiently stable features of the environment are made effective through operant conditioning during the life time of the individual, whose power in dealing with his world is thus vastly increased.

The Feelings of Reinforcers. The fact that operant conditioning, like all

---

physiological processes, is a product of natural selection throws light on the question of what kinds of consequences are reinforcing and why. It is commonly said that a thing is reinforcing because it feels, looks, sounds, smells, or tastes good, but from the point of view of evolutionary theory a susceptibility to reinforcement is due to its survival value and not to any associated feelings.

The point may be made for the reinforcers which play a part in the conditioning of reflexes. Salivation is elicited by certain chemical stimuli on the tongue (as other secretions are elicited by other stimuli in later stages of digestion) because the effect has contributed to the survival of the species. A person may report that a substance tastes good, but it does not elicit salivation because it tastes good. Similarly, we pull our hand away from a hot object, but not because the object *feels* painful. The behavior occurs because appropriate mechanisms have been selected in the course of evolution. The feelings are merely collateral products of the conditions responsible for the behavior.

The same may be said of operant reinforcers. Salt and sugar are critical requirements, and individuals who were especially likely to be reinforced by them have more effectively learned and remembered where and how to get them and have therefore been more likely to survive and transmit this susceptibility to the species. It has often been pointed out that competition for a mate tends to select the more skillful and powerful members of a species, but it also selects those more susceptible to sexual reinforcement. As a result, the human species, like other species, is powerfully reinforced by sugar, salt, and sexual contact. This is very different from saying that these things reinforce *because* they taste or feel good.

Feelings have dominated the discussion of rewards and punishments for centuries. One reason is that the conditions we report when we say that a taste, odor, sound, picture, or a piece of music is delicious, pleasant, or beautiful are part of the immediate situation, whereas the effect they may have in changing our behavior is much less salient—and much less likely to be "seen," because the verbal environment cannot establish good contingencies. According to the philosophy of hedonism, people act to achieve pleasure and escape from or avoid pain, and the effects referred to in Edward L. Thorndike's famous Law of Effect were feelings: "satisfying" or "annoying." The verb "to like" is a synonym of "to be pleased with;" we say "If you like" and "If you please" more or less interchangeably.

Some of these terms refer to other effects of reinforcers—satisfying, for example, is related to satiation—but most refer to the bodily states generated by reinforcers. It is sometimes possible to discover what reinforces a person simply by asking him what he likes or how he feels about things. What we learn is similar to what we learn by testing the effect of a reinforcer: he is talking about what has reinforced him in the past or what he sees himself "going for." But this does not mean that his feelings are causally effective; his answer reports a collateral effect.

The expressions "I like Brahms," "I love Brahms," "I enjoy Brahms," and

"Brahms pleases me" may easily be taken to refer to feelings, but they can be regarded as statements that the music of Brahms is reinforcing. A person of whom the expressions are true will listen to the radio when it plays Brahms rather than turn it off, buy and play records of Brahms, and go to concerts where Brahms is played. The expressions have antonyms ("I dislike Brahms," "I hate Brahms," I detest Brahms," and "Brahms bores me"), and a person for whom Brahms is thus aversive will act to avoid or escape from hearing him. These expressions do not refer to instances of reinforcement but rather to a general susceptibility or the lack of it.

The allusion to what is felt needs to be carefully examined. Feelings are especially plausible when the experience is directed toward a living person. The statement "I love my wife" seems to be a report of feelings, but it also involves a probability of action. We are disposed to do to a person we love the things he likes or loves to have done. We are not disposed to do to a person we dislike (or especially to a person we hate) the things he likes or loves to have done; on the contrary we are disposed to do the things he dislikes or hates to have done. With respect to a person with whom we interact, then, to "love" is to behave in ways having certain kinds of effects, possibly with accompanying conditions which may be felt.

Wants, Needs, Desires, Wishes. Some mentalistic terms refer to conditions which affect both the susceptibility for reinforcement and the strength of already reinforced behavior. We use "want" to describe a shortage: a hungry man wants food in the simple sense that food is wanting. "Needs" originally meant violent force, restraint, or compulsion, and we still make a distinction between wanting to act (because of positively reinforcing consequences) and needing to act (because not acting will have aversive consequences), but for most purposes the terms are interchangeable. We say that a car needs gasoline and much less idiomatically, that gasoline is wanting, but to say that a person "wants to get out" suggests aversive control. The significant fact is that a person who needs or wants food is particularly likely to be reinforced by food and that he is particularly likely to engage in any behavior which has previously been reinforced with food. A person under aversive control is particularly likely to be reinforced if he escapes and to engage in any behavior which has led to escape.

If we know the level of deprivation or aversive stimulation, we can more accurately predict how reinforcing a given event will be and how likely it is that a person will engage in relevant behavior. The knowledge has long been used for purposes of control. People have been made hungry so that they will "work for food" and so that they can be reinforced with food, as they have been made miserable so that they will act in ways which reduce their misery.

3.

B. F. SKINNER

Operant Conditioning. To get at the core of Thorndike's Law of Effect, we need to clarify the notion of "probability of response." This is an extremely important concept; unfortunately, it is also a difficult one. In discussing human behavior, we often refer to "tendencies" or "predispositions" to behave in particular ways. Almost every theory of behavior uses some such term as "excitatory potential," "habit strength," or "determining tendency." But how do we observe a tendency? And how can we measure one?

If a given sample of behavior existed in only two states, in one of which it always occurred and in the other never, we should be almost helpless in following a program of functional analysis. An all-or-none subject matter lends itself only to primitive forms of description. It is a great advantage to suppose instead that the *probability* that a response will occur ranges continuously between these all-or-none extremes. We can then deal with variables which, unlike the eliciting stimulus, do not "cause a given bit of behavior to occur" but simply make the occurrence more probable. We may then proceed to deal, for example, with the combined effect of more than one such variable.

[3] Skinner, B. F. (1953). Reprinted with the permission of Macmillan Publishing Company from *Science and Human Behavior*, pp. 62–66, by B. F. Skinner. Copyright © 1953 by Macmillan Publishing Company, renewed 1981 by B. F. Skinner.

The everyday expressions which carry the notion of probability, tendency, or predisposition describe the frequencies with which bits of behavior occur. We never observe a probability as such. We say that someone is "enthusiastic" about bridge when we observe that he plays bridge often and talks about it often. To be "greatly interested" in music is to play, listen to, and talk about music a good deal. The "inveterate" gambler is one who gambles frequently. The camera "fan" is to be found taking pictures, developing them, and looking at pictures made by himself and others. The "highly sexed" person frequently engages in sexual behavior. The "dipsomaniac" drinks frequently.

In characterizing a man's behavior in terms of frequency, we assume certain standard conditions: he must be able to execute and repeat a given act, and other behavior must not interfere appreciably. We cannot be sure of the extent of a man's interest in music, for example, if he is necessarily busy with other things. When we come to refine the notion of probability of response for scientific use, we find that here, too, our data are frequencies and that the conditions under which they are observed must be specified. The main technical problem in designing a controlled experiment is to provide for the observation and interpretation of frequencies. We eliminate, or at least hold constant, any condition which encourages behavior which competes with the behavior we are to study. An organism is placed in a quiet box where its behavior may be observed through a one-way screen or recorded mechanically. This is by no means an environmental vacuum, for the organisms will react to the features of the box in many ways; but its behavior will eventually reach a fairly stable level, against which the frequency of a selected response may be investigated.

To study the process which Thorndike called stamping in, we must have a "consequence." Giving food to a hungry organism will do. We can feed our subject conveniently with a small food tray which is operated electrically. When the tray is first opened, the organism will probably react to it in ways which interfere with the process we plan to observe. Eventually, after being fed from the tray repeatedly, it eats readily, and we are then ready to make this consequence contingent upon behavior and to observe the result.

We select a relatively simple bit of behavior which may be freely and rapidly repeated, and which is easily observed and recorded. If our experimental subject is a pigeon, for example, the behavior of raising the head above a given height is convenient. This may be observed by sighting across the pigeon's head at a scale pinned on the far wall of the box. We first study the height at which the head is normally held and select some line on the scale which is reached only infrequently. Keeping our eye on the scale we then begin to open the food tray very quickly whenever the head rises above the line. If the experiment is conducted according to specifications, the result is invariable: we observe an immediate change in the frequency with which the head crosses the line. We also observe, and this is of some importance theoretically, that higher lines are now being crossed. We may advance almost immediately to a higher line in determining when food is to be presented. In a minute or two, the bird's posture has changed so that the top of the head seldom falls below the line which we first chose.

When we demonstrate the process of stamping in this relatively simply way, we see that certain common interpretations of Thorndike's experiment are superfluous. The expression "trial-and-error learning," which is frequently associated with the Law of Effect, is clearly out of place here. We are reading something into our observations when we call any upward movement of the head a "trial," and there is no reason to call any movement which does not achieve a specified consequence an "error." Even the term "learning" is misleading. The statement that the bird "learns that it will get food by stretching its neck" is an inaccurate report of what has happened. To say that it has acquired the "habit" of stretching its neck is merely to resort to an explanatory fiction, since our only evidence of the habit is the acquired tendency to perform the act. The barest possible statement of the process is this: we make a given consequence contingent upon certain physical properties of behavior (the upward movement of the head), and the behavior is then observed to increase in frequency.

It is customary to refer to any movement of the organism as a "response." The word is borrowed from the field of reflex action and implies an act which, so to speak, answers a prior event—

the stimulus. But we may make an event contingent upon behavior without identifying, or being able to identify, a prior stimulus. We did not alter the environment of the pigeon to *elicit* the upward movement of the head. It is probably impossible to show that any single stimulus invariably precedes this movement. Behavior of this sort may come under the control of stimuli, but the relation is not that of elicitation. The term "response" is therefore not wholly appropriate but is so well established that we shall use it in the following discussion.

A response which has already occurred cannot, of course, be predicted or controlled. We can only predict that *similar* responses will occur in the future. The unit of a predictive science is, therefore, not a response but a class of responses. The word "operant" will be used to describe this class. The term emphasizes the fact that the behavior *operates* upon the environment to generate consequences. The consequences define the properties with respect to which responses are called similar. The term will be used both as an adjective (operant behavior) and as a noun to designate the behavior defined by a given consequence.

A single instance in which a pigeon raises its head is a *response*. It is a bit of history which may be reported in any frame of reference we wish to use. The behavior called "raising the head," regardless of when specific instances occur, is an *operant*. It can be described, not as an accomplished act, but rather as a set of acts defined by the property of the height to which the head is raised. In this sense an operant is defined by an effect which may be specified in physical terms; the "cut-off" at a certain height is a property of behavior.

The term "learning" may profitably be saved in its traditional sense to describe the reassortment of responses in a complex situation. Terms for the process of stamping in may be borrowed from Pavlov's analysis of the conditioned reflex. Pavlov himself called all events which strengthened behavior "reinforcement" and all the resulting changes "conditioning." In the Pavlovian experiment, however, a reinforcer is paired with a *stimulus*; whereas in operant behavior it is contingent upon a *response*. Operant reinforcement is therefore a separate process and requires a separate analysis. In both cases, the strengthening of behavior which results from reinforcement is appropriately called "conditioning." In operant conditioning we "strengthen" an operant in the sense of making a response more probable or, in actual fact, more frequent. In Pavlovian or "respondent" conditioning we simply increase the magnitude of the response elicited by the conditioned stimulus and shorten the time which elapses between stimulus and response. (We note, incidentally, that these two cases exhaust the possibilities: an organism is conditioned when a reinforcer (1) accompanies another stimulus or (2) follows upon the organism's own behavior. Any event which does neither has no effect in changing a probability of response.) In the pigeon experiment, then, food is the *reinforcer* and presenting food when a response is emitted is the *reinforcement*. The *operant* is defined by the property upon which reinforcement is contingent—the height to which the head must be raised. The change in frequency with which the head is lifted to this height is the process of *operant conditioning.*

While we are awake, we act upon the environment constantly, and many of the consequences of our actions are reinforcing. Through operant conditioning the environment builds the basic repertoire with which we keep our balance, walk, play games, handle instruments and tools, talk, write, sail a boat, drive a car or fly a plane. A change in the environment—a new car, a new friend, a new field of interest, a new job, a new location—may find us unprepared, but our behavior usually adjusts quickly as we acquire new responses and discard old.

4.

B. F. SKINNER

What Events Are Reinforcing? In dealing with our fellow men in everyday life and in the clinic and laboratory, we may need to know just how reinforcing a specific event is. We often begin by noting the extent to which our own behavior is reinforced by the same event. This practice frequently miscarries; yet it is still commonly believed that reinforcers can be identified apart from their effects upon a particular organism. As the term is used here, however, the only defining characteristic of a reinforcing stimulus is that it reinforces.

The only way to tell whether or not a given event is reinforcing to a given organism under given conditions is to make a direct test. We observe the frequency of a selected response, then make an event contingent upon it and observe any change in frequency. If there is a change, we classify the event as reinforcing to the organism under the existing conditions. There is nothing circular about classifying events in terms of their effects; the criterion is both empirical and objective. It would be circular, however, if we then went on to assert that a given event strengthens an operant *because* it is reinforcing. We achieve a certain success in guessing at reinforcing powers only because we have in a sense made a crude survey; we have gauged the reinforcing effect of a stimulus upon ourselves and assume the same effect upon others. We are successful only when we resemble the organism under study and when we have correctly surveyed our own behavior.

Events which are found to be reinforcing are of two sorts. Some reinforcements consist of *presenting* stimuli, of adding something—for example, food, water, or sexual

[4] Skinner, B. F. (1953). Reprinted with the permission of the Free Press, a division of Macmillan, Inc. from *Science and Human Behavior,* pp. 72–75, by B. F. Skinner. Copyright © 1953 by Macmillan Publishing Company, renewed 1981 by B. F. Skinner.

contact—to the situation. These we call *positive* reinforcers. Others consist of *removing* something—for example a loud noise, a very bright light, extreme cold or heat, or electric shock—from the situation. These we call *negative* reinforcers. In both cases the effect of reinforcement is the same—the probability of response is increased. We cannot avoid this distinction by arguing that what is reinforcing in the negative case is the *absence* of the bright light, loud noise, and so on; for it is absence after presence which is effective, and this is only another way of saying that the stimulus is removed. . . .

A survey of the events which reinforce a given individual is often required in the practical application of operant conditioning. In every field in which human behavior figures prominently—education, government, the family, the clinic, industry, art, literature, and so on—we are constantly changing probabilities of response by arranging reinforcing consequences. The industrialist who wants employees to work consistently and without absenteeism must make certain that their behavior is suitably reinforced—not only with wages but with suitable working conditions. The girl who wants another date must be sure that her friend's behavior in inviting her and in keeping the appointment is suitably reinforced. To teach a child to read or sing or play a game effectively, we must work out a program of educational reinforcement in which appropriate responses "pay off" frequently. If the patient is to return for further counsel, the psychotherapist must make sure that the behavior of coming to him is in some measure reinforced.

We evaluate the strength of reinforcing events when we attempt to discover what someone is "getting out of life." What consequences are responsible for his present repertoire and for the relative frequencies of the responses in it? His responses to various topics of conversation tell us something, but his everyday behavior is a better guide. We infer important reinforcers from nothing more unusual than his "interest" in a writer who deals with certain subjects, in stores or museums which exhibit certain objects, in friends who participate in certain kinds of behavior, in restaurants which serve certain kinds of food, and so on. The "interest" refers to the probability which results, at least, in part, from the consequences of the behavior of "taking an interest." We may be more nearly sure of the importance of a reinforcer if we watch the behavior come and go as the reinforcer is alternately supplied and withheld, for the change in probability is then less likely to be due to an incidental change of some other sort. The behavior of associating with a particular friend varies as the friend varies in supplying reinforcement. If we observe this covariation, we may then be fairly sure of "what this friendship means" or "what our subject sees in his friend."

This technique of evaluation may be improved for use in clinical and laboratory investigation. A direct inventory may be made by allowing a subject to look at an assortment of pictures and recording the time he spends on each. The behavior of looking at a picture is reinforced by what is seen in it. Looking at one picture may be more strongly reinforced than looking at another, and the times will vary accordingly. The information may be valuable if it is necessary for any reason to reinforce or extinguish our subject's behavior.

Literature, art and entertainment, are contrived reinforcers. Whether the public buys books, tickets to performances, and works of art depends upon whether those books, plays, concerts, or pictures are reinforcing. Frequently the artist confines himself to an exploration of what is reinforcing to himself. When he does so his work "reflects his own individuality," and it is then an accident (or a measure of his universality) if his book or play or piece of music or picture is reinforcing to others. Insofar as commercial success is important, he may make a direct study of the behavior of others. . . .

We cannot dispense with this survey simply by asking a man what reinforces him. His reply may be of some value, but it is by no means necessarily reliable. A reinforcing connection need not be obvious to the individual reinforced. It is often only in retrospect that one's tendencies to behave in particular ways are seen to be the result of certain consequences, and . . . the relation may never be seen at all even though it is obvious to others.

There are, of course, extensive differences between individuals in the events which prove to be reinforcing. The differences between species are so great as scarcely to arouse interest; obviously what is reinforcing to a horse need not be reinforcing to a dog or a man. Among the members of a species, the extensive differences are less likely to be due to hereditary endowment, and to that extent may be traced to circumstances in the history of the individual. The fact that organisms evidently inherit the capacity to be reinforced by certain kinds of events does not help us in predicting the reinforcing effect of an untried stimulus. Nor does the relation between the reinforcing event and deprivation or any other condition of the organism endow the reinforcing event with any particular physical property. It is especially unlikely that events which have *acquired* their power to reinforce will be marked in any special way. Yet such events are an important species of reinforcer.

Education: Teaching and Learning

COMMENTARY

It frequently goes unnoticed that B. F. Skinner made a major contribution to education. One of his most important research areas was in the development of programmed instruction. He was, for example, a pioneer in the development of the teaching machine. In all of these developments, Skinner's major concern was to apply the principles of contingency and reinforcement to educational methods and practices.

Observing that teachers were important controlling agents in the lives of their students and in the society at large, Skinner sought to provide teachers access to the important principles of operant conditioning so that their controlling techniques would be more effective, educationally sound, and in the best interest of students' learning and development.

In the application of operant techniques to classroom learning, Skinner emphasized the importance of positive reinforcement, and he cautioned against the use of punishment as a way of promoting student learning and reaching educational goals. Skinner viewed punishment as antithetical to any sound educational purpose or practice.

Skinner's programmed instruction has evolved to include the use of audio and video presentations, recordings, films, and the development of textbooks designed to follow the programmed format. Essentially, whatever the mode of instruction, students are presented with discrete stimuli to which they must make a response. After the response, students get immediate "feedback" as to the correctness of their answers.

Programmed instruction is designed to follow some important principles of learning. Among these are:

1. Each student is able to advance at his or her own pace.
2. Moving from the simple to the complex, there is a progressive mastery of the material, leading to the frequent reinforcement of "being right."
3. There is an absence of negative feedback and punishment.

In this technology of teaching, learning is "shaped" to aid the student in meeting a progressive sequence of learning goals. This approach follows the same conditioning principles that Skinner used in shaping and strengthening, through successive approximations, the behavior of laboratory animals. By identifying the component skills, correct responses are sequentially reinforced, leading to the ultimate conceptual grasp and understandings desired. In spite of the positive and progressive nature of programmed instruction, there have been some major criticisms.

1. Programmed instruction tends to isolate the student, and recent research has demonstrated the positive impact of student interaction and shared experience on learning.
2. Many disciplines and subject matter areas are not so clearly defined as to allow for the programming of hierarchically linked concepts.
3. In programmed instruction, learning is defined primarily in behavioral terms, thus ignoring the student's experiences, personal meanings, and creative responses. Programmed instruction is, after all, also programmed learning. This approach is seen by many as a mechanistic one and a limiting influence on student growth and intellectual development.

1.

B. F. SKINNER

In an American school if you ask for the salt in good French, you get an A. In France you get the salt. The difference reveals the nature of educational control. Education is the establishing of behavior which will be of advantage to the individual and to others at some future time. The behavior will eventually be reinforced in many of the ways we have already considered; meanwhile reinforcements are arranged by the educational agency for the purposes of conditioning. The reinforcers it uses are artificial, as such expressions as "drill," "exercise," and "practice," suggest.

Education emphasizes the acquisition of behavior rather than its maintenance. Where religious, governmental, and economic control is concerned with making certain kinds of

[1] Skinner, B. F. (1953). Reprinted with the permission of Macmillan Publishing Company from *Science and Human Behavior*, pp. 402–407, by B. F. Skinner. Copyright © 1953 by Macmillan Publishing Company, renewed 1981 by B. F. Skinner.

behavior more probable, educational reinforcement simply makes special forms more probable under special circumstances. In preparing the individual for situations which have not as yet arisen, discriminative operants are brought under the control of stimuli which will probably occur in these situations. Eventually, noneducational consequences determine whether the individual will continue to behave in the same fashion. Education would be pointless if other consequences were not eventually forthcoming, since the behavior of the controllee at the moment when he is being educated is of no particular importance to any one.

Educational Agencies and Their Techniques of Control. The immediate family functions as an educational agency in teaching the child to walk, to talk, to play, to eat in a given way, to dress himself, and so on. It uses the primary reinforcers available to the family: food, drink, and warmth, and such conditioned reinforcers as attention, approval, and affection. The family sometimes engages in education for obvious reasons—for example, because the child is converted into a useful member. The "pride" which a parent takes in the achievements of his children does not provide an explanation, since the term simply describes the fact that the achievement of a child is reinforcing. This fact appears to depend upon the culture. The individual continues to receive many forms of casual instruction from members of the group outside his family, where the variables available to the group are similar to those in ethical control. . . . Certain forms of behavior are classified as good or right and

others as bad or wrong and are reinforced accordingly. It is not always clear why this is done, however. An extension of ethical control to education may, like family pride, have special advantages for the group, in which case it can be explained only through an analysis of cultural practices. . . .

The artisan teaches an apprentice because in so doing he acquires a useful helper, and industries teach those who work for them for a similar reason. The reinforcers are usually economic. When a government engages in military training to improve the efficiency of its armed forces, the techniques are usually based upon punishment or the threat of punishment. When religious agencies turn to education to supplement other techniques, they also use the variables peculiarly under their control. The educational agency, then, is not distinguished by the nature of its variables but in the use to which they are put. There is a difference between the use of economic power to induce an apprentice to work and to induce him to acquire effective forms of behavior, between the use of the threat of punishment to induce a soldier to fight and to induce him to fight effectively, and between the use of the power peculiarly available to the religious agency to reinforce pious behavior and to teach a catechism.

The Educational Institution. A more explicit educational agency requires special treatment. Education is a profession, the members of which engage in education primarily because of economic reinforcement. As in many other professions, reinforcements supplied by the ethical group are also often important: teaching is not only a way of earning a living, it is "a good thing to do." In explaining the presence of educational institutions in a given community, then, we have to explain the behavior of those who pay for or approve those who teach. What is received by them in return?

The private tutor extends family education, and the family pays for his services for the same reason it educates its children directly, The private school is a collaborative effort of the same sort. Religious or trade schools are similar extensions of the activities of other agencies. In explaining the public education, certain immediate benefits to the group as a whole may be pointed out. The lower grades of the public schools take over the educational function of the family, supervise the children during part of the day, generate behavior which is useful to the family and community and which permits the family to escape censure. Comparable results from the education of older children are not always clear, and this fact raises a practical as well as a theoretical difficulty. The explicit educational agency is not found in every culture, and the extent to which a given group supports it may vary widely from time to time. When those who supply the ultimate power, economic or otherwise, do not receive sufficient reinforcement for doing so, they withdraw their support. Yet educators seldom attempt to increase the return benefits or to make them more effective as reinforcers.

Aside from any immediate return we have to note the possible long-term effect of education. Like family pride or education by members of the group, the explicit educational institution may be explained by a different sort of consequence to the group. . . .

The reinforcers used by established educational institutions are familiar: they consist of good grades, promotions, Phi Beta Kappa keys, diplomas, degrees, and medals, all of which are associated with the generalized reinforcer of approval. The spelling bee is a familiar device which makes approval or other social reinforcers explicitly contingent upon scholastic behavior. The same technique is represented by modern quiz programs in which "knowledge is reinforced for its own sake." A certain exchange value is evident when the recently educated individual is offered a job or is automatically admitted to membership in certain controlling groups. The educational agency usually wields no economic power itself, however, except for prizes, fellowships, and scholarships. Some reinforcers may be available in the form of privileges. The institution may also have the support of the family which makes primary or conditioned reinforcers contingent upon a level of scholastic achievement—for example, by granting a special allowance to the student who maintains a certain average. During World War II some military education was taken over by educational institutions, and a new and important reinforcer then became available to the teacher in the form of military advancement.

The venerable place of punishment in educational control is represented by the birch rod and the cane, as well as by condoning of certain forms of disciplinary violence—for example, hazings. Extreme forms of physical punishment have now been generally abandoned, but we have noted the general rule that when one aversive consequence is dropped, another is often created to take its place. Just as wages paid on a fixed-interval schedule may eventually be used to supply aversive stimulation in the form of a threat of dismissal, so the teacher of small children who does not spank may nevertheless threaten to withdraw approval or affection in a form of aversive control. In the same way, the positive reinforcers available to schools and colleges are often used as the basis for conditioned aversive stimulation in the form of a threat of failure or dismissal.

By-products of control through punishment have always been conspicuous features of educational institutions. Hell-raisings, riots, hazings, and truancy are forms of counter aggression or escape. . . . Somewhat more neurotic by-products are common. The advantages to be gained in turning to other techniques of control are therefore obvious. But one mode of control cannot be given up until something else is ready to take its place, and there is evidence that the educational institution at the moment lacks adequate control. Not only has the educator relinquished the birch rod; he can no longer borrow discipline from family practices based on aversive control. As more and more people are educated, the honorific reinforcements of education are weakened; fewer special advantages are not contingent upon education. With increasing social security the economic consequences of an education are also less important; relatively fewer students are out to "make good" in amassing wealth or at least in escaping the threat of a destitute old age.

Educational institutions have, therefore, turned to alternative methods of control. The teacher, often unwillingly, uses the sources of power available to him in personal control to make himself or his teaching interesting; in other words, he becomes an entertainer. Textbooks are supplied with pictures and diagrams which resemble expositions of the subject matter in magazines or the press, and lectures are supplemented with demonstrations and "visual aids." Especially favorable circumstances for the execution of the behavior to be controlled by the educational institution are arranged: libraries are designed to make books more readily accessible, laboratories are expanded and improved, facilities are provided for field trips and periods of study in especially favorable locations. Subjects which are not easily adapted to these techniques are often minimized or discarded.

The term "progressive education" roughly describes a concerted effort to find substitutes for the spurious reinforcements of educational control. Consequences of the sort which will eventually govern the behavior of the student are brought into the educational situation. Under the traditional system the student who is reinforced for speaking French correctly by an A is eventfully reinforced, if at all, when he enjoys books written in French or communicates effectively in a French-speaking community. In progressive education, these "natural" or "functional" reinforcements are employed by the educational agency as soon as possible. Similarly, the student who is studying science is reinforced as soon as possible by his increasing competence in dealing with nature. By permitting a wider choice of what is to be studied, the probability is increased that scholastic behavior will receive such noneducational reinforcement at an early date. It has perhaps always been characteristic of good education to introduce "real" consequences, but progressive education has made an effort to do this as often and as soon as possible. A common objection has been that certain fields of study are thus unduly emphasized at the expense of others in which disciplinary training with merely education reinforcement cannot be avoided.

The continued reinforcers of the educational agency may be made more effective by pointing up the connection with natural contingencies to be encountered later. By informing the student of the advantages to be gained from education, education itself may be given reinforcing value. Many educational institutions have therefore turned to counseling and various forms of therapy as auxiliary techniques.

2.

B. F. SKINNER

The teacher doesn't have too many reinforcers at her disposal. That's one of the tragedies of education. There are a number of contrived reinforcers, such as prizes or tokens, pats on the back, approval, attention, and that sort of thing. But the important thing is that the child sees that he is progressing toward some ultimately desirable state, even if only the state of getting through school. Any little indication of progress, such as being right so that you can move on to the next step, is enough. I don't define a reinforcer in any biological sense. Some reinforcers have an obvious relevance to biological conditions; some don't. The human organism is reinforced simply by being effective. It is reinforcing to the student to be right, but in a contemporary classroom he is seldom right and therefore receives little reinforcement. Possibly, for this type of student, something a little more important than being right must be brought into play, but there are other things which can be used. . . .

. . . I think educators have done a very good job, given the resources at their disposal and the attitudes of the public toward them. But they can do much more. Teaching machines are only one aspect of a whole technology of teaching . . . Devices of many kinds will certainly be used and for very good reasons. One is to get away

<hr>

[2] Evans, Richard I. (1968). *B. F. Skinner: The Man and His Ideas.* New York: E. P. Dutton and Co., Inc., pp. 61–62, 70–71.

from aversive control. There is an article in this morning's paper saying that teachers in New York are no longer going to be allowed to assign homework as punishment. Schoolwork is considered *punishment.* You'll find teachers who excuse students from schoolwork as a *reward.* That's just the wrong way around. Additional homework ought to be rewarding, and if you want to punish someone, you should deprive him of the opportunity to study. But this is as unthinkable as using positive reinforcement to control traffic violations. We are committed to a punitive system, and we are experiencing all the byproducts of it: dropouts, truants, vandalism, and so on. But to effect a change you've got to arrange much better schedules of reinforcement than the teacher can possibly arrange when working with a large group of students. If you had an individual tutor for each student, it's conceivable that standard methods could be appropriately employed. But

you don't, and so you have to work out other ways in which the student will be appropriately reinforced to shape his behavior progressively toward the goals of education. A technology of teaching should emphasize individual instruction. Educators pay lip service to that; they advocate individual instruction. But their practices are as regimented as they can possibly be. A state board specifies exactly what the student should be studying all the way through the system. Nothing could be more regimented than that, but we know they aren't going to learn what is specified and so we're not worried. We now solve the problem of regimentation by teaching badly. With proper instrumentation, and with a system based on proper teaching methods, it should be possible to allow the individual to follow his own bent and to work at his own speed. The good student could move quickly, and the slow student, who is not necessarily unintelligent, could work at his own effective pace.

3.

B. F. SKINNER

A Solution. We could solve our major problems in education if students learned more during each day in

school. That does not mean a longer day or year or more homework. It simply means using time more efficiently. Such a solution is not considered in any of the reports I have mentioned—whether from the National Institute of Education, the American Association for the Advancement of Science, the National Research

[3] B. F. Skinner. "The Shame of American Education," *The American Psychologist* 39:9 (September 1984), pp. 950–952. Copyright © 1984 by the American Psychological Association. Reprinted by permission.

Council, or the National Academies of Sciences and Engineering. Nevertheless, it is within easy reach. Here is all that needs to be done.

1. Be clear about what is to be taught. When I once explained to a group of grade-school teachers how I would teach children to spell words, one of them said, "Yes, but can you teach spelling?" For him, students spelled words correctly not because they had learned to do so but because they had acquired a special ability. When I told a physicist colleague about the Roanoke experiment in teaching algebra, he said, "Yes, but did they learn algebra?" For him, algebra was more than solving certain kinds of problems; it was a mental faculty. The more words you learn to spell, the easier it is to spell new words, and the more problems you solve in algebra the easier it is to solve new problems. What eventually emerges is often intuition. We do not know what it is, but we can certainly say that no teacher has ever taught it directly, nor has any student ever displayed it without first learning to do the kinds of things it supposedly replaces.

2. Teach first things first. It is tempting to move too quickly to final products. I once asked a leader of the "new math" what he wanted students to be able to do. He was rather puzzled and then said, "I suppose I just want them to be able to follow a logical line of reasoning." That does not tell a teacher where to start or, indeed, how to proceed at any point. I once asked a colleague what he wanted his students to do as a result of having taken his introductory course in physics. "Well," he said, "I guess I've never thought about it that way." I'm afraid he spoke for most of the profession.

Among the ultimate but useless goals of education is "excellence." A candidate for president recently said that he would let local communities decide what that meant. "I am not going to try to define excellence for them," he said, and wisely so. Another useless ultimate goal is "creativity." It is said that students should do more than what they have been taught to do. They should be creative. But does it help to say that they must acquire creativity? More than 300 years ago, Molière wrote a famous line: "I am asked by the learned doctors for the cause and reason why opium puts one to sleep, to which I reply that there is in it a soporific virtue, the nature of which is to lull the senses." Several years ago an article in *Science* pointed out that 90 percent of scientific innovations were accomplished by fewer than 10 percent of scientists. The explanation, it was said, was that only a few scientists possess creativity. Molière audiences laughed. Eventually some students behave in creative ways, but they must have something to be creative with and that must be taught first. Then they can be taught to multiply the variations that give rise to new and interesting forms of behavior. (Creativity, incidentally, is often said to be beyond a science of behavior, and it *would* be if that science were a matter of stimulus and response. By emphasizing the selective action of consequences, however, the experimental analysis of behavior deals with the creation of behavior precisely as Darwin dealt with the creation of species.)

3. Stop making all students advance at essentially the same rate. The phalanx was a great military invention, but it has long been out of date, and it should be out of date in American schools. Students are still expected to move from kindergarten through high school in twelve years, and we all know what is wrong: Those who could move faster are held back, and those who need more time fall farther and farther behind. We could double the efficiency of education with one change alone—by letting each student move at his or her own place. (I wish I could blame this costly mistake on developmental psychology, because it is such a beautiful example of its major principle, but the timing is out of joint.)

No teacher can teach a class of thirty or forty students and allow each to progress at an optimal speed. Tracking is too feeble a remedy. We must turn to individual instruments for part of the school curriculum. The report of the convocation held by the National Academies of Sciences and Engineering refers to "new technologies" that can be used to extend the educational process, to supplement the teacher's role in new and imaginative ways," but that is scarcely an enthusiastic endorsement of technology. Thirty years ago educational television was promising, but the promise has not been kept. The report alludes to "computer-aided instruction" but calls it the latest "rage of education" and insists that "the primary use of the computer is for drill." (Properly programmed instruction is *never* drill if that means going over material again and again until it is learned.) The report also contains a timid allusion to "low-cost teaching stations that

can be controlled by the learner," but evidently these stations are merely to give the student access to video material rather then to programs.

4. Program the subject matter. The heart of the teaching machine, call it what you will, is the programming of instruction—an advance not mentioned in any of the reports I have cited. Standard texts are designed to be read by the students, who then discuss what they say with a teacher or take a test to see how much has been learned. Material prepared for individual study is different. It first induces students to say or do the things they are to learn to say or do. Their behavior is thus "primed" in the sense of being brought out for the first time. Until the behavior has acquired more strength, it may need to be prompted. Primes and prompts must then be carefully "vanished" until the behavior occurs without help. At that point the reinforcing consequences of being right are more effective in building and sustaining an enduring repertoire.

Working through a program is really a process of discovery, but not in the sense in which that word is currently used in education. We discover many things in the world around us, and that is usually better than being told about them, but as individuals, we can discover only a very small part of the world. Mathematics has been discovered very slowly and painfully over thousands of years. Students discover it as they go through a program, but not in the sense of doing something for the first time in history. Trying to teach mathematics or science as if the students themselves were discovering things for the first time is not an efficient way of teaching the very skills with which, in the long run, a student may, with luck, actually make a genuine discovery.

When students move through well-constructed programs at their own pace, the so-called problem of motivation is automatically solved. For thousands of years students have studied to avoid the consequences of not studying. Punitive sanctions still survive, disguised in various ways, but the world is changing, and they are no longer easily imposed. The great mistake of progressive education was to try to replace them with natural curiosity. Teachers were to bring the real world into the classroom to arouse the students' interest. The inevitable result was a neglect of subjects in which children were seldom naturally interested—in particular, the so-called basics. One solution is to make some of the natural reinforcers—goods or privileges—artificially contingent upon basic behavior, as in a token economy. Such contingencies can be justified if they correct a lethargic or disordered classroom, but there should be no lethargy or disorder. It is characteristic of the human species that successful action is automatically reinforced. The fascination of video games is adequate proof. What would industrialists not give to see their workers as absorbed in their work as young people in a video arcade? What would teachers not give to see their students applying themselves with the same eagerness? (For that matter, what would any of us not give to see ourselves as much in love with our work?) But there is no mystery; it is all a matter of the scheduling of reinforcements.

A good program of instruction guarantees a great deal of successful action.

Students do not need to have a natural interest in what they are doing, and subject matters do not need to be dressed up to attract attention. No one really cares whether Pac-Man gobbles up all those little spots on the screen. As soon as the screen is cleared, the player covers it again with little spots to be gobbled up. What is reinforcing is successful play, and in a well-designed instructional program, students gobble up their assignments. I saw them doing that when I visited the project in Roanoke. The director, Allen Calvin, and I entered a room in which thirty or forty eighth-grade students were at their desks using rather crude teaching machines. When I said I was surprised that they paid no attention to us, Calvin proposed a better demonstration. He went up to the teacher's platform, jumped in the air, and came down with a loud bang. Not a single student looked up. Students do not have to be made to study. Reinforcement is enough, and good programming provides it.

The Teacher. Individually programmed instruction has much to offer teachers and makes very few demands upon them. Paraprofessionals may take over some of their chores. That is not a reflection on teachers or a threat to their profession. There is much that only teachers can do, and they can do it as soon as they have been freed of unnecessary tasks.

Some things they can do are talk to and listen to students and read what students write. . . .

If given a chance, teachers can also be interesting and sympathetic companions. It is a difficult assignment in a classroom in which order is maintained by punitive sanctions. the word *discipline* has come a long way from its association with *disciple* as one who understands.

Success and progress are the very stuff on which programmed instruction feeds. They should also be the stuff that makes teaching worthwhile as a profession. Just as students must not only learn but know that they are learning, so teachers must not only teach but know that they are teaching. Burnout is usually regarded as the result of abusive treatment by students, but it can be as much the results of looking back upon a day in the classroom and wondering what one has accomplished.

SECTION D

Design of a Culture

COMMENTARY

In the spring of 1968 my son Tom announced that he was going to spend his spring break at Twin Oaks in Louisa, Virginia. Twin Oaks was, and is, an experimental community designed to apply the principles of operant conditioning to a microcosmic society as set forth in Skinner's book, *Walden II*, a fictional account of the design of an ideal, or utopian, community. Frightened by the notion of communes, we made every effort to dissuade him from what we perceived as a reckless venture. Tom, however, was not to be deterred. Leaving us a long note, the essence being "I'm old enough to make my own decisions, and this is something I'm going to do," Tom left early one morning with two friends for Twin Oaks. A week later, he returned from his visit without the deleterious effects we had feared and without any further interest in Twin Oaks.

Perhaps the ultimate expression and application of Skinner's work on operant conditioning lies in the design, management, and control of society. Cultural or environmental engineering suggests that by applying the scientifically established behavioral principles to a larger society, a utopian ideal could be established. Having rejected the idea of autonomous man, Skinner's primary interest was in extending his operant conditioning principles to the design and control of the environment to create and shape behavior for the benefit of both the individual and society. Skinner believed that the greatest deterrent to the development of a utopian society was to be found in the deeply entrenched belief in autonomous man and in relying on such illusory concepts as freedom, dignity, and responsibility as guiding forces in the evolution of culture. These fictions, Skinner believed,

190

only interfered with any serious attempt to establish a society based on benevolent controls and carefully selected environmental reinforcements. For Skinner, therefore, culture represented little more than a set of reinforcement contingencies. He believed, however, that if these controls were not based on a scientific analysis of behavior, they were destined to be haphazard, hit or miss, and in the long run ineffective.

1.

B. F. SKINNER

The interpretation of the complex world of human affairs in terms of an experimental analysis is no doubt often oversimplified. Claims have been exaggerated and limitations neglected. But the really great oversimplification is the traditional appeal to states of mind, feelings, and other aspects of the autonomous man which a behavioral analysis is replacing. The ease with which mentalistic explanations can be invented on the spot is perhaps the best gauge of how little attention we should pay to them. And the same may be said for traditional practices. The technology which has emerged from an experimental analysis should be evaluated only in comparison with what is done in other ways. What, after all, have we to show for nonscientific or prescientific good judgment, or common sense, or the insights gained through personal experience? It is science or nothing, and the only solution to simplification is to learn how to deal with complexities.

A science of behavior is not yet ready to solve all our problems, but it is a science in progress, and its ultimate adequacy cannot now be judged. When critics assert that it cannot account for this or that aspect of human behavior, they usually imply that it will never be able to do so, but the analysis continues to develop and is in fact much further advanced than its critics usually realize.

The important thing is not so much to know how to solve a problem as to know how to look for a solution. The scientists who approached President Roosevelt with a proposal to build a bomb so powerful that it could end the Second World War within a few days could not say that they knew how to build it. All they could say was that they knew how to go about finding out. The behavioral problems to be solved in the world today are no doubt more complex than the practical use of nuclear fission, and the basic science by no means as far advanced, but we know where to start looking for solutions.

A proposal to design a culture with the help of a scientific analysis often leads to Cassandran prophecies of disaster. The culture will not work as planned, and unforeseen consequences may be catastrophic. Proof is seldom offered, possibly because history seems to be on the side of failure: many plans have gone wrong, and possibly just because they were planned. The threat in a designed culture, said Mr Krutch, is that the unplanned "may never erupt again." But it is hard to justify the trust which is placed in accident. It is true that accidents have been responsible for almost everything that men have achieved to date, and they will no doubt continue to contribute to human accomplishments, but there is no virtue in an accident as such. The unplanned also goes wrong. The idiosyncrasies of a jealous ruler who regards any disturbance as an offense against him may have an accidental survival value if law and order are maintained, but the military strategies of a paranoid leader are of the same provenance and may have an entirely different effect. The industry which arises in the unrestrained pursuit of happiness may have an accidental survival value when war material is suddenly needed, but it may also exhaust natural resources and pollute the environment.

If a planned culture necessarily meant uniformity or regimentation, it might indeed work against further evolution. If men were very much alike, they would be less likely to hit upon or design new practices, and a culture which made people as much alike as possible might slip into a standard pattern from which there would be no escape. That would be bad design, but if we are looking for variety, we should not fall back upon accident. Many accidental cultures have been marked by uniformity and regimentation. The exigencies of administration in governmental, religious, and economic systems breed uniformity, because it simplifies the problem of control. Traditional educational establishments specify what the student is to learn at what age and administer tests to make sure that the specifications are met. The codes of governments and religions are usually quite explicit and allow little room for diversity or change. The only hope is *planned* diversification, in which the importance of variety is recognized. The breeding of plants and animals moves toward uniformity when uniformity is important (as in simplifying agriculture or animal husbandry), but it also requires planned diversity.

Planning does not prevent useful accidents. For many thousands of years people used fibers (such as cotton, wool, or silk) from sources which were accidental in the sense that they were the products of contingencies of survival not closely related to the contingencies which made them useful to men. Synthetic fibers, on the other hand, are explicitly designed; their usefulness is taken into account. But the production of synthetic fibers does not make the evolution of a new kind of cotton, wool, or silk any less likely. Accidents still occur, and indeed, are furthered by those investigating new possibilities. It might be said that science maximizes accidents. The physicist does not confine himself to the temperatures which occur accidentally in the world at large, he produces a continuous series of temperatures over a very wide range. The behavioral scientist does not confine himself to the schedules of reinforcement which happen to occur in nature, he constructs a great variety of schedules, some of which might never arise by accident. There is no virtue in the accidental nature of an accident. A culture evolves as new practices appear and undergo selection, and we cannot wait for them to turn up by chance.

Another kind of opposition to a new cultural design can be put this way: "I wouldn't like it," or in translation, "The culture would be aversive and would not reinforce me in the manner to which I am accustomed." The word reform is in bad odor, for it is usually associated with the destruction of reinforcers—"the Puritans have cut down the maypoles and the hobbyhorse is forgot"—but the design of a new culture is necessarily a kind of reform, and it almost necessarily means a change of reinforcers. To eliminate a threat, for example, is to eliminate the thrill of escape; in a better world no one will "pluck this flower, safely . . . out of this nettle, danger." The reinforcing value of rest, relaxation, and leisure is necessarily weakened as labor is made less compulsive. A world in which there is no need for moral struggle will offer none of the reinforcement of a successful outcome. No convert to a religion will enjoy Cardinal Newman's release from "the stress of a great anxiety." Art and literature will no longer be based on such contingencies. We shall not only have no reason to admire people who endure suffering, face danger, or struggle to be good, it is possible that we shall have

little interest in pictures or books about them. The art and literature of a new culture will be about other things. . . .

There are, of course, good reasons why the control of human behavior is resisted. The commonest techniques are aversive, and some sort of counter-control is to be expected. The controllee may move out of range (the controller will work to keep him from doing so), or he may attack, and ways of doing so have emerged as important steps in the evolution of cultures. Thus, members of a group establish the principle that it is wrong to use force and punish those who do so with any available means. Governments codify the principle and call the use of force illegal, and religions call it sinful, and both arrange contingencies to suppress it. When controllers then turn to methods which are nonaversive but have deferred aversive consequences, additional principles emerge. The group calls it wrong to control through deception, for example, and governmental and religious sanctions follow.

We have seen that the literatures of freedom and dignity have extended these countercontrolling measures in an effort to suppress all controlling practices even when they have no aversive consequences or have offsetting reinforcing consequences. The designer of a culture comes under fire because explicit design implies control (if only the control exerted by the designer). The issue is often formulated by asking: Who is to control? And the question is usually raised as if the answer were necessarily threatening. To prevent the misuse of controlling power, however, we must look not at the controller himself but at the contingencies under which he engages in control.

We are misled by differences in the conspicuousness of controlling measures. The Egyptian slave, cutting stone in a quarry for a pyramid, worked under the supervision of a soldier with a whip, who was paid to wield the whip by a paymaster, who was paid in turn by a Pharaoh, who had been convinced of the necessity of an inviolable tomb by priests, who argued to this effect because of the sacerdotal privileges and power which then came to them, and so on. A whip is a more obvious instrument of control than wages, and wages are more conspicuous than sacerdotal privileges, and privileges are more obvious than the prospect of an affluent future life. There are related differences in the results. The slave will escape if he can, the soldier or paymaster will resign or strike if the economic contingencies are too weak, the Pharaoh will dismiss his priests and start a new religion if his treasury is unduly strained, and the priests will shift their support to a rival. We are likely to single out the conspicuous examples of control, because in their abruptness and clarity of effect, they seem to start something, but it is a great mistake to ignore the inconspicuous forms.

The relation between the controller and the controlled is reciprocal. The scientist in the laboratory, studying the behavior of a pigeon, designs contingencies and observes their effects. His apparatus exerts a conspicuous control on the pigeon, but we must not overlook the control exerted by the pigeon. The behavior of the pigeon has determined the design of the apparatus and the procedures in which it is used. Some such reciprocal control is characteristic of all science. As Francis Bacon put it, nature to be commanded must be obeyed. The scientist who designs a cyclotron is under the control of the particles he is studying. The behavior with which a parent controls his child, either aversively or through positive reinforcement, is shaped and maintained by the child's responses. A psychotherapist changes the behavior of his patient in ways which have been shaped and maintained by his success in changing that behavior. A government or religion prescribes and imposes sanctions selected by their effectiveness in controlling citizen or communicant. An employer induces his employees to work industriously and carefully with wage systems determined by their effects on behavior. The classroom practices of the teacher are shaped and maintained by the effects on his students. In a very real sense, then, the slave controls the slave driver, the child the parent, the patient the therapist, the citizen the government, the communicant the priest, the employee the employer, and the student the teacher. . . .

The archetypal pattern of control for the good of the controllee is the benevolent dictator, but it is no explanation to say that he acts benevolently because he feels benevolent, and we naturally remain suspicious until we can point to contingencies which generate benevolent behavior. Feelings of benevolence or compassion may accompany that behavior, but they may also arise from irrelevant conditions. They are therefore no guarantees that a controller will necessarily control well with respect to either himself or others because he feels compassionate. It is said that

Ramakrishna, walking with a wealthy friend, was shocked by the poverty of some villagers. He exclaimed to his friend, "Give these people one piece of cloth and one good meal each, and some oil for their heads." When his friend at first refused, Ramakrishna shed tears. "You wretch," he cried, ". . . I'm staying with these people. They have no one to care for them. I won't leave them." We note that Ramakrishna was concerned not with the spiritual condition of the villagers but with clothing, food, and protection against the sun. But his feelings were not a by-product of effective action; with all the power of his samadhi he had nothing to offer but compassion. Although cultures are improved by people whose wisdom and compassion may supply clues to what they do or will do, the ultimate improvement comes from the environment which makes them wise and compassionate.

The great problem is to arrange effective countercontrol and hence to bring some important consequences to bear on the behavior of the controller. Some classical examples of a lack of balance between control and countercontrol arise when control is delegated and countercontrol then becomes ineffective. Hospitals for psychotics and homes for retardates, orphans, and old people are noted for weak countercontrol, because those who are concerned for the welfare of such people often do not know what is happening. Prisons offer little opportunity for countercontrol, as the commonest controlling measures indicate. Control and countercontrol tend to become dislocated when control is taken over by organized agencies. Informal contingencies are subject to quick adjustments as their effects change, but the contingencies which organizations leave to specialists may be untouched by many of the consequences. Those who pay for education, for example, may lose touch with what is taught and with the methods used. The teacher is subject only to the countercontrol exerted by the student. As a result, a school may become wholly autocratic or wholly anarchistic, and what is taught may go out of date as the world changes or be reduced to the things students will consent to study. There is a similar problem in jurisprudence when laws continue to be enforced which are no longer appropriate to the practices of the community. Rules never generate behavior exactly appropriate to the contingencies from which they are derived, and the discrepancy grows worse if the contingencies change while the rules remain inviolate. Similarly, the values imposed on goods by economic enterprises may lose their correspondence with the reinforcing effects of the goods, as the latter change. In short, an organized agency which is insensitive to the consequences of its practices is not subject to important kinds of countercontrol.

Self-government often seems to solve the problem by identifying the controller with the controlled. The principle of making the controller a member of the group he controls should apply to the designer of a culture. A person who designs a piece of equipment for his own use presumably takes the interests of the user into account, and the person who designs a social environment in which is to live will presumably do the same. He will select good or values which are important to him and arrange the kind of contingencies to which he can adapt. In a democracy the controller is found among the controlled, although he behaves in different ways in the two roles. We shall see later that there is a sense in which a culture controls itself, as a person controls himself, but the process calls for careful analysis. . . .

The intentional design of a culture and the control of human behavior it implies are essential if the human species is to continue to develop. Neither biological nor cultural evolution is any guarantee that we are inevitably moving toward a better world. Darwin concluded the *Origin of Species* with a famous sentence: "And as natural selection works solely by and for the good of each being, all corporeal and mental environments will tend to progress towards perfection." And Herbert Spencer argued that "the ultimate development of the ideal man is logically certain" (though Medawar has pointed out that Spencer changed his mind when thermodynamics suggested a different kind of terminus in the concept of entropy). Tennyson shared the eschatological optimism of his day in pointing to that "one far off divine event toward which the whole creation moves." But extinct species and extinct cultures testify to the possibility of miscarriage.

Survival value changes as conditions change. For example, a strong susceptibility to reinforcement by certain kinds of foods, sexual contact, and aggressive damage was once extremely important. When a person spent a good part of each day in searching for food, it was important that he quickly learn where to find it or how to catch it, but with the advent of agriculture and animal husbandry

and ways of storing food, the advantage was lost, and the capacity to be reinforced by food now leads to overeating and illness. When famine and pestilence frequently decimated the population, it was important that men should breed at every opportunity, but with improved sanitation, medicine, and agriculture, the susceptibility to sexual reinforcement now means overpopulation. At a time when a person had to defend himself against predators, including other people, it was important that any sign of damage to a predator should reinforce the behavior having that effect, but with the evolution of organized society the susceptibility to that kind of reinforcement has become less important and may now interfere with more useful social relations. It is one of the functions of a culture to correct for these innate dispositions through the design of techniques of control, and particularly of self-control, which moderate the effects of reinforcement.

Even under stable conditions a species may acquire nonadaptive or maladaptive features. The process of operant conditioning itself supplies an example. A quick response to reinforcement must have had survival value, and many species have reached the point at which a single reinforcement has a substantial effect. But the more rapidly an organism learns, the more vulnerable it is to adventitious contingencies. The accidental appearance of a reinforcer strengthens any behavior in progress and brings it under the control of current stimuli. We call the result superstitious. So far as we know, any species capable of learning from a few reinforcements is subject to superstition, and the consequences are often disastrous. A culture corrects for this defect when it devises statistical procedures which offset the effects of adventitious contingencies and bring behavior under the control of only those consequences which are functionally related to it.

What is needed is more "intentional" control, not less, and this is an important engineering problem. The good of a culture cannot function as the source of genuine reinforcers for the individual, and the reinforcers contrived by cultures to induce their members to work for their survival are often in conflict with personal reinforcers. The number of people explicitly engaged in improving the design of automobiles, for example, must greatly exceed the number of those concerned with improving life in city ghettos. It is not that the automobile is more important than a way of life, but rather that the economic contingencies which induce people to improve automobiles are very powerful. They arise from the personal reinforcers of those who manufacture automobiles. No reinforcers of comparable strength encourage the engineering of the pure survival of a culture. The technology of the automobile industry is also, of course, much further advanced than a technology of behavior. These facts simply underline the importance of the threat posed by the literatures of freedom and dignity.

2.

B. F. SKINNER

The Evolution of a Culture. The social environment I have been referring to is usually called a culture, though a culture is often defined in other ways—as a set of customs or manners, as a system of values and ideas, as a network of communication, and so on. As a set of contingencies of reinforcement maintained by a group, possibly formulated in rules or laws, it has a clear-cut physical status, a continuing existence beyond the lives of members of the group, a changing pattern as practices are added, discarded, or modified, and, above all, power. A culture so defined *controls* the behavior of the members of the group that practices it.

It is not a monolithic thing, and we have no reason to explain it by appealing to a group mind, idea, or will. If there are indeed "seventy-three elements of culture common to every human society still existing or known to history," then there must be seventy-three practices or kinds of practices in every set of contingencies called a culture, each of which must be explained

────────
[2] Skinner, B. F. (1976). From *About Behaviorism*, pp. pp. 223–227, by B. F. Skinner. Copyright © 1974 by B. F. Skinner. Reprinted by permission of Alfred A. Knopf, Inc.

in terms of conditions prevailing before the culture emerged as such. Why do people develop a language? Why do they practice some kind of marriage? Why do they maintain moral practices and formulate them in codes? Some answers to questions of this sort are to be found in the biological characteristics of the species, others in "universal features" of the environments in which people live.

The important thing about a culture so defined is that it evolves. A practice arises as a mutation, it affects the chances that the group will solve its problems, and if the group survives, the practice survives with it. It has been selected by its contribution to the effectiveness of those who practice it. Here is another example of that subtle process called selection, and it has the same familiar features. Mutations may be random. A culture need not have been designed, and its evolution does not show a purpose.

The practices which compose a culture are a mixed bag, and some parts may be inconsistent with others or in open conflict. Our own culture is sometimes called sick, *and in a sick society, man will lack a sense of identity and feelings of competence; he will see the suspension of his own thought structures . . . to enter into a more fruitful relationship with those around him as betrayal; he will approach the world of human interaction with a sense of real despair; and only when he has been through that despair and learnt to know himself will he attain as much of what is self-fulfilling as the human condition allows.*

In translation: a sick society is a set of contingencies which generates disparate or conflicting behaviors suggesting more than one self, which does not generate the strong behavior with which a feeling of competence is associated, which fails to generate successful social behavior and hence leads a person to call the behavior of others betrayal, and which, supplying only infrequent reinforcement, generates the condition felt as despair. Another writer has said that our culture is "in convulsions owing to its state of value contradiction, its incorporation of opposing and conflicting values," but we may say that the values, here as elsewhere, refer to reinforcers, and that it is the contingencies of which they are a part which are opposing and conflicting.

The society will be "cured" if it can be changed in such a way that a person is generously and consistently reinforced and therefore "fulfills himself" by acquiring and exhibiting the most successful behavior of which he is capable. Better ways of teaching (introduced for whatever reason, possibly only because of immediate consequences for teacher or student) will make a more effective use of the human genetic endowment. Better incentive conditions (introduced for whatever reasons, possibly only in the interests of management or labor) mean more and better goods and more enjoyable working conditions. Better ways of governing (introduced for whatever reason, possibly merely in the interests of governed or governor) mean less time wasted in personal defense and more time for other things. More interesting forms of art, music, and literature (created for whatever reason, possibly simply for the immediate reinforcement of those creating or enjoying them) mean fewer defections to other ways of life.

In a well-known passage in *The Descent of Man,* Darwin wrote:

Obscure as is the problem of the advance of civilization, we can at least see that the nation which produced, during a lengthened period, the greatest number of highly intellectual, energetic, brave, patriotic, and benevolent men, would generally prevail over less favored nations.

The point survives when the appeal to character is corrected by speaking of "a nation which maintains a social environment in which its citizens behave in ways called intelligent, energetic, brave, patriotic, and benevolent." Darwin was speaking of the survival value of a culture.

There are remarkable similarities in natural selection, operant conditioning, and the evolution of social environments. Not only do all three dispense with a prior creative design and a prior purpose, they invoke the notion of survival as a value. What is good for the species is what makes for its survival. What is good for the individual is what promotes his well-being. What is good for a culture is what permits it to solve its problems. There are, as we have seen, other kinds of values, but they eventually take second place to survival.

The notion of evolution is misleading—and it misled both Herbert Spencer and Darwin—when it suggests that the good represented by survival will naturally work itself out. Things go wrong under all three contingencies of selection, and they may need to be put right by explicit design. Breeding practices have long represented a kind of intervention in the evolution of the species, and geneticists are now talking about changing genetic codes. The behavior of the individual is easily changed by designing new contingencies of reinforcement. New cultural practices are explicitly designed in such fields as education, psychotherapy, penology, and economic incentives.

The design of human behavior implies, of course, control, and possibly the question most often asked of the behaviorist is this: Who is to control? The question represents the age-old mistake of looking to the individual rather than to the world in which he lives. It will not be a benevolent dictator, a compassionate therapist, a devoted teacher, or a public-spirited industrialist who will design a way of life in the interests of everyone. We must look instead at the conditions under which people govern, give help, teach, and arrange incentive systems in particular ways. In other words, we must look to the culture as a social environment. Will a culture evolve in which no individual will be able to accumulate vast power and use it for his own aggrandizement in ways which are harmful to others? Will a culture evolve in which individuals are not so much concerned with their own actualization and fulfillment that they do not give serious attention to the future of the culture? These questions, and many others like them, are the questions to be asked rather than *who* will control and to what *end.* No one steps outside the causal stream. No one really intervenes. Mankind has slowly but erratically created environments in which people behave more effectively and no doubt enjoy the feelings which accompany successful behavior. It is a continuing process.

CHAPTER VII

The Social Learning Theory of Albert Bandura

BIOGRAPHICAL SKETCH

Albert Bandura was born in Canada on December 4, 1925, in a small town in northern Alberta. His parents were wheat farmers of Polish descent.

In 1949 Bandura received his B.A. from the University of British Columbia with a major in psychology. His undergraduate degree was followed by the M.A. and Ph.D. at the University of Iowa, which offered a highly recognized graduate program in learning theory. Bandura completed his Ph.D. at Iowa in 1952. In 1953, following a postdoctoral year of study at the Wichita (Kansas) Guidance Center, he took a position at Stanford University, where he has remained throughout his career. In 1974 he was awarded an endowed chair at Stanford, the David Starr Jordan Professor of Social Science in Psychology.

Although his early work focused on clinical psychology and psychotherapy, Bandura has become more widely known for his work on aggressive behavior and the role of modeling and observational learning in personality development and behavior. His early views on modeling and social learning were presented in an early publication, *Social Learning and Personality Development* (1963) with R. Walters. His most recent major contribution came in 1986 with the publication of *Social Foundations of Thought and Action: A Social Cognitive Theory*. Bandura has also published other books and many important articles.

In addition to being a prolific writer, Bandura has received many awards and recognitions for his pioneering research work in social learning theory and cognition. In 1972 he received a Guggenheim Fellowship and was awarded, the same year, the Distinguished Scientist Award by the Clinical

Division of the American Psychological Association. In 1974 he was recognized for his outstanding achievements by being elected president of the American Psychological Association. In 1977 he received the James McKeen Cattell Award. In 1980 Bandura was presented with the Distinguished Contribution Award by the International Society for Research on Aggression.

Bandura continues his active professional life as a researcher, writer, and teacher, while finding time to enrich his life through his interests in opera and hiking. Albert Bandura is married to Virginia Wanns, whom he met at the University of Iowa. They have two daughters.

Bandura has spent his entire career developing a social cognitive learning theory and applying it to personality development and behavior. Through his impressive record of research and scholarship, Bandura has established himself as the leading figure in this area. He has had a decided impact on most areas of psychology, but especially in the fields of clinical and developmental psychology.

Reciprocal Determinism:
The Triadic Model

COMMENTARY

Albert Bandura has played a leading role in the demise of the behaviorist tradition in American psychology. More than this, with his concept of reciprocal determinism, he has been instrumental in bringing about a certain reconciliation in psychology; a reconciliation between behaviorism and the "third force" humanistic psychology.

While Bandura's primary orientation is identified as being within the behaviorist tradition, his social-cognitive theories and research have, nevertheless, dramatically transformed the simplistic views of personality development presented by B. F. Skinner and other classical behaviorists. These one-dimensional views of determinism, stressing the importance of environmental reinforcement while rejecting the validity of internal variables in motivation and behavior, have been largely abandoned.

Bandura's model of reciprocal determinism recognizes the complexity of human personality and behavior. In addition to environmental and behavioral determinants, Bandura introduced a self-system which focuses attention on the importance of symbolic processes, the agency of self-efficacy, and the potential for self-reinforcement and self-regulation. His model of reciprocal determinism includes, therefore, the *interaction* and integration of three crucial variables in determining personality and behavior: *behavior, personal (internal) variables,* and *environmental events.* According to Bandura, neither behavior, personal variables, nor environmental forces alone is responsible for personality development. It is the *interaction* of these three causal forces and the individual's capacity to integrate them that is at the heart of Bandura's theory. Everything, therefore, even fortuitous happenings, enters the interlocking system of reciprocal determinism. All three of these interactional processes leading to self-directed behavior are centered on the carefully researched concepts of *observational learning* and *modeling*, which are also presented in this chapter. Although the environment continues to play a substantial role in Bandura's theory, there is a measure of both determinism *and* freedom in his conception of personality development.

1.

ALBERT BANDURA

One-Sided Determinism

Over the years the locus of the causes of human behavior has been debated vigorously in terms of dispositional and environmental determinants, which are often portrayed as operating in an unidirectional manner. Exponents of *environmental determinism* study and theorize about how behavior is controlled by situational influences. The view of unidirectional environmental determinism has been carried to its extreme in the more radical forms of behaviorism. In this one-sided determinism, acts are regulated by current external stimuli and the residuum of past environmental inputs. The environment thus reappears as an autonomous force that automatically shapes, orchestrates, and controls behavior. Whatever illusions are made to two-way processes, environmental rule

clearly emerges as the reigning metaphor in this view of reality.

Theorists favoring personal determinism seek the causes of human behavior in dispositional sources in the form of instincts, drives, traits, and other motivational forces within the individual. Existentialists, who stress the human capacity for conscious judgment and intentional action, contend that people determine what they become by their own free choices. In extreme formulations of cognitivism, thought supplants actuality in the explanation of human affect and action. The words of the Stoic philosopher Epictetus are widely quoted . . . as testimony for the power of thought over social reality: "Men are disturbed not by things but by the views which they take of them." . . .

One-sided Interactionism

Most contemporary theorists subscribe to some form of interactional model of causality that portrays

[1] Albert Bandura, *Social Foundations of Thought and Action: A Social Cognitive Theory,* © 1986, pp. 22–23. Reprinted by permission of Prentice Hall, Englewood Cliffs, New Jersey.

behavior as a product of personal and situational influences. . . .

In the unidirectional view of interaction, persons and situations are treated as independent entities that unite in unspecified ways to produce behavior. A basic problem with this conception is that personal and environmental factors do not function as independent determinants; rather, they determine each other. People create, alter, and destroy environments. The changes they produce in environmental conditions, in turn, affect their behavior and the nature of future life.

The partially bidirectional conception of interaction acknowledges that persons and situations affect each other. But it treats influences relating to behavior as flowing in only one direction—the person-situation interchange unidirectionally produces the behavior, but the behavior itself does not affect the ongoing transaction between the person and the situation. A major limitation of this conception is that, except for their social stimulus value, persons cannot affect the environment other than through their actions. Their actions take the dominant role in how people influence the situations which, in turn, will affect their thoughts, emotional reactions, and behavior. It is difficult to conceive a behavior as the off-spring of an intimate exchange between a behaviorless person and the environment. This would be analogous to an immaculate conception. Behavior is interacting and exerting influence at the meeting and is active throughout events, rather than being procreated by a union of a behaviorless person and a situation. In short, behavior is an interacting determinant, not a detached by-product that plays no role in the production process.

2.

ALBERT BANDURA

Model of Causation

Triadic Reciprocal Determinism. . . . Social cognitive theory favors a model of causation involving triadic reciprocal determinism. In this model of reciprocal causation, behavior, cognition and other personal factors, and

environmental influences all operate as interacting determinants that influence each other bidirectionally (Figure 1). Reciprocal causation does not mean that the different sources of influence are of equal strength. Some may be stronger than others. Nor do the reciprocal influences all occur simultaneously. It takes time for a causal factor to exert its influence and activate reciprocal influences.

---

[2] Bandura, A. (1989) "Social Cognitive Theory," excerpt from *Annals of Child Development*, Vol. 6, R. Vasta, ed. Greenwich, Conn: JAI Press, pp. 2–6.

FIGURE 1. Schematization of Triadic Reciprocal Determinism.
B signifies behavior; P the cognitive, biological, and other internal events that can affect
perceptions and actions; and E the external environment.

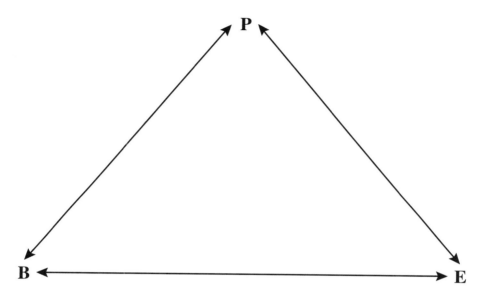

Let us consider briefly the major interactional links between the different subsystems of influence. The P↔B segment of reciprocal causation reflects the interaction between thought, affect and action. Expectations, beliefs, self-perceptions, goals and intentions give shape and direction to behavior. What people think, believe, and feel, affects how they behave. . . . The natural and extrinsic effects of their actions, in turn, partly determine their thought patterns and emotional reactions. The personal factor also encompasses the biological properties of the organism. Physical structure and sensory and neural systems affect behavior and impose constraints on capabilities. Sensory systems and brain structures are, in turn, modifiable by behavioral experiences.

The E↔P segment of reciprocal causation is concerned with the interactive relation between personal characteristics and environmental influences. Human expectations, beliefs, emotional bents and cognitive competencies are developed and modified by social influences that convey information and activate emotional reactions through modeling, instruction and social persuasion. People also evoke different reactions from their social environment by their characteristics, such as their age, size, race, sex and physical attractiveness, quite apart from what they say and do. People similarly activate different social reactions depending on their socially conferred roles and status. For example, children who have a reputation as tough aggressors will elicit different reactions from their peers than those reputed to be unassertive. Thus, by their social status and observable characteristics people can affect their social environment before they say or do anything. The social reactions so elicited affect the recipients' conceptions of themselves and others in ways that either strengthen or alter the environmental bias. . . .

The B↔E segment of reciprocal causation in the triadic system represents the two-way influence between behavior and the environment. In the transactions of everyday life, behavior alters environmental conditions and is, in turn, altered by the very conditions it creates. The environment is not a fixed entity that inevitably impinges upon individuals. When mobility is constrained, some aspects of the physical and social environment may encroach on individuals whether they like it or not. But most aspects of the environment do not operate as an influence until they are activated by appropriate behavior. Lecturers do not influence students unless they attend their classes, hot stove tops do not burn unless they are touched, parents usually do not praise their children unless they do something praiseworthy. The aspect of the potential environment that becomes the actual environment for given individuals thus depends on how they behave.

Because of the bidirectionality of influence between behavior and environmental circumstances, people are both products and producers of their environment. They affect the nature of their experienced environment through selection and creation of situations. People tend to select activities and associates from the vast range of possibilities in terms of their acquired preferences and competencies. . . . Through their actions, people create as well as select environments. Aggressive persons produce hostile environments wherever they go, whereas those who act in a more friendly manner generate an amiable social milieu. Thus, behavior determines which of the many potential environmental influences will come into play and what forms they will take. Environmental influences, in turn, partly determine which forms of behavior are developed and activated. The growing recognition of reciprocal causation has altered the way in which socialization is viewed. One-sided developmental analyses of how parents influence their children have given way to transactional analyses of how parents and children influence each other.

Determinants of Life Paths

Psychological theories of human development focus heavily on the growth of capabilities, especially during the earlier formative years when changes occur rapidly. However, the fundamental issues of what determines human life paths has received little attention. Knowledge of the level to which various capabilities have developed does not, in itself, tell us much about the course personal lives will take.

When human development is viewed from a lifespan perspective, the influential determinants include a varied succession of life events that vary in their power to affect the direction lives take. . . . Many of these determinants include age-graded social influences that are provided by custom within familial, educational, and other institutional systems. Some involve biological conditions that exercise influence over persons' futures. Others are unpredictable occurrences in the physical environment. Still others involve irregular life events such as career changes, divorce, migration, accidents, and illness.

Social and technological changes alter, often considerably, the kinds of life events that become customary in the society. Indeed, many of the major changes in social and economic life are ushered in by innovations of technology. Life experiences under the same sociocultural conditions at a given period will differ for people who encounter them at different points in their lifespan. Thus, for example, economic depression will have different effects on those entering adulthood than on those who pass through such adverse conditions at a young age. Major sociocultural changes that make life markedly different such as economic adversities that alter livelihoods and opportunity structures, military conflicts, cultural upheavals, new technologies and political changes that modify the character of the society can have a strong impact on life courses.

Whatever the social conditions might be, there is still the task of explaining the varied directions that personal lives take at any given time and place. This requires a personal, as well as a social, analysis of life paths. Analysis of behavioral patterns across the lifespan reveals that, in addition to the prevailing sociocultural influences, fortuitous events often exert an important influence on the course of human lives. There are many fortuitous elements in the events people encounter in their daily lives. They are often brought together through a fortuitous constellation of events, when their paths would otherwise never be crossed. In such chance encounters, the separate paths in which people are moving have their own chain of causal determinants, but their intersection occurs fortuitously rather than through deliberate plan. The profusion of separate chains of events provides innumerable opportunities for fortuitous intersections. It is such chance encounters that often play a prominent role in shaping the course of career pursuits, forming marital partnerships, and altering the future direction of other aspects of human lives. To cite but a single example, an editor arrives for a talk on the psychology of chance encounters and grabs a seat that happens to be next to a woman psychologist as the lecture hall rapidly fills up. This chance meeting eventually led to their marriage. With only a slight change of time of entry, seating constellations would have altered and this particular social intersect would probably not have occurred. A marital partnership was thus fortuitously formed at a talk devoted to fortuitous determinants of life paths! As this incident illustrates, some of the most important determinants of life paths often arise through the most trivial of circumstances.

Many chance encounters touch people only lightly, others leave more lasting effects, and still others thrust people into new trajectories of life. Psychology cannot foretell the occurrences of fortuitous encounters, however sophisticated its knowledge of human behavior. The unforeseeability and bracing power of fortuitous influences make the specific course of lives neither easily predictable nor easily controllable. Fortuity of influence does not mean that behavior is undetermined. Fortuitous influences may be unforeseeable, but having occurred they enter as evident factors in causal chains in the same way as prearranged influences do.

A science of psychology does not have much to say about the occurrence of fortuitous intersections, except that personal attributes and particular social affiliations and milieus make some types of encounters more probable than others. The everyday activities of delinquent gangs and college enrollees will bring them into fortuitous contact with different types of persons. However, psychology can provide the basis for predicting the nature, scope, and strength of the impact such encounters will have on human lives. The power of fortuitous influences to inaugurate enduring change is determined by the reciprocal influence of personal proclivities and social factors. . . .

Knowledge of the factors, whether planned or fortuitous, that can alter the course of life paths provides guides for how to foster valued futures. At the personal level, it requires cultivating the capabilities for exercising self-directedness.

These include the development of competencies, self-beliefs of efficacy to exercise control, and self-regulatory capabilities for influencing one's own motivation and actions. Such personal resources expand freedom of action, and enable people to serve as causal contributors to their own life course by selecting, influencing, and constructing their own circumstances.

With such skills, people are better able to provide supports and direction for their actions, to capitalize on planned or fortuitous opportunities, to resist social traps that lead down detrimental paths, and to disengage themselves from such predicaments should they become enmeshed in them.

To exercise some measure of control over one's developmental course requires, in addition to effective tools of personal agency, a great deal of social support. Social resources are especially important during formative years when preferences and personal standards are in a state of flux, and there are many conflicting sources of influence with which to contend. To surmount the obstacles and stresses encountered in the life paths people take, they need social supports to give incentive, meaning, and worth to what they do. . . . the life paths that realistically become open to individuals are also partly determined by the nature of societal opportunity structures. To the extent that societal systems provide aidful means and resources, they increase people's opportunities to influence the course of their lives.

In social cognitive theory, people are neither driven by inner forces nor automatically shaped and controlled by the environment. As we have already seen, they function as contributors to their own motivation, behavior, and development within a network of reciprocally interacting influences. . . .

Learning Through Observation and Modeling

COMMENTARY

Ironically, while highlighting the shortcomings of simplistic behavioral theories of learning and personality development, the recognition by social learning theorists of a much greater complexity in human learning and behavior seems to call for some basic construct or principle that confers integration and establishes order and coherence among all of these complex variables and their interactions.

The legacy of traditional behaviorism is most evident in Bandura's theory in the absence of some holistic or global construct in personality. For example, there is no concept of a "sovereign motivation" or some central source of energy in social-learning theory that we find, for instance, in Adler's striving for superiority, in Maslow's and Rogers' self-actualization theories, and to some extent in the theories of Erikson and Allport.

While recognizing the importance of internal variables, thus moving closer to the humanistic position, these variables are conceived by Bandura as subfunctions and without any reference or connection to some overarching unity or holistic view of the "self" or "self-concept" that other theorists have seen as a primary integrating agency in personality. Could we not have such a concept in Bandura's theory without detracting from the other causal variables?

In addition, in social learning theory there is no place among our cognitive functions for a creative process issuing forth, innately, from the mind itself and independent of all prior reinforcements and experiences. Many of our most creative works and important discoveries seem to represent this little-understood attribute of cognitive functioning. In such cases, consciousness seems to transcend reinforcement patterns and the given of prior experience.

The closest Bandura comes to such an independent component of mind is in his discussion of creative modeling. He suggests here that in creative modeling we lend our own uniqueness and individuality to the process that gives impetus to the emergence of innovation and new styles. Bandura's treatment of uniqueness, however, follows the same principles of modeling as in any other learning. Perhaps the evolution of social learning theory will move in the direction of some recognition of this creative emergence as an expression of an independent quality of mind and as an additional variable in the complicated process of human growth and development.

Finally, the complex variables in learning and development that have been identified in the research of Bandura and other social learning theorists seem unrelated to any moral, ethical, or existential dimensions of personality, except insofar as they are explained in much the same way as any other learning. Following the principles of observational learning and modeling, therefore, personality is seen as a vast array of potentialities that may, depending upon the interaction of many complex variables, go in any direction. Social learning theory, therefore, seems quite compatible with the new postmodern construction and its emphasis on multiplicity within personality and a rejection of any notion of the "self" as a unified and cohesive entity.

1.

ALBERT BANDURA

Learning Through Modeling

Learning would be exceedingly laborious, not to mention hazardous, if people had to rely solely on the effects of their own actions to inform them what to do. Fortunately, most human behavior is learned observationally through modeling: from observing others one forms an idea of how new behaviors are performed, and on later occasions this coded information serves as a guide for action. Because people can learn from example what to do, at least in approximate form, before performing any behavior, they are spared needless errors.

Processes of Observational Learning

According to social learning theory, modeling influences produce learning principally through their informative function. During exposure observers

[1] Albert Bandura, *Social Learning Theory*, © 1977, pp. 22–29. Reprinted by permission of Prentice Hall, Englewood Cliffs, New Jersey.

acquire mainly symbolic representations of the modeled activities which serve as guides for appropriate performances. In this conceptualization . . . observational learning is governed by four component processes.

Attentional Processes

People cannot learn much by observation unless they attend to, and perceive accurately the significant features of the modeled behavior. Attentional processes determine what is selectively observed in the profusion of modeling influences to which one is exposed and what is extracted from such exposures. A number of factors, some involving the observers' characteristics, others involving the features of the modeled activities themselves, and still others involving the structural arrangement of human interactions, regulate the amount and types of observational experiences.

Among the various attentional determinants, associational patterns are clearly of major importance. The people with whom one regularly associates, either through preference or imposition, delimit the types of behavior that will be repeatedly observed and hence learned most thoroughly. Opportunities for learning aggressive conduct, for example, differ markedly for members of assaultive gangs and for members of groups exemplifying pacific lifestyles.

Within any social group some individuals are likely to command greater attention than others. Modeled conduct varies in effectiveness. The functional value of the behaviors displayed by different models is therefore highly influential in determining which

models people will observe and which they will disregard. Attention to models is also channeled by their interpersonal attraction. Models who possess engaging qualities are sought out, while those lacking pleasing characteristics are generally ignored or rejected.

Some forms of modeling are so intrinsically rewarding that they hold the attention of people of all ages for extended periods. This is nowhere better illustrated than in televised modeling. The advent of television has greatly expanded the range of models available to children and adults alike. Unlike their predecessors, who were limited largely to familial and subcultural sources of modeling, people today can observe and learn diverse styles of conduct within the comfort of their homes through the abundant symbolic modeling provided by the mass media. Models presented in televised form are so effective in capturing attention that viewers learn much of what they see without requiring any special incentives. . . .

Retention Processes

People cannot be much influenced by observation of modeled behavior if they do not remember it. A second major process involved in observational learning concerns retention of activities that have been modeled at one time or another. In order for observers to profit from the behavior of models when they are no longer present to provide direction, the response patterns must be represented in memory in symbolic form. Through the medium of symbols, transitory modeling experiences can be maintained in permanent memory. It is the advanced capacity for symbolization that enables humans to learn much of their behavior by observation. . . .

After modeled activities have been transformed into images and readily utilizable verbal symbols, these memory codes serve as guides for performance. . . . Observers who code modeled activities into either words, concise labels, or vivid imagery learn and retain behavior better than those who simply observe or are mentally preoccupied with other matters while watching.

In addition to symbolic coding, rehearsal serves as an important memory aid. When people mentally rehearse or actually perform modeled response patterns, they are less likely to forget them if they neither think about them nor practice what they have seen. Many behaviors that are learned observationally cannot be easily established by overt enactment because of either social prohibitions or lack of opportunity. It is therefore of considerable interest that mental rehearsal, in which individuals visualize themselves performing the appropriate behavior, increases proficiency and retention. . . .

Motor Reproduction Processes

The third component of modeling involves converting symbolic representations into appropriate actions. To understand this response guidance function requires analysis of the ideomotor mechanisms of performance. Behavioral reproduction is achieved by organizing one's responses spatially and temporally in accordance with the modeled patterns. For purposes of analysis, behavioral enactment can be separated into cognitive organization of responses, their initiation, monitoring, and refinement on the basis of informative feedback.

In the initial phase of behavioral enactment, responses are selected and organized at the cognitive level. The amount of observational learning that will be exhibited behaviorally partly depends on the availability of component skills. Learners who possess the constituent elements can easily integrate them to produce the new patterns; but if some of these response components are lacking, behavioral reproduction will be faulty. When deficits exist, then the basic sub-skills required for complex performances must first be developed by modeling and practice.

There are other impediments at the behavioral level to doing what one has learned observationally. Ideas are rarely transformed into correct actions without error on first attempt. Accurate matches are usually achieved by corrective adjustments of preliminary efforts. Discrepancies between the symbolic representation and execution serve as cues for corrective action. A common problem in learning complex skills, such as golfing or swimming, is that performers cannot fully observe their responses, and must therefore rely upon vague kinesthetic cues or verbal reports of onlookers. It is difficult to guide actions that are only partially observable or to identify the corrections needed to achieve a close match between representation and performance.

Skills are not perfected through observation alone, nor are they developed solely by trial-and-error fumbling. A golf instructor, for example, does not provide beginners with golf balls and clubs and wait for them to discover the golf swing. In most everyday learning, people usually achieve a close approximation of the new behavior by modeling, and they refine it through self-corrective adjustments on the basis of informative feedback from performance and from focused demonstrations of segments that have been only partially learned.

Motivational Processes

Social learning theory distinguishes between acquisition and performance because people do not enact everything they learn. They are more likely to adopt modeled behavior if it results in outcomes they value than if it has unrewarding or punishing effects. Observed consequences influence modeled conduct in much the same way. Among the countless responses acquired observationally, those behaviors that seem to be effective for others are favored over behaviors that are seen to have negative consequences. The evaluative reactions that people generate toward their own behavior also regulate which observationally learned responses will be performed. . . .

Because of the numerous factors governing observational learning, the provision of models, even prominent ones, will not automatically create similar behavior in others. One can produce imitative behavior without considering the underlying processes. A model who repeatedly demonstrates desired responses, instructs others to reproduce the behavior, prompts them physically when they fail, and then rewards them when they succeed, may eventually produce matching responses in most people. If, on the other hand, one seeks to explain the occurrence of modeling and to achieve its effects predictably, one has to consider the various determining factors discussed above. In any given instance, then, the failure of an observer to match the behavior of a model may result from any of the following: not observing the relevant activities, inadequately coding modeled events for memory representation, failing to retain what was learned, physical inability to perform, or experiencing insufficient incentives.

2.

ALBERT BANDURA

Modeling Determinants

Of the numerous predictive cues that influence behavior at any given

[2] Albert Bandura, *Social Learning Theory,* © 1977, pp. 87–89. Reprinted by permission of Prentice Hall, Englewood Cliffs, New Jersey.

moment, none is more common or effective than the actions of others. People applaud when others clap, they laugh when others laugh, they exit from social events when they see others leaving, and on countless other occasions their behavior is prompted and channeled by modeling influences.

The actions of others acquire predictive value through correlated consequences in much the same way as do nonsocial physical and symbolic stimuli. Modeling cues prompt similar conduct when behaving like others produces rewarding outcomes, but they elicit divergent behavior when actions dissimilar to the model are reinforced. Because people usually display behavior of proven value, following good examples is much more efficacious than tedious trial and error. Thus, by relying on the actions of knowledgeable models, novices can act appropriately in diverse settings and at different events without having to discover what constitutes acceptable conduct from the shocked or pleased reactions of witnesses to their groping performances. The dictum "When in Rome do as the Romans do" underscores the functional value of modeling cues.

People differ in the degree to which their behavior is guided by modeling influences, and not all models are equally effective in eliciting the types of behavior they themselves exemplify. Responsiveness to modeling cues is largely determined by three factors, which in turn derive their activating power largely from correlative relationships to response outcomes. These include the characteristics of models, the attributes of observers, and the response consequences associated with matching behavior.

With regard to the characteristics of models, those who have high status, competence, and power are more effective in prompting others to behave similarly than are models of lower standing. . . .

It is not difficult to explain why status enhances the cueing function of modeled conduct. The behavior of models who have gained distinction is more likely to be successful, and hence to have greater functional value for observers, than that of models who are relatively low in vocational, intellectual, or social competence. When following different models produces divergent effects, the models' characteristics and symbols of status assume informative value in signifying the probable consequences of behavior exemplified by the different models.

In situations in which people are uncertain about the wisdom of a modeled course of action, they must rely on such cues as general appearances, speech, style, age, symbols of socioeconomic success, and signs of expertise as indicators of past successes. The effects of a model's status tend to generalize from one area of behavior to another, as when prominent athletes express preferences for breakfast cereals as though they were nutrition experts. Unfamiliar persons likewise gain influence by their similarity to models whose behavior proved successful in the past.

3.

ALBERT BANDURA

Creative Modeling

Contrary to common belief, innovative patterns can emerge through the modeling process. When exposed to diverse models, observers rarely pattern their behavior exclusively after a single source, nor do they adopt all the attributes even of preferred models. Rather, observers combine aspects of various models into new amalgams that differ from the individual sources. . . .

In the case of social behavior, children within the same family may develop dissimilar personality characteristics by drawing upon different parental and sibling attributes. Successive modeling, in which observers later serve as sources of behavior for new members, would most likely produce a gradual imitative evolution of new patterns bearing little resemblance to those exhibited by the original models. In homogeneous cultures, where all models display similar styles of behavior, behavior may undergo little or no change throughout a series of successive models. It is diversity in modeling that fosters behavioral innovation.

Modeling probably contributes most to creative development in the inception of new styles. Once initiated, experiences with the new forms create further evolutionary changes. A partial departure from tradition thus eventually becomes a new direction. The progression of creative careers through distinct periods provides notable examples of this process. In his earliest works, Beethoven adopted the classical forms of Haydn and Mozart, though with greater emotional expressiveness which foreshadowed the direction of his artistic development. Wagner fused Beethoven's symphonic mode with Weber's naturalistic enchantment and Meyerbeer's dramatic virtuosity to evolve a new operatic form. Innovators in other endeavors in the same manner initially draw upon the contributions of others and build from their experiences something new.

The discussion thus far has analyzed creativity through the innovative synthesis of different sources of influence. While existing practices furnish some of the ingredients for the new, they also impede innovation. As long as familiar routines serve adequately, there is little incentive to consider alternatives. The unconventional is not only unexplored, but is usually negatively received when introduced by the more venturesome. Modeling influences can weaken conventional inclinations by exemplifying novel responses to common situations. People exposed to divergently thinking models are indeed more innovative than those exposed to models who behave in a stereotyped conventional fashion. . . . Although innovative modeling generally enhances creative ideas in others, there are some limits to this influence.

[3] Albert Bandura, *Social Learning Theory,* © 1977, pp. 48–52. Reprinted by permission of Prentice Hall, Englewood Cliffs, New Jersey.

When models are unusually productive and observers possess limited skills, their creative efforts may be self-devalued by the unfavorable comparison. Prolific creative modeling can thus dissuade the less talented. . . .

Diffusion of Innovation

Modeling also plays a prime role in spreading new ideas and social practices within a society, or from one society to another. Successful diffusion of innovation follows a common pattern: new behavior is introduced by prominent examples, it is adopted at a rapidly accelerating rate, and it then either stabilizes or declines depending upon its functional value. The general pattern of diffusion is similar, but the mode of transmission, the speed and extent of adoption, and the lifespan of innovations varies for different forms of behavior.

Social learning theory distinguishes between two processes in the social diffusion of innovation. These are the acquisition of innovative behaviors and their adoption in practice. With regard to acquisition, modeling serves as the major vehicle for transmitting new styles of behavior. The numerous factors that determine observational learning, discussed earlier, apply equally to the rapid promulgation of innovations.

Symbolic modeling usually functions as the principal conveyance of innovations to widely dispersed areas. This is especially true in the early stages of diffusion. Newspapers, magazines, radio, and television inform people of new practices and their likely benefits or risks. . . .

Modeling affects adoption of innovations in several different ways. It instructs people in new styles of behavior through social, pictorial, or verbal display. Observers are initially reluctant to embark on new undertakings that involve risks until they see the advantages gained by early adopters. Modeled benefits accelerate diffusion by weakening the restraints of the more cautious potential adopters. As acceptance spreads, the new gains further social support. Models not only exemplify and legitimate innovations, they also serve as advocates by encouraging others to adopt them.

The acquisition of innovations is necessary but not sufficient for their adoption in practice. Social learning theory recognizes a number of factors that determine whether people will act on what they have learned. Stimulus inducements serve as one set of activators. In the consumer field, for example, advertising appeals are used extensively to stimulate consumers to purchase new products. Fashion industries saturate the market with new styles and reduce the availability of the fashions they wish to supplant. Different sources of mass communication furnish prompts from time to time for new technologies, ideologies, and social practices. The more pervasive the stimulus inducements, the greater the likelihood that learned innovations will be tried.

Adoptive behavior is highly susceptible to reinforcement influences. People will espouse innovations that produce tangible advantages. However, because benefits cannot be experienced until the new practices are tried, the promotion of innovations draws heavily upon anticipated and vicarious reinforcement. Advocates of new technologies and ideologies create expectations that they offer better solutions than do established ways. Promoters rely on vicarious reinforcement to increase the likelihood that observers will respond in the recommended manner. In positive appeals, adoptive behavior is depicted as resulting in a host of rewarding effects. Commercials promise that drinking certain beverages or using a particular hair lotion will win the admiration of attractive people, enhance job performance, bolster positive self-images, actualize individualism and authenticity, tranquilize irritable nerves, and arouse the affections of spouses. Negative appeals portray the adverse consequences of failure to pursue the recommended practices. Vicarious punishment, however, is a less reliable means of promoting adoptive behavior. . . .

Many innovations serve as a means of gaining attention and status. People who strive to distinguish themselves from the common and the ordinary adopt new styles in clothing, grooming, recreational activities, and conduct, thereby achieving distinctive status. As the popularity of the new behavior grows, it loses its status—conferring value until eventually it, too, becomes commonplace. Widespread imitation thus instigates further inventiveness to preserve status differentiations.

Self-Efficacy

COMMENTARY

While certain links to behaviorism remain in aspects of Bandura's theory, his concept of *self-efficacy* has clearly broken all ties with the tenets of behaviorism.

While Bandura's concept of self-efficacy parallels similar concepts found in other theories and in "common sense" constructs—for example, self-esteem, self-regard, self-image and self-confidence—Bandura's concept, unlike most others, has been subjected to careful research to identify the variables involved in self-efficacy development and its role in personality. Indeed, all of Bandura's constructs have been subjected to the same rigorous scientific scrutiny. Among personality theorists this is an unparalleled achievement and is largely responsible for the recognition and great respect extended to Bandura and his work, even by those psychologists and theorists of other persuasions.

Put quite simply, self-efficacy is what a person believes he or she is capable of doing or accomplishing. Self-efficacy, therefore, represents the judgments or self-appraisals we make concerning our ability to learn, perform, accomplish, or execute a defined task. Such tasks may range from making high grades to learning to play tennis. This construct may remind the reader of the classic children's story *The Little Engine Who Could*. "I think I can, I think I can, I think I can."

In Bandura's triadic model of reciprocal determinism (the interaction of person variables, environmental variables, and behavior variables), self-efficacy clearly represents an important internal or person variable and

218

also quite clearly illustrates the workings of reciprocal determinism. In college, for example, a student's feelings of high self-efficacy (person variable) will lead to high grades (behavior variable) which, in turn, will bring positive and supportive responses from teachers (environmental variable). These interactions will act in a feedback fashion to further strengthen self-efficacy in the student. Success, in other words, breeds success. Bandura has demonstrated, therefore, that perceived self-efficacy is a potent factor in determining motivation and quality of behavior that leads to success or failure in many undertakings.

In some respects, self-efficacy comes close to resembling a global construct of the "self" or self-concept. It is, nevertheless, conceived of by Bandura as just another important sub-function and never operates as an autonomous agent in the personality. In other words, it is never independent from other person, environmental, and behavior variables. It could be said, however, that self-efficacy is Bandura's most encompassing, global construct.

The reader will recall from the biographical sketch that Bandura's early interests and research focused on clinical psychology and psychotherapy. He brings these early interests back into his work with his concept of self-efficacy. Bandura sees the primary goal of psychotherapy as one of strengthening and expanding self-efficacy. His behavior therapy techniques, addressing specific behavioral issues, are designed to do this.

1.

ALBERT BANDURA

Self-Efficacy Appraisal

Among the types of thoughts that affect action, none is more central or pervasive than people's judgments of their capabilities to exercise control over events that affect their lives. The

self-efficacy mechanism plays a central role in human agency. . . . Self-judgments of operative capabilities function as one set of proximal determinants of how people behave, their thought patterns, and the emotional reactions they experience in taxing situations. In their daily lives, people continuously have to make decisions about what courses of action to pursue and how long to continue those they

---

[1] Bandura, A. (1989). "Social Cognitive Theory," in *Annals of Child Development*, Vol. 6, R. Vasta, ed. Greenwich Conn.: JAI Press, Inc., pp. 42–43.

have undertaken. Because acting on misjudgments of personal efficacy can produce adverse consequences, accurate appraisal of one's own capabilities has considerable functional value.

It is partly on the basis of judgments of personal efficacy that people choose what to do, how much effort to invest in activities and how long to persevere in the face of obstacles and failure experiences. People's judgments of their capabilities additionally influence whether their thought patterns are self-hindering or self-enhancing, and how much stress and despondency they experience during anticipatory and actual transaction with the environment. . . .

As previously noted, accurate appraisal of one's own capabilities is highly advantageous and often essential for effective functioning. Very young children lack knowledge of their own capabilities and the demands and potential hazards of different situations. They would repeatedly get themselves into dangerous predicaments were it not for the guidance of others. Adult watchfulness and guidance sees young children through this early formative period until they gain sufficient knowledge of what they can do and what different situations require in the way of skills. With development of cognitive self-reflective capabilities, self-efficacy judgment increasingly supplants external guidance.

Beginnings of Perceived Causal Efficacy

Children's exploratory experiences and observation of the performances of others provide the initial basis for developing a sense of causal efficacy. However, newborns' immobility and limited means of action upon the physical and social environment restrict their domain of influence. The initial experiences that contribute to development of a sense of personal agency are tied to infants' ability to control the sensory stimulation from manipulable objects and the attentive behavior of those around them. Infants behave in certain ways, and certain things happen. Shaking a rattle produces predictable sounds, energetic kicks shake their cribs, and screams bring adults.

Realization of causal efficacy requires both self-observation and recognition that one's actions are part of oneself. By repeatedly observing that certain environmental events occur with action, but not in its absence, infants learn that actions produce effects. Infants who experience success in controlling environmental events become more attentive to their own behavior and more competent in learning new efficacious responses than do infants for whom the same environmental events occur regardless of how they behave. . . .

2.

ALBERT BANDURA

Perceived Self-Efficacy as a Generative Capability

Efficacy in dealing with one's environment is not simply a matter of knowing what to do. Nor is it a fixed act that one does or does not have in one's behavioral repertoire, any more than one would construe linguistic efficacy in terms of a collection of words or a colony of fixed sentences in a verbal repertoire. Rather, efficacy involves a generative capability in which cognitive, social, and behavioral subskills must be organized into integrated courses of action to serve innumerable purposes. Success is often attained only after generating and testing alternative forms of behavior and strategies, which require perseverant effort. Self-doubters are quick to abort this generative process if their initial efforts prove deficient. . . .

Competent functioning requires both skills and self-beliefs of efficacy to use them effectively. Operative efficacy calls for continuously improvising multiple subskills to manage ever changing circumstances, most of which contain ambiguous, unpredictable and often stressful elements. Even routinized activities are rarely performed in exactly the same way. Initiation and regulation of transactions with the environment are, therefore, partly governed by judgments of operative capabilities—what

people think they can do under given circumstances. Perceived self-efficacy is defined as people's judgments of their capabilities to organize and execute courses of action required to attain designated types of performances. It is concerned not with the skills one has but with judgments of what one can do with whatever skills one possesses.

Judgments of personal efficacy are distinguished from response-outcome expectations. Perceived self-efficacy is a judgment of one's capability to accomplish a certain level of performance, whereas an outcome expectation is a judgment of the likely consequence such behavior will produce. For example, the belief that one can jump six feet is an efficacy judgment; the anticipated social recognition, applause, trophies, and self-satisfactions for such a performance constitute the outcome expectations.

An outcome is the consequence of an act, not the act itself. Serious confusions arise when an act is misconstrued as an outcome of itself, as when jumping six feet is viewed as consequence. An act must be defined by the criteria that state what it is, for example, a leap upward of a designated height. To regard a six-foot high jump as an outcome would be to misinterpret the specification criteria of an act as the consequences that flow from it. If an act is defined as a six-foot leap, then a six-foot leap is the realization of the act, not a consequent of it. Failure to complete a designated act (e.g., knocking off a crossbar by failing to jump six

---

[2] Albert Bandura, *Social Foundations of Thought and Action: A Social Cognitive Theory,* © 1986, pp. 391–392. Reprinted by permission of Prentice Hall, Englewood Cliffs, New Jersey.

feet) cannot be the outcome of the act because it was never fully executed. The failed jump is an incomplete act that produces its own divergent collection of outcomes, be they social, physical, or self-evaluative. . . .

Efficacy and outcome judgments are differentiated because individuals can believe that a particular course of action will produce certain outcomes, but they do not act on that outcome belief because they question whether they can actually execute the necessary activities. Thus, expectations that high grades gain students entry to medical school and that medical practice yields high incomes will not steer undergraduates into premedical programs who have serious self-doubts that they can master the science requirements.

3.

ALBERT BANDURA

Sources of Self-Efficacy Information

Self-knowledge about one's efficacy, whether accurate or faulty, is based on four principal sources of information: performance attainments; vicarious experiences of observing the performances of others; verbal persuasion and allied types of social influences that one possesses certain capabilities; and physiological states from which people partly judge their capableness, strength, and vulnerability to dysfunction. Any given influence, depending on its form, may draw on one or more sources of efficacy information.

Enactive Attainment

. . . Successes raise efficacy appraisals; repeated failures lower them, especially if the failures occur early in the course of events and do not reflect lack of effort or adverse external circumstances. The weight given to new experiences depends on the nature and strength of the preexisting self-perception into which they must be integrated. After a strong sense of self-efficacy is developed through repeated successes, occasional failures are unlikely to have much effect on judgments of one's capabilities. People who are assured of their capabilities are more likely to look to situational factors, insufficient effort, or poor strategies as the causes. . . . Failures that are overcome by determined effort can instill robust percepts of self-efficacy through experience that one can eventually master even the most difficult obstacles.

Once established, enhanced self-efficacy tends to generalize to other situations. . . .

Vicarious Experience

People do not rely on enactive experience as the sole source of information about their capabilities. Self-efficacy appraisals are partly

[3] Albert Bandura, *Social Foundations of Thought and Action: A Social Cognitive Theory,* © 1986, pp. 399–401. Reprinted by permission of Prentice Hall, Englewood Cliffs, New Jersey.

influenced by vicarious experiences. . . . They persuade themselves that if others can do it, they should be able to achieve at least some improvement in performance. By the same token, observing that others perceived to be similarly competent fail despite high effort lowers observer's judgments of their own capabilities. . . .

There are several conditions under which self-efficacy appraisals are especially sensitive to vicarious information. The amount of uncertainty about one's capabilities is one such factor. Perceived self-efficacy can be readily changed by relevant modeling influences when people have had little prior experience on which to base evaluations of their personal competence. . . .

Although vicarious experiences are generally weaker than direct ones, vicarious forms can produce significant, enduring changes through their effects on performance. People convinced vicariously of their inefficacy are inclined to behave in ineffectual ways that, in fact, generate confirmatory behavioral evidence of inability. Conversely, modeling influences that enhance perceived self-efficacy can weaken the impact of direct experiences of failure. . . .

Verbal Persuasion

Verbal persuasion is widely used to try to talk people into believing they possess capabilities that will enable them to achieve what they seek. Social persuasion alone may be limited in its power to create enduring increases in self-efficacy, but it can contribute to successful performance if the heightened appraisal is within realistic bounds. People who are persuaded verbally that they possess the capabilities to master given tasks are likely to mobilize greater sustained effort than if they harbor self-doubts and dwell on personal deficiencies when difficulties arise. To the extent that persuasive boosts in self-efficacy lead people to try hard enough to succeed, they promote development of skills and a sense of personal efficacy. . . . However, the raising of unrealistic beliefs of personal competence only invites failures that will discredit the persuaders and will further undermine the recipient's perceived self-efficacy.

It is probably more difficult to produce enduring increases in perceived efficacy by persuasory means than to undermine it. Illusory boosts in self-efficacy are readily disconfirmed by the results of one's actions. But those who have been persuaded of their inefficacy tend to avoid challenging activities and give up quickly in the face of difficulties. By restricting choice behavior and undermining effort, self-disbeliefs can create their own validation.

Physiological State

People rely partly on information from their physiological state in judging their capabilities. They read their somatic arousal in stressful or taxing situations as ominous signs of vulnerability to dysfunction. Because high arousal usually debilitates performance, people are more inclined to expect success when they are not beset by aversive arousal than if they are tense and viscerally agitated. Fear reactions generate further fear through anticipatory self-arousal. By conjuring up fear-provoking thoughts about their ineptitude, people can rouse themselves to elevated levels of distress that produce the very dysfunctions they fear. . . .

Cognitive Processing of Self-Efficacy Information

Information that is relevant for judging personal capabilities—whether conveyed enactively, vicariously, persuasively, or physiologically—is not inherently enlightening. Rather, it becomes instructive only through cognitive appraisal. A distinction must, therefore, be drawn between information conveyed by environmental events and information as selected, weighted, and integrated into self-efficacy judgments. A host of factors, including personal, social, situational, and temporal circumstances under which events occur, affect how personal experiences are cognitively appraised. For this reason, even noteworthy performance attainments do not necessarily boost perceived self-efficacy.

Nor are self-percepts that have served protective functions for years quickly discarded. Those who question their coping efficacy are more likely to distrust their positive experiences than to risk encounters with threats they judge they cannot adequately control. When experience contradicts firmly held judgments of self-efficacy, people may not change their beliefs about themselves if the conditions of performance are such as to lead them to discount the import of the experience. . . .

The cognitive processing of efficacy information involves two separable functions: The first concerns the types of information people attend to and use as indicators of personal efficacy. Each of the four modes of conveying information has its distinctive set of efficacy indicators. The second concerns the combination rules or heuristics they employ for weighing and integrating efficacy information from different sources in forming their self-efficacy judgments.

Self-Reinforcement and Self-Management

COMMENTARY

Bandura recognizes both an external system of controls and an internal self-system. As we have seen, these inner and outer determinants interact in a reciprocal fashion. It is the self-system, however, that prevents us from responding like "weather vanes" and establishes a certain unity and self-consistency in attitudes and behavior. This unity is not created by some autonomous agency or sovereign system but, rather, is fashioned by self-generated cognitive processes that interact and intersect with other causal forces. It is from these self-generated cognitive and symbolic processes that we receive the power to create our own reinforcements and establish a large measure of control over our lives.

The concept of self-reinforcement and self-management represents another significant departure from the radical behaviorism of B. S. Skinner and other early behaviorists. These concepts form an important aspect of Bandura's more flexible view of the many causal forces, both internal and external, that help shape behavior and personality.

There seem to be two major sources of self-reinforcement. First, there is the reinforcement (sense of pleasure, pride, reward, etc.) that comes from increased self-esteem and self-efficacy generated within us by success or progress toward our goals. Second, the individual may create his/her own reinforcement system, selecting those rewards from the environment upon successful achievement or performance.

The possibility for self-reinforcement and self-directed behavior changes, returning a large measure of power and control to the individual, is of great significance in Bandura's theory and leads to some important practical applications.

A good way to experience several of Bandura's principles in action is to plan and implement a self-management program. One aspect of your present behavior you may wish to alter is your study behavior (or some undesirable habit or behavior such as smoking, poor eating habits, etc.). The following steps are recommended.

1. *Identify your goal.* What, specifically, do you wish to change about your current study habits? For example, do you need to increase length of study time for each day, increase the length of each study period, increase your concentration by decreasing interruptions, etc.?
2. *Establish a baseline record.* Keep a record, for one week, of your current study habits, including the exact times you study and the conditions under which you study.
3. *Alter your environment.* This involves altering the situations that contribute to your inefficient study behavior. For example, you might go to the library each night instead of suffering the interruptions and noises of studying in your room.
4. *Develop an incentive program.* Once you have altered your environment and are beginning to establish satisfactory study routines and behaviors, introduce an attractive incentive program into your schedule. Build in some rewarding experience to follow the successful completion of the desired study behavior. The major self-reinforcement will come, of course, from the sense of accomplishment, self-control, and other positive feelings you have after altering your study habits and the increased feeling of competence that comes with improved grades.
5. *Maintain your gains.* Continue your self-management program until your new behaviors become second nature to you and are as habitual as your previous behavior was.

ALBERT BANDURA

Self-Reinforcement

. . . If actions were determined solely by external rewards and punishments, people would behave like weather vanes, constantly shifting in different directions to conform to the momentary influences impinging upon them. They would act corruptly with unprincipled individuals and honorably with righteous ones, and liberally with libertarians and dogmatically with authoritarians.

Albert Bandura, *Social Learning Theory,* © 1977, pp. 128–133. Reprinted by permission of Prentice Hall, Englewood Cliffs, New Jersey.

Examination of social interactions however—aside from strong coercive pressures—would reveal that people hold firmly to ideological positions rather than undergo compliant behavior reversals. Anyone who attempted to change a pacifist into an aggressor or a devout religionist into an atheist would quickly come to appreciate the existence of personal sources of behavior control.

The notion that behavior is regulated by its consequences is usually misinterpreted to mean that actions are at the mercy of situational influences. Theories that explain human behavior as solely the product of external rewards and punishments present a truncated image of people because they possess self-reactive capacities that enable them to exercise some control over their own feelings, thoughts, and actions. Behavior is therefore regulated by the interplay of self-generated and external sources of influence.

Behavior is commonly performed in the absence of immediate external reinforcement. Some activities are maintained by anticipated consequences, but most are under self-reinforcement control. In this process, people set certain standards of behavior for themselves and respond to their own actions in self-rewarding or self-punishing ways.

The act of writing is a familiar example of a behavior that is continuously self-regulated through evaluative self-reinforcement. Authors do not need someone sitting at their sides selectively reinforcing each written statement until a satisfactory manuscript is produced. Rather, they possess a standard of what constitutes an acceptable piece of work. Ideas are generated and phrased in thought several times before anything is committed to paper. Initial constructions are successively revised until authors are satisfied with what they have written. The more exacting the personal standards, the more extensive are the corrective improvements. Self-editing often exceeds external requirements of what would be acceptable to others. Indeed, some people are such critical self-editors that they essentially paralyze their own writing efforts. Others who lack suitable standards exercise little self-correction.

Because of their symbolizing and self-reactive capacities, humans are less dependent upon immediate external supports for their behavior. Including self-reinforcement processes in learning theory thus greatly increases the explanatory power of reinforcement principles as applied to human functioning.

Component Processes In Self-Regulation

Self-reinforcement refers to a process in which individuals enhance and maintain their own behavior by rewarding themselves with rewards that they control whenever they attain self-prescribed standards. Because behavior can also be reduced by negative self-reactions, the broader term self-regulation will be used to encompass both the enhancing and reducing effects of self-reactive influences.

. . . Self-regulated reinforcement increases performance mainly through its motivational function. By making self-reward conditional upon attaining a certain level of performance, individuals create self-inducements to persist in their efforts until their performances match self-prescribed standards. The level of self-motivation generated by this means will vary according to the type and value of the incentives and the nature of the performance standards. . . .

Behavior generates self-reactions through a judgmental function which includes several subsidiary processes. Whether a given performance will be regarded as rewardable or punishable depends upon the personal standards against which it is evaluated. Actions that measure up to internal standards give rise to positive appraisals, while those that fall short are judged negatively.

For most activities there are no absolute measures of adequacy. The time in which a mile is run, the scores obtained on tasks, or the size of charitable contributions, do not convey in themselves sufficient information for self-appraisal. When adequacy is defined relationally, performances are evaluated by comparing them with those of others. Thus, a student who scores 115 points on an examination and who wants to be in the upper 10% of the group would have no basis for making either a positive or a negative self-assessment without knowing the accomplishments of the other students. In performances gauged by social criteria, self-appraisals require relational comparisons of at least three sources of information to judge a given performance: absolute performance level, one's own personal standards, and a social referent.

The referential comparisons may take different forms for different tasks. For some regular activities, standard norms based on representative groups are used to determine one's relative standing. More often, however, people compare themselves to particular associates in similar situations. Performance judgments will therefore vary substantially depending upon the level of ability of those chosen for comparison: self-estimates are enhanced when comparison is made to others of lesser ability, and diminished when the accomplishments of the more talented are used to set the relative standard of adequacy.

One's previous behavior is continuously used as the reference against which ongoing performance is judged. In this process, it is self-comparison that supplies the measure of adequacy. Past performance determines self-appraisal mainly through its effects on standard setting. After a given level of performance is attained, it is no longer challenging, and new self-satisfactions are sought through progressive improvement. People tend to raise their performance standards after success and to lower them to more realistic levels after repeated failure.

The view is widely endorsed that social learning practices should be structured so that people come to judge themselves in reference to their own capabilities and standards, rather than by comparing themselves with others. In competitive, individualistic societies, however, where one person's success represents another person's failure, social comparison figures prominently in self-appraisal. The standards by which behavior is judged take other forms in societies organized around a collectivist ethic. Comparison processes still operate to some extent under such arrangements, but self-appraisal is primarily in terms of one's relative contribution to common goals and the level of group accomplishment.

Self-appraisals of performances set the occasion for self-produced consequences. Favorable judgments give rise to rewarding self-reactions, whereas unfavorable appraisals activate punishing self-responses. Performances that are regarded as having no personal significance do not generate any reactions one way or another. Much human behavior is regulated through self-evaluative consequences as expressed variously by self-satisfaction, self-pride, self-dissatisfaction, and self-criticism. People also get themselves to do things they would otherwise put off by making tangible outcomes conditional upon goal attainment.

CHAPTER VIII

The Dispositional-Trait Theory of Gordon Allport

BIOGRAPHICAL SKETCH

Gordon Allport was born in Montezuma, Ohio, on November 11, 1897. His father was a hard-working physician who strongly believed in the Protestant work ethic. His mother, a school teacher, strongly encouraged Gordon and his three older brothers in their education and in intellectual explorations.

In 1915, after graduating from a high school in Cleveland, Ohio, where his family had moved, Allport followed brother Floyd to Harvard. Floyd had graduated from Harvard two years earlier, and was also to become a famous psychologist. Allport received his A.B. degree in 1919 with major study in economics and philosophy.

Following his graduation, an opportunity to teach at Robert College in Istanbul, Turkey, convinced him that he would enjoy teaching. After his year at there, Allport returned to Harvard on a fellowship to complete his Ph.D. in psychology. He received his degree in 1922 at the age of 24. The prophetic title of his dissertation was *An Experimental Study of the Traits of Personality*. Following this accomplishment, Allport spent the next two years studying psychology in Germany under famous Gestalt psychologists and in England at Cambridge University. He returned to Harvard in 1924, where he developed and taught, in the Department of Social Ethics, the first course in personality ever offered in the United States. The title of this course was Personality: Its Psychological and Social Aspects.

In June 1925 Allport married Ada Lufkin Gould. They had one child, Robert, who later became a pediatrician. Following his marriage, Allport accepted an assistant professorship at Dartmouth College in 1926, where he remained for four years. Following his years at Dartmouth, Allport was offered an assistant professorship at Harvard. He accepted this offer and returned once again to his alma mater, where he established a long and distinguished career in the Department of Social Relations. Allport remained at Harvard until his death from lung cancer on October 9, 1967.

Allport, the gadfly of American psychology, took issue with all established psychological theories of his day, particularly behaviorism and psychoanalysis. While accepting, in eclectic fashion, the contributions these theories had to offer, Allport believed with almost religious fervor that these theories, with their focus on the past, pathology, and environmentalism, largely ignored or grossly distorted the essence of the human personality, thus obscuring the individuality, uniqueness, and integrity of the individual.

His major work *Personality: A Psychological Interpretation* (1937), revised and reissued as *Pattern and Growth in Personality* (1961), presents both his eclecticism and his pioneering efforts to free psychology from its many rigidities.

Perhaps the most influential American psychologist of the twentieth century, Allport, through his teaching and writings, had a far-reaching impact on the ideas and theories of other psychologists. Along with Maslow, Rogers, Moustakas, May, and others, he was also an important force in the emergence of humanistic psychology in the sixties.

Gordon Allport was loved and respected by his students. In 1963 he was honored with the presentation of two bound volumes of the publications of fifty-five of his former Ph.D. students.

Trait Theory and the Dispositions

COMMENTARY

For years Gordon Allport has been identified as a trait theorist. He was the first psychologist to emphasize the existence and importance of traits in personality. He viewed them as psychological entities and as the most valid units of analysis in personality study. Allport was also the first to give the term *trait* some empirical foundation and scientific legitimacy. If we are to keep pace with Allport's theoretical developments, however, we must withdraw the label trait theorist. Allport, himself, felt uncomfortable with the label, and he rejected it as inappropriate. The term *trait* became too suggestive of a general characteristic held in common by a group of people and did not address Allport's primary interest in the uniqueness of personality, the focus of much of his later work.

Allport became much more concerned with those attributes of personality that created distinctiveness and individuality, and he realized that the designation of *trait* for both group and individual characteristics was misleading. He did not want to confuse a common trait around which a group of individuals may be compared with the special significance and uniqueness of the trait as it functions within the individual.

The first selection, taken from a presentation given by Allport in 1929, is a very early essay and represents one of Allport's first attempts to formulate a trait theory. In it, he tries to give some comprehensive definition of *trait* and to rescue the term from confusion with habits and attitudes and from general and misleading appropriation.

In this essay he limits the term trait to "a generalized response-unit in which resides the distinctive quality of behavior that reflects personality."

A trait, therefore, represents a disposition to act in a similar way in a wide range of situations and circumstances. Traits, in other words, ensure a certain constancy in personality as well as uniqueness. Early on, therefore, Allport saw the trait as a basic structural unit of personality that makes for both uniqueness and consistency of personality.

Allport recognized that a trait may have a universal as well as a unique, individual aspect. That is, we may examine a trait as a distribution within a given population, as a group phenomenon, and measure it accordingly, i.e., following the psychology of individual differences we may administer a measure of extraversion, for example, to a group of people for the purpose of obtaining norms and percentiles. We can then proceed to compare and contrast individual scores. Using this approach we arbitrarily isolate the trait for study without any regard for its meaning and unique functioning within a given individual.

We may also study this trait of extraversion as a unique and integrated personal characteristic. Allport stresses that it is in this approach that the unique *combination* of traits and their interactions help us understand the "patterned individuality" of personality.

In the later selections, Allport has moved quite far in his thinking from the material of his 1929 essay. He has clarified the ambiguity in the term *trait* by distinguishing between common traits, those traits that can be isolated and used for individual comparison, and the personal dispositions. This new dispositional psychology focuses attention on the uniqueness of traits within a given personality as they interact with other traits and become integrated as systems and sub-systems within the individual. He further recognizes that some personal dispositions are more central than others to the individual personality and more provocative in the sense that they seek to be expressed, developed, and integrated into the personality. Finally, Allport distinguishes between the cardinal, the central, and the secondary or peripheral dispositions.

1.

GORDON ALLPORT

What is a Trait of Personality?

At the heart of all investigation of personality lies the puzzling problem of the nature of the unit or element that is the carrier of the distinctive behavior of man. *Reflexes* and *habits* are too specific in reference and connote constancy rather than consistency in behavior. *Attitudes* are ill-defined and, as employed by various writers, refer to determining tendencies that range in inclusiveness from the *Aufgabe* to the *Weltanschaung.* Dispositions and tendencies are even less definitive. But *traits*, although appropriated by all manner of writers for all manner of purposes, may still be salvaged, I think, and may be limited in their reference to a certain definite conception of a generalized response-unit in which resides the distinctive quality of behavior that reflects personality. Foes as well as friends of the doctrine of traits will gain from a more consistent use of the term.

The doctrine itself has never been explicitly stated. It is my purpose, with the aid of eight criteria, to define *trait* and to state the logic and some of the evidence for the admission of this concept to good standing in psychology.

1. *A trait has more than nominal existence.* A trait may be said to have the same kind of existence that a habit of

¹ Allport, G. (1960). From *Personality and Social Encounter,* pp. 131–135, by Gordon Allport. Copyright © 1960 by Gordon Allport. Reprinted by permission of Beacon Press.

a complex order has. Habits of a complex, or higher, order have long been accepted as household facts in psychology. There is no reason to believe that the mechanics that produces such a habit . . . stops short of producing the more generalized habits which are here called traits of personality.

2. *A trait is more generalized than a habit.* Within a personality there are, of course, many independent habits; but there is also so much integration, organization and coherence among habits that we have no choice but to recognize great systems of interdependent habits. If the habit of brushing one's teeth can be shown, statistically or genetically, to be unrelated to the habit of dominating a tradesman, there can be no question of a common trait involving both these habits; but, if the habit of dominating a tradesman can be shown, statistically or genetically, to be related to the habit of bluffing one's way past guards, there is the presumption that a common trait of personality exists that includes these two habits. Traits may conceivably embrace anywhere from two habits to a legion of habits. In this way, there may be said to be both major, widely extensified traits and minor, less generalized traits in the same personality.

3. *A trait is dynamic, or at least determinative.* The stimulus is not the crucial determinant in behavior that expresses personality; the trait itself is decisive. Once formed, a trait seems to have the capacity of directing responses to stimuli into characteristic

channels. This emphasis upon the dynamic nature of traits, ascribing to them a capacity for guiding the specific response, is variously recognized by many writers. . . .

From this general point of view, traits might be called "derived drives" or "derived motives." Whatever they are called, they may be regarded as playing a motivating role in each act, thus endowing the separate adjustments of the individual to specific stimuli with that *adverbial* quality that is the very essence of personality . . .

4. *The existence of a trait may be established empirically or statistically.* In order to know that a person has a habit, it is necessary to have evidence of repeated reactions of a constant type. Similarly, in order to know that an individual has a trait, it is necessary to have evidence of repeated reactions that, though not necessarily constant in type, seem none the less to be consistently a function of the same underlying determinant. If this evidence is gathered casually by mere observation of the subject or through the reading of a case history or biography, it may be called empirical evidence.

More exactly, of course, the existence of a trait may be established with the aid of statistical techniques that determine the degree of coherence among the separate responses. Although this employment of statistical aid is highly desirable, it is not necessary to wait for such evidence before speaking of traits, any more than it would be necessary to refrain from speaking of the habit of biting fingernails until the exact frequency of the occurrence is known. Statistical methods are at present better suited to intellective than to conative functions,

and it is with the latter that we are chiefly concerned in our studies of personality.

5. *Traits are only relatively independent of each other.* The investigator desires, of course, to discover what the fundamental traits of personality are—that is to say, what broad trends in behavior do exist independently of one another. Actually, with the test methods and correlational procedures in use, completely independent variation is seldom found. In one study, expansion correlated with extroversion to the extent of +.39; ascendance with conversatism, +.22; humor with insight, +.83; and so on. This overlap may be due to several factors, the most obvious being the tendency of the organism to react in an integrated fashion: when concrete acts are observed or tested, they reflect not only the trait under examination but also, and simultaneously, other traits. Several traits may thus converge into a final common path. It seems safe, therefore, to predict that traits can never be completely isolated for study, since they never show more than a relative independence of one another.

In the instance just cited, it is doubtful whether humor and insight (provided their close relationship is verified in subsequent studies) represent distinct traits. In the future, it may be possible to agree upon a certain magnitude of correlation, below which it will be acceptable to speak of separate traits, and above which only one trait will be recognized. If only one trait is indicated, it will presumably represent a broadly generalized disposition. For example, if humor and insight cannot be established as independent traits, it will be necessary to recognize a more inclusive trait and name it, perhaps, "sense of proportion."

6. *A trait of personality, psychologically considered, is not the same as moral quality.* A trait of personality may or may not coincide with some well-defined, conventional social concept. Extroversion, ascendance, social participation and insight are free from preconceived moral significance, largely because each is a word newly coined or adapted to fit a psychological discovery. It would be ideal if we could, in this way, find our traits first and then name them. But honesty, loyalty, neatness and tact, though encrusted with social significance, *may* likewise represent true traits of personality. The danger is that, in devising scales for their measurement, we may be bound by the conventional meanings and thus be led away from the precise integration as it exists in a given individual. Where possible, it would be well for us to find our traits first and then seek devaluated terms with which to characterize our discoveries.

7. *Acts, and even habits, that are inconsistent with a trait are not proof of the nonexistence of the trait.* The objection most often considered fatal to the doctrine of traits has been illustrated as follows: "An individual may be habitually neat with respect to his person and characteristically slovenly in his handwriting or the care of his desk."

In the first place, this observation fails to state that there are cases frequently met where a constant level of neatness is maintained in all of a person's acts, giving unmistakable empirical evidence that the trait of neatness is, in some people at least, thoroughly and permanently integrated. Not everyone will show the same degree of integration in respect to a given trait. What is a major trait in one personality may be a minor trait, or even nonexistent, in another personality.

In the second place, there may be opposed integrations—that is, contradictory traits—in a single personality. The same individual may have traits both of neatness and of carelessness, of ascendance *and* of submission, although these will frequently be of unequal strength.

In the third place, there are in every personality instances of acts that are unrelated to existent traits, the product of the stimulus and the attitude of the moment. Even the characteristically neat person may become careless when he is hurrying to catch a train. But to say that not all of a person's acts reflect some higher integration is not to say that no such higher integrations exist.

8. *A trait may be viewed either in the light of the personality that contains it or in the light of its distribution in the population at large.* Each trait has both its unique and its universal aspect. In its unique aspect, the trait takes its significance entirely from the role it plays in the personality as a whole. In its universal aspect, the trait is arbitrarily isolated for study, and a comparison is made between individuals in respect to it. From this second point of view, traits merely extend the familiar field of the psychology of individual differences.

2.

GORDON ALLPORT

Scarcely anyone questions the existence of traits as the fundamental units of personality. Common speech presupposes them. This man, we say, is *gruff* and *shy*, but a *hard worker*; that woman is *fastidious, talkative, and stingy.* Psychologists, too, talk in these terms. One psychologist recently wrote a letter of recommendation for a former student characterizing him as *ambitious, friendly*, an *enthusiastic teacher*, but having a quick temper. Even in their technical research in personality most investigators have some kind of trait doctrine. At the same time, psychologists know that common sense is sometimes a faulty guide, and the issue of traits is one of the areas where common sense, even if fundamentally correct, needs to be critically examined and refined.

The Case Against Traits

For one thing, trait-names, such as those in the preceding paragraph, imply too much. The young teacher is not always "friendly;" he is not uniformly "ambitious" in every direction; his "enthusiasm" surely depends on what and whom he is teaching.

During World War II the Office of Strategic Services established an Assessment Center where candidates for foreign secret-service work were examined. After testing and studying a man for several days, several psychologists would try to discover his traits and predict whether they would fit him or unfit him for such a sensitive assignment. The research staff found their tasks enormously difficult, and the reason they gave may be taken as a classic statement of the limitations of any trait-doctrine.

It is easy to predict precisely the outcome of the meeting of one known chemical with another known chemical in an immaculate test tube. But where is the chemist who can predict what will happen to a known chemical if it meets an unknown chemical in an unknown vessel? . . . How, then, can a psychologist foretell with any degree of accuracy the outcome of future meetings of one barely known personality with hundreds of other undesignated personalities in distant, undesignated cities, villages, fields and jungles that are seething with one knows not what potential harms and benefits? [OSS Assessment Staff, *Assessment of Men* (New York: Holt, Rinehart & Winston, 1948), p. 8.]

This criticism is so true and so telling that we must admit at the outset that *no trait theory can be sound unless it allows for, and accounts for, the variability of a person's conduct.* Pressures from the surrounding environment, the companions he is with, and the countercurrents in the person himself may delay, augment, distort, or inhibit completely the conduct that we would normally expect to issue from a person's traits.

All this is true; yet in a person's stream of activity there is, besides a variable portion, likewise a constant

[2] Allport, G. (1961). *Pattern and Growth in Personality.* New York: Holt, Rinehart and Winston, pp. 332–334. Reprinted by permission of the author's estate.

portion; and it is the constant portion we seek to designate with the concept of trait.

The basic principle of behavior is its continuous flow, each successive act representing a mobilizing of much energy for a particular purpose in hand. Only one integrated activity takes place at any one time, and this activity is the result of a final convergence of relevant energies and pressures. In other words, a given act is the product of the interaction of many determining forces, of which traits are only one.

The only thing we can observe is the *act*, and no act is the product of only one trait. When you write a letter, there may enter into this bit of behavior all sorts of determining factors: a sense of duty, a certain homesickness for your friend, a request you wish to make of him, the fact that you now have leisure to write, the availability of pen and paper, as well as the presence of memories, emotions, associations relevant to the activity. Such elaborate convergence of determining tendencies

prevents us from saying that any single activity is the exclusive product of one or more traits. Traits are one of the factors that determine a present act, and they make that act seem "characteristic" of the person; but they are never the sole determinant.

Traits, unlike the "faculties" or "powers" of earlier psychology, are not "little men within the breast" who pull the strings of behavior. Traits are looser tendencies, each expression of a trait being slightly different because it confronts other determining conditions. Furthermore, after an act takes place, there is "feedback" to the nervous system, and in the future a trait will never be precisely the same as it was previously. Thus *continuous flow* is the primary fact. Yet we know that traits exist because, in spite of the continuous flow and change, there is considerable constancy in a person's mode of behavior. We can say that certain acts are characteristic of him. Traits underlie what is "characteristic" in conduct.

3.

GORDON ALLPORT

Personal Dispositions

For a moment we shall continue our discussion of trait-names. Some of

these, we find, are derived from individual historical or fictional characters: *quixotic, narcistic, . . . chauvinistic, sadistic, puckish, a quisling.* Some are spelled with capital letters, *Boswellian, Lesbian, Chesterfieldian, Rabelaisian, Pickwickian, Emersonian, Falstaffian, Homeric, Faustian.*

---

[3] Allport, G. (1961). *Pattern and Growth in Personality.* New York: Holt, Rhinehart and Winston, pp. 358–361. Reprinted by permission of the author's estate.

We say a person is *Christlike, a Don Juan, a Beau Brummell, a Xantippe.* In all of these cases, and many more like them, we note that some particular outstanding characteristic of a single person gave us a new label to apply occasionally (not often) to other people.

In such instances we are not dealing with a common trait. It would be absurd to try to compare all people—or any large number of them—on a scale designed to measure the peculiar *fastidious exhibitionism* of a Beau Brummell or the *sexual cruelty* of a Marquis de Sade. Yet the very fact that we now name the characteristic shows that we have abstracted it from the individual life with the intention of applying it to other lives to which it may fit. Words are general. Even if we say "this boy," we are using two abstract words to point to a particular. Only a proper name, such as Franklin Roosevelt, comes near to designating one unique personal event in nature.

The Uniqueness of Personal Dispositions

We come again to the proposition that seems so shocking to science. Franklin Roosevelt was a unique historical event in nature, and the fabulously complex organization of his mental processes and nervous system was likewise unique. It could not be otherwise considering the individuality of his inheritance, the individuality of his life experience. Even the subsystems of his personality were ultimately unique. When confronted with this unassailable logic, one outraged psychologist exclaimed, "I think it is nonsense to say that no two men ever have the same trait. I mean, of course it is true, but it is one of those truths that can't be accepted." We reply: Unfortunately, this is one truth that the study of personality *must* accept, however great the difficulties it creates.

In order to keep the problem distinct from that of common traits, we shall adopt a different terminology. We could with propriety speak of *individual* (or of *personal*) traits as distinct from common traits, for there is similarity between the two conceptions (both, for example, refer to a complex level of organization). Yet for purposes of clarity we shall designate the individual unit not as a trait, but as a *personal disposition* (and shall occasionally use the abbreviation p.d.).

Much that we have said concerning common traits applies also to personal dispositions. Both are broad (generalized) determining tendencies; both differ in the same way from habits, attitudes, and types; both refer to the level of analysis most suitable to the study of personality; the existence of both is inferred by the occurrence of activities having "functional equivalence."

But there are differences. It makes no sense to speak of the "normal distribution" of p.d.'s, since each is unique to one person. Trait-names fit common traits better than they fit p.d.'s (Generally several words are needed to designate a disposition, as when we say, "Little Susan has a peculiar anxious helpfulness all her own;" or, "He will do anything for you if it doesn't cost him any effort.")

Our contention is that, if correctly diagnosed, p.d.'s reflect the personality structure accurately, whereas common traits are categories into which the individual is forced.

For example, by common trait methods, we find that Peter stands high in *aesthetic interest* and *anxiety,* but low in *leadership* and *need-achievement.* The truth is that all these common traits have a special coloring in his life, and—still more important—they interact with one another. Thus it might be more accurate to say that his personal disposition is a kind of *artistic and self-sufficient solitude.* His separate scores on common traits do not fully reflect this pattern.

But, one asks, is it not "more scientific" to work with common traits? We shall answer this question gradually. For the moment we merely insist that common traits are at best approximations. Often they fail to reflect the structure of a given personality. . . .

Let the reader bear in mind that we are not condemning the common trait-approach. Far from it. When we wish to compare people with one another, it is the only approach possible. Furthermore, the resulting scores, and the profiles, are up to a point illuminating. We are simply saying that there is a second, more accurate way, of viewing personality: namely, the internal patterning (the morphogenesis) of the life considered as a unique product of nature and society.

We view personality—in the only way it can be intelligibly viewed—as a network of organization, composed of systems within systems, some systems of small magnitude and somewhat peripheral to the central or propriate structure, other systems of wider scope at the core of the total edifice; some easy to set into action, others more

dormant; some so culturally conforming that they can readily be viewed as "common;" others definitely idiosyncratic. But in the last analysis this network—employing billions and billions of nerve cells, fashioned by a one-time heredity and by environmental experiences never duplicated—is ultimately unique.

The diehard nomothetic scientist replies, "Well, everything in the world is unique—every stone in the meadow, every old shoe, every mouse; but they are all composed of the same elements." Uniqueness appears when common elements appear in different proportions. Organic chemistry is chiefly concerned with the various combinations of six or seven elements, and it has been estimated that about three million combinations of these few elements are possible. Allowing for still more elements (including common traits) we can ultimately account for the final uniqueness of every person.

My answer is this: Personality exists only at a post-elementary state; it exists only when the common features of human nature have already interacted with one another and produced unique, self-continuing, and evolving systems. This is not to say that the search for common elements or common human functions is undesirable. For the most part the science of psychology does this and nothing else. I insist only that if we are interested in *personality,* we must go beyond the elementaristic and reach into the morphogenic realm.

4.

GORDON ALLPORT

Cardinal, Central, and Secondary Dispositions

In every personality there are p.d.'s of major significance and p.d.'s of minor significance. Occasionally some p.d. is so pervasive and so outstanding in a life that it deserves to be called a cardinal disposition. Almost every act seems traceable to its influence. The list of terms . . . derived from the proper names of historical and fictional characters (even allowing for exaggeration and oversimplification) suggests what is meant by cardinal dispositions. No such disposition can remain hidden, an individual is known by it, and may become famous for it. Such a master quality has sometimes been called the eminent trait, the ruling passion, the master-sentiment, the unity-thema, or the radix of a life.

It is an unusual personality that possesses one and only one cardinal disposition. Ordinarily the foci of a life seem to lie in a handful of distinguishable central p.d.'s. How many is the question we shall ask presently. Central dispositions are likely to be those that we mention in writing a careful letter of recommendation . . .

On a still less important level we may speak of secondary p.d.'s—less conspicuous, less generalized, less consistent, and less often called into play

than central dispositions. Secondary p.d.'s are likely to be more peripheral and less propriate than central p.d.'s.

It goes without saying that these three gradations are arbitrary and are phrased mainly for convenience of discourse. In reality there are all possible degrees of organization, from the most circumscribed and unstable to the most pervasive and firmly structured. It is helpful, however, to have these distinctions at hand when we wish to speak roughly of the relative prominence and intensity of various dispositions in a given personality.

How Many Dispositions Has a Person?

How many dispositions has a person is a most audacious question, and can be answered in only a preliminary and speculative way. For many reasons the question is audacious: Behavior is in continuous flow; dispositions never express themselves singly; people manifest contradictory dispositions in contradictory situations; furthermore, diagnostic methods are too ill developed to enable us to discover the answer.

Still, a few guesses can be made on the basis of partial evidence, provided we confine ourselves to the level of cardinal or central p.d.'s. We shall not even venture a guess concerning secondary dispositions.

We turn first to the realm of biography. In his definitive life of William James, Ralph Barton Perry writes that

---

[4] Allport, G. (1961). *Pattern and Growth in Personality.* New York: Holt, Rhinehart and Winston, pp. 365–367. Reprinted by permission of the author's estate.

in order to understand this fascinating figure it is necessary to deal with eight leading "traits: or "ingredients." He first lists four "morbid" dispositions—tendencies which, taken by themselves, would prove to be severe handicaps: (1) hypochondria, (2) preoccupation with exceptional mental states, (3) marked oscillations of mood, and (4) repugnance to the processes of exact thought. Blended with these morbid p.d.'s and redeeming them are four "benign" dispositions: (5) sensibility, (6) vivacity, (7) humanity, (8) sociability. The labels Perry uses are of course, common trait names; but he defines them in such a way that the peculiar Jamesian flavor of each is brought out. What is important for our purposes is the fact that, even after a most exhaustive study of a complex personality, Perry feels that a limited number of major dispositions (in this case eight) adequately covers the major structure of the life.

Let us consider a bit of experimental evidence. We asked 93 students "to think of some one individual of your own sex whom you know well;" and then "to describe him or her by writing words, phrases, or sentences that express fairly well what seem to you to be the essential characteristics of this person." The phrase essential characteristic was defined as "any trait, quality, tendency, interest, etc., that you regard as of major importance to a description of the person you select."

The average number listed by students was 7.2. Only 10 percent of the writers felt that they needed more than 10 items to describe their friend's "essential characteristics."

These are only suggestive bits of evidence, but they open a momentous possibility. *When psychology develops adequate diagnostic methods for discovering the major lines along which a particular personality is organized (personal dispositions), it may turn out that the number of such foci will normally vary between five and ten.* We state this proposition as a hypothesis subject to eventual scientific testing.

The Functional Autonomy
of Motives

COMMENTARY

In the history of psychology few articles have had such an impact as the 1937 publication of Gordon Allport's article "The Functional Autonomy of Motives" in the *American Journal of Psychology*. Few journal articles alter the course of psychological thought. This one did. The concept of the functional autonomy of motives is Allport's most distinctive professional contribution. Simply stated, the theory asserts that one's current motives have become independent (functionally autonomous) from the original energies and needs that helped form or create them. In other words, to put it even more simply, the quality and character of our motivations change as we grow up and mature. Today this idea sounds more like "common sense" than revolutionary, but when Allport advanced this theory in 1937 it created one of the more interesting controversies in psychology. To understand why this was such a radical view of human motivation and why the psychoanalysts and behaviorists were so upset by it we must place the appearance of Allport's article in historical context.

From the turn of the century, motivation theory had been dominated by the myopic "unchanging energies" view of psychoanalysis and behaviorism. Psychoanalytic theory had firmly established the position that we are motivated by the unconscious demons of our past and by our strivings to reduce the ubiquitous tensions created by the instinctual drives. In a reductionistic fashion, therefore, all motivations, throughout our lives, were to be understood in the light of these primitive and unconscious forces.

The stimulus-response psychology of earlier behaviorism offered their own "unchanging energies" theory. Without the Freudian dynamics, they also explained human motivations with a tension-reduction model. This theory related all motivation to the reduction of tension created by the various drive states. The primary and secondary reinforcers became the scaffolding upon which the more complex "higher order" motives were built. At the time of Allport's article, therefore, psychology was locked into these "unchanging energy" theories that could not adequately account for the conscious, complex, and contemporary motivational systems exhibited by mature adults. In his article, it was Allport's intention to "rock the boat" of motivation theory so that psychology could give a more accurate accounting of the motivations of mature and healthy individuals.

One of the important principles we find throughout Allport's work is the principle of *discontinuity*. This principle is clearly in evidence in his concept of functional autonomy. Allport makes a sharp, qualitative distinction between the motivations of the neurotic vs. the healthy, the child vs. the adult, and the immature vs. the mature personalities. There is a qualitative difference in the motivational lives of individuals within these groups, and the principle of functional autonomy, therefore, will only apply to the motivations of individuals in the latter groups. In other words, the motivations of children, neurotics, and the immature are largely unconscious, linked to archaic patterns and energies, and follow more closely the unchanging energy principles of psychoanalysis and behaviorism.

While recognizing the enormous contribution of Allport's concept, I would, nevertheless, like to raise one issue with the functional autonomy of motives. In this theory Allport seems to suggest that *all* motives have some historical links to earlier, more primitive energies, needs, reinforcements, or desires. He was, of course, trying to bridge the gap between psychoanalytic and behavior theory and a more growth-oriented open-systems theory. Perhaps there are, however, even in children, some motivations that emerge spontaneously out of other resources that have no connection whatsoever, historical or otherwise, to these primitive and archaic systems, or "seed motives," as Allport called them. I am thinking of my son here. When he was six years old, he spent much of his summer watching a house being built near our home. At the end of that summer he announced that he wanted to be a carpenter and to build houses. From that time forward much of his life was directed by that goal. He sought opportunities to help neighbors with home projects. In high school he took the home building option in a vocational education program. After a two-year liberal arts experience, he transferred to a university that offered a degree that enabled him to learn all aspects of home construction. Immediately after graduation he got a job with a home builder, and today he is the vice-president and operations manager of that company.

Now one might argue that my son's original motive or desire was linked to some Oedipal resolution or a transference phenomenon which included skilled men doing "real" work, and a father who can hardly drive a nail and who gets nervous in a hardware store. I doubt it. I am inclined to think that that defining summer of largely vicarious learning tapped into latent skills, interests, and attributes of my son's personality that served as a catalyst for a fundamental life direction. I hesitate to believe that my son's experience was a case of the functional autonomy of a motive, with some historical link to a more primitive need or purpose.

In any case the issue is worthy of conjecture.

1.

GORDON ALLPORT

Functional Autonomy of Motives

We turn now to one general law of motivation that allows fully for the concrete uniqueness of personal motives, and observes all other criteria for an adequate theory of motivation. It is by no means the only valid principle pertinent to the development of human motives; nor does it explain *all* motivation. It is, however, our attempt to escape the limitations of uniform, rigid, abstract, backward-looking theories, and to recognize the spontaneous, changing, forward-looking, concrete character that much adult motivation surely has.

Functional autonomy regards adult motives as varied, and as self-sustaining, contemporary systems, growing out of antecedent systems, but functionally independent of them. Just as a child gradually outgrows dependence on his parents, becomes self-determining, and outlives his parents,

so it is with many motives. The transition may be gradual but it is nonetheless drastic. As the individual (or the motive) matures, the bond with the past is broken. The tie is historical, not functional.

Such a theory is obviously opposed to all conceptions of "unchanging energies." It declines to view the energies of adults as infantile or archaic in nature. Motivation is always contemporary. The life of modern Athens is *continuous* with the life of the ancient city, but in no sense *depends* upon it for its present "go." The life of a tree is continuous with that of its seed, but the seed no longer sustains and nourishes the full-grown tree. Earlier purposes lead into later purposes, but are abandoned in the latter's favor.

Let us take a few commonplace examples. An ex-sailor has a craving for the sea, a musician longs to return to his instrument after an enforced absence, a miser continues to build up his useless pile. Now the sailor may have first acquired his love for the sea as an incident in his struggle to earn a living. The sea was "secondary

[1] Allport, G. (1961). *Pattern and Growth in Personality.* New York: Holt, Rinehart and Winston. pp. 226–229. Reprinted by permission of the author's estate.

reinforcement" for his hunger drive. But now the ex-sailor is perhaps a wealthy banker; the original motive is destroyed, and yet the hunger for the sea persists and even increases in intensity. The musician may first have been stung by a slur on his inferior performance into mastering his instrument; but now he is safely beyond these taunts, and finds that he loves his instrument more than anything else in the world. The miser perhaps learned his habit of thrift in dire necessity, but the miserliness persists and becomes stronger with the years even after the necessity has been relieved.

Workmanship is a good example. A good workman feels compelled to do a clean-cut job even though his income no longer depends on maintaining high standards. In fact, in a day of jerry-building his workmanlike standards may be to his economic disadvantage. Even so, he cannot do a slipshod job. Workmanship is not an instinct, but so firm is the hold it may acquire on a man that it is no wonder Veblen mistook it for one.

A businessman, long since secure economically, works himself into ill-health, perhaps even back into poverty, for the sake of carrying on his plans. Hard work, once a means to an end, becomes an end in itself.

Neither necessity nor reason can make a person contented on an isolated country farm after he is adapted to active, energetic city life. Citified habits urge him to a frenzied existence, even though health may demand the simpler life.

The pursuit of literature, the development of good taste in clothes, the use of cosmetics, strolls in the public park, or a winter in Miami may first serve, let us say, the interests of sex. But every one of these "instrumental" activities may become an interest in itself, held for a lifetime, even after they no longer serve the erotic motive.

Some mothers bear their children unwillingly, dismayed at the thought of drudgery in the future. The "parental instinct" is wholly lacking. The mother may be held to her child-tending by fear of what her critical neighbors will say, or by fear of the law, or perhaps by a dim hope that the child will provide security for her in her old age. Gross as these motives may be, they hold her to her work until gradually, through the practice of devotion, her burden becomes a joy. As her love for the child develops, her earlier practical motives are lost. In later years not one of these original motives may operate. The tenacity of the maternal sentiment is proverbial, even when, as in this case, it can be shown to be not an original but an acquired motive.

Let us add one more example. Many boys choose occupations that follow in their fathers' footsteps. Also, most young boys go through a period of passionate "father identification." Joe, let us say, is the son of a famous politician. As a young lad he imitates everything his father does, even perhaps giving "speeches." Years pass and the father dies. Joe is now middle-aged and is deeply absorbed in politics. He runs for office, perhaps the self-same job his father held. What, then, motivates Joe today? Is it his earlier father fixation: Conceivably yes, for Joe may never have outgrown his Oedipal complex (trying to be like Daddy in order to win his mother's affection). If Joe's political activity today is of this neurotic variety we shall probably find him behaving in a compulsive, rigid, even maladaptive manner. The chances, however, are that his interest in politics has outgrown its roots in "father identification." There is historical continuity but no longer any functional continuity. Politics is now his dominant passion; it is his style of life; it is a large part of Joe's personality. The original seed has been discarded.

All our illustrations have one feature in common. The adult interest we describe began as something else. In all cases the activity that later became motivational was at first instrumental to some other end (i.e., to some earlier motive). What was once extrinsic and instrumental becomes intrinsic and impelling. The activity once served a drive or some simple need; it now serves itself, or in a larger sense, serves the self-image (self-ideal) of the person. Childhood is no longer in the saddle; maturity is.

Functional autonomy, then, refers to any acquired system of motivation in which the tensions involved are not of the same kind as the antecedent tensions from which the acquired system developed.

2.

GORDON ALLPORT

Propriate Functional Autonomy

Although personality contains many such self-maintaining systems, its principal energies are master systems of motivation that confer more unity on personality than disparate perseverating systems can do. Our account . . . cannot be complete until we relate the concept of functional autonomy to the propriate functions of personality. Let us consider a few examples from this level of functional autonomy.

1. *Ability often turns into interest.* It is an established fact that ordinarily people like to do what they can do well (the correlation between abilities and interests is high). Now the original reason for learning a skill may not be interest at all. For example, a student who first undertakes a field of study in college because it is required, because it pleases his parents, or because it comes at a convenient hour may end by finding himself absorbed in the topic, perhaps for life. The original motives may be entirely lost. What was a means to an end becomes an end in itself.

It is true that rewards are often given to an able person for exercising his talents. But does he exercise them

---

[2] Allport, G. (1961). *Pattern and Growth in Personality.* Holt, Rinehart and Winston: pp. 235–237. Reprinted by permission of the author's estate.

merely to get a reward? It seems unlikely. No such motivation accounts for the drive behind genius. For the genius, creative passion itself is the motive. How hollow to think of Pasteur's concern for reward, or for health, food, sleep, or family, as the root of his devotion to his work. For long periods of time he was oblivious of them all, losing himself in the white heat of research. And the same passion is seen in the histories of geniuses who in their lifetimes received little or no reward for their work: Galileo, Mendel, Schubert, van Gogh, and many others.

It is important to note that major life-interests are seldom clearly formed or even indicated in childhood (musical prodigies being an exception). . . .

Clearly youthful interests are less stable than adult interests. Further, it seems safe to say that the interests of most children, even into the teens, are very much like those of other children, whereas adults grow in uniqueness (individuation). The ruling passions of adults are exceedingly diverse. One man is absorbed in business and golf; another, in religion and art. An old woman in a home for the aged pivots her life solely on the hope that "some people may remember me kindly."

Whether we shall call these propriate motives *interests, sentiments, values,* or something, else, does not for the moment matter. Whatever we call them, they are acquired preeminent motives. Since the tensions involved are not of the same kind as the tensions of the seed motives, they are, by our definition, functionally autonomous.

2. *Acquired interests and values have selective power.* . . . what a person perceives, remembers, and thinks is in large part determined by his own propriate formations. As an interest grows it creates a lasting tensional condition that leads to congruent conduct, and also acts as a silent agent for selecting and directing whatever is related to the interest. . . .

3. *Self-image and life-style are organizing factors.* It would be an error to think of interests as single and separate mainsprings. Together they form a complex self-image or life-style which is also functionally autonomous. It evolves gradually in the course of life, and day by day guides and unifies all, or at least many, of a person's transactions with life.

I am speaking here of the highest levels of organization in personality. Most theories of personality (especially those postulating "unchanging energies") overlook the motivational power of higher-level formations. My position is that, although lower-level self-maintaining (perseverative) systems exist, the more important instance of functional autonomy is found in the complex propriate organization that determines the "total posture" of a mature life-system.

Expressive Movement and Behavior

COMMENTARY

In the majority of texts on personality theory, little or no attention is given to Allport's interest in expressive movement and behavior, but such behaviors are an important feature of his theory.

Allport was always looking for the unique attributes of personality, to identify individual styles and expressions. He sought to penetrate below the surface aspects of personality to capture its individual "flavor" and uniqueness. Allport was interested, therefore, in all forms of expressive behavior, including handwriting, doodles, gestures, and gait. He believed that such expressions provided us with an infallible signature of the person's unique style and individuality. Thus, Allport made an early contribution to the current interest in body language and nonverbal behavior. Allport contrasted these expressive behaviors with coping behaviors and strategies. While every act contains both an expressive and a coping component, these latter behaviors are more peripheral and external to the individual, designed to alter and manage the environment and meet the conscious needs of the moment. Coping behavior, Allport emphasized, is task-oriented and reflects a large degree of conformity and cultural conditioning. Expressive behaviors, on the other hand, are more unconscious in their origin and expression. They are more purposeless and spontaneous, revealing deeper personality structures and traits that are not expressed in coping behaviors. In short, they represent the more creative features of the personality. Hence, the expressive movements and behaviors are a fundamental component of the individual's personal dispositions and contribute to the "patterned uniqueness" of personality.

249

Much of our important learning in life is accomplished by following models and rules. We learn, through practice, to play the piano, or to play baseball, or to write by attending to authorities, listening to and watching the experts, and following the prescribed rules for skill development. Ultimately, however, if we are to express our individual natures, we must break away from our tutors, from *their* rules and conventions, and exhibit our own special style and unique way of doing things. Real achievement and success often depends upon the emergence of these expressive features of personality. Allport encourages us to respect and develop our own uniqueness.

GORDON ALLPORT

Expressive Movement and Behavior

Suppose that you go to a lecture delivered by a stranger. The lecture may be on any topic at all—let us say it is on "expressive behavior." You go primarily to hear *what* the lecturer will say, only secondarily, if at all, to note how he will say it. You are concerned with the content of his views, with the way he will cope with the topic. He, too, will be intent on the subject matter. Both of you are focused on this high-level process of communication.

But while the lecturer is speaking, a lower level process of communication is under way. Even if you are not particularly interested, you note—especially at the start of the lecture—many things about the speaker. He is tall, fairly young, neatly dressed, slender,

incessantly active; he speaks rapidly but in a voice that is high and raspy. He repeats his phrases, smiles frequently, mops his brow though it is not hot, and scrawls illegibly on the blackboard.

Almost immediately—whether you wish to do so or not—you make some inferences about him as a person. The inferences are fleeting, fringe-like, usually unimportant. You think to yourself, "He is insecure, on the make, self-centered, but learned, humorous though slightly cynical; on the whole I don't like him and I pity his wife." Your judgments are shadowy and perhaps all wrong. But you cannot help making them and he by his *expressive movement* cannot help prompting them.

Before the lecture is ended, and especially if you hear many lectures by the same man, you become so accustomed to him that you pay no more attention to his manner. You tend to

Allport, G. (1961). *Pattern and Growth in Personality*. New York: Holt, Rinehart and Winston, pp. 460–491. Reprinted by permission of the author's estate.

discount his style of expression and pay attention almost exclusively to his high-level communication, to what he is saying, how competent he is, and what it all means to you.

Sometimes, of course, we do become directly interested in manner, in style, in the expressive aspect of behavior. We put aside our usual preoccupation with content, with the intellectual, purposive, coping aspects of life. We ask ourselves what do this person's voice, speech, facial expression, style of clothing, handwriting, posture, gait, and pattern of gestures signify? We sometimes think—and rightly—that the *how* of behavior can be more revealing than the *what*. The *adverbial* manner of an act tells us much about the person we are dealing with.

Expression Defined

The term *expression* is used in psychology with at least three different meanings. First is the common-sense use. We say that a man expresses an opinion, or a preference, or a point of view. That is, he tells us directly and deliberately something about his ideas or himself. We also say that an artist, a musician, or a dancer is expressing his feelings as well as some symbolized meaning in his production. Whether intellectual or artistic, this type of expression is deliberate and conscious. It normally is our chief channel for understanding other personalities.

The term has a more limited meaning when it refers to such bodily changes as blushing, laughing, dilation of the pupil, quaking of the knees. Darwin's *The Expression of Emotions in Men and Animals*, first published in 1872, established this meaning firmly.

In this sense expression signifies involuntary response to emotional stimuli.

The third use of the term is subtler. . . . It refers to one's manner or style of behaving. Unlike the first meaning, it has nothing to do with the *what* of an act, but only with the *how*. Unlike the second meaning, it has nothing to do with the release of emotional tension; instead, it deals with the oblique mirroring of personal traits. Of course, all three types of expression tell us something about a person, but for analytic clarity it is important to make the distinction.

We can define expressive movement simply as *one's manner of performing adaptive acts*. From our point of view, every single act a person performs has both its expressive and its adaptive (coping) aspects, sometimes more of one, sometimes more of the other. Let us examine this proposition more closely.

Expressive Versus Coping Behavior

Every act that we perform copes with our environment. Even rest and sleep and play are no exceptions. There is a *task* in hand (the *what* of behavior). We must repair a lock, seek relaxation, summon a doctor, answer a question, or blink a speck of dust from our eyes. To cope with the task we employ our reflexes and habits or call upon our skills, our judgment and knowledge. But into this stream of activity there enter deeper trends in our nature. There are *styles* of repairing locks, calling a doctor, relaxing, answering a question, or blinking the eye. Every action betrays *both* a coping and an expressive aspect. One may think of coping as the *predicate* of action (what we are doing); expression as the *adverb* of action (how we are doing it). . . .

Some of the differences between coping and expressive behavior may be summarized as follows:

a. Coping is purposive and specifically motivated; expressive behavior is not.
b. Coping is determined by the needs of the moment and by the situation; expressive movement reflects deeper personal structure.
c. Coping is formally elicited, expressive behavior spontaneously "emitted."
d. Coping can be more readily controlled (inhibited, modified, conventionalized); expressive behavior is harder to alter and often uncontrollable. (Changing our style of handwriting, e.g., can be kept up for only a short time.)
e. Coping usually aims to change the environment; expressive behavior aims at nothing, though it may incidentally have effects (as when our manner of answering questions in an interview creates a good impression and lands us the job).
f. Typically coping is conscious, even though it may employ automatic skills; expressive behavior generally lies below the threshold of our awareness. . . .

Genesis of Expressive Behavior

If a young child is irritable he shows it openly in almost every movement he makes: he cries, fusses, whines, slaps. His expressiveness is diffuse and massive. An adult, by contrast, may show his irritable nature only by his restless fingers or shifting eyes. The growing differentiation and localizing of movement as a person matures is true not only of skilled coping but also of expression.

The fact that expression tends with growing maturity to become confined to limited regions of the body has important consequences for personality assessment. For one thing, it means that various features of expression are of unequal significance in different people. Some faces are open books; some are "poker faces." For some people gestures are merely conventional; for others, highly individual. Sometimes the style of clothing or the handwriting seems "just like" the person; in other cases, entirely nonexpressive. One person reveals himself primarily in his speech; another, in his posture and gait; a third, in his style of clothing or ornamentation. As a promising hypothesis we suggest that every person has one or two leading expressive features which reveal his true nature. If this is so, it is somewhat futile to study all people by the same cues, e.g., voice, eyes, or handwriting. The cue that is revealing for one person is not necessarily revealing for another.

Every child is exposed to standard forms of expression which tend to limit his individual impulses in movement. He learns to write from a standard model, to play the piano or to dance according to rules. . . . His handwriting acquires "graphic maturity," his musical interpretation and his dancing steps are his own. Even the stenographer in time modifies her system of shorthand, and the physician, when no longer an intern, comes to practice his art in his own manner. But all people remain conventional to some degree. What is important is the extent to which they break through the prescriptions of training and convention, and develop their own stamp of individuality. And, as we have said, the stamp may be more apparent in some expressive features than in others.

The child, and especially the adolescent, is likely to adopt expressive styles by imitation. The small boy who envies the worldliness of the street-corner gang imitates their carefree manner of tilting the cap and spitting. The adolescent girl wears her hair as her favorite actress does. The college student apes the mannerisms of some coach or professor. Such superficial imitation is of psychological interest. At heart the youth wants the basic skills or attributes of his model. He is too young to attain them, and so he settles for the external expression of these attributes—for the kind of necktie or the haircut worn by the boss, for the swagger or stance of the athletic hero.

With maturity many of these imitative mannerisms are dropped. The office boy grown up to worldly wisdom can wear whatever necktie he likes; he no longer needs to ape the boss. And yet occasionally mannerisms in adulthood may be vestigial, indicating more the past history of one's development than its present state. Perhaps an expressive habit has become fixed by a kind of perseverative functional autonomy. In such a case we are dealing with a residue of earlier life, and should evaluate it as such. Thus if an adult has a habit of averting his eyes, biting his nails, or picking his nose, he *may* be evincing present conflict and present trends, or he *may* be carrying out a dissociated perseverative mannerism from childhood. Only close study will tell. . . .

Posture, Gesture, Gait

The position and movements of the limbs reflect the influence of coping, cultural convention, and personality. The traffic policeman stops the flow of vehicles with his left arm and motions to pedestrians with his right. In this case the nature of the task and cultural convention are largely responsible for the pattern of motion. But even in this highly prescribed sequence we may detect subtle individuality of expression, sometimes suggesting friendliness, boredom, or arrogance.

Take posture. Man differs from the apes by his standing posture, a fact that has enormous consequences for his mobility and intelligence. An anthropological investigation indicates that the human body is capable of assuming about one thousand different steady postures. "Steady" means a static position that one can maintain comfortably for some time. To some extent these preferred positions depend on cultural habits (e.g., whether or not chairs are used), but still to a large extent the posture one finds congenial is a matter of his own choosing. Posture during sleep is also a highly stable personal characteristic . . . Limbs in action are still more revealing, although here too we must read through the coping and cultural components. Culture, we know, has a marked influence on hand gesticulation. Some movements, on the other hand, are more culture-free. . . .

Gait is a topic of special fascination. In the Apocrypha we read: "The attire of the body, and the laughter of the 'teeth, and the gait of the man, shew what he is." But here again controlled analysis is just beginning. Wilsmann suggests that there are seven measurable attributes in gait: regularity, speed, pressure, length of stride, elasticity, definiteness of direction, and variability. To this list he adds an attribute pertaining to the total swing which he calls rhythm.

Over and over again in all the channels of expression the problem of rhythm recurs. It is a poorly defined concept. Sometimes it refers to the periodicity of some aspect of the movement pattern. But usually the term points to an unanalyzed (and perhaps unanalyzable) effect created by the whole pattern of movement. "Rhythm," like "style," is as yet a vague and nonoperational concept. . . .

Handwriting is, of all the forms of expression, by far the most popular. Graphologists may make a living by "reading character from handwriting." Psychologists increasingly, if somewhat reluctantly, are turning their attention to this field of investigation. For one thing, they have invented clever instruments for measuring the three dimensions of script—its vertical length, its width, and its pressure.

There is a strong case to be made for handwriting analysis. It is, as proponents argue, not merely handwriting, but also "brain writing," influenced by all manner of expressive neural impulses giving individual flavor to the coping movements of the hand. As "crystallized gesture," it is by all odds the most accessible of expressive movements for study; all other movements are fugitive and more difficult

to measure. Part, but not all, of the popularity of studying handwriting is due to its easy availability.

Critics who say flatly that there is "nothing in graphology" are simply wrong. Many studies show that graphologists are in fact able to diagnose some characteristics above chance. And it is not only professionals who have skill; probably all of us have to some extent. For example, it is commonly found that a random sample of people can tell the sex of writers correctly from script alone in about 70 percent of the cases. Though far from perfect, this degree of success is above chance.

If some critics claim too little for graphology, enthusiasts certainly claim too much. Sometimes charlatanry is involved, as when a graphologist gives us a "reading" of a well-known political figure or actress. The characteristics reported are probably not discovered from the script at all but merely repeat common knowledge about the personage in question.

Charlatans aside, many workers in the field make serious attempts to discover the most appropriate dimensions of handwriting for use. Broadly speaking, there is a quarrel between those who favor specific graphic signs and those who look only at molar features of script. The former group might claim, e.g., that a forward slant indicates "sympathy," or that writing uphill signifies "optimism," or that a person who writes "o" open at the top is "open" and "generous." This is the graphic-sign approach, and probably is less valid. . . .

One problem that urgently needs exploration is this: what aspects of personality can be validly determined from script and what aspects cannot be? One study shows, for example, that a person's outstanding values can be fairly well identified (e.g., whether he is a markedly religious person), but we certainly cannot decide from handwriting alone whether the writer is Catholic, Baptist, or Jew. And also, in line with our argument. . . . we must expect some people to reveal more of their personal traits in handwriting than others. A librarian, for example, might give an inexpressive script, but a revealing voice or gait.

These limitations lead us to our main conclusion: All avenues of expression deserve study. We dare not rest our practice of psychodiagnosis on any one "monosymptomatic" feature. To study expression adequately we should explore all channels.

Style

Originally *style* meant a pen or inscribing tool (stylus). It came later to mean handwriting, and then the whole flavor of a written, or any other, work in its entirety. Since man is, in a sense, a fusion of all his works, the French are wont to say, *Le style est l'homme même.*

For the psychologist the term means the complex and complete pattern of expressive behavior. It concerns the whole of activity, not merely special skills or single regions, unless, of course, we specifically limit the term by speaking of a style of *handwriting* or a *style of speaking.*

Each painter has a style of his own; so, too, each composer, musician, ball player, novelist, housewife, and mechanic. From style alone we recognize compositions by Chopin, paintings by Dali, and pastry by Aunt Sally. In all these cases we are speaking of the close tie between expressive layers of personality and highly integrated forms of coping. Style applies to the *personal idiom* that marks coping activity.

The Mature Personality

COMMENTARY

Gordon Allport's interests, training, and background were never focused on the unhealthy and the pathological in personality. He was neither a clinician nor a psychotherapist. While other psychologists sought to understand the dynamics of pathology and to apply their principles as a general psychology, Allport sought, rather, to distinguish neurotic from normal functioning and to establish the intrinsic features of normality. Increasingly, as Allport's ideas and conceptual development matured, he turned his attention to the possibility of an even higher level of development and integration—the healthy or mature personality. It was as if he were searching for some ultimate integration of his work, some capstone expression of all of his ideas and theories.

Attempts to formulate the criteria for normality were prominent in the 1940s and 1950s. In the decades following, this earlier work gradually led to a conceptual advance that recognized the healthy, mature personality as qualitatively different from the "merely normal." Allport's work was instrumental in this development.

Many theoretical contributions to this recognition of the healthy personality were also made by Abraham Maslow, Carl Rogers, and others. Although coming from different backgrounds and representing different perspectives and approaches, these theorists reached a remarkable consensus as to the essential attributes of the healthy or mature individual. The reader is encouraged to compare their views.

Certainly, after studying Allport and moving through the readings, we may take an educated guess as to the important principles that guided Allport's formulation of the concept of the mature personality.

1. In the mature personality, motives are conscious.
2. In the mature personality, motives are contemporary.
3. In the mature personality, the development of motives follows a process leading to functional autonomy.
4. In the mature personality, there is a focus on future goals.
5. In the mature personality, motives seek a creative tension rather than tension reduction.

We could list other specifics to Allport's theory of maturity but we will let Allport speak for himself in the selections that follow.

One final thought in this commentary. We must remember that the mature or healthy individual is not a collection of separate and discrete characteristics but is a unified personality with these core attributes forming an integrated and functioning whole. Allport helped us to appreciate this important fact more than any other psychologist.

GORDON ALLPORT

The Mature Personality

We now turn to the task of summarizing in our own way the criteria of maturity. . . . It is arbitrary to say they are six in number. Yet six seems to give a reasonable balance between distinctions too fine and too coarse for our purpose.

Extension of the Sense of Self

The sense of self built up gradually in infancy is not fully formed in the

first three, or ten, years of life. It continues to expand with experience as one's circle of participation becomes larger. As Erikson points out, adolescence is an especially critical time. Battling against "identity-diffusion," the youth wants to know just who he is. Which facts and experiences and roles are for him appropriate, which peripheral, or not suited at all to his life-style?

Puppy love illustrates the point. It focalizes powerful but discordant impulses: sexual tonicity, assertive and submissive tendencies, ambitions, esthetic interests, family sentiment, even religious emotion. But what is

Allport, G. (1961). *Pattern and Growth in Personality.* New York: Holt, Rinehart and Winston, pp. 283–296, 300–301. Reprinted by permission of the author's estate.

important is that this intimate surge attaches itself to another person. The boundaries of self are rapidly extended. The welfare of another is as important as one's own; better said, the welfare of another is *identical* with one's own.

It is not only adolescent love that enlarges the "oneliness:" new ambitions, new memberships, new ideas, new friends, new recreations and hobbies, and, above all, one's vocation become incorporated into the sense of self. They are now factors in one's identity.

Here we clearly need the principle of functional autonomy. To the mature person, life is more than food, drink, safety, mating; more than anything that can be directly, or even indirectly, related to "drive-reduction." Unless a person develops strong interests "outside himself" (and yet still part of himself) he lives closer to the animal level than to the human level of existence. We are, of course, speaking here of *propriate* (and not merely perseverative) functional autonomy.

Let us put the matter another way. The criterion of maturity we are now examining calls for authentic participation by the person in some significant spheres of human endeavor. To be participant is not the same as being *merely* active. . . .

True participation gives direction to life. Maturity advances in proportion as lives are decentered from the clamorous immediacy of the body and of egocenteredness. Self-love is a prominent and inescapable factor in every life, but it need not dominate. Everyone has self-love, but only self-extension is the earmark of maturity.

Warm Relating of Self to Others

The social adjustment of the mature person is marked by two quite different kinds of warmth. On the one hand, by virtue of self-extension, such a person is capable of great intimacy in his capacity for love—whether the attachment is in family life or in deep friendship. On the other hand, he avoids gossipy, intrusive, and possessive involvements with people (even his own family). He has a certain detachment which makes him respectful and appreciative of the human condition of all men. This type of warmth may be called *compassion*.

Both intimacy and compassion require that one not be a burden or nuisance to others, nor impede their freedom in finding their own identity. Constant complaining and criticizing, jealousy and sarcasm are toxic in social relationships. A woman of marked maturity was asked what she considered the most important rule of life. She answered, "Do not poison the air that other people have to breathe."

This respect for persons as persons is achieved through an imaginative extension of one's own rougher experiences in life. One comes to know that all mortals are in the same human situation: they did not ask to come into the world; they are saddled with an urge to survive and are buffeted by drives and passions; they encounter failure, suffer, but somehow carry on. No one knows for sure the meaning of life; everyone is growing older as he sails to an unknown destination. All lives are pressed between two oblivions. No wonder the poet cries, "Praise the Lord for every globule of human compassion."

It is here that we encounter tolerance and the "democratic character structure" so often advanced as earmarks of maturity. By contrast the immature person feels, as it were, that only he himself has the distinctively human experiences of compassion, fear, and preference. He and his kind matter; no one else. His church, his lodge, his family, and his nation make a safe unit, but all else is alien, dangerous, to be excluded from his petty formula for survival.

More should be said about the deeper personal attachments. It is safe to assert that no one, mature or immature, can ever love or be loved enough. But it seems that the less mature person wants to be loved rather more than he wants to give love. When he gives love it is usually on his own terms, which is to say that strings are attached: the other must pay for the privilege. A possessive, crippling love—such as some parents burden their children with—is common enough but unwholesome for both giver and receiver. It is a hard lesson for a parent to learn—or for a wife, husband, lover, or friend—that he should desire the other's company, wish him well, and accept him for what he is, without placing iron bonds of obligation upon him. . . .

Emotional Security (Self-Acceptance)

We readily note the difference between the person who has emotional poise and one who is emotionally clamorous and who gives way to outbursts of anger and passion—including overindulgence in alcohol and obsessive outbursts of profanity and obscenity. The egotist, the roué, the infantile person have not passed successfully through the normal stages of development. They are still preoccupied with bits and pieces of emotional experience.

Many writers speak of *self-acceptance*. This feature of maturity includes the ability to avoid overreaction to matters pertaining to segmental drives. One accepts his sex drive and does the best he can to handle it with the minimum of conflict in himself and with society; he does not constantly seek the salacious and the scatological, nor is he prudish and repressed. Everyone has fears, both of immediate dangers and of ultimate death, but these can be handled with acceptance. If not, there develops a neurotic preoccupation with the danger of knives, of high places, with health foods and medicines, with self-protective superstitions and rituals.

Especially important is the quality called "frustration tolerance." Irritations and thwartings occur daily. The immature adult, like the child, meets them with tantrums of temper, or with complaining, blaming others, and self-pity. By contrast, the mature person puts up with frustration, takes the blame on himself (by being "intropunitive") if it is appropriate to do so. He can bide his time, plan to circumvent the obstacle, or, if necessary, resign himself to the inevitable. It is definitely not true that the mature person is always calm and serene, nor is he always cheerful. His moods come and go; he may even be temperamentally pessimistic and depressed. But he has learned to live with his emotional states in such a way that they do not betray him into impulsive acts nor interfere with the well-being of others.

He probably could not do so unless he had evolved a continuous sense of security in his life. His early childhood experiences of "basic trust" will have something to do with this development. And at later stages he has somehow learned that not every pinprick to his pride is a mortal wound, and not every fear portends disaster. The sense of security is by no means absolute. No one has control of time, tide, taxes, death, or disaster. As the sense of self expands, one takes on new risks and new chances of failure. But these insecurities are somehow held with a sense of proportion. One becomes cautious without panic. Self-control is a reflection of a sense of proportion. The mature person expresses his conviction and feelings with consideration for the convictions and feelings of others; and he does not feel threatened by his own emotional expressions or by theirs. Such a sense of proportion is not an isolated attribute in personality. It comes about because one's outlook is generally of a realistic order, and because one possesses integrative values that control and gate the flow of emotional impulse. . . .

Realistic Perception, Skills, and Assignments

Thought, . . . is an integral part of personality. One might say that the life of feeling and emotion is the warp and that higher mental processes are the woof of the fabric.

We have already seen that the everyday perceptions and cognitions of the sound personality are on the whole marked by efficiency and accuracy. One might say that the sound person has "sets" that lead to veridicality to a greater degree than do persons not so sound. Maturity does not bend reality to fit one's needs and fantasies.

Does this fact mean that no person can be healthy and mature unless he has a high IQ? There is truth, but also danger, in such a judgment. Manifestly a sturdy minimum is required of memory ability, verbal (symbolic) power, and general problem-solving capacity. To be mature means to have these basic intellectual abilities. Yet the equation is not reversible. Plenty of people with high intelligence lack the emotional balance and intellectual organization that constitute a wholesome personality. . . .

Not only are the perceptions mostly veridical, and cognitive operations accurate and realistic, but appropriate skills are available for solving objective problems. An otherwise sound person who lacks the know-how of his trade—be it mechanics, statecraft, or housekeeping—will not have the security of the means for self-extension that maturity requires. Although we often find skillful people who are immature, we never find mature people without problem-pointed skills.

Along with veridicality and skill we must list the capacity to lose oneself in one's work. . . . Mature people are problem centered. Something objective is worth doing. What this means is that egoistic impulses of drive-satisfaction, pleasure, pride, defensiveness, can all be forgotten for long stretches while a task takes over. This particular criterion can be related to the goal of "responsibility" which is stressed by existential thinkers. . . .

In short, a mature person will be in close touch with what we call the "real world." He will see objects, people, and situations for what they are. And he will have important work to do. . . .

Self-Objectification: Insight and Humor

To achieve the good life, said Socrates, there is one paramount rule: *know thyself.* This is not an easy assignment. Santayana wrote, "Nothing requires a rarer intellectual heroism than willingness to see one's equation written out." Lord Chesterfield was perhaps too self-satisfied when he wrote to his son, "I know myself (no common piece of knowledge, let me tell you). I know what I can, what I cannot, and consequently, what I ought to do."

Most people *think* they have good self-insight. In various courses in psychology 96 percent of the students claimed to have average or better than average insight, only 4 percent admitting possible deficiency. Since we think about ourselves so much of the time it is comforting to assume that our thinking is veridical—that we really know the score.

The term *insight* (often called *self-insight*) comes from psychiatric usage according to which a mental patient, who knows that he (and not everybody else) is suffering from disorientation, is credited with insight. Extending this usage to the normal population, we may say that accurate self-knowledge is a dimension where people occupy positions ranging from high self-insight to little or none. . . .

How is the psychologist to tell whether or not an individual has insight? According to an old adage, Everyman has three characters:

1. that which he has;
2. that which he thinks he has;
3. that which others think he has.

Ideally, insight is to be measured by the ratio between the second item and the first, for what a man thinks he is in relation to what he really is provides a perfect definition and index of his insight. Practically, however, proof positive of what a man is in the biophysical sense is difficult to obtain. Ultimately, therefore, the most practicable index becomes the ratio between the second and third items—the relation of what a man thinks he is to what others (especially the psychologist who studies him) think he is. If the man objects that all the world, including the psychologist, is wrong about him, he cannot be disproved. In such a case the evaluation of his insight must be left to heaven.

Psychologists know that there are certain correlates of insight. For example, those who are aware of their own objectionable qualities are much less likely to attribute them to other people, that is to say, they are less given to "projection" than are those lacking insight. Also, people with high insight are better judges of other people and are likely to be accepted by them. There is likewise evidence that those with good insight are on the average relatively high in intelligence. We recall also that students rated high in "soundness" stood high on insight.

Humor. Perhaps the most striking correlate of insight is the sense of humor. In one unpublished study where subjects rated one another on a large number of traits, the correlation between ratings on insight and humor turned out to be .88. Such a high coefficient means either that personalities with marked insight are also high in humor, or else that the raters were not able to distinguish between the two qualities. In either case the result is important. . . .

The sense of humor must be distinguished sharply from the cruder sense of the comic. The latter is a common possession of almost all people, children as well as adults. What is ordinarily considered funny—on the stage, in comic strips, on TV—consists usually of absurdities, horse play, or puns. For the most part it consists in the degradation of some imagined opponent. The aggressive impulse is only slightly disguised. Aristotle, Hobbes, and many others have seen in this "sudden glory" of one's own ego the secret of all laughter. Related to aggressive wit (which derides the other fellow) is laughter at the risqué which seems due to the release of suppressions. Aggression and sex are at the basis of much that we call comic.

A young child has a keen sense of the comic, but seldom if ever laughs at himself. Even during adolescence the youth is more likely to view his failings with acute suffering than with laughter. There is evidence that people who are less intelligent, who have low esthetics and theoretical values, prefer the comic and lack a sense of humor based on the real relationships in life.

The reason why insight and humor march hand in hand is probably because at bottom they are a single phenomenon—the phenomenon of self-objectification. The man who has the most complete sense of proportion concerning his own qualities and cherished values is able to perceive their incongruities and absurdities in certain settings.

It is only fair to state that up to now psychologists have had very little success in measuring either insight or the sense of humor. We are dealing here with the subtler reaches of personality—a territory which we hope psychologists will explore with more success in the future than in the past.

Affectation. The precise opposite of the criterion we are describing is the tendency of some people to appear outwardly to be something they cannot be. The affected person is not aware that his deception is transparent, or that his pose is unbecoming. We have spoken of the adolescent's bent for trying on all manner of "identities" for size. The mature person, by contrast, unless he is deliberately play-acting for fun, knows that he cannot counterfeit a personality.

It is true that most of us try to put our best foot forward, and even pretend to virtues and achievements that stretch the truth. But the mature person does not let this social effort collide too seriously with his true nature. Insight and humor keep such egotism in check.

The Unifying Philosophy of Life

Humor, we have said, is indispensable to a mature outlook on life. But it is never sufficient. An exclusively humorous philosophy of existence would lead to cynicism. Everything would be regarded as trivial, displaced, and incongruous. Reason would be distrusted, and all serious solutions rejected. Although the cynic may find amusement along the way, he is at bottom a lonely soul, for he lacks the companionship of a life-goal.

Maturity requires, in addition to humor, a clear comprehension of life's purpose in terms of an intelligible theory. Or, in brief, some form of a unifying philosophy of life. . . .

Religious Sentiment. When we speak of a person's "unifying philosophy of life" we are likely to think first of his religion.

But here an immediate distinction must be drawn. The religious sentiments of many people—perhaps of most people—are decidedly immature. Often they are holdovers from childhood. They are self-centered constructions in which a deity is adopted who favors the immediate interests of the individual, like a Santa Claus or an overindulgent father. Or the sentiment may be of tribal sort: "My church is better than your church. God prefers my people to your people." In cases of this sort religion merely serves self-esteem. It is utilitarian and incidental in the life. It is a defense mechanism (often an escape mechanism) and does not embrace and guide the life as a whole. It is an "extrinsic" value in the sense that the person finds it "useful" in serving his immediate ends. . . . In short, we certainly cannot say that the religious sentiment is always a unifying philosophy of life.

At the same time the religious sentiment may be of such an order that it does provide an inclusive solution to life's puzzles in the light of an intelligible theory. It can do so if the religious quest is regarded as an end-in-itself, as the value underlying all things and

desirable for its own sake. By surrendering himself to this purpose (not by "using" it), religion becomes an "intrinsic" value for the individual and as such is comprehensive and integrative and motivational.

It may help to understand the religious sentiment thus defined if we compare it with humor. In one respect only are they alike. Both set a worrisome event in a new frame of reference, smashing, as it were, the context of literal-mindedness. Both humor and religion shed new light on life's troubles by taking them out of the routine frame. To view our problems humorously is to see them as of little consequence; to view them religiously is to see them in a serious scheme of changed meaning. In either case a new perspective results.

In all other respects they are different. Humor depends on seeing incongruity in events; religion sees an ultimate congruity. Since experiences cannot possibly be regarded at any one time as of great moment and as trivial it follows that we cannot be simultaneously both reverent and jesting. We may joke and pray about the same disturbing events in life, but never at the same time.

What keeps the religious person from becoming a cynic—as thoroughgoing humorists must be—is the conviction that at bottom something is more important than laughter, namely, the fact that he the laugher, as well as the laughter itself, have a place in the scheme of things. When this important issue is decided there is still plenty of room for jesting. In fact, a case might be made for the superior sense of humor of the religious person who has settled once and for all what things are sacred and of ultimate value, for nothing else in the world then needs to be taken seriously. He can see that hosts of happenings are ludicrous, that men and women, including himself, are given to amusing vanities, actors upon a stage. To him nothing in their coming and going is of consequence unless it happens to touch the matter of their ultimate value in the scheme of things.

CHAPTER IX

The Self-Actualization Theory of Abraham Maslow

BIOGRAPHICAL SKETCH

Dr. Abraham Maslow, internationally known educator and psychologist, was born in Brooklyn on April 1, 1908. He received his B.A., M.A., and Ph.D. (1943) degrees from the University of Wisconsin.

Out of his vigorous research and prolific writing has come much of the inspiration and impetus for the contemporary "third force" humanistic psychology movement, with its emphasis upon freeing psychology from its rigidities in order to create a more human science. The name Abraham Maslow has become synonymous with these new concerns for a broader, more humanistically oriented psychology. These concerns, given little attention by existing theories and systems, are devoted to topics such as creativity, healthy personality, love and play, spontaneity, personal growth, and higher levels of consciousness. Dr. Maslow explored and expanded all of these areas in his research and writings.

Throughout his distinguished career, Dr. Maslow taught and lectured at major colleges and universities throughout the United States, Canada, and Mexico. In 1967–68 his outstanding accomplishments and contributions to the field of psychology were honored through his election to the presidency of the American Psychological Association.

In addition to his classic work in motivation theory, *Motivation and Personality*, Dr. Maslow's major publications include *Toward a Psychology of Being; Religions, Values, and Peak Experiences: The Psychology of Science*; an edited volume, *New Knowledge in Human Values;* and a posthumously published book, *The Farther Reaches of Human Nature.* He was on the editorial boards of many leading journals, and his articles, too numerous to mention, have appeared in a great variety of publications.

Dr. Maslow's longest academic tenure was at Brandeis University. He went to Brandeis University in 1951 where he served as chairperson of the Psychology Department for ten years. In 1969, at the peak of his career and influence, Dr. Maslow took a leave of absence from Brandeis to accept a four-year research grant from the W. P. Laughlin Foundation in Menlo Park, California. During the period of this grant, Dr. Maslow intended to develop "the philosophy of democratic politics, economics, and ethics which is generated by the humanistic psychology. . . ." After a year of work under this grant, Dr. Maslow died of a heart attack on June 8, 1979.

Deficiency vs. Growth Motivation

COMMENTARY

George Leonard has observed that Abraham Maslow has done more to change our view of human nature and human possibilities than has any other American psychologist of the past fifty years. Leonard's appraisal of Maslow's work suggests that Maslow ranks with Freud in importance as a revolutionary force in the history of psychology. Maslow drastically altered the theory of human motivation by suggesting, through his hierarchy of needs theory, that human beings have an innate tendency (need) to move to higher levels of growth, health, and creativity, As with Freud, therefore, Maslow's ideas have not only been of theoretical importance but have altered the way we think of ourselves.

Prior to Maslow's presentation of the hierarchy of human needs and his theory of self-actualization, human motivation was seen largely in terms of unconscious forces (the Freudian view), tension reduction models, and operantly conditioned tendencies, none of which are concerned with human potentials and creative living. Thus, based on his distinction between deficiency motivation and growth motivation, and drawing upon his pioneering study of psychologically healthy individuals, Maslow began to create a psychology of healthy personality. This is, perhaps, his greatest contribution.

In the following selections, Maslow discusses the qualitative distinctions between deficiency motivation and growth motivation, presents some theoretical and research support for his theory of growth motivation, and lists the major characteristics of healthy (self-actualizing) personalities.

One of the interesting paradoxes of human development is that we must live with two contradictory impulses: the need to establish integration, order, and stability and the need for differentiation, growth, and change.

Within the personality there is always a dialectic tension between these two dynamic principles of development. In the final selections on safety and growth, Maslow addresses some of the issues in this inherent developmental conflict.

- What prevents growth?
- Why is it so hard and painful for some of us to grow forward?
- Why do we fear the development and expression of our own potentials?
- Why are we so ambivalent toward actualizing our highest possibilities?
- Why (and how) do we move from one satisfying level of development (safety) to a new and higher level (growth)?

Maslow attaches great importance to these questions because he feels that, ultimately, we are destined to be unhappy and unsuccessful unless we can transcend the repressive and inhibiting forces of safety and pursue a course of growth and becoming.

1.

ABRAHAM MASLOW

The concept "basic need" can be defined in terms of the questions which it answers and the operations which uncovered it. . . . My original question was about psychopathogenesis. "What makes people neurotic?" My answer (a modification of and, I think, an improvement upon the analytic one) was, in brief, that neurosis seemed at its core, and in its beginning, to be a deficiency disease; that it was born out of being deprived of certain satisfactions which I called needs

in the same sense that water and amino acids and calcium are needs, namely that their absence produces illness. Most neuroses involved, along with other complex determinants, ungratified wishes for safety, for belongingness and identification, for close love relationships and for respect and prestige. My "data" were gathered through twelve years of psychotherapeutic work and research and twenty years of personality study. One obvious control research (done at the same time and in the same operation) was on the effect of replacement therapy which showed, with many complexities, that when these deficiencies were eliminated, sicknesses tended to disappear.

These conclusions, which are now in effect shared by most clinicians, therapists, and child psychologists (many of them would not phrase it as I have) make it more possible year by year to define need, in a natural, easy, spontaneous way, as a generalization of actual experiential data. . . .

The long-run deficiency characteristics are then the following. It is a basic or instinctoid need if

1. its absence breeds illness,
2. its presence prevents illness,
3. its restoration cures illness,
4. under certain (very complex) free choice situations, it is preferred by the deprived person over the satisfactions,
5. it is found to be inactive, at a low ebb, or functionally absent in the healthy person.

Two additional characteristics are subjective ones, namely, conscious or unconscious yearning and desire, and feeling of lack or deficiency, as of something missing on the one hand, and, on the other, palatability. ("It tastes good.") . . .

In recent years more and more psychologists have found themselves compelled to postulate some tendency to growth or self-perfection to supplement the concepts of equilibrium, homeostasis, tension-reduction, defense and other conserving motivations. This was so for various reasons.

1. *Psychotherapy.* The pressure toward health makes therapy possible. It is an absolute *sine qua non.* If there were no such trend, therapy would be inexplicable to the extent that it goes beyond the building of defenses against pain and anxiety. . . .

2. *Brain-injured soldiers.* Goldstein's work . . . is well known to all. He found it necessary to invent the concept of self-actualization to explain the reorganization of the person's capacities after injury.

3. *Psychoanalysis.* Some analysts . . . have found it impossible to understand even neuroses unless one postulates that they are a distorted version of an impulse toward growth, toward perfection of development, toward the fulfillment of the person's possibilities.

4. *Creativeness.* Much light is being thrown on the general subject of creativeness by the study of healthy growing and grown people, especially when contrasted with sick people. Especially does the theory of art and art education call for a concept of growth and spontaneity. . . .

5. *Child Psychology.* Observation of children shows more and more clearly that healthy children *enjoy* growing and moving forward, gaining new skills, capacities and powers. This is in flat contradiction to that version of Freudian theory which conceives of every child as hanging on desperately to each adjustment that it achieves and to each state of rest or equilibrium. According to this theory, the reluctant and conservative child has continually to be kicked upstairs, out of its comfortable, preferred state of rest *into* a new frightening situation.

While this Freudian conception is continually confirmed by clinicians as largely true for insecure and frightened children, and while it is partially true for all human beings, in the main it is *untrue* for healthy, happy, secure children. In these children we see clearly an eagerness to grow up, to mature, to drop the old adjustment as outworn, like an old pair of shoes. We see in them with special clarity not only the eagerness for the new skill but also the most obvious delight in repeatedly enjoying it. . . .

For the writers in these various groups, . . . growth, individuation, autonomy, self-actualization, self-development, productiveness, self-realization, are all crudely synonymous, designating a vaguely perceived area rather than a sharply defined concept. In my opinion, it is *not* possible to define this area sharply at the present time. Nor is this desirable either, since a definition which does not emerge easily and naturally from well-known facts is apt to be inhibiting and distorting rather than helpful, since it is quite likely to be wrong or mistaken if made by an act of the will, on a priori grounds. We just don't know enough about growth yet to be able to define it well.

Its meaning can be *indicated* rather than defined, partly by positive pointing, partly by negative contrast, i.e., what is *not*. For example, it is not the same as equilibrium, homeostasis, tension-reduction, etc. . . .

This present treatment, however, derives mostly from a direct study of psychologically healthy individuals. This was undertaken not only for reasons of intrinsic and personal interest but also to supply a firmer foundation for the theory of therapy, of pathology and therefore of values. The true goals of education, of family training, of psychotherapy, of self-development, it seems to me, can be discovered only by such a direct attack. The end product of growth teaches us much about the processes of growth. In a recent book I have described what was learned from this study and in addition theorized very freely about various possible consequences for general psychology of this kind of direct study of good rather than bad human beings, of healthy rather than sick people, of the positive as well as the negative. (I must warn you that the data cannot be considered reliable until someone else repeats the study. The possibilities of projection are very real in such a study and of course are unlikely to be detected by the investigator himself.) I want now to discuss some of the differences that I have observed to exist between the motivational lives of healthy people and of others, i.e., people motivated by growth needs contrasted with those motivated by the basic needs.

So far as motivational status is concerned, healthy people have sufficiently gratified their basic needs for safety, belongingness, love, respect, and self-esteem so that they are motivated primarily by trends to self-actualization (defined as on-going actualization of potentials, capacities, and talents, as fulfillment of mission (or call, fate, destiny, or vocation), as intrinsic nature, as an unceasing trend toward unity, integration or synergy within the person). . . .

These healthy people are . . . defined by describing their clinically observed characteristics. These are:

1. Superior perception of reality.
2. Increased acceptance of self, of others and nature.
3. Increased spontaneity.

4. Increase in problem-centering.
5. Increased detachment and desire for privacy.
6. Increased autonomy, and resistance to enculturation.
7. Greater freshness of appreciation, and richness of emotional reaction.
8. Higher frequency of peak experiences.
9. Increased identification with the human species.
10. Changed (the clinician would say, improved) interpersonal relations.
11. More democratic character structure.
12. Greatly increased creativeness.
13. Certain changes in the value system. . . .

If we define growth as the various processes which bring the person toward ultimate self-actualization, then this conforms better with the observed fact that it is going on *all* the time in the life history. It discourages also the stepwise, *all* or none, saltatory conception of motivational progression toward self-actualization in which the basic needs are completely gratified, one by one, before the next higher one emerges into consciousness. Growth is seen then not only as progressive gratification of basic needs to the point where they "disappear," but also in the form of specific growth motivations over and above these basic needs, e.g., talents, capacities, creative tendencies, constitutional potentialities. We are thereby helped also to realize that basic needs and self-actualization do not contradict each other any more than do childhood and maturity. One passes into the other and is a necessary prerequisite for it.

2.

ABRAHAM MASLOW

Defense and Growth

Just how does growth take place? Why do children grow or not grow? How do they know in which directions to grow? How do they get off in the direction of pathology?

After all, the concepts of self-actualization, growth and self are all high-level abstractions. We need to get closer to actual processes, to raw data, to concrete, living happenings.

These are far goals. Healthily growing infants and children don't live for the sake of far goals or for the distant future; they are too busy enjoying themselves and spontaneously living for the moment. They are *living*, not *preparing* to live. How can they manage, just being, spontaneously, not *trying* to grow, seeking only to enjoy the present activity, nevertheless to move

² Maslow, A. (1968). *Toward a Psychology of Being,* 2nd ed., pp. pp. 44–47. Copyright © 1968 by D. Van Nostrand. Reprinted by permission.

forward step by step? I.e., to grow in a healthy way? To discover their real selves? How can we reconcile the facts of Being with the facts of Becoming? Growth is not in the pure case a goal out ahead, nor is self-actualization, nor is the discovery of Self. In the child, it is not specifically purposed; rather it just happens. He doesn't so much search as find. The laws of deficiency-motivation and of purposeful coping do not hold for growth, for spontaneity, for creativeness.

The danger with a pure Being-psychology is that it may tend to be static, not accounting for the facts of movement, direction and growth. We tend to describe states of Being, of self-actualization, as if they were Nirvana states of perfection. Once you're there, you're there, and it seems as if all you could do is to rest content in perfection.

The answer I find satisfactory is a simple one, namely, that growth takes place when the next step forward is subjectively more delightful, more joyous, more intrinsically satisfying than the previous gratification with which we have become familiar and even bored: that the only way we can ever know what is right for us is that it feels better subjectively than any alternative. The new experience validates *itself* rather than by any outside criterion. It is self-justifying, self-validating.

We don't do it because it is good for us, or because psychologists approve, or because somebody told us to, or because it will make us live longer, or because it is good for the species, or because it will bring external rewards, or because it is logical. We do it for the same reason that we choose one dessert over another. I have already described this as a basic mechanism for falling in love, or for choosing a friend, i.e., kissing one person gives more delight than kissing the other, being friends with *a* is more satisfying subjectively than being friends with *b*.

In this way, we learn what we are good at, what we really like or dislike, what our tastes and judgment and capacities are. In a word, this is the way in which we discover the Self and answer the ultimate questions Who am I? What am I?

The steps and the choices are taken out of pure spontaneity, from within outward. The healthy infant or child, just Being, as *part* of his Being, is randomly, and spontaneously curious, exploratory, wondering, interested. Even when he is non-purposeful, non-coping, expressive, spontaneous, not motivated by any deficiency of the ordinary sort, he tends to try out his powers, to reach out, to be absorbed, fascinated, interested, to play, to wonder, to manipulate the world. *Exploring, manipulating, experiencing,* being interested, choosing, delighting, *enjoying* can all be seen as attributes of pure Being, and yet lead to Becoming, though in a serendipitous way, fortuitously, unplanned, unanticipated. Spontaneous, creative experience can and does happen without expectations, plans, foresight, purpose, or goal. It is only when the child sates himself, becomes bored, that he is ready to turn to other, perhaps "higher," delights.

Then arises the inevitable questions. What holds him back? What prevents growth? Wherein lies the conflict? What is the alternative to growth forward? Why is it so hard and painful for some to grow forward? Here we must become more fully aware of the fixative and regressive power of ungratified deficiency-needs, of the attractions of safety and security, of the functions of defense and protection against pain, fear, loss, and threat, of the need for courage in order to grow ahead.

Every human has *both* sets of forces within him. One set clings to safety and defensiveness out of fear, tending to regress backward, hanging on to the past, *afraid* to grow away from the primitive communication with the mother's uterus and breast, *afraid* to take chances, *afraid* to jeopardize what he already has, *afraid* of independence, freedom and separateness. The other set of forces impels him forward toward wholeness of Self and uniqueness of Self, toward full functioning of all his capacities, toward confidence in the face of the external world at the same time that he can accept his deepest, real, unconscious Self.

I can put all this together in a schema, which though very simple, is also very powerful, both heuristically and theoretically. This basic dilemma or conflict between the defensive forces and the growth trends I conceive to be existential, imbedded in the deepest nature of the human being, now and forever into the future. If it is diagrammed like this:

Safety $\longleftarrow$ (Person) $\longrightarrow$ Growth

then we can very easily classify the various mechanisms of growth in an uncomplicated way as

a. Enhancing the growthward vectors, e.g., making growth more attractive and delight producing.
b. Minimizing the fears of growth.
c. Minimizing the safetyward vectors, i.e., making it less attractive.
d. Maximizing the fears of safety, defensiveness, pathology and regression.

We can then add to our basic schema these four sets of valences:

Enhance the dangers   Enhance the attractions

Safety $\longleftarrow$ (Person) $\longrightarrow$ Growth

Minimize the attractions Minimize the dangers

Therefore we can consider the process of healthy growth to be a never-ending series of free choice situations, confronting each individual at every point throughout his life, in which he must choose between the delights of safety and growth, dependence and independence, regression and progression, immaturity and maturity. Safety has both anxieties and delights; growth has both anxieties and delights. We grow forward when the delights of growth and anxieties of safety are greater than the anxieties of growth and the delights of safety.

3.

ABRAHAM MASLOW

The Jonah Complex

. . . We have, all of us, an impulse to improve ourselves, an impulse toward actualizing more of our potentialities, toward self-actualization, or full humanness, or human fulfillment, or whatever term you like. Granted this, then what holds us up? What blocks us?

One such defense against growth that I'd like to speak about specially— because it hasn't been noticed much— I shall call the Jonah Complex.

In my own notes I had at first labeled this defense the "fear of one's own greatness" or the "evasion of one's destiny" or the "running away from one's own best talents." I had wanted to stress as bluntly and sharply as I could the non-Freudian point that we fear our best as well as our worst, even though in different ways. It is certainly possible for most of us to be greater than we are in actuality. We all have unused potentialities or not fully developed ones. It is certainly true that many of us evade our constitutionally suggested vocations (call, destiny, task in life, mission). So often we run away from the responsibilities dictated (or rather suggested) by nature, by fate, even sometimes by accident, just as Jonah tried— in vain—to run from *his* fate.

We fear our highest possibilities (as well as our lowest ones). We are

generally afraid to become that which we can glimpse in our most perfect moments, under the most perfect conditions, under conditions of greatest courage. We enjoy and even thrill to the godlike possibilities we see in ourselves in such peak moments. And yet we simultaneously shiver with weakness, awe, and fear before these very same possibilities.

I have found it easy enough to demonstrate this to my students simply by asking, "Which of you in this class hopes to write the great American novel, or to be a Senator, or Governor, or President? Who wants to be a Secretary-General of the United Nations? Or a great composer? Who aspires to a be a saint, like Schweitzer, perhaps? Who among you will be a great leader?" Generally everybody starts giggling, blushing, and squirming until I ask, "If not you, then who else?" Which of course is the truth. And in this same way, as I push my graduate students toward these higher levels of aspiration, I'll say, "what great book are you now secretly planning to write?" And then they often blush and stammer and push me off in some way. But why should I not ask that question? Who else will write the books on psychology except psychologists? So I can ask, "Do you not plan to be a psychologist?" "Well, yes." "Are you in training to be a mute or an inactive psychologist? What's the advantage of that? That's not a good path to self-actualization. No, you must want to be a first-class psychologist, meaning the best, the very best you are

[3] Maslow, A. (1971). From *The Farther Reaches of Human Nature*, pp. 35–39 by Abraham Maslow. Copyright © 1971 by Bertha G. Maslow. Used by permission of Viking Penguin, a division of Penguin Books USA, Inc.

capable of becoming. If you deliberately plan to be less than you are capable of being, then I warn you that you'll be deeply unhappy for the rest of your life. You will be evading your own capacities, your own possibilities."

Not only are we ambivalent about our own highest possibilities, we are also in a perpetual and I think universal—perhaps even *necessary*—conflict and ambivalence over these same highest possibilities in other people, and in human nature in general. Certainly we love and admire good men, saints, honest, virtuous, clean men. But could anybody who has looked into the depths of human nature fail to be aware of our mixed and often hostile feelings toward saintly men? Or toward very beautiful women or men? Or toward great creators? Or toward our intellectual geniuses? It is not necessary to be a psychologist to see this phenomenon— let us call it "Counter-valuing." Any reading of history will turn up plenty of examples, or perhaps even I could say that any such historical search might fail to turn up a single exception throughout the whole history of mankind. We surely love and admire all the persons who have incarnated the true, the good, the beautiful, the just, the perfect, the ultimately successful. And yet they also make us uneasy, anxious, confused, perhaps even a little jealous or envious, a little inferior, clumsy. They usually make us lose our aplomb, our self-possession, and self-regard. (Nietzsche is still our best teacher here.)

Here we have a first clue. My impression so far is that the greatest people, simply by their presence and by being what they are, make us feel aware of our lesser worth, whether or not they intend to. If this is an unconscious effect, and we are not aware of why we feel stupid or ugly of inferior whenever such a person turns up, we are apt to respond with projection, i.e., we react as if he were *trying* to make us feel inferior. . . . Hostility is then an understandable consequence. It looks to me so far as if conscious awareness tends to fend off this hostility. That is, if you are willing to attempt self-awareness and self-analysis of your *own* counter-valuing, i.e., of your unconscious fear and hatred of true, good, beautiful, etc., people, you will very likely be less nasty to them. And I am willing also to extrapolate to the guess that if you can learn to love more purely the highest values in others, this might make you love these qualities in yourself in a less frightened way. . . . We become more aware of the universality of the fear of direct confrontation with a god or with the godlike. In some religions death is the inevitable consequence. Most preliterate societies also have places or objects that are taboo because they are too sacred and *therefore too dangerous.* . . . Mostly it comes down to awe before the highest and best. (I want to stress that this awe is intrinsic, justified, *right*, suitable, rather than some sickness or failing to get "cured of.")

But here again my feeling is that this awe and fear need not be negative alone, something to make us flee or cower. These are also desirable and enjoyable feelings capable of bringing us even to the point of highest ecstasy and rapture. Conscious awareness, insight, and "working through," à la Freud, is the answer here too I think. This is the best path I know to the acceptance of our highest powers, and whatever elements of greatness or goodness or wisdom or talent we may have concealed or evaded.

A helpful sidelight for me has come from trying to understand why peak experiences are ordinarily transient and brief. The answer becomes clearer and clearer. *We are just not strong enough to endure more!* It is just too shaking and wearing. So often people in such ecstatic moments say, "It's too much," or "I can't stand it," or "I could die." And as I get the descriptions, I sometimes feel, Yes, they *could* die. Delirious happiness cannot be borne for long. Our organisms are just too weak for any large doses of greatness, just as they would be too weak to endure hour-long sexual orgasms, for example.

The word "peak-experience" is more appropriate than I realized at first. The acute emotion must be climactic and momentary and it *must* give way to nonecstatic serenity, calmer happiness, and the intrinsic pleasures of clear, contemplative cognition of the highest goods. . . .

Doesn't this help us to understand our Jonah Complex? It is partly a justified fear of being torn apart, of losing control, of being shattered and disintegrated, even of being killed by the experience. Great emotions after all can in *fact* overwhelm us. The fear of surrendering to such an experience, a fear which reminds us all of the parallel fears found in sexual frigidity, can be understood better I think through familiarity with the literature of psychodynamics and depth psychology, and of the psychophysiology and medical psychomatics of emotion. . . .

For some people this evasion of one's own growth, setting low levels of aspiration, the fear of doing what one is capable of doing, voluntary self-crippling, pseudostupidity, mock-humility are in fact defenses against grandiosity, arrogance, sinful pride, hubris. There are people who cannot manage that graceful integration between the humility and the pride which is absolutely necessary for creative work. To invent or create you must have the "arrogance of creativeness" which so many investigators have noticed. But, of course, if you have only the arrogance without the humility, then you are in fact paranoid. You *must* be aware not only of the godlike possibilities within, but also of the existential human limitations. You must be able simultaneously to laugh at yourself and at all human pretensions. If you can be amused by the worm trying to be a god, then in fact you may be able to go on trying and being arrogant without fearing paranoia or bringing down upon yourself the evil eye. This is a good technique.

May I mention one more such technique that I saw at its best in Aldous Huxley, who was certainly a great man in the sense I've been discussing, one who was able to accept his talents and use them to the full. He managed it by perpetually marveling at how interesting and fascinating everything was, by wondering like a youngster at how miraculous things are, by saying frequently, "Extraordinary! Extraordinary!" He could look out at the world with wide eyes, with unabashed innocence, awe, and fascination, which is a kind of admission of smallness, a form of humility, and then proceed calmly and unafraid to the great task he set for himself.

Self-Actualization

COMMENTARY

What is the source of our desire to strive for the best that is within us? In answering this question, humanistic biologists, psychologists, and organismic theorists have made a persuasive case for the presence of an innate growth force or self-actualizing tendency within the personality. The Nobel Prize winning biochemist, Albert Szent Gyoergyi, came to the conclusion that there is "an innate 'drive' in living matter to perfect itself." Some personality theorists base the weight of their entire theory on the premise that there is an innate tendency or striving within us to achieve wholeness, perfection, or some form of self-realization. Carl Rogers, for example, puts it this way:

I would reaffirm . . . my belief that there is one central source of energy in the human organism; that it is a function of the whole organism rather than of some portion of it; and that it is perhaps best conceptualized as a tendency toward fulfillment, toward actualizing, toward maintenance and enhancement of the organism.

It was Kurt Goldstein, the psychiatrist and neurologist, who first used the term *self-actualization.* He discussed the evolution of the personality in terms of this sovereign tendency, or drive, which he observed in his research on brain-damaged patients. According to Goldstein, all other characteristics and motives of the organism are in the service of this sovereign tendency toward self-actualization.

It was Abraham Maslow, however, who presented us with the first research and theoretical model of self-actualization. With his publication

Self-Actualizing People: A Study of Psychological Health in 1950 and his hierarchy of needs theory, Abraham Maslow gave us a more empirical foundation for the various theories of self-actualization. In the following selections he talks about his early work, discusses some practical ways in which self-actualization can be achieved, and redefines self-actualization in terms of the peak experience.

1.

ABRAHAM MASLOW

The Beginnings of Self-Actualization Studies

My investigations on self-actualization were not planned to be research and did not start out as research. They started out as the effort of a young intellectual to try to understand two of his teachers whom he loved, adored, and admired and who were very, very wonderful people. It was a kind of high-IQ devotion. I could not be content simply to adore, but sought to understand why these two people were so different from the run-of-the-mill people in the world. These two people were Ruth Benedict and Max Wertheimer. They were my teachers after I came with a Ph.D from the West to New York City, and they were most remarkable human beings. My training in psychology equipped me not at all for understanding them. It was as if they were not quite people but

something more than people. My own investigations began as a prescientific or nonscientific activity. I made descriptions and notes on Max Wertheimer, and I made notes on Ruth Benedict. When I tried to understand them, think about them, and write about them in my journal and my notes, I realized in one wonderful moment that their two patterns could be generalized. I was talking about a kind of person, not about two noncomparable individuals. There was wonderful excitement in that. I tried to see whether this pattern could be found elsewhere, and I did find it elsewhere, in one other person after another.

By ordinary standards of laboratory research, i.e., of rigorous and controlled research, this simply was not research at all. My generalization grew out of *my* selection of certain kinds of people. Obviously, other judges are needed. So far, one man has selected perhaps two dozen people whom he liked or admired very much and thought were wonderful people and then tried to figure them out and found that he was able to describe a syndrome—the kind of pattern that seemed to fit all of them. These were people only from Western cultures, people selected with all kinds of built-in biases. Unreliable as it is, that was the only operational definition of self-actualizing people as I described them in my first publication on the subject.

. . . in fact everything I know adds up to corroborative support, though not replicated support, for that study. I personally feel very confident about its major conclusions. I cannot conceive of any research that would make major changes in the pattern, though I am sure there will be minor changes. I have made some of those myself. But my confidence in my rightness is not a scientific datum. . . . The conclusions are in the realm of prescience, but the affirmations are set forth in a form that can be put to test. In that sense, they are scientific.

The people I selected for my investigation were older people, people who had lived much of their lives out and were visibly successful. We do not yet know about the applicability of the findings to young people. We do not know what self-actualization means in other cultures, although studies of self-actualization in China and in India are now in process. We do not know what the findings of these new studies will be, but of one thing I have no doubt: When you select out for careful study very fine and healthy people, strong people, creative people, saintly people, sagacious people—in fact, exactly the kind of people I picked out—then you get a different view of mankind. You are asking how tall can people grow, what can a human being become? . . .

Behaviors Leading to Self-Actualization

What does one do when he self-actualizes? Does he grit his teeth and squeeze? What does self-actualization mean in terms of actual behavior, actual procedure? I shall describe eight ways in which one self-actualizes.

First, self-actualization means experiencing fully, vividly, selflessly, with full concentration and total absorption. It means experiencing without the self-consciousness of the adolescent. At this moment of experiencing, the person is wholly and fully human. This is a self-actualizing moment. This is a moment when the self is actualizing itself. As individuals, we all experience such moments occasionally. As counselors, we can help clients to experience them more often. We can encourage them to become totally absorbed in something and to forget their poses and their defenses and their shyness—to go at it "whole-hog." From the outside, we can see that this can be a very sweet moment. In those youngsters who are trying to be very tough and cynical and sophisticated, we can see the recovery of some of the guilelessness of childhood; some of the innocence and sweetness of the face can come back as they devote themselves fully to a moment and throw themselves fully into the experiencing of it. The key word for this is "selflessly," and our youngsters suffer from too little selflessness and too much self-consciousness, self-awareness.

Second, let us think of life as a process of choices, one after another. At each point there is a progression choice and a regression choice. There may be a movement toward defense, toward safety, toward being afraid; but over on the other side, there is the growth choice. To make the growth choice instead of the fear choice a dozen times a day is to move a dozen times a day toward self-actualization. *Self-actualization is an ongoing process*; it means making each of the many single choices about whether to lie or be honest, whether to steal or not to steal at a particular point, and it means to make each of these choices a growth choice. This is movement toward self-actualization.

Third, to talk of self-actualization implies that there is a self to be actualized. A human being is not a *tabula rasa*, not a lump of clay or Plasticine. He is something which is already there, at least a "cartilaginous" structure of some kind. A human being is, at minimum, his temperament, his biochemical balances, and so on. There is a self, and what I have sometimes referred to as "listening to the impulse voices" means letting the self emerge. Most of us, most of the time (and especially does this apply to children, young people), listen not to ourselves but to Mommy's interjected voice or Daddy's voice or the voice of the Establishment, of the Elders, of authority or of tradition.

As a simple first step toward self-actualization, I sometimes suggest to my students that when they are given a glass of wine and asked how they like it, they try a different way of responding. First, I suggest that they *not* look at the label on the bottle. Thus they will not use it to get any cue about whether or not they *should* like it. Next, I recommend that they close their eyes if possible and that they "make a hush." Now they are ready to look within themselves and try to shut out the noise of the world so that they may savor the wine on their tongues and look to the "Supreme Court" inside themselves. Then, and only then, they may come out and say, "I like it" or "I don't like it." A statement so arrived at is different from the usual kind of phoniness that we all indulge in. At a recent party, I caught myself looking at the label of a bottle and assuring my hostess that she had indeed selected a very good Scotch. But then I stopped myself: What was I saying? I know little about Scotches. All I knew was what the advertisements said. I had no idea whether this one was good or not; yet this is the kind of thing we all do. Refusing to do it is part of the ongoing process of actualizing oneself. Does *your* belly hurt? Or does it feel good? Does this taste good on *your* tongue? Do *you* like lettuce?

Fourth, when in doubt, be honest rather then not. I am covered by that phrase "when in doubt," so that we need not argue too much about diplomacy. Frequently, when we are in doubt we are not honest. Clients are not honest much of the time. They are playing games and posing. They do not take easily to the suggestion to be honest. Looking within oneself for many of the answers implies taking responsibility. That is in itself a great step toward actualization. This matter of responsibility has been little studied. It doesn't turn up in our textbooks, for who can investigate responsibility in white rats? Yet it is an almost tangible part of psychotherapy. In psychotherapy, one can see it, can feel it, can know the moment of responsibility. Then there is a clear knowing of what it feels like. This is one of the great steps. Each time one takes responsibility, this is an actualizing of the self.

Fifth, we have talked so far of experiencing without self-awareness, of making the growth choice rather than the fear choice, of listening to the impulse voices, and of being honest and taking responsibility. All these are steps toward self-actualization, and all of them guarantee better life choices. A person who does each of these little things each time the choice point comes will find that they add up to better choices about what is constitutionally right for him. He comes to know what his destiny is, who his wife or husband will be, what his mission in life will be. One cannot choose wisely for a life unless he dares to listen to himself, *his own self*, at each moment in life, and to say calmly, "No, I don't like such and such."

The art world, in my opinion, has been captured by a small group of opinion- and taste-makers about whom I feel suspicious. That is an *ad hominem* judgment, but it seems fair enough for people who set themselves up as able to say, "You like what I like or else you are a fool." We must teach people to listen to their own tastes. Most people don't do it. When standing in a gallery before a puzzling painting, one rarely hears, "That is a puzzling painting." We had a dance program at Brandeis University not too long ago—a weird thing altogether, with electronic music, tapes, and people doing surrealistic and Dada things. When the lights went up everybody looked stunned, and nobody knew what to say. In that kind of situation most people will make some smart chatter instead of saying, "I would like to think about this." Making an honest statement involves daring to be different, unpopular, nonconformist. If clients, young or old, cannot be taught about being prepared to be unpopular, counselors might just as well give up right now. To be courageous rather than afraid is another version of the same thing.

Sixth, self-actualization is not only an end state but also the process of actualizing one's potentialities at any time, in any amount. It is, for example, a matter of becoming smarter by studying if one is an intelligent person. Self-actualization means using one's intelligence. It does not mean doing some far-out thing necessarily, but it may mean going through an arduous and demanding period of preparation in order to realize one's possibilities. Self-actualization can consist of finger exercises at a piano keyboard. Self-actualization means working to do well the thing that one wants to do. To become a second rate physician is not a good path to self-actualization. One wants to be first-rate or as good as he can be.

Seventh, peak experiences . . . are transient moments of self-actualization. They are moments of ecstasy which cannot be bought, cannot be guaranteed, cannot even be sought. One must be, as C. S. Lewis wrote, "surprised by joy." But one can set up the conditions so that peak experiences are more likely, or one can perversely set up the conditions so that they are less likely. Breaking up an illusion, getting rid of a false notion, learning what one is not good at, learning what one's potentialities are *not*— these are also part of discovering what one is in fact. . . .

Eighth, finding out who one is, what he is, what he likes, what he doesn't like, what is good for him and what is bad, where he is going and what his mission is—opening oneself up to himself—means the exposure of psychopathology. It means identifying defenses, and after defenses have been identified, it means finding the courage to give them up. This is painful because defenses are erected against something which is unpleasant. But giving up the defenses is worthwhile. If the psychoanalytic literature has taught us nothing else, it has taught us that repression is not a good way of solving problems. . . .

Put all these points together, and we see that self-actualization is not a matter of one great moment. It is not true that on Thursday at four o'clock the trumpet blows and one steps into the pantheon forever and altogether. Self-actualization is a matter of degree, of little accessions accumulated one by one. Too often our clients are inclined to wait for some kind of inspiration to strike so that they can say, "At 3:23 on this Thursday I became self-actualized!" People selected as self-actualizing subjects, people who fit the criteria, go about it in these little ways: they listen to their own voices; they take responsibility; they are honest; and they work hard. They find out who they are and what they are, not only in terms of their mission in life, but also in terms of the way their feet hurt when they wear such and such a pair of shoes and whether they do or do not like eggplant or stay up all night if they drink too much beer. All they know is what the real self means. They find their own biological natures, their congenital natures, which are irreversible or difficult to change.

2.

ABRAHAM MASLOW

Redefinition of Self-Actualization

. . . Any person in any of the peak experiences takes on temporarily many of the characteristics which I found in self-actualizing individuals. That is, for the time they become self-actualizers. We may think of it as a passing characterological change if we wish, and not just as an emotional-cognitive-expressive state. Not only are these his happiest and most thrilling moments, but they are also moments of greatest maturity, individuation, fulfillment—in a word, his healthiest moments.

This makes it possible for us to redefine self-actualization in such a way as to purge it of its static and typological short comings, and to make it less a

---

[2] Maslow, A. (1968). *Toward a Psychology of Being*, 2nd ed., pp. 97–98. Copyright © 1968 by D. Van Nostrand. Reprinted by permission.

kind of all-or-none pantheon into which some rare people enter at the age of 60. We may define it as an episode, or a spurt in which the powers of the person come together in a particularly efficient and intensely enjoyable way, and in which he is more integrated and less split, more open for experience, more idiosyncratic, more perfectly expressive or spontaneous, or fully functioning, more creative, more humorous, more ego-transcending, more independent of his lower needs, etc. He becomes in these episodes more truly himself, more perfectly actualizing his potentialities, closer to the core of his Being, more fully human.

Such states or episodes can, in theory, come at any time in life to any person. What seems to distinguish these individuals I have called self-actualizing people, is that in them these episodes seem to come far more frequently and intensely and perfectly than in average people. This makes self-actualization a matter of degree and of frequency rather than an all-or-none affair, and thereby makes it more amenable to available research procedures. We need no longer be limited to searching for those rare subjects who may be said to be fulfilling themselves most of the time. In theory at least we may also search *any* life history for episodes of self-actualization, especially those of artists, intellectuals and other especially creative people, of profoundly religious people, and of people experiencing great insights in psychotherapy or in other important growth experiences.

D-Love and B-Love

COMMENTARY

The need for love and belonging is the third deficiency need in Maslow's hierarchy of needs. As is characteristic of the deficiency needs, this "need" for love has a demanding quality and a self-centered orientation. Motivations, needs, and behaviors at the level of self-actualization, however, become *qualitatively* different from the motives, needs, and behaviors at the deficiency level. This qualitative difference between deficiency motivation and growth motivation is nowhere better illustrated than in the nature of love at the being or self-actualizing level of personality development. The self-centered "needing" and striving is gone, and the person becomes capable of a deeper, more satisfying love relationship. The capacity to love and be loved is heightened, and the neurotic tendencies common to deficiency love relationships are no longer present. The qualities of spontaneity, respect, admiration, intimacy, openness, and enjoyment become readily available within the relationship.

In the following selections, Maslow contrasts the characteristics and dynamics of B-love (love for the being of another person, unneeding love, unselfish love) with D-love (deficiency love, love need, selfish love) and he responds to the conventional wisdom that "love is blind."

1.

ABRAHAM MASLOW

Needing Love and Unneeding Love

The love need as ordinarily studied . . . is a deficit need. It is a hole which has to be filled, an emptiness into which love is poured. If this healing necessity is not available, severe pathology results; if it *is* available at the right time, in the right quantities and with proper style, then pathology is averted. Intermediate states of pathology and health follow upon intermediate states of thwarting or satiation. If the pathology is not too severe and if it is caught early enough, replacement therapy can cure. That is to say the sickness, "love-hunger," can be cured in certain cases by making up the pathological deficiency. Love hunger is a deficiency disease, like salt hunger or the avitaminoses.

The healthy person, not having this deficiency, does not need to receive love except in steady, small, maintenance doses and he may even do without these for periods of time. But if motivation is entirely a matter of satisfying deficits and thus getting rid of needs, then a contradiction appears. Satisfaction of the need should cause it to disappear, which is to say that people who have stood in satisfying love relationships are precisely the people who should be *less* likely to give and to receive love! But clinical study of healthier people, who have been love-

need-satiated, show that although they need less to *receive* love, they are more able to *give* love. In this sense, they are *more* loving people . . .

I have already described in a preliminary fashion the contrasting dynamics of B-love (love for the Being of another person, unneeding love, unselfish love) and D-love (deficiency-love, love need, selfish love). At this point, I wish only to use these two contrasting groups of people to exemplify and illustrate some of the generalizations made above.

1. B-love is welcomed into consciousness, and is completely enjoyed. Since it is non-possessive, and is admiring rather than needing, it makes no trouble and is practically always pleasure-giving.

2. It can never be sated; it may be enjoyed without end. It usually grows greater rather than disappearing. It is intrinsically enjoyable. It is end rather than means.

3. The B-love experience is often described as being the same as, and having the same effects as the aesthetic experience or the mystic experience. . . .

4. The therapeutic and psychogogic effects of experiencing B-love are very profound and widespread. Similar are the characterological effects of the relatively pure love of a healthy mother for her baby, or the perfect love of their God that some mystics have described.

[1] Maslow, A. (1968). *Toward a Psychology of Being,* 2nd ed., pp. 41–43. Copyright © 1968 by D. Van Nostrand. Reprinted by permission.

5. B-love is, beyond the shadow of a doubt, a richer, "higher," more valuable subjective experience than D-love (which all B-lovers have also previously experienced). This preference is also reported by my other older, more average subjects, many of whom experience both kinds of love simultaneously in varying combinations.

6. D-love can be gratified. The concept "gratification" hardly applies at all to admiration-love for another person's admiration-worthiness and love-worthiness.

7. In B-love there is a minimum of anxiety-hostility. For all practical human purposes, it may even be considered to be absent. There *can*, of course, be anxiety-for-the-other. In D-love one must always expect some degree of anxiety-hostility.

8. B-lovers are more independent of each other, more autonomous, less jealous or threatened, less needful, more individual, more disinterested, but also simultaneously more eager to help the other toward self-actualization, more proud of his triumphs, more altruistic, generous and fostering.

9. The truest, most penetrating perception of the other is made possible by B-love. . . . So impressive is this, and so often validated by other people's later experience, that, far from accepting the common platitude that love makes people blind, I become more and more inclined to think of the *opposite* as true, namely that non-love makes us blind.

10. Finally, I may say that B-love, in a profound but testable sense, creates the partner. It gives him a self-image, it gives him self-acceptance, a feeling of love-worthiness, all of which permit him to grow. It is a real question whether the full development of the human being is possible without it.

2.

ABRAHAM MASLOW

When does Love sometimes bring blindness? When does it mean *greater* and when lesser perspicuity?

The point at which a corner is turned is when the love becomes so great and so pure (unambivalent) for the object itself that *its* good is what we want, not what it can do for us, i.e., when it passes beyond being means and becomes an end (with our permission). As with the apple tree for instance: We can love *it* so much that we don't want it to be anything else; we are happy it is as it is. Anything that interferes with it ("butts in") can do *only* harm and make it

[2] Maslow, A. (1971). From *The Farther Reaches of Human Nature*, pp. 142–144 by Abraham Maslow. Copyright © 1971 by Bertha G. Maslow. Used by permission of Viking Penguin, a division of Penguin Books USA, Inc.

less an apple tree, or less perfectly living by its own intrinsic, inherent rules. It can look so perfect that we are afraid to touch it for fear of lessening it. Certainly, if it is seen as perfect, there is no possibility of improving it. As a matter of fact, the effort to improve (or decorate, etc.) is itself a proof that the object is seen as less than perfect, that the picture of "perfect development" in the improver's head is conceived by him to be better than the final end of the apple tree itself; i.e., he can do better than the apple tree, he knows better; he can shape it better than it can itself. So we feel half-consciously that the dog improver is not really a dog-lover. The real dog-lover will be enraged by the tail cropping, the ear cropping or shaping, the selective breeding that makes this dog fit a pattern from some magazine, at the cost of making it nervous, sick, sterile, unable to give birth normally, epileptic, etc. (And yet such people do call themselves dog-lovers.) Same for people who train dwarf-trees, or teach bears to ride a bicycle, or chimpanzees to smoke cigarettes.

Real love then is (sometimes at least) noninterfering and nondemanding and can delight in the thing itself; therefore, it can gaze at the object without guile, design, or calculation of any selfish kind. This makes for less abstracting (or selecting of parts or attributes or single characteristics of the object), less viewing of less-than-the-whole, less atomizing or dissecting. This is the same as saying that there is less active or Procrustean structuring, organizing, shaping, molding, or fitting-to-theory, or to a preconception; i.e., the object

remains more whole, more unified, which amounts to saying, more itself. The object is less measured against criteria of relevance or irrelevance, importance or unimportance, figure or ground, useful or useless, dangerous or not-dangerous, valuable or valueless, profit or no-profit, good or bad, or other criteria of selfish human perceiving. Also the object is less apt to be rubricized, classified, or placed in a historical sequence, or seen as simply a member of a class, as a sample, or instance of a type.

This means that all the (unimportant as well as important) aspects or characteristics of (holistic) parts of the object (peripheral as well as central) are more apt to be given equal care or attention, and that *every* part is apt to be delightful and wonderful; B-love, whether of a lover, or a baby or a painting or a flower, almost always guarantees this kind of distributed looking-with-care-intense-and-fascinated.

Seen in this holistic context, little flaws are apt to be seen as "cute," charming, endearing, *because* idiosyncratic, because they give character and individuality to the object, because they make it what-it-is-rather-than-something-else, perhaps also *just* because they are unimportant, peripheral, nonessential.

Therefore, the B-lover (B-cognizer) will see details that will evade the D-lover or nonlover. Also he will more easily see the *per se* nature of the object itself, in its own right and in its own style of being. Its own delicate and cartilaginous structure is more likely to be yielded to be receptive looking, which is nonactive, noninterfering, less arrogant. That is, its perceived shape is more determined by its own shape when B-cognized than when a structure is imperiously imposed upon it by the perceiver, who will therefore be more likely to be too brusque, too impatient, too much the butcher hacking a carcass apart, for his own appetite, too much the conqueror demanding unconditional surrender, too much the sculptor modeling clay which has no structure of its own.

The Peak Experience

COMMENTARY

In his study of self-actualizing individuals, Maslow made the important discovery that the mystical or transcendent experience was a common one for many of them. He included the peak experience, therefore, as one of the primary characteristics of the self-actualizing personality. Maslow also discovered that, while the peak experience is much more common among self-actualizers, it may also be experienced by others as well. In his later years, Maslow devoted much of his time to the study of peak experiences, and the concept became increasingly important to his theory of self-actualization. He discovered that the peak experience was not just a discrete and fortuitous happening in the life of the individual but, rather, was an intense episode of self-actualization (whether experienced by a self-actualizer or not) and an integrating center in one's identity formation.

In addition to studying the peak experience in the lives of famous and highly developed personalities, Maslow also researched this special experience by having college students respond to the following instructions.

I would like you to think of the most wonderful experience or experiences in your life, happiest moments, ecstatic moments, moments of rapture, perhaps from being in love, or from listening to music or suddenly "being hit" by a book or painting or from some great creative moment. First list these. And then try to tell me how you feel in such acute moments, how you feel differently from the way you feel at other times, how you are at the moment a different person in some ways.

These instructions help us get a feeling for the nature of the psychological-emotional transformation that Maslow called the peak experience and make it easier to identify our own similar experiences.

In the following selections, Maslow discusses the triggers for peak experiences, their impact on personality development, and the religious dimension of the experience.

1.

ABRAHAM MASLOW

Triggers for Peak Experiences

In our investigations of peak experiences, we found many, many triggers, many kinds of experiences that would set them off. Apparently most people, or almost all people, have peak experiences, or ecstasies. The question might be asked in terms of the single most joyous, happiest, most blissful moment of your whole life. You might ask questions of the kind I asked. How did you feel different about yourself at that time? How did the world look different? What did you feel like? What were your impulses? How did you change if you did? I want to report that the two easiest ways of getting peak experiences (in terms of simple statistics in empirical reports) are through music and through sex. I will push aside sex education, as such discussions are premature—although I am sure that one day we will not giggle over it, but will take it quite seriously and teach children that like music, like love, like insight, like a beautiful

¹ Maslow, A. (1971). From *The Farther Reaches of Human Nature*, pp. 175–177 by Abraham Maslow. Copyright © 1971 by Bertha G. Maslow. Used by permission of Viking Penguin, a division of Penguin Books USA, Inc.

meadow, like a cute baby, or whatever, that there are many paths to heaven, and sex is one of them, and music is one of them. These happen to be the easiest ones, the most widespread, and the ones that are easiest to understand.

For our purposes in identifying and studying peak experiences, we can say it is justified to make a list of kinds of triggers. The list gets so long that it becomes necessary to make generalizations. It looks as if any experience of real excellence, of real perfection, of any moving toward the perfect justice or toward perfect values tends to produce a peak experience. Not always. But this is the generalization I would make for the many kinds of things that we have concentrated on. Remember, I am talking here as a scientist. This doesn't sound like scientific talk, but this is a new kind of science. . . . We know just how to encourage peak experiences; we know the best way for women to have children in such a fashion that the childbearing mother is apt to have a great and mystical experience, a religious experience if you wish—an illumination, a revelation, an insight. That is what they call it, by the way, in the interviews—to simply become a different kind of person because, in a fair number of peak experiences, there ensues what I have called the "cognition of being."

We must make a new vocabulary for all these untilled, these unworked problems. This "cognition of being" means really the cognition that Plato and Socrates were talking about; almost, you could say, a technology of happiness, of pure excellence, pure truth, pure goodness, and so on. Well, why not a technology of joy, of happiness? I must add that this is the only known technique for inducing peak experiences in fathers. It had occurred to us, as my wife and I had first gotten to these surveys in college students, that many triggers were discovered. One of them was that while women talked about peak experiences from having children, men didn't. Now we have a way to teach men also to have peak experiences from childbirth. This means, in a certain condensed sense, being changed, seeing things differently, living in a different world, having different cognitions, in a certain sense, some move toward living happily ever after. Now these are data, various paths to mystical experiences. I think that I had better pass them by as they are so numerous.

So far, I have found that these peak experiences are reported from what we might call "classical music." I have not found a peak experience from John Cage or from an Andy Warhol movie, from abstract-expressionistic kind of painting, or the like. I just haven't. The peak experience that has reported the great joy, the ecstasy, the visions of another world, or another level of living, has come from classical music—the great classics. Also I must report that this melts over, fuses over, into dancing or rhythm. So far as this realm of research is concerned, there really isn't much difference between them; they melt into each other. I may add, even, that when I was talking about music as a path to peak experiences, I included dancing. For me they have already melted together. The rhythmic experience, even the very simple rhythmic experience—the good dancing of a rumba, or the kinds of things that the kids do with drums: I don't know whether you want to call that music, dancing, rhythm, athletics, or something else. The love for the body, awareness of the body, and a reverence of the body—these are clearly good paths to peak experiences. These in turn are good paths (not guaranteed, but statistically likely to be good paths) to the "cognition of being," to the perceiving of the platonic essences, the intrinsic values, the ultimate values of being, which in turn is a therapeutic-like help toward both the curing-of-sicknesses kind of therapy and also the growth toward self-actualization, the growth toward full humanness.

2.

ABRAHAM MASLOW

The Aftereffects of Peak-Experiences

Completely separable from the question of the external validity of cognition in the various peak-experiences, is that of the aftereffects upon the person of these experiences which in still another sense, may be said to validate the experience. I have no controlled research data to present. I have only the general agreement of my subjects that there *were* such effects, my own conviction that there were, and the complete agreement of all the writers on creativeness, love, insight, mystic experience and aesthetic experience. On these grounds I feel justified in making at least the following affirmatives or propositions, all of which are testable.

1. Peak-experiences may and do have some therapeutic effects in the strict sense of removing symptoms. I have at least two reports—one from a psychologist, one from an anthropologist—of mystic or oceanic experiences so profound as to remove certain neurotic symptoms forever after. Such conversion experiences are of course plentifully recorded in human history but so far as I know have never received the attention of psychologists or psychiatrists.
2. They can change the person's view of himself in a healthy direction.
3. They can change his view of other people and his relations to them in many ways.
4. They can change more or less permanently his view of the world, or of aspects or parts of it.
5. They can release him for greater creativity, spontaneity, expressiveness, idiosyncrasy.
6. He remembers the experience as a very important and desirable happening and seeks to repeat it.
7. The person is more apt to feel that life in general is worthwhile, even if it is usually drab, pedestrian, painful or ungratifying, since beauty, excitement, honesty, play, goodness, truth and meaningfulness have been demonstrated to him to exist. That is, life itself is validated, and suicide and death-wishing must become less likely.

Many other effects could be reported that are *ad hoc* and idiosyncratic, depending on the particular person, and his particular problems which he considers to be solved or seen in a new light as the result of his experience.

I think that these aftereffects can *all* be generalized and a feeling for them communicated if the peak-experience could be likened to a visit to a personally defined Heaven from which the person then returns to earth. Desirable aftereffects of such an experience, some universal and some individual, are then seen to be very probable.

---
[2] Maslow. A. (1968). *Toward a Psychology of Being*, 2nd ed., pp. 101–102. Copyright © 1968 by D. Van Nostrand. Reprinted by permission.

CHAPTER X

The Phenomenological Self-Theory of Carl Rogers

BIOGRAPHICAL SKETCH

Dr. Carl Rogers was born on January 8, 1902. A Phi Beta Kappa graduate of the University of Wisconsin, he entered Union Theological Seminary in 1924 where he spent two important and formative years. Later, he began taking courses at Teachers College, Columbia University, where he completed his Ph.D. degree in 1931, after several years of experience as a clinical psychologist and child guidance worker in Rochester, New York. In 1939–40, during his last year in Rochester, Dr. Rogers served as director of the Rochester Guidance Center. It was out of the early experience and experimentation in Rochester that came Rogers' first major publication, *Clinical Treatment of the Problem Child* (1939).

Following the years in Rochester, which served as an important base for later explorations, Dr. Rogers held increasingly prominent positions in psychology and positions of leadership in counseling centers. In 1940 he went to Ohio State University as Professor of Psychology. During his tenure at Ohio State he published his first major presentation on client-centered counseling, *Counseling and Psychotherapy* (1942).

In 1945 Dr. Rogers became professor of psychology and executive secretary of the Counseling Center, University of Chicago. He remained at the University of Chicago until 1957, when he took a professorial position at the University of Wisconsin in the Departments of Psychology and Psychiatry.

During the Chicago years, Dr. Rogers stimulated and directed many important research projects on his emerging theories of personality and new approach to psychotherapy. Dr. Rogers' next major publication,

Client-Centered Therapy (1951), developed, in large part, out of these experiences and research studies at the University of Chicago. In addition to these publications Dr. Rogers published *On Becoming a Person* (1961); *The Therapeutic Relationship and Its Impact: A Study of Psychotherapy with Schizophrenics* (with E. T. Gendlin, D. J. Kiesler, and C. B. Truax, 1967); and *Man and the Science of Man* (edited with William. R. Coulson, 1968). Reflecting his interest in the problems of education and in the personal growth possibilities of small group interaction, he published *Freedom to Learn: A View of What Education Might Become* (1969) and *Carl Rogers on Encounter Groups* (1970). Dr. Rogers has also written other books and articles too numerous to mention. Many of his works have been translated into foreign languages, especially Japanese and French.

In 1963 Dr. Rogers became a resident fellow at Western Behavioral Sciences Institute in La Jolla, California. His last position was as resident fellow of the Center for Studies of the Person, La Jolla, California, which he established. Rogers died on February 4, 1987, following surgery for a broken hip.

Dr. Rogers was one of the most important and esteemed psychologists of our time. He served as president of the American Psychological Association and is the only American psychologist to be awarded both of the major awards of that association. In 1956 Dr. Rogers received the Award for Professional Achievement, also from the American Psychological Association.

For several years prior to his death Rogers became more and more involved in the encounter-group movement, extending its application to promote peace and international understanding throughout the world. He led workshops and encounter groups in many countries in an attempt to heal divisive conflict and promote harmony and peaceful coexistence.

Vigorous professional activity did not mark the limit of Carl Rogers' interest. As a dedicated photographer, he took pictures in many parts of the world. Another major hobby was gardening, with a special fondness for the tuberous begonia.

The Therapeutic Relationship

COMMENTARY

No one is more imminently qualified to discuss the therapeutic or helping relationship than Carl Rogers. His person-centered approach to psychotherapy evolved out of years of clinical experience and extensive research on the therapeutic process and the core conditions which facilitate personality growth. He was the first researcher to use transcriptions of actual therapy sessions to study these conditions. These investigations identified important features of the therapeutic relationship and led to important data regarding the role of the self-concept in maladaptive behavior and in the process of personality change. Rogers thus opened up the construct of the *self* and the therapeutic process as legitimate areas for empirical investigation.

In the selections that follow, Rogers defines the helping relationship and discusses the important characteristics or qualities of the helper that facilitate growth and personality change within the relationship. In this discussion, Rogers goes beyond his own core conditions of congruence, unconditional positive regard, and empathic understanding to discuss other important features of the helping relationship.

It is important to note Rogers' important hypothesis that these characteristics are not confined to the formal client-therapist relationship but are applicable to all types of relationships. As Rogers states (*On Becoming a Person*, p. 37.):

There seems every reason to suppose that the therapeutic relationship is only one instance of interpersonal relations, and that the same lawfulness governs all such relationships.

In other words, all relationships concerned with facilitating growth appear to respond to the facilitative conditions outlined by Rogers. This broad hypothesis, far-reaching in its implications, includes such relationships as the parent-child, teacher-student, husband-wife, and, perhaps, friends and lovers as well.

CARL ROGERS

The Characteristics of a Helping Relationship

My interest in psychotherapy has brought about in me an interest in every kind of helping relationship. By this term I mean a relationship in which at least one of the parties has the intent of promoting the growth, development, maturity, improved functioning, improved coping with life of the other. The other, in this sense, may be one individual or a group. To put it in another way, a helping relationship might be defined as one in which one of the participants intends that there should come about, in one or both parties, more appreciation of, more expression of, more functional use of the latent inner resources of the individual.

Now it is obvious that such a definition covers a wide range of relationships which usually are intended to facilitate growth. It would certainly include the relationship between mother

and child, father and child. It would include the relationship between the physician and his patient. The relationship between teacher and pupil would often come under this definition, though some teachers would not have the promotion of growth as their intent. It includes almost all counselor-client relationships, whether we are speaking of educational counseling, vocational counseling, or personal counseling. In this last-mentioned area it would include the wide range of relationships between the psychotherapist and hospitalized psychotic, the therapist and the troubled or neurotic individual, and the relationship between the therapist and the increasing number of so-called "normal" individuals who enter therapy to improve their own functioning or accelerate their personal growth. . . .

But what are the characteristics of those relationships which *do* help, which do facilitate growth? And at the other end of the scale is it possible to discern those characteristics which make a relationship unhelpful, even though it was the sincere intent to promote growth and development? It is to these questions, particularly the first, that I would like to take you with me over some of the paths I have explored, and to tell you where I am, as of now, in my thinking on these issues. . . .

Let me list a number of these questions and considerations.

1. Can I *be* in some way which will be perceived by the other person as trustworthy, as dependable or consistent in some deep sense? Both research and experience indicate that this is very important, and over the years I have found what I believe are deeper and better ways of answering this question. I used to feel that if I fulfilled all the outer conditions of trustworthiness—keeping appointments, respecting the confidential nature of the interviews, etc.—and if I acted consistently the same during the interviews, then this condition would be fulfilled. But experience drove home the fact that to act consistently acceptant, for example, if in fact I was feeling annoyed or skeptical or some other non-acceptant feeling, was certain in the long run to be perceived as inconsistent or untrustworthy. I have come to recognize that being trustworthy does not demand that I be rigidly consistent but that I be dependably real. The term "congruent" is one I have used to describe the way I would like to be. By this I mean that whatever feeling or attitude I am experiencing would be matched by my awareness of that attitude. When this is true, then I am a unified or integrated person in that moment, and hence I can *be* whatever I deeply *am*. This is a reality which I find others experience as dependable.

2. A very closely related question is this: Can I be expressive enough as a person that what I am will be communicated unambiguously? I believe that most of my failures to achieve a helping relationship can be traced to unsatisfactory answers to these two questions. When I am experiencing an attitude of annoyance toward another person but am unaware of it, then my communication contains contradictory messages. My words are giving one message, but I am also in subtle ways communicating the annoyance I feel and this confuses the other person and makes him distrustful, though he too may be unaware of what is causing the difficulty. When as a parent or a therapist or a teacher or an administrator I fail to listen to what is going on in me, fail because of my defensiveness to sense my own feelings, then this kind of failure seems to result. It has made it seem to me that the most basic learning for anyone who hopes to establish any kind of helping relationship is that it is safe to be transparently real. If in a given relationship I am reasonably congruent, if no feelings relevant to the relationship are hidden either to me or the other person, then I can be almost sure that the relationship will be a helpful one. . . .

3. A third question is: Can I let myself experience positive attitudes toward this other person—attitudes of warmth, caring, liking, interest, respect? It is not easy. I find in myself, and feel that I often see in others, a certain amount of fear of these feelings. We are afraid that if we let ourselves freely experience these positive feelings toward another we may be trapped by them. They may lead to demands on us or we may be disappointed in our trust,

and these outcomes we fear. So as a reaction we tend to build up distance between ourselves and others—aloofness, a "professional" attitude, an impersonal relationship.

I feel quite strongly that one of the important reasons for the professionalization of every field is that it helps to keep this distance. In the clinical areas we develop elaborate diagnostic formulations, seeing the person as an object. In teaching and in administration we develop all kinds of evaluative procedures, so that again the person is perceived as an object. In these ways, I believe, we can keep ourselves from experiencing the caring which would exist if we recognized the relationship as one between two persons. It is a real achievement when we can learn, even in certain relationships or at certain times in those relationships, that it is safe to care, that it is safe to relate to the other as a person for whom we have positive feelings.

4. Another question the importance of which I have learned in my own experience is: Can I be strong enough as a person to be separate from the other? Can I be a sturdy respecter of my own feelings, my own needs, as well as his? Can I own and, if need be, express my own feelings as something belonging to me and separate from his feelings? Am I strong enough in my own separateness that I will not be downcast by his depression, frightened by his fear, nor engulfed by his dependency? Is my inner self hardy enough to realize that I am not destroyed by his anger, taken over by his need for dependence, nor enslaved by his love, but that I exist separately from him with feelings and rights of my own? When I can freely feel this strength of

being a separate person, then I find that I can let myself go much more deeply in understanding and accepting him because I am not fearful of losing myself.

5. The next question is closely related. Am I secure enough within myself to permit his separateness? Can I permit him to be what he is—honest or deceitful, infantile or adult, despairing or over-confident? Can I give him the freedom to be? Or do I feel that he should follow my advice, or remain somewhat dependent on me, or mold himself after me? . . .

6. Another question I ask myself is: Can I let myself enter fully into the world of his feelings and personal meanings and see these as he does? Can I step into his private world so completely that I lose all desire to evaluate or judge it? Can I enter it so sensitively that I can move about in it freely, without trampling on meanings which are precious to him? Can I sense it so accurately that I can catch not only meanings of his experience which are obvious to him, but those meanings which are only implicit, which he sees only dimly or as confusion? Can I extend this understanding without limit? I think of the client who said, "Whenever I find someone who understands *a part* of me at the time, then it never fails that a point is reached where I know they're *not* understanding me again. . . . What I've looked for so hard is for someone to understand."

For myself I find it easier to feel this kind of understanding, and to communicate it to individual clients than to students in a class or staff members in a group in which I am involved. There is a strong temptation to set students "straight," or to point out to a staff member the errors in his thinking. Yet when I can permit myself to understand in these situations, it is mutually rewarding. And with clients in therapy, I am often impressed with the fact that even a minimal amount of empathic understanding—a bumbling and faulty attempt to catch the confused complexity of the client's meaning—is helpful, though there is no doubt that it is most helpful when I can see and formulate clearly the meanings in his experiencing which for him have been unclear and tangled.

7. Still another issue is whether I can be acceptant of each facet of this other person which he presents to me. Can I receive him as he is? Can I communicate this attitude? Or can I only receive him conditionally, acceptant of some aspects of his feelings and silently or openly disapproving of other aspects? It has been my experience that when my attitude is conditional, then he cannot change or grow in those respects in which I cannot fully receive him. And when—afterward and sometimes too late—I try to discover why I have been unable to accept him in every respect, I usually discover that it is because I have been frightened or threatened in myself by some aspect of his feelings. If I am to be more helpful, then I must myself grow and accept myself in these respects.

8. A very practical issue is raised by the question: Can I act with sufficient sensitivity in the relationship that my behavior will not be perceived as a threat? The work we are beginning to do in studying the physiological concomitants of psychotherapy confirms the research . . . in indicating how easily individuals are threatened at a physiological level. The psychogalvanic reflex—the measure of skin conductance—takes a sharp dip when the therapist responds with some word which is just a little stronger than the client's feelings. And to a phrase such as, "My you *do* look upset," the needle swings almost off the paper. My desire to avoid even such minor threats is not due to hypersensitivity about my client. It is simply due to the conviction based on experience that if I can free him as completely as possible from external threat, then he can begin to experience and to deal with the internal feelings and conflicts which he finds threatening within himself.

9. A specific aspect of the preceding question but an important one is: Can I free him from the threat of external evaluation? In almost every phase of our lives—at home, at school, at work—we find ourselves under the rewards and punishments of external judgments. "That's good"; "that's naughty." "That's worth an A"; "that's a failure." "That's good counseling"; "that's poor counseling." Such judgments are a part of our lives from infancy to old age. I believe they have a certain social usefulness to institutions and organizations such as schools and professions. Like everyone else I find myself all too often making such evaluations. But, in my experience, they do not make for personal growth and hence I do not believe that they are a part of a helping relationship. Curiously enough a positive evaluation is as threatening in the long run as a negative one, since to inform someone that he is good implies that you also have the right to tell him he is bad. So I have come to feel that the more I can keep a

relationship free of judgment and evaluation, the more this will permit the other person to reach the point where he recognizes that the locus of evaluation, the center of responsibility, lies within himself. The meaning and value of his experience is in the last analysis something which is up to him, and no amount of external judgment can alter this. So I should like to work toward a relationship in which I am not, even in my own feelings, evaluating him. This I believe can set him free to be a self-responsible person.

10. One last question: Can I meet this other individual as a person who is in process of *becoming*, or will I be bound by his past and by my past? If, in my encounter with him, I am dealing with him as an immature child, an ignorant student, a neurotic personality, or a psychopath, each of these concepts of mine limits what he can be in the relationship. . . . If I accept the other person as something fixed, already diagnosed and classified, already shaped by his past, then I am doing my part to confirm this limited hypothesis. If I accept him as a process of becoming, then I am doing what I can to confirm or make real his potentialities.

Congruence, Unconditional Positive Regard, and Empathic Understanding

COMMENTARY

No one since Freud has had a greater impact on the theory and practice of psychotherapy than Carl Rogers. Early in his career he presented the radical claim, supported by his Chicago research on client-therapist interaction, that there were only three therapeutic conditions necessary *and* sufficient for client growth and change. Further, Rogers asserted that client progress in psychotherapy was virtually assured if this therapeutic triad was provided by the therapist and communicated to the client.

Rogers' research findings and resulting claims sparked widespread and heated controversy. Depending on one's bias and perspective he was either praised or ridiculed for his unorthodox views.

To practice his three conditions seemed, to many, to be deceptively simple. All the therapist had to do was sit quietly and communicate acceptance, honesty, and empathy, and it was then the responsibility of the client to change. Since reflection of client feelings was, and is, a major technique, client-centered therapists were frequently considered to be little more than parrots in such interactions. In fact, Rogers' person-centered therapy, whatever value we want to assign to its efficacy, is extremely demanding and difficult in practice. It takes much sensitivity and skill to understand the client's inner world of experience and to communicate this understanding effectively and with sensitivity.

In order to appreciate the impact of Rogers' three necessary and sufficient conditions for therapeutic change and growth, it is important to view them within their theoretical context. The internal actualizing tendency provides the client with the power and intrinsic motivation to change. The therapeutic climate created by the "magic triad" releases and strengthens these inner resources, allowing the client to move toward becoming a more fully functioning person.

It must be said that while many have accepted Rogers' three conditions as very necessary for effective therapy, there has been more resistance in recent years to viewing them as sufficient conditions. The controversy continues.

In the selections that follow, Rogers presents his three necessary and sufficient conditions for therapeutic change and discusses the reasons for their powerful impact on the lives of clients. The first brief selection represents one of Rogers' earliest attempts to state his hypothesis.

1.

CARL ROGERS

The Necessary and Sufficient Conditions of Therapeutic Personality Change

As I have considered my own clinical experience and that of my colleagues, together with the pertinent research which is available, I have drawn out several conditions which seem to me to be necessary to initiate constructive personality change, and which, taken together, appear to be sufficient to inaugurate that process. As I have worked on this problem I have found myself surprised at the simplicity of what has emerged. The statement which follows is not offered with any assurance as to its correctness, but with the expectation that it will have the value of any theory, namely that it states or

implies a series of hypotheses which are open to proof or disproof, thereby clarifying and extending our knowledge of the field.

Since I am not, in this paper, trying to achieve suspense, I will state at once, in severely rigorous and summarized terms, the six conditions which I have come to feel are basic to the process of personality change. ... It is hoped that this brief statement will have much more significance to the reader when he has completed the paper. Without further introduction let me state the basic theoretical position.

For constructive personality change to occur, it is necessary that these conditions exist and continue over a period of time.

1. Two persons are in psychological contact.
2. The first, whom we shall term the client, is in a state of incongruence, being vulnerable or anxious.

[1] Rogers, C. R. "The Necessary and Sufficient Conditions of Therapeutic Personality Change." *Journal of Consulting Psychology* 21:2 (1957), pp. 95–96.

3. The second person, whom we shall term the therapist, is congruent or integrated in the relationship.
4. The therapist experiences unconditional positive regard for the client.
5. The therapist experiences an empathic understanding of the client's internal frame of reference and endeavors to communicate this experience to the client.

6. The communication to the client of the therapist's empathic understanding and unconditional regard is to a minimal degree achieved.

No other conditions are necessary. If these six conditions exist, and continue over a period of time, this is sufficient. The process of constructive personality change will follow.

2.

CARL ROGERS

What We Know About Psychotherapy

It has been found that personal change is facilitated when the psychotherapist is what he *is*, when in the relationship with his client he is genuine and without "front" or facade, openly being the feelings and attitudes which at that moment are flowing *in* him. We have coined the term "congruence" to try to describe this condition. By this we mean that the feelings the therapist is experiencing are available to him, available to his awareness, and he is able to live these feelings, be them, and able to communicate them if appropriate. No one fully achieves this condition, yet the more the therapist is able to listen acceptantly to what is going on within himself, and the more he is able to be the complexity of his

feelings, without fear, the higher the degree of congruence.

To give a commonplace example, each of us senses this quality in people in a variety of ways. One of the things which offends us about radio and TV commercials is that it is often perfectly evident from the tone of voice that the announcer is "putting on," playing a role, saying something he doesn't feel. This is an example of incongruence. On the other hand each of us knows individuals whom we somehow trust because we sense that they are being what they are, that we are dealing with the person himself, not with a polite or professional front. It is this quality of congruence which we sense which research has found to be associated with successful therapy. The more genuine and congruent the therapist in the relationship, the more probability there is that change in personality in the client will occur.

---

[2] Rogers, Carl R., *On Becoming a Person*, pp. 61–64. Copyright © 1961 by Houghton Mifflin Company. Used with permission.

Now the second condition. When the therapist is experiencing a warm, positive and acceptant attitude toward what *is* in the client, this facilitates change. It involves the therapist's genuine willingness for the client to be whatever feeling is going on in him at that moment—fear, confusion, pain, pride, anger, hatred, love, courage or awe. It means that the therapist cares for the client in a non-possessive way. It means that he prizes the client in a total rather than a conditional way. By this I mean that he does not simply accept the client when he is behaving in certain ways, and disapprove of him when he behaves in other ways. It means an outgoing positive feeling without reservations, without evaluations. The term we have come to use for this is unconditional positive regard. Again research studies show that the more this attitude is experienced by the therapist, the more likelihood there is that therapy will be successful.

The third condition we may call empathic understanding. When the therapist is sensing the feelings and personal meanings which the client is experiencing in each moment, when he can perceive these from "inside," as they seem to the client, and when he can successfully communicate something of that understanding to his client, then this third condition is fulfilled.

I suspect each of us has discovered that this kind of understanding is extremely rare. We neither receive it nor offer it with any great frequency. Instead we offer another type of understanding which is very different. "I understand what is wrong with you;" "I understand what makes you act that way;" or "I too have experienced your trouble and I reacted very differently;" these are the types of understanding which we usually offer and receive, an evaluative understanding from the outside. But when someone understands how it feels and seems to be *me*, without wanting to analyze me or judge me, then I can blossom and grow in that climate. And research bears out this common observation. When the therapist can grasp the moment-to-moment experiencing which occurs in the inner world of the client as the client sees it and feels it, without losing the separateness of his own identity in this empathic process, then change is likely to occur.

Studies with a variety of clients show that when these three conditions occur in the therapist, and when they are to some degree perceived by the client, therapeutic movement ensues, the client finds himself painfully but definitely learning and growing, and both he and his therapist regard the outcome as successful. It seems from our studies that it is attitudes such as these rather than the therapist's technical knowledge and skill, which are primarily responsible for therapeutic change.

The Dynamics of Change

You may well ask, "But why does a person who is seeking help change for the better when he is involved, over a period of time, in a relationship with a therapist which contains these elements? How does this come about?" Let me try very briefly to answer this question.

The reactions of the client who experiences for a time the kind of therapeutic relationship which I have described are a reciprocal of the therapist's attitudes. In the first place, as he finds someone else listening acceptantly to his feelings, he little by little becomes able to listen to himself. He begins to receive the communications from within himself—to realize that he is angry, to recognize when he is frightened, even to realize when he is feeling courageous. As he becomes more open to what is going on within him he becomes able to listen to feelings which he has always denied and repressed. He can listen to feelings which have seemed to him so terrible, or so disorganizing, or so abnormal, or so shameful, that he has never been able to recognize their existence in himself.

While he is learning to listen to himself he also becomes more acceptant of himself. As he expresses more and more of the hidden and awful aspects of himself, he finds the therapist showing a consistent and unconditional positive regard for him and his feelings. Slowly he moves toward taking the same attitude toward himself, accepting himself as he is, and therefore ready to move forward in the process of becoming.

And finally as he listens more accurately to the feelings within, and becomes less evaluative and more acceptant toward himself, he also moves toward greater congruence. He finds it possible to move out from behind the facades he has used, to drop his defensive behaviors, and more openly to be what he truly is. As these changes occur, as he becomes more self-aware, more self-acceptant, less defensive and more open, he finds that he is at last free to change and grow in the directions natural to the human organism.

Conditions of Worth

COMMENTARY

Rogers' concept of conditions of worth plays a crucial role in his theory of personality development. Its significant presence or absence in the life of the child forms a major link in a sequence of forces leading to a state of incongruence and possible neurosis or to a more integrated and fully functioning personality.

The imposition of conditions of worth upon the child leads to a denial or distortion of important self-experiences in order to receive positive regard from parents. Certain experiences, therefore, are valued and incorporated into the self-structure only if they are perceived to meet parental approval. The child thus disregards his/her own experiences and organismic evaluations. This denial-distortion of important self-experiences may bring about a serious disruption in the child's natural organismic valuing process. The child's responses to conditions of worth, therefore, often result in a divided self which Rogers refers to as a state of incongruence.

It must be emphasized that very few of us have experienced unconditional acceptance. Rather, it is the frequency and severity of imposed conditions of worth upon the child that is the crucial factor.

In the following selection, Rogers outlines the development of conditions of worth and illustrates the sequence of experiences that lead either to the development of incongruence or a healthy state of congruence within the personality.

1.

CARL ROGERS

The Development of Conditions of Worth

1. When *self-experiences* of the individual are discriminated by significant others as being more or less worthy of *positive regard*, then *self-regard* becomes similarly selective.

2. When a *self-experience* is avoided (or sought) solely because it is less (or more) worthy of *self-regard*, the individual is said to have acquired a *condition of worth*.

3. If an individual should *experience* only *unconditional positive regard*, then no *conditions of worth* would develop, *self-regard* would be unconditional, the needs for *positive regard* and *self*-regard would never be at variance with *organismic evaluation*, and the individual would continue to be *psychologically adjusted*, and would be fully functioning. This chain of events is hypothetically possible, and hence important theoretically, though it does not appear to occur in actuality.

The infant learns to need love. Love is very satisfying, but to know whether he is receiving it or not he must observe his mother's face, gestures, and other ambiguous signs. He develops a total gestalt as to the way he is regarded by his mother and each new experience of love or rejection tends to alter the whole gestalt. Consequently each behavior on his mother's part such as a specific disapproval of a specific behavior tends to be experienced as disapproval in general. So important is this to the infant that he comes to be guided in his behavior not by the degree to which an experience maintains or enhances the organism, but by the likelihood of receiving maternal love.

Soon he learns to view himself in much the same way, liking or disliking himself as a total configuration. He tends, quite independently of his mother or others, to view himself and his behavior in the same way they have. This means that some behaviors are regarded positively which are not actually experienced organically as satisfying. Other behaviors are regarded negatively which are not actually experienced as unsatisfying. It is when he behaves in accordance with these introjected values that he may be said to have acquired conditions of worth. He cannot regard himself positively, as having worth, unless he lives in terms of these conditions. He now reacts with adience or avoidance toward certain behaviors solely because of these introjected conditions of self-regard, quite without reference to the organismic consequences of these behaviors. This is what is meant by living in terms of introjected values (the phrase formerly used) or conditions of worth.

It is not theoretically necessary that such a sequence develop. If the infant always felt prized, if his own feelings

¹ Rogers, C. (1959). "A Theory of Therapy, Personal, and Interpersonal Relationships as Developed in the Client-Centered Framework," in S. Koch, ed., *Psychology: A Study of Science*, Vol. III, pp. 224–226. Copyright © 1959 by McGraw-Hill, Inc. Reprinted by permission of McGraw-Hill.

were always accepted even though some behaviors were inhibited, then no conditions of worth would develop. This could at least theoretically be achieved if the parental attitude was genuinely of this sort: "I can understand how satisfying it feels to you to hit your baby brother (or to defecate when and where you please, or to destroy things) and I love you and am quite willing for you to have those feelings. But I am quite willing for me to have my feelings, too, and I feel very distressed when your brother is hurt, (or annoyed or sad at other behaviors) and so I do not let you hit him. Both your feelings and my feelings are important, and each of us can freely have his own." If the child were thus able to retain his own organismic evaluation of each experience, then his life would become a balancing of these satisfactions. Schematically he might feel, "I enjoy hitting baby brother. It feels good. I do not enjoy mother's distress. That feels dissatisfying to me. I enjoy pleasing her." Thus his behavior would sometimes involve the satisfaction of pleasing mother. But he would never have to disown the feelings of satisfaction or dissatisfaction which he experienced in this differential way.

2.

CARL ROGERS

I am inwardly pleased when I have the strength to permit another person to be his own realness and to be separate from me. I think that is often a very threatening possibility. In some ways I have found it an ultimate test of staff leadership and of parenthood. Can I freely permit this staff member or my son or my daughter to become a separate person with ideas, purposes, and values which may not be identical with my own? I think of one staff member this past year who showed many flashes of brilliance but who clearly held values different from mine and behaved in ways different from the ways in which I would behave. It was a real struggle, in which I feel I was only partially successful, to let him be himself, to let him develop as a person entirely separate from me and my ideas and my values. Yet to the extent that I was successful, I was pleased with myself, because I think this permission to be a separate person is what makes for the autonomous development of another individual.

I am angry with myself when I discover that I have been subtly controlling and molding another person in my own image. This has been a very painful part of my professional

---

[2] Rogers, C. (1970). *A Way of Being*, pp. 18–19. Copyright © 1961 by Houghton Mifflin Company. Used with permission.

experience. I hate to have "disciples," students who have molded themselves meticulously into the pattern that they feel I wish. Some of the responsibility I place with them but I cannot avoid the uncomfortable probability that in unknown ways I have subtly controlled such individuals and made them into carbon copies of myself, instead of the separate professional persons they have every right to become.

Trusting Your Own Experience

COMMENTARY

Why do we find it so difficult, at times, to chose, to make decisions, to know what we really want and need? Allen Wheelis, expressing an existential view, suggests that in important matters we prefer not to choose, prefer that the deeper issues in our lives are removed from choice and hence from our freedom and responsibility. But is our difficulty in choosing merely a reflection of this existential dilemma?

From the position of his personality theory, Carl Rogers believes that the inability to make decisions or the inability to choose wisely comes as a result of sacrificing the organismic and inherent wisdom of our own experience for the wishes and opinions of others in order to receive positive regard. Thus, the organismic valuing process, listening and responding to our own experiences, is weakened and we have less and less faith in its validity. In the extreme, we may be cut off entirely from our own experiencing, not really knowing what we are feeling, wanting, and needing.

Trusting one's own experience is an important characteristic of Rogers' fully functioning person and represents a state of congruence. It is also a major direction taken by clients in psychotherapy. In the following selections, Rogers discusses the issue of trusting one's own experience within the context of his person-centered psychotherapy.

1.

CARL ROGERS

Trust

Therapy seems to mean a getting back to basic sensory and visceral experience. Prior to therapy the person is prone to ask himself, often unwittingly, "What do others think I should do in this situation?" "What would my parents or my culture want me to do?" "What do I think *ought* to be done?" He is thus continually acting in terms of the form which should be imposed upon his behavior. This does not necessarily mean that he always acts in *accord* with the opinions of others. He may indeed endeavor to act so as to contradict the expectations of others. He is nevertheless acting *in terms* of the expectations (often introjected expectations) of others. During the process of therapy the individual comes to ask himself, in regard to ever-widening areas of his life-space, "How do I experience this?" "What does it mean to *me*?" "If I behave in a certain way how do I symbolize the meaning which it *will* have for me?" He comes to act on a basis of what may be termed realism—a realistic balancing of the satisfactions and dissatisfactions which any action will bring to himself.

Perhaps it will assist those who, like myself, tend to think in concrete and clinical terms, if I put some of these ideas into schematized formulations

---

[1] Rogers, Carl R., *On Becoming a Person*, pp. 103–106. Copyright © 1961 by Houghton Mifflin Company. Used with permission.

of the process through which various clients go. For one client this may mean: "I have thought I must feel only love for my parents, but I find that I experience both love and bitter resentment." Perhaps I can be that person who freely experiences both love *and* resentment." For another client the learning may be: "I have thought I was only bad and worthless. Now I experience myself at times as one of much worth; at other times as one of little worth or usefulness. Perhaps I can be a person who experiences varying degrees of worth." For another: "I have held the conception that no one could really love me for myself. Now I experience the affectional warmth of another for me. Perhaps I can be a person who is lovable by others—perhaps I *am* such a person." For still another: "I have been brought up to feel that I must not appreciate myself—but I do. I can cry for myself, but I can enjoy myself, too. Perhaps I am a richly varied person, whom I can enjoy and for whom I can feel sorry." Or, to take the last example from Mrs. Oak, "I have thought that in some deep way I was bad, that the most basic elements in me must be dire and awful. I don't experience that badness, but rather a positive desire to live and let live. Perhaps I can be that person who is, at heart, positive."

What is it that makes possible anything but the first sentence of each of these formulations? It is the addition of awareness. In therapy the person adds to ordinary experience the full and undistorted awareness of his experiencing—of his sensory and visceral reactions. He ceases, or at least decreases, the distortion of experience in awareness. He can be aware of what he is actually experiencing, not simply what he can permit himself to experience after a thorough screening through a conceptual filter. In this sense the person becomes for the first time the full potential of the human organism, with the enriching element of awareness freely added to the basic aspect of sensory and visceral reaction. The person comes to *be* what he *is*, as clients so frequently say in therapy. What this seems to mean is that the individual comes to *be*—in awareness what he *is*—in experience. He is, in other words, a complete and fully functioning human organism.

Already I can sense the reactions of some of my readers. "Do you mean that as a result of therapy, man becomes nothing but a human *organism*, a human *animal*? Who will control him? Who will socialize him? Will he then throw over all inhibitions? Have you merely released the beast, the id, in man?" To which the most adequate reply seems to be, "In therapy the individual has actually *become* a human organism, with all the richness which that implies. He is realistically able to control himself, and he is incorrigibly socialized in his desires. There is no beast in man. There is only man in man, and this we have been able to release."

So the basic discovery of psychotherapy seems to me, if our observations have any validity, that we do not need to be afraid of being "merely" homo sapiens. It is the discovery that if we can add to the sensory and visceral experiencing which is characteristic of the whole animal kingdom, the gift of a free and undistorted awareness of which only the human animal seems fully capable, we have an organism which is beautifully and constructively realistic. We have then an organism which is as aware of the demands of the culture as it is of its own physiological demands for food or sex—which is just as aware of its desire for friendly relationships as it is of its desire to aggrandize itself—which is just as aware of its delicate and sensitive tenderness toward others as it is of its hostilities toward others. When man's unique capacity of awareness is thus functioning freely and fully, we find that we have, not an animal whom we must fear, not a beast who must be controlled, but an organism able to achieve, through the remarkable integrative capacity of its central nervous system, a balanced, realistic, self-enhancing, other-enhancing behavior as a resultant of all these elements of awareness. To put it another way, when man is less than fully man—when he denies to awareness various aspects of his experience—then indeed we have all too often reason to fear him and his behavior, as the present world situation testifies. But when he is most fully man, when he is his complete organism, when awareness of experience, that peculiarly human attribute, is most fully operating, then he is to be trusted, then his behavior is constructive. It is not always conventional. It will not always be conforming. It will be individualized. But it will also be socialized.

2.

CARL ROGERS

An Increasing Trust in His Organism

Still another characteristic of the person who is living the process of the good life appears to be an increasing trust in his organism as a means of arriving at the most satisfying behavior in each existential situation. Again, let me try to explain what I mean.

In choosing what course of action to take in any situation, many people rely upon guiding principles, upon a code of action laid down by some group or institution, upon the judgment of others (from wife and friends to Emily Post), or upon the way they have behaved in some similar past situation. Yet as I observe the clients whose experiences in living have taught me so much, I find that increasingly such individuals are able to trust their total organismic reaction to a new situation because they discover to an ever-increasing degree that if they are open to their experience, doing what "feels right" proves to be a competent and trustworthy guide to behavior which is truly satisfying.

As I try to understand the reason for this, I find myself following this line of thought. The person who is fully open to his experience would have access to all of the available data in the situation on which to base his behavior; the social demands, his own complex and possibly conflicting needs, his

memories of similar situations, his perception of the uniqueness of this situation, etc., etc. The data would be very complex indeed. But he could permit his total organism, his consciousness participating to consider each stimulus, need, and demand, its relative intensity and importance, and out of this complex weighing and balancing, discover that course of action which would come closest to satisfying all his needs in the situation. An analogy which might come close to a description would be to compare this person to a giant electronic computing machine. Since he is open to his experience, all of the data from his sense impressions, from his memory, from previous learning, from his visceral and internal states, is fed into the machine. The machine takes all of these multitudinous pulls and forces which are fed in as data, and quickly computes the course of action which would be the most economical vector of need satisfaction in this existential situation. This is the behavior of our hypothetical person.

The defects which in most of us make this process untrustworthy are the inclusion of information which does not belong to this present situation, or the exclusion of information which does. It is when memories and previous learnings are fed into the computations as if they were this reality, and not memories and learnings, that erroneous behavioral answers arise. Or when certain threatening experiences are inhibited from awareness, and hence are withheld from the

---

[2] Rogers, Carl R., *On Becoming a Person*, pp. 189–191. Copyright © 1961 by Houghton Mifflin Company. Used with permission.

computation or fed into it in distorted form, this too produces error. But our hypothetical person would find his organism thoroughly trustworthy, because all of the available data would be used, and it would be present in accurate rather than distorted form. Hence his behavior would come as close as possible to satisfying all his needs—for enhancement, for affiliation with others, and the like.

In this weighing, balancing, and computation, his organism would not by any means be infallible. It would always give the best possible answer for the available data, but sometimes data would be missing. Because of the element of openness to experience, however, any errors, any following of behavior which was not satisfying, would be quickly corrected. The computations, as it were, would always be in process of being corrected, because they would be continually checked in behavior.

Perhaps you will not like my analogy of an electronic computing machine. Let me return to the clients I know. As they become more open to all of their experiences, they find it increasingly possible to trust their reactions. If they "feel like" expressing anger they do so and find that this comes out satisfactorily, because they are equally alive to all of their other desires for affection, affiliation, and relationship. They are surprised at their own intuitive skill in finding behavioral solutions to complex and troubling human relationships. It is only afterward that they realize how surprisingly trustworthy their inner reactions have been in bringing about satisfactory behavior.

Index